Lecture Notes in Computer Science   12471

More information about this series at http://www.springer.com/series/7407

Alex Orailoglu · Matthias Jung ·
Marc Reichenbach (Eds.)

Embedded Computer Systems: Architectures, Modeling, and Simulation

20th International Conference, SAMOS 2020
Samos, Greece, July 5–9, 2020
Proceedings

 Springer

Editors
Alex Orailoglu
Department of Computer Science
and Engineering
University of California San Diego
La Jolla, CA, USA

Matthias Jung
Department of Electrical
and Computer Engineering
Fraunhofer IESE
Kaiserslautern, Germany

Marc Reichenbach
Department of Computer Science
Friedrich-Alexander University
Erlangen, Germany

ISSN 0302-9743   ISSN 1611-3349   (electronic)
Lecture Notes in Computer Science
ISBN 978-3-030-60938-2   ISBN 978-3-030-60939-9   (eBook)
https://doi.org/10.1007/978-3-030-60939-9

LNCS Sublibrary: SL1 – Theoretical Computer Science and General Issues

This Springer imprint is published by the registered company Springer Nature Switzerland AG
The registered company address is: Gewerbestrasse 11, 6330 Cham, Switzerland

Preface

For 20 years, SAMOS has brought together researchers from both academia and industry to the quiet and inspiring mediterranean island of Samos, Greece, which is different to many other conference locations.

This year, 35 papers from 13 countries were submitted to the regular conference. Each paper was thoroughly reviewed by four reviewers. A first round of discussions was initiated online, followed by a remote Technical Program Committee (TPC) meeting that decided the final paper selection. Out of the 35 submissions, 16 papers were selected by the TPC for the technical program of the conference.

The conference program included 9 papers in two special sessions on (1) "Innovative Architectures for Security," organized by Francesco Regazzoni (University of Amsterdam, The Netherlands), and (2) "European Projects on Embedded and High Performance Computing for Health Applications," organized by Giampaolo Agosta (Politecnico di Milano, Italy).

In 2020, unfortunately, we could not experience the spirit of SAMOS due to the global COVID-19 pandemia. There were no physical presentations, no lively discussions in panels, and no social activities which were usually used to deepen the discussions of the morning conference sessions, since SAMOS XX was held as a virtual event. We want to thank all the authors who trusted in the conference, submitted their papers, and prepared their presentation as excellent videos. Moreover, we want to thank the TPC for carefully reviewing the submitted papers, so that we could still provide an excellent, high-quality virtual program. Although it was a fully virtual event, the participants discussed the presentations using the commenting feature of the SAMOS website. We sincerely hope that in 2021 we can celebrate the 20th anniversary of SAMOS again in person.

July 2020

Alex Orailoglu
Matthias Jung
Marc Reichenbach

Organization

General Chair

Alex Orailoglu   University of California, San Diego, USA

Program Chairs

Matthias Jung   Fraunhofer IESE, Germany
Marc Reichenbach   University of Erlangen-Nuremberg, Germany

Special Session Chairs

Innovative Architectures for Security

Francesco Regazzoni   University of Amsterdam, The Netherlands

European Projects on Embedded and High Performance Computing for Health Applications

Giovanni Agosta   Politecnico di Milano, Italy

Submission Chair

Andy D. Pimentel   University of Amsterdam, The Netherlands

Web Chair

Jasmin Jahic   University of Kaiserslautern, Germany

Proceedings Chair

Carlo Galuzzi   Swinburne University of Technology, Australia

Publicity Chairs

Andy D. Pimentel   University of Amsterdam, The Netherlands
Matthias Jung   Fraunhofer IESE, Germany

Finance Chair

Carlo Galuzzi   Swinburne University of Technology, Australia

Steering Committee

Shuvra Bhattacharyya   University of Maryland, USA, and IETR, France
Holger Blume   Leibniz Universität Hannover, Germany
Ed F. Deprettere   Leiden University, The Netherlands
Nikitas Dimopoulos   University of Victoria, Canada
Carlo Galuzzi   Swinburne University of Technology, Australia
Georgi N. Gaydadjiev   Maxeler Technologies, UK
John Glossner   Optimum Semiconductor Technologies, USA
Walid Najjar   University of California, Riverside, USA
Andy D. Pimentel   University of Amsterdam, The Netherlands
Olli Silvén   University of Oulu, Finland
Dimitrios Soudris   National Technical University of Athens, Greece
Jarmo Takala   Tampere University of Technology, Finland
Stephan Wong   Delft University of Technology, The Netherlands

Program Committee

Holger Blume   Leibniz Universitat Hannover, Germany
Luigi Carro   Universidade Federal do Rio Grande do Sul, Brazil
Jeronimo Castrillon   Dresden University of Technology, Germany
Ricardo Chaves   INESC-ID, Portugal
Francesco Conti   Università di Bologna, Italy
Vassilios V. Dimakopoulos   University of Ioannina, Greece
Giorgos Dimitrakopoulos   Democritus University of Thrace, Greece
Nikitas Dimopoulos   University of Victoria, Canada
Lide Duan   University of Texas at San Antonio, USA
Holger Flatt   Fraunhofer IOSB, Germany
Carlo Galuzzi   Swinburne University of Technology, Australia
Georgi N. Gaydadjiev   Maxeler Technologies, UK
Andreas Gerstlauer   The University of Texas at Austin, USA
Michael Glaß   University of Erlangen-Nuremberg, Germany
John Glossner   Optimum Semiconductor Technologies Inc., USA
Diana Goehringer   Ruhr-Universität Bochum, Germany
Ann Gordon-Ross   University of Florida, USA
Xinfei Guo   University of Virginia, USA
Rajiv Gupta   University of California, Riverside, USA
Soonhoi Ha   Seoul National University, South Korea
Frank Hannig   University of Erlangen-Nuremberg, Germany
Christian Haubelt   University of Rostock, Germany
Pekka Jääskeläinen   Tampere University of Technology, Finland
Matthias Jung   Fraunhofer IESE, Germany
Christoforos Kachris   Athens Information Technology, Greece
Georgios Keramidas   Technical Educational Institute of Western Greece, Greece
Leonidas Kosmidis   Barcelona Supercomputing Center, Spain

Angeliki Kritikakou	Inria, Irisa, France
Kevin Martin	Université Bretagne Sud, France
John McAllister	Queen's University Belfast, UK
Paolo Meloni	Università degli Studi di Cagliari, Italy
Alexandre Mercat	Tampere University of Technology, Finland
Daniel Mueller-Gritschneder	Technical University of Munich, Germany
Walid Najjar	University of California, Riverside, USA
Chrysostomos Nicopoulos	University of Cyprus, Cyprus
Alex Orailoglu	University of California, San Diego, USA
Andrés Otero	Universidad Politécnica de Madrid, Spain
Gianluca Palermo	Politecnico di Milano, Italy
Francesca Palumbo	Università degli Studi di Cagliari, Italy
Anuj Pathania	National University of Singapore, Singapore
Guillermo Paya-Vaya	Leibniz Universität Hannover, Germany
Maxime Pelcat	European University of Brittany, France
Andy Pimentel	University of Amsterdam, The Netherlands
Oscar Plata	University of Malaga, Spain
Dionisios Pnevmatikatos	ICS-FORTH and University of Crete, Greece
Francesco Regazzoni	ALaRI, Switzerland
Marc Reichenbach	University of Erlangen-Nuremberg, Germany
Ruben Salvador	CentraleSupélec, IETR, France
Carlo Sau	Università degli studi di Cagliari, Italy
Muhammad Shafique	Karlsruhe Institute of Technology, Germany
Magnus Själander	Uppsala University, Norway
Dimitrios Soudris	National Technical University of Athens, Greece
Ioannis Sourdis	Chalmers University of Technology, Sweden
Leonel Sousa	Universidade de Lisboa, Portugal
Todor Stefanov	Leiden University, The Netherlands
Christos Strydis	Erasmus University Medical Center, The Netherlands
Sander Stuijk	Eindhoven University of Technology, The Netherlands
Wonyong Sung	Seoul National University, South Korea
Jarmo Takala	Tampere University of Technology, Finland
Jean-Pierre Talpin	Inria, Irisa, France
George Theodoridis	University of Patras, Greece
Stavros Tripakis	University of California, Berkeley, USA
Theo Ungerer	University of Augsburg, Germany
Carlos Valderrama	University of Mons-Hainaut, Belgium
Norbert Wehn	University of Kaiserslautern, Germany
Stefan Weithoffer	IMT Atlantique, France
Stephan Wong	Delft University of Technology, The Netherlands
Roger Woods	Queen's University Belfast, UK
Hoeseok Yang	Ajou University, South Korea

Secondary Reviewers

Achmad, Rachmad Vidya
Danopoulos, Dimitrios
Di Mauro, Alfio
Grützmacher, Florian
Khalid, Faiq
Marantos, Charalampos
Multanen, Joonas
Neubauer, Kai
Ozen, Elbruz

Panagiotou, Sotirios
Paulin, Gianna
Siddiqi, Muhammad Ali
Vasilakis, Evangelos
Willig, Michael
Wulf, Cornelia
Zahedi, Mahdi
Zhang, Mingqi

Contents

SPECIAL SESSION: European Projects on Embedded and High Performance Computing for Health Applications

Fast Performance Estimation and Design Space Exploration of SSD Using AI Techniques

Jangryul Kim and Soonhoi Ha[✉]

Seoul National University, Seoul, Republic of Korea
{urmydata,sha}@snu.ac.kr

Abstract. SSD has become an indispensable element in today's computer systems, and their architecture is constantly evolving with new host interfaces for higher performance and larger storage capacities thanks to incessant flash technology development. As the complexity of SSD architecture increases, it is necessary to use a systematic methodology for architecture design. In this paper, we propose a novel methodology to explore the design space of an SSD based on a genetic algorithm at the early design stage. The key technical challenge in the design space exploration (DSE) is fast and accurate performance estimation or fitness evaluation in the genetic algorithm. To tackle this challenge, we propose two performance estimation methods. One is based on the scheduling of the task graph abstracted from the firmware and the other one is based on a neural network (NN) regression model. While the NN-based method is faster, the accuracy of the NN-based method depends on the training data set that consists of hardware configurations and performance. The scheduling-based performance estimator is used to generate the training data set fast. The viability of the proposed methodology is confirmed by comparison with a state-of-the-art SSD simulator in terms of accuracy and speed for design space exploration.

Keywords: Performance estimation · Design space exploration · Solid State Drives

1 Introduction

Solid State Drive (SSD) is becoming the major storage element in computer systems as it is constantly evolving with new host interfaces for higher performance and larger storage capacities thanks to incessant flash technology development. A today's SSD itself can be regarded as an embedded computer system that consists of multiple cores and non-trivial memory systems, running the firmware under real-time constraints. As the complexity of SSD architecture grows, for the design of a new SSD architecture, it is necessary to use a systematic methodology to explore the design space that is defined by several axes such as the number of cores, the DRAM cache configuration, clock frequencies, mapping of firmware

© Springer Nature Switzerland AG 2020
A. Orailoglu et al. (Eds.): SAMOS 2020, LNCS 12471, pp. 1–17, 2020.
https://doi.org/10.1007/978-3-030-60939-9_1

to cores. And we need to consider multiple objectives, performance, power, and cost, to find the Pareto optimal solutions in the design space exploration (DSE).

Fast and accurate performance estimation is the key technical challenge in the design space exploration of an embedded system. Since the system behavior of an SSD is very dynamic, it is not feasible to estimate the performance analytically. The behavior depends on the types of command, read or write, and on the data size. Access conflict to a shared resource is non-deterministic and the cache hit ratio of a DRAM cache is not predictable.

Thus simulation has been popularly used for performance estimation of SSD. An SSD simulator can predict the performance by constructing the simulation model of the system and running the firmware on the simulator. There is a trade-off between accuracy and speed in the simulation-based performance estimation. For timed simulation, it is necessary to make a simulation model for each hardware component and perform cycle level timing simulation to accurately estimate the contention delay on shared resources. But an accurate simulator is not adequate to use for exploring the design space of SSD since we have to build a new simulator for each architecture candidate and perform cycle-level simulation, which will take prohibitively long simulation time. Thus in the proposed methodology, we prune the design space fast to select a few architecture candidates and compare them by simulation for detailed evaluation.

To prune the design space at the early design phase, we use a genetic algorithm that is a popular AI-based meta-heuristic to generate high-quality solutions to optimization problems by relying on bio-inspired operators such as mutation and crossover. Initially, a set of candidate solutions is randomly generated and the fitness of each solution is computed. In each generation, we select a portion of the population with higher fitness value than the unselected ones and apply mutation and crossover operators to produce the population of the next generation. Iterating this genetic process is expected to generate solutions with converged fitness values eventually.

For fast and accurate fitness evaluation, we propose two performance estimations methods: scheduling-based method and machine-learning-based method. In the scheduling-based method, we model the firmware of SSD as a task graph where a task represents a function module and arcs represent the dependency between tasks. We map the tasks onto hardware components and schedule them according to the execution scenario of the firmware. For performance estimation, we need to profile the execution time of a task on each processing element beforehand by cycle-accurate simulation. With the profiled execution time information of each task on the mapped component, we can estimate the latency of the firmware for each input command from the schedule diagram.

In the machine-learning-based method, we construct a neural network (NN) model that predicts performance with a set of hardware configuration parameters. Finding a good network model is a problem to solve in this method. Since the accuracy of a neural network model depends on the size of the training data set, how to obtain the training set is another problem. It is necessary to generate the data set quickly for fast model construction. We use the schedule-based method to generate the training data set fast.

In summary, we propose a novel AI-based DSE methodology using the genetic algorithm for the design of SSD. For fitness value evaluation, an NN-based performance estimation method is devised. For the generation of the training data set, we propose to use another performance estimation method based on the scheduling of the task graph, an abstracted model of the firmware, onto the hardware components. The accuracy and the speed of our two proposed performance estimation methods are compared with an open-source state-of-the-art SSD simulator, Amber [6], that we use the baseline SSD simulator in this work. The main goal of the proposed methodology is to prune the design space at the early design stage and to produce a few candidate architectures that need to be evaluated in more detail with a cycle-accurate but slow SSD simulator or with hardware emulators.

2 Related Work

As the SSD architecture evolves constantly, the SSD simulation technique needs to be improved to support new features for accurate simulation. Early SSD simulators such as DiskSim [2], FlashSim [13], and SSDSim [7] are mostly trace-driven simulators that mainly focus on the performance estimation of FTL (flash translation layer) algorithm with relatively simple modeling on the hardware and the firmware. They are not suitable for DSE. VSSIM [20] is a QEMU-based simulator that enables the user to flexibly model the hardware components and change the firmware algorithms. By modeling the communication with the host side, the host performance, as well as the SSD behavior, can be estimated. Since it uses a virtual machine, however, execution speed is slow. Also, It does not support PCIe interface and NVMe protocol supported by recent SSDs. SSDExplorer [22] is a virtual platform for the DSE of SSD. By using SystemC modeling, it allows the user to mix multiple levels of abstraction in a unified simulation framework. While it supports fine-grained DSE, it has the same drawbacks of simulation-based DSE: modification of the simulation model for each candidate architecture and slow simulation speed. In fact, the design space explored in their work is rather limited.

SimpleSSD [10], MQSim [18], and Amber [6] have been recently released as open-source simulators, enabling more accurate performance prediction than the previous simulators. They all include the host interface in the simulation model supporting the NVMe protocol, and improve the simulation accuracy with more detailed modeling of hardware and software components. In particular, SimpleSSD and Amber provide both a full-system version that works with gem5 for host simulation and a standalone version that can simulate the SSD architecture with a given trace input file or a request generator. While they focus on simulation accuracy, the simulation speed is not fast enough for exploring the design space.

Yoo et al. [21] have proposed an analytical model to explore the design space for the flash memory configuration, not for the entire SSD architecture. Chen et al. [3] have proposed an analytical model of SSD based on queueing theory for high-level performance estimation.

However, none of the above-mentioned works for SSD use the well-established automated DSE method which is provided by [16]. They do not mention DSE but explore the design space manually at most. However, manual DSE requires too much effort because the design space of an SSD is complex and it is difficult to determine how and what factors affect performance. In summary, there exists no previous work on automated design space exploration of an SSD architecture to the best of our knowledge.

With the explosive development of deep learning techniques, several approaches based on neural network have been proposed for performance estimation in various application domains. Oyamada et al. [14] proposed an NN-based approach to predict software performance after classifying applications using control flow graphs. An approach proposed by Wu et al. [19] performed performance and power estimation of GPGPU using K-means clustering and neural network classifier. Ipek et al. [9] and Ozisikyilmaz et al. [15] have addressed the problem of microprocessor performance prediction with a neural network. They showed that performance estimation over a wider range of design space is possible with a set of training data that covers a smaller design space. They used an analytical tool, SimPoint [17], to reduce the simulation time and to generate the training data.

Meanwhile, Kim et al. [12] presented a method of measuring utilization of SSD using machine learning techniques, Support Vector Machine and LASSO Generalized Linear Model, to predict I/O saturation for load balancing in multiple storage architecture. Huang et al. [8] proposed a black-box model of SSD using a statistical machine learning algorithm. These approaches are not applicable to the DSE of an SSD. To the best of our knowledge, no previous work exists that uses an NN-based performance estimation for exploring the SSD design space in the early stage of design.

3   Background

3.1   Overall Structure of SSD

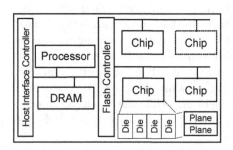

Fig. 1. SSD architecture

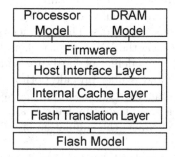

Fig. 2. Software structure of the Amber simulator

Figure 1 shows a simplified architecture of an SSD that is composed of four main hardware modules: host interface, a multi-core processor, DRAM cache, and flash memory. To process multiple commands concurrently, the flash memory module is configured to exploit the internal parallelism maximally with various techniques such as channel striping and die interleaving. Besides, SSD performance can be increased by using more cores, increasing the DRAM bandwidth, and/or adding a special hardware logic at the cost of area and power consumption. Thus it is required to consider many issues simultaneously in the design of an SSD.

3.2 Amber Simulator

As the baseline SSD simulator in the current implementation, we use the Amber [6] that is an open-source state-of-the-art simulator. In fact, it is the only open-source simulator that supports performance variation as the number of cores changes, which is the required feature for our design space exploration. Nonetheless, it is noteworthy that the proposed methodology does not depend on a specific SSD simulator. Figure 2 shows the software structure of Amber. In Amber, the processor, DRAM, and flash memory are modeled in detail and the SSD firmware is implemented in a layered structure with Host Interface Layer (HIL), Internal Cache Layer (ICL), and Flash Translation Layer (FTL). Processor cores are assigned to each layer. The HIL is responsible for communication with the host, the ICL is for internal caching using DRAM, and the FTL is for flash access management with various functionalities such as address translation and garbage collection. Amber provides a detailed configuration file in which a user can alter some configuration parameters such as the number of cores and clock frequencies. Thus we may explore a limited region of the entire design space with Amber by varying the configuration parameters. The standalone version provides a request generator that generates an input trace with the desired input pattern such as random read with 4 KB sized block or sequential write with 128 KB sized block.

4 Proposed Methodology

The proposed methodology consists of four major steps. In the first step, the firmware is abstracted and transformed into a task graph. With the task graph, we build a scheduling-based performance estimation tool that estimates the performance by scheduling the tasks onto the hardware components in the next step. In the third step, we make a neural network model for analytical performance estimation and train the model with the data set that is generated by the scheduling-based performance estimation tool. Finally, we automatically explore the design space with a GA-based technique where the fitness evaluation of each candidate solution is performed analytically by neural network regression. The third step is used in the NN-based DSE flow that is presented in Fig. 3. As explained earlier, we may use the scheduling-based performance estimation (step 2) for fitness evaluation in the genetic algorithm, skipping step 3. The output of the proposed methodology is a set of architecture candidates that will be compared by detailed simulation.

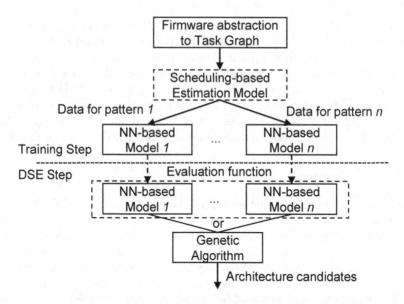

Fig. 3. NN-based DSE flow of the proposed methodology

4.1 Firmware Abstraction to Task Graph

By analyzing the call graph of the firmware and the source code, we first represent the firmware structure with a hierarchical flow chart manually. By clustering some blocks in the flow chart, the level of abstraction is raised to construct a high-level task graph as illustrated in Fig. 4. In the transformed task graph, a task is a unit of mapping onto hardware resources. The orange, blue, and red boxes represent tasks that belong to the HIL, ICL, and FTL layer, respectively. The purple boxes mean access to shared resources such as DRAM and flash memory.

Next, we identify the execution sequence of tasks, called *scenario* in this paper, for each command. The scenarios are obtained by running the firmware on the Amber simulator with various input patterns. In addition, we profile the execution time of each task and the statistics of the dynamic behavior during simulation. Two example scenarios are shown in the lower left part of Fig. 4 for the case when the input command is a random read of 4 KB sized blocks with two cache conditions, hit and miss, respectively. The execution time of a task may depend on the scenario. Note that even though the set of scenarios and the profiling information are obtained by simulation, it is a one-time effort to be taken before design space exploration. Although this paper focuses on finding an architecture that is suitable for a given firmware, the proposed performance estimation technique can be used to evaluate the firmware algorithms by transforming them into task graphs and profiling tasks.

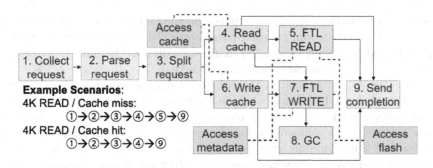

Fig. 4. High-level task graph of the firmware (Color figure online)

4.2 Scheduling-Based Performance Estimation

For a given input trace of commands associated with scenarios and a given system configuration, we can estimate the performance by mapping and scheduling the tasks onto hardware resources. Figure 5 displays an example schedule diagram for an input trace of 4 KB random read with three cache hits and two cache misses. The horizontal axis represents the time and the vertical axis represents the hardware components that tasks are mapped to.

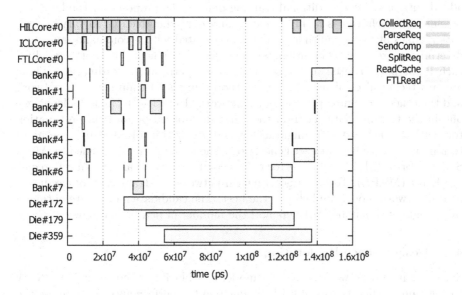

Fig. 5. Scheduling of tasks onto hardware resources

We may generate the input traces randomly based on the same statistics of the dynamic behavior as that obtained in the profiling stage. The maximum number of outstanding commands depends on the I/O depth parameter that is included in the system configuration parameter. The hardware configuration is easily changed by adding or deleting hardware components and the frequency change is reflected in the execution time of tasks.

Unlike the Amber simulator, this scheduling-based performance estimation does not need the address information in the input trace. Since an SSD exploits the internal parallelism of the flash memory, however, its performance depends on the addresses. To compensate for this omission, a flash mapping policy is considered in the scheduling. For sequential read and write access requests, we assume die interleaving when mapping tasks into flash memory modules, which minimizes the resource conflict in flash memory. On the other hand, for random accesses, access conflict to flash die is modeled by random mapping.

4.3 Neural Network-Based Performance Estimation

Even though we may explore the design space with the scheduling-based performance estimation that is much faster than simulation, it is still cumbersome to generate an input trace and perform scheduling for each candidate system architecture. Hence we propose a neural network regression model to estimate the performance analytically. The input to the neural network is a set of system configuration parameters as listed in the first column of Table 1 and the output is the estimated throughput performance. More configuration parameters can be added with associated additional training data in the proposed method.

Since the behavior is highly dynamic and unpredictable due to varying execution times of tasks, multiple scenarios associated with a command, and non-deterministic resource contention, we make a separate neural network model for each input pattern used in the schedule-based performance estimation. There are two technical challenges in this method. One is to train a neural network and the other is to find a proper neural network. To tackle the first challenge, we obtain the training data set from the scheduling-based performance estimation tool with varying system configurations as illustrated in Fig. 3, which is a novel technique for training data set generation. The loss function is defined by Mean Squared Error (MSE) and the error rate is computed by Mean Absolute Percentage Error (MAPE). To find a good neural network, we train a set of candidate neural network models and choose the best. The candidate models are obtained by changing the number of layers and the number of neurons per layer.

4.4 Design Space Exploration

Since the neural network regression model is a black-box model, it is not easy to determine which factors affect how much on the performance. We explore the design space with a genetic algorithm (GA), a popular meta-heuristic for the optimization problem, in the proposed methodology since an exhaustive search method is not scalable and there exist GA solvers readily available. An individual represents a candidate system configuration and the fitness function is defined as the estimated performance that is evaluated by the trained neural network model obtained from the previous step. The scheduling-based performance estimator can be used for fitness evaluation instead of the neural network model. In the current implementation, we set the maximum number of generations to 10,000 and stop evolution if the fitness value does not change during 300 generations. The population size is set to 32, and uniform crossover with mixing ratio of 0.5 and one-point mutation are performed with the rate of crossover and mutation to be 0.9 and 0.7, respectively.

5   Experiments

5.1   Set-Up

All experiments have been conducted on a system consisting of Ubuntu 18.04.2 LTS, Intel Core i9-9900KF CPU @ 3.60 GHz with 64 GB RAM. While the scheduling-based estimator is manually implemented in C++, we use Keras [4] with the TensorFlow environment [1] to construct an NN-based model, and the DEAP framework [5] to implement the genetic algorithm. We use four different input patterns, 4K random read/write and 128K sequential read/write, which are popular patterns used for performance evaluation of SSD architectures and pruning the design space in the early design phase. For an example SSD configuration, Intel 750 400 GB SSD configuration is assumed as the baseline that is modeled in the Amber simulator.

Table 1. Configuration parameters explored in the DSE

Parameters	Values
Number of HIL cores	1, 2, 3
Number of ICL cores	1, 2, 3
Number of FTL cores	1, 2, 3
Frequency of HIL cores	<u>200</u>, 400, 600, <u>800</u> MHz
Frequency of ICL cores	<u>200</u>, 400, 600, <u>800</u> MHz
Frequency of FTL cores	<u>200</u>, 400, 600, <u>800</u> MHz
Number of DRAM banks	8, <u>16</u>
Frequency of DRAM channel	<u>533</u>, 667, 800, <u>933</u> MHz
I/O depths	1, 4, 8, 12, 16, 20, 24, 28, 32

5.2   Scheduling-Based Performance Estimator

In the first experiment, the scheduling-based performance estimator is compared with the Amber simulator in terms of accuracy and speed. Comparisons are made by varying the configuration parameters shown in Table 1. We could cover only a small subset of the whole design space that is supported by Amber configuration

parameters. Since cores take a large share of the power consumption, we vary
the number cores and their operating frequencies. We assume that all cores have
the same clock frequency and the number of DRAM banks is not varying due to
the limitation of the Amber simulator. The underlined values are not included
in this experiment. As for the input trace, the request generator provided by
the Amber simulator is used. For scheduling-based performance estimation, a
simplified request generator which does not include address information is used
with the same statistics on the dynamic behavior by random modeling. The total
data size is set to 1 GB.

The experimental results are displayed in Table 2. The error rate is calcu-
lated by $(|Throughput_{Simulator} - Throughput_{Model}|)/Throughput_{Simulator}$. It
is observed that the average error rate is around 10%, which is a reasonable price
we had to pay to gain the significant estimation speed we believe. The main cause
of error comes from the abstracted input trace without address information and
statistical modeling of dynamic behavior in the scheduling-based method. The
estimation speed of the scheduling-based method takes a few seconds at the minimum and it is at least 10 times faster than the simulator. Remind that we need
to modify the simulator or change undisclosed related parameters to explore the

Table 2. Comparison between the Amber simulator and the proposed scheduling-based
performance estimator

Patterns	Error rate (%)				Speed up
	Avg	Min	Max	Std	
4K random read	4.37	0.08	15.91	3.07	45.69
4K random write	10.79	0.12	28.71	4.93	36.91
128K sequential read	12.02	0.34	25.15	3.39	10.72
128K sequential write	8.95	3.08	24.87	5.56	54.06

Table 3. Comparison between the scheduling-based and the neural network-based
estimator

Patterns	Test set ratio	MAPE (%)		
		Avg	Min	Max
4K random read/write	50%	1.41/1.58	0.97/1.23	2.07/1.95
	70%	1.58/2.29	1.03/1.56	2.20/2.74
	90%	2.56/2.43	1.51/1.73	4.04/2.82
	95%	3.86/2.60	3.18/2.24	4.82/3.01
128K sequential read/write	50%	0.35/0.29	0.24/0.09	0.51/0.70
	70%	0.50/0.44	0.30/0.22	0.88/0.91
	90%	0.94/0.66	0.48/0.31	1.54/1.30
	95%	1.24/1.04	0.81/0.64	1.70/1.54

design space that is not covered by simulator configuration parameters, which is not considered in this experiment.

5.3   Neural Network-Based Performance Estimation

In the second experiment, we compare the proposed NN-based performance estimator with the scheduling-based performance estimator in terms of accuracy and speed. To find the best network model, we change the number of fully connected layers in the hidden layer from 1 to 5 and the number of neurons to 32, 64, 128, and 256. Each candidate neural network is trained with a fixed learning rate of 0.01 and a batch size of 512 during 100 epochs. Whether to add a batch normalization layer between fully connected layers is considered as an option. The ratio of the training set, validation set, and test set was randomly selected with the ratio of 4:1:5. We repeat this process 3 times and take the average. The resultant neural network for 4K random read case consists of three fully connected layers of 32 neurons. Meanwhile, for other patterns, the network consists of two fully connected layers of 64 neurons, one batch normalization layer between them.

With the chosen neural networks, we compared the NN-based estimator with the scheduling-based estimator in terms of MAPE and the result is shown in Table 3. Since the neural network regression accuracy is expected to increase as the size of the training set increases, the comparison is made with varying size of the training set. On the second column of the table, the size of the training set is (1 - test set size) multiplied by the total design space. The result is obtained after 10 repetitions for each case.

Table 4. Comparison between the Amber simulator and the proposed neural network-based estimator which is trained with the data generated by the scheduling-based estimator

Patterns	Error rate (%)			
	Avg	Min	Max	Std
4K random read	4.49	0.01	15.76	2.75
4K random write	8.95	0.01	43.66	7.88
128K sequential read	11.54	0.56	21.15	2.73
128K sequential write	10.18	3.07	26.45	6.60

Note that the accuracy degrades very smoothly as the training size decreases. With only 5% of the training data, the average accuracy error of neural network regression is less than 4% for 4K random read/write and less than 1.3% for 128K sequential read/write. The maximum error is less than 5% for the former case and 2% and for the latter. On the other hand, the NN-based estimation takes a few milliseconds so that the estimation speed is three orders of magnitude faster than the scheduling-based estimation.

In addition, we compare the NN-based estimator with the Amber simulator in terms of the error rate. As shown in Table 4, the error rate is similar to that of the scheduling-based method, except for the 4K random write case that has larger variation of error rates but similar average rate. Since the objective of the DSE in the early design phase is selecting a few candidate architectures that need to be evaluated in more detail with a cycle-accurate but slow SSD simulator, such increased variation does not affect the viability of the NN-based estimation technique, we believe.

5.4   Design Space Exploration

The design space explored in this work is defined by the configuration parameters displayed in Table 1. The proposed DSE technique based on GA produces Pareto-optimal system configurations with two objective functions, throughput, and core power. As explained above, the throughput performance is estimated by the proposed NN-estimator. On the other hand, the core power, which depends on the number of cores and the clock frequency, is computed as follows, assuming that the voltage is proportional to frequency for simplicity [11]. A more accurate formula could be defined for a given core type.

$$Power \propto \sum_{i \in cores} (n_i \cdot f_i^3) \tag{1}$$

where i is the type of cores, n_i is the number of cores of i type, and f_i is the frequency of the i-type core.

We conducted DSE separately for two input patterns of 4K random read and 128K sequential read using the neural network model with the least error rate in Table 3. Figure 6 shows the Pareto-optimal solutions for each case, varying the I/O depth. In the figure, each line represents the Pareto front for a given input pattern and an I/O depth, with a legend. For example, $randr\_1$ means 4K random read when I/O depth is one. Each point on the line is associated with a system configuration that is omitted in the figure.

In the case of 4K random read, when the I/O depth is 1, 4, and 8, the input intensity is relatively loose and the throughput performance is saturated with a few cores. And the gain of increasing the frequency or the number of cores is not significant. On the other hand, when the I/O depth is 16 and 32, the gain of increasing the frequency and the number of cores is outstanding. In particular, the HIL core affects the performance most; large improvement in Fig. 6 is due to increasing the number of HIL cores.

Meanwhile, there is no noticeable difference in the case of 128K sequential read except when the I/O depth is one. This is because the prefetch logic that is activated for sequential read in the firmware becomes saturated even at relatively low I/O depth. So it is not necessary to use many resources for the sequential read.

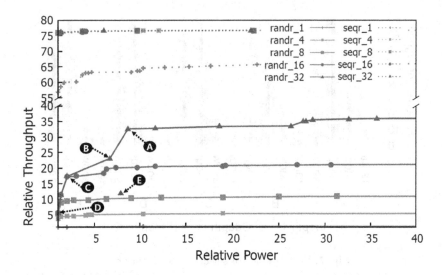

Fig. 6. Pareto front of system configurations for various input patterns

Table 5. Selected four Pareto-optimal configurations and default configuration

Configuration	Cores (Num/Freq (MHz))			Relative power
	HIL core	ICL core	FTL core	
A	3/400	1/200	1/200	8.67
B	2/400	1/200	1/200	6.00
C	3/200	1/200	1/200	1.67
D	1/200	1/200	1/200	1.00
E	1/400	1/400	1/400	8.00

Table 5 shows selected four Pareto-optimal configurations and one configuration which is not on Pareto-front marked in Fig. 6. In the Intel 750 SSD
configuration defined in Amber, the number of HIL core is zero, meaning that
the latency is zero for tasks mapped on HIL part, while the numbers of the ICL
core and the FTL core are both 1 and the clock frequency is set to 400 MHz. To
profile the execution time of tasks mapped on the HIL core, we set the number of
HIL core to be 1 and make it as the default configuration E for comparison. The
selected Pareto-optimal configurations are ordered in the order of power where
configuration D is the baseline with the least power consumption. The other
three Pareto-optimal configurations show clear trade-offs between the throughput performance and the relative power. Meanwhile, default configuration E
consumes more power than B and C but has lower performance on $randr\_32$.

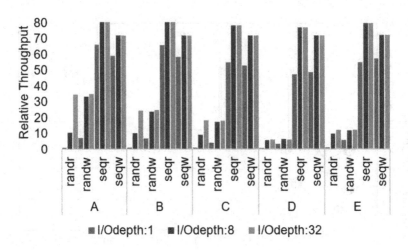

Fig. 7. Performance of selected configurations

Even if the configuration is Pareto-optimal for a given input pattern, it may not be Pareto-optimal for the other input patterns. Thus, in order to explore the design space of SSD that should support various input patterns, it is necessary to compare the configurations with various input patterns. Figure 7 shows the relative throughput among the five configurations of Table 5 with four different input patterns. Configuration E shows poor performance comparing B which uses less power than E. Among the Pareto-optimal configurations, the performance difference of sequential case is not significant according to the power change except for D. But the difference is noticeable in the case of a random case.

5.5   Design Space Exploration Time

There are three possible methods to explore the design space in the proposed methodology. In the first method, we can explore the whole design space exhaustively using the scheduling-based estimator. The second is to use the scheduling-based estimator in the proposed GA-based DSE. The last method is to use the NN-based estimator in the GA-based DSE. The DSE time of each method can be formulated as follows:

$$T_{method1} = T_{scheduling-based} \times N_{space},$$
$$T_{method2} = T_{scheduling-based} \times N_{evaluation}, \qquad (2)$$
$$T_{method3} = 5\% \times T_{method1} + T_{network} + T_{NN-basedDSE}$$

where $T_{scheduling-based}$ is the average execution time of scheduling-based estimator, N_{space} and $N_{evaluation}$ are the number of design points in the entire design space and the evaluated points in the GA, respectively. For the third method, the first term is the time to obtain the training set from the scheduling-based performance estimation, taking only 5% of the data for the training set generation. The second term, $T_{network}$, is the time to find a set of good neural networks and training and the last term is the actual NN-based DSE time with the GA.

Table 6. Execution time of each method

Patterns	Execution time (hours)		
	Method 1	Method 2	Method 3
4K random read	137.10	58.12	7.61 (89/6/5%)
4K random write	119.34	28.33	6.71 (88/7/5%)
128K sequential read	487.56	60.00	25.13 (97/2/1%)
128K sequential write	70.02	22.04	4.25 (79/11/10%)

Table 6 compares the DSE time among the three methods of DSE. Comparison between the first and the second method shows that the GA-based DSE is faster than the exhaustive search by about 2 to 8 times. Using the NN-based estimation gives another significant speed-up over the scheduling-based estimator. In the third method, how much portion of the time is taken for each term in Eq. 2 is shown in the parenthesis. Time to generate the training data set takes the most while and the GA-based DSE takes the least. The DSE time gap among three methods will grow as the design space increases. In case the design space is not large, any DSE method could be used since the DSE time will not be significant in the whole design process of SSD.

6   Conclusion

In this work, we propose a novel methodology to explore the wide design space of SSD whose complexity is constantly increasing in the early design phase. Since the fast performance estimation is a key technical ingredient of DSE, we propose two performance estimation methods, scheduling-based estimation, and NN-based estimation. Even though the scheduling-based estimation can be used for DSE directly, NN-based estimation is preferred for scalable DSE since the DSE time is much faster. For scheduling-based estimation, it is necessary to construct a task graph, an abstracted SW structure of the firmware. The scheduling-based performance estimation is more than ten times faster than the Amber simulator that is used as the baseline SSD simulator in this work, paying about 10% accuracy loss. The proposed scheduling-based estimator is used to generate the training set for the NN-based estimator. The viability of the proposed methodology is confirmed by several experiments, including DSE conducted with an example SSD, Intel 750 400 GB SSD configuration that is supported in Amber.

Acknowledgement. This work is supported by Memory Division, Semiconductor Business, Samsung Electronics.

References

1. Abadi, M., et al.: TensorFlow: large-scale machine learning on heterogeneous systems (2015)
2. Bucy, J., et al.: The DiskSim simulation environment version 4.0 reference manual (2008)
3. Chen, Z., et al.: Explore the design space of solid state drive by an analytical model. In: 2011 Sixth Annual Chinagrid Conference, pp. 81–88. IEEE (2011)
4. Chollet, F., et al.: Keras. https://keras.io (2015)
5. Fortin, F.A., et al.: DEAP: evolutionary algorithms made easy. J. Mach. Learn. Res. **13**, 2171–2175 (2012)
6. Gouk, D., et al.: Amber*: enabling precise full-system simulation with detailed modeling of all SSD resources. In: 2018 51st Annual IEEE/ACM International Symposium on Microarchitecture (MICRO), pp. 469–481. IEEE (2018)
7. Hu, Y., et al.: Performance impact and interplay of SSD parallelism through advanced commands, allocation strategy and data granularity. In: Proceedings of the International Conference on Supercomputing, pp. 96–107. ACM (2011)
8. Huang, H.H., et al.: Performance modeling and analysis of flash-based storage devices. In: 2011 IEEE 27th Symposium on Mass Storage Systems and Technologies (MSST), pp. 1–11. IEEE (2011)
9. Ipek, E., et al.: Efficiently exploring architectural design spaces via predictive modeling. ACM SIGOPS Oper. Syst. Rev. **41**, 195–206 (2006)
10. Jung, M., et al.: SimpleSSD: modeling solid state drives for holistic system simulation. IEEE Comput. Archit. Lett. **17**(1), 37–41 (2017)
11. Keller, B.: Opportunities for fine-grained adaptive voltage scaling to improve system-level energy efficiency. Master's thesis, EECS Department, University of California, Berkeley (2015)
12. Kim, J., et al.: Machine learning based performance modeling of flash SSDs. In: Proceedings of the 2017 ACM on Conference on Information and Knowledge Management, pp. 2135–2138. ACM (2017)
13. Kim, Y., et al.: FlashSim: a simulator for NAND flash-based solid-state drives. In: 2009 First International Conference on Advances in System Simulation, pp. 125–131. IEEE (2009)
14. Oyamada, M.S., et al.: Accurate software performance estimation using domain classification and neural networks. In: Proceedings of the 17th Symposium on Integrated Circuits and System Design, pp. 175–180. ACM (2004)
15. Ozisikyilmaz, B., et al.: Machine learning models to predict performance of computer system design alternatives. In: 2008 37th International Conference on Parallel Processing, pp. 495–502. IEEE (2008)
16. Panerati, J., et al.: Optimization strategies in design space exploration. In: Ha, S., Teich, J. (eds.) Handbook of Hardware/Software Codesign, pp. 189–216. Springer, Netherlands (2017). https://doi.org/10.1007/978-94-017-7267-9_7
17. Sherwood, T., et al.: Automatically characterizing large scale program behavior. ACM SIGARCH Comput. Archit. News **30**(5), 45–57 (2002)
18. Tavakkol, A., et al.: MQSim: a framework for enabling realistic studies of modern multi-queue {SSD} devices. In: 16th {USENIX} Conference on File and Storage Technologies ({FAST} 2018), pp. 49–66 (2018)

19. Wu, G., et al.: GPGPU performance and power estimation using machine learning. In: 2015 IEEE 21st International Symposium on High Performance Computer Architecture (HPCA), pp. 564–576. IEEE (2015)
20. Yoo, J., et al.: VSSIM: virtual machine based SSD simulator. In: 2013 IEEE 29th Symposium on Mass Storage Systems and Technologies (MSST), pp. 1–14. IEEE (2013)
21. Yoo, J., et al.: Analytical model of SSD parallelism. In: 2014 4th International Conference on Simulation and Modeling Methodologies, Technologies and Applications (SIMULTECH), pp. 551–559. IEEE (2014)
22. Zuolo, L., et al.: SSDExplorer: a virtual platform for fine-grained design space exploration of solid state drives. In: Proceedings of the Conference on Design, Automation & Test in Europe, p. 284. European Design and Automation Association (2014)

Combining Task- and Data-Level Parallelism for High-Throughput CNN Inference on Embedded CPUs-GPUs MPSoCs

Svetlana Minakova$^{(\boxtimes)}$, Erqian Tang, and Todor Stefanov

LIACS, Leiden University, Leiden, The Netherlands
{s.minakova,e.tang,t.p.stefanov}@liacs.leidenuniv.nl

Abstract. Nowadays Convolutional Neural Networks (CNNs) are widely used to perform various tasks in areas such as computer vision or natural language processing. Some of the CNN applications require high-throughput execution of the CNN inference, on embedded devices, and many modern embedded devices are based on CPUs-GPUs multiprocessor systems-on-chip (MPSoCs). Ensuring high-throughput execution of the CNN inference on embedded CPUs-GPUs MPSoCs is a complex task, which requires efficient utilization of both task-level (pipeline) and data-level parallelism, available in a CNN. However, the existing Deep Learning frameworks utilize only task-level (pipeline) or only data-level parallelism, available in a CNN, and do not take full advantage of all embedded MPSoC computational resources. Therefore, in this paper, we propose a novel methodology for efficient execution of the CNN inference on embedded CPUs-GPUs MPSoCs. In our methodology, we ensure efficient utilization of both task-level (pipeline) and data-level parallelism, available in a CNN, to achieve high-throughput execution of the CNN inference on embedded CPUs-GPUs MPSoCs.

Keywords: Convolutional Neural Networks · Dataflow models · SDF · CSDF · Mapping · Hight throughput

1 Introduction

Convolutional Neural Networks (CNNs) are biologically inspired graph computational models, characterized by high degree of available parallelism. Due to their ability to handle large, unstructured data, CNNs are widely used to perform various tasks in areas such as computer vision and natural language processing [1]. The CNNs execution typically includes two phases: training and inference [1]. At the training phase the optimal CNN parameters are established. At the inference phase, a trained CNN is applied to the actual data and performs the task for which the CNN is designed. Due to the high complexity of state-of-the-art CNNs, their training and inference phases are usually performed by high-performance

© Springer Nature Switzerland AG 2020
A. Orailoglu et al. (Eds.): SAMOS 2020, LNCS 12471, pp. 18–35, 2020.
https://doi.org/10.1007/978-3-030-60939-9_2

platforms, and provided as cloud services. However, some applications, e.g. [2–4], require high-throughput execution of the CNNs inference, which cannot be provided as a cloud service. These applications are typically deployed on embedded devices.

Many modern embedded devices are based on multi-processor systems-on-chip (MPSoCs) [5]: complex integrated circuits, that consist of processing elements with specific functionalities. Due to their specific design, MPSoCs offer energy-efficient and high-performance solutions for applications running on embedded devices. In addition to hosting various processing elements, capable of running the CNN inference, such as central processing units (CPUs), embedded graphics processing units (embedded GPUs), and field-programmable gate arrays (FPGAs), MPSoCs integrate many other components, such as communication network components and video accelerators, that allow to deploy the entire embedded application on a single chip. Therefore, MPSoCs seem to be a promising solution for the deployment of the CNN inference phase on embedded devices.

However, achieving high-throughput execution of the computationally-intensive CNN inference phase on embedded CPUs-GPUs MPSoCs is a complex task.

On the one hand, a high-throughput CNN inference execution requires effective utilization of the parallelism, available in a CNN. The parallelism available in a CNN can be divided into two different types: task-level (pipeline) and data-level parallelism. The parallelism, available among CNN layers, hereinafter referred as task-level parallelism [6], involves execution of several CNN layers in a parallel pipelined fashion, where each layer may perform computations, different from the computations, performed by other CNN layers. Utilization of this type of parallelism allows to reduce the overall computation time, and increase the overall CNN inference throughput, compared to sequential execution of CNN layers [7]. The parallelism, available within a CNN layer, hereinafter referred as data-level parallelism [6], involves the same computation, e.g., Convolution, performed by a CNN layer over the CNN layer input data partitions. Utilization of this type of parallelism allows to improve the CNN inference throughput by accelerating the execution of individual CNN layers [8–12].

When the CNN inference is executed on an embedded CPUs-GPUs MPSoC, the CNN computational workload is distributed among the heterogeneous MPSoC processors: embedded CPUs and GPUs. The CPUs are more suitable for handling task-level parallelism, compared to GPUs, whereas GPUs are more suitable for handling data-level parallelism, compared to CPUs [13]. Thus, for efficient execution of the CNN inference on an embedded MPSoC, the task-level parallelism should be handled by the CPUs, available in an embedded MPSoC, i.e., different CNN layers should, if possible, be executed on different CPUs, and the overall CNN computational workload should be balanced among the CPUs [14]. Additionally, the data-level parallelism, available within CNN layers, should be handled by embedded GPUs, i.e., the embedded CPUs should offload data-parallel computations within the CNN layers onto the embedded GPUs, thereby accelerating the computations within CNN layers for further improvement of the CNN inference throughput, already achieved by efficient task-level parallelism exploitation. Thus, efficient execution of the CNN inference on an embedded CPUs-GPUs MPSoC involves efficient exploitation of both task-level parallelism and data-level parallelism, available in the CNN.

On the other hand, effective utilization of task- and data-level parallelism requires proper communication and synchronization between tasks, executed on different processors of an embedded MPSoC. In this respect, attempting to utilize an unnecessary large amount of CNN parallelism on limited embedded MPSoC resources, results in unnecessary communication and synchronization overheads, that reduce the CNN inference throughput. Thus, to achieve high CNN inference throughput, the CNN inference, executed on an embedded MPSoC, should utilize the right amount of parallelism, which matches the computational capacity of the MPSoC.

Based on the discussion above, we argue, that efficient execution of the CNN inference on a CPUs-GPUs embedded MPSoC requires:

1. efficient handling of the task-level parallelism, available in a CNN, by CPUs;
2. CPU workload balancing;
3. efficient handling of the data-level parallelism, available in a CNN, by GPUs;
4. efficient exploitation of task- and data-level parallelism, which matches the computational capacity of an embedded MPSoC.

However, the existing Deep Learning (DL) frameworks [7–12,15–18], that enable execution of the CNN inference on embedded CPUs-GPUs MPSoCs, only partially satisfy requirements (1) to (4), mentioned above. These frameworks can be divided into two main groups. The first group includes frameworks [7] and [18], that exploit only task-level parallelism, available in a CNN, and efficiently utilize only embedded CPUs. Thus, these frameworks satisfy requirements (1) and (2), mentioned above, and do not satisfy requirement (3). The second group includes frameworks [8–12,15–17], that exploit only data-level parallelism, available in a CNN, and efficiently utilize only embedded GPUs. Thus, these frameworks satisfy requirement (3), mentioned above, but do not satisfy requirements (1) and (2). Moreover, all frameworks [7–12,15–18] directly utilize the CNN computational model to execute the CNN inference on embedded CPUs-GPUs MPSoCs. The large amount of parallelism, available in a CNN model, typically does not match the limited computational capacity of embedded CPUs-GPUs MPSoC. Thus, frameworks [7–12,15–18] do not satisfy requirement (4), mentioned above.

Therefore, in this paper, we propose a novel methodology for efficient execution of the CNN inference on embedded CPUs-GPUs MPSoCs. Our methodology consists of three main steps. In Step 1 (Sect. 4.1), we convert a CNN model into a functionally equivalent Synchronous Dataflow (SDF) model [19]. Unlike the CNN model, the SDF model explicitly specifies task- and data-level parallelism, available in a CNN, as well as it explicitly specifies the tasks communication and synchronization mechanisms, suitable for efficient mapping and execution of a CNN on an embedded MPSoC. Thus, a conversion of a CNN model into a SDF model is necessary for efficient mapping and execution of a CNN on an embedded CPUs-GPUs MPSoC. In Step 2 (Sect. 4.2), we propose to utilize a Genetic Algorithm [20], to find an efficient mapping of the SDF model, obtained on Step 1, on an embedded CPUs-GPUs MPSoC. The mapping, obtained by the Genetic Algorithm, describes the distribution of the CNN inference computational workload on an embedded MPSoC, that satisfies requirements (1) to (3), mentioned above. In Step 3 (Sect. 4.3), we use the mapping, obtained in Step 2, to convert a CNN model into a final platform-aware executable Cyclo-Static Dataflow (CSDF) application model [21]. The CSDF model, obtained in Step 3, describes the CNN inference as an application, efficiently distributed over embedded MPSoC processors and exploiting the right amount of task- and data-level parallelism, which matches the computational capacity of an embedded MPSoC. Thus, our methodology satisfies all requirements (1) to (4), mentioned above, to take full advantage of the CPU and GPU resources, available in an MPSoC. Moreover, as we show by experimental results (Sect. 5), our methodology enables high-throughput execution of the CNN inference on embedded CPUs-GPUs MPSoCs.

Paper Contributions

In this paper, we propose a novel methodology for execution of the CNN inference on embedded CPUs-GPUs MPSoCs (Sect. 4), which takes full advantage of all CPU and GPU resources, available in an MPSoC, and ensures high-throughput CNN inference execution on CPUs-GPUs MPSoCs. The exploitation of task-level (pipeline) parallelism, available among CNN layers, together with data-level parallelism, available within CNN layers, for high-throughput execution of the CNN inference on embedded MPSoCs, is our main novel contribution. Other important novel contributions are: (1) the automated conversion of a CNN model into a SDF model, suitable for searching for an efficient mapping of a CNN onto an embedded MPSoC (Sect. 4.1); (2) the automated conversion of a CNN model into a functionally equivalent platform-aware executable CSDF model, which efficiently utilizes CPUs-GPUs embedded MPSoC computational resources (Sect. 4.3); (3) taking state-of-the-art CNNs from the ONNX models zoo [22] and mapping them on a Nvidia Jetson MPSoC [23], we achieve a 20% higher throughput, when the CNN inference is executed with our methodology, compared to the throughput of the CNN inference, executed by the best-known and state-of-the-art Tensorrt DL framework [12] for Nvidia Jetson MPSoCs (Sect. 5).

2 Related Work

The well-known Deep Learning (DL) frameworks, such as TensorFlow [8], Caffe2 [9] and others [10] and some of the Deep Learning frameworks for embedded devices such as [11,12,15–17] efficiently exploit data-level parallelism, available in a CNN, for efficient utilization of embedded GPUs. However, these frameworks do not exploit task-level parallelism, available in a CNN. They execute the

CNN inference layer-by-layer, i.e., at every computational step only one CNN layer is executed. Such layer-by-layer execution of CNN layers is performed either on a single CPU, which utilizes GPU devices for acceleration, or on all available embedded CPUs. Thus, at every computational step, either some of the embedded CPUs are not utilized, or embedded GPUs are not utilized. Therefore, these frameworks cannot take full advantage of all CPU and GPU resources and cannot achieve high CNN inference throughput, typically required for the CNN inference, executed on embedded MPSoCs [2–4]. Unlike these frameworks, our methodology exploits together both task-level parallelism and data-level parallelism, available in the CNN. In our methodology, the CNN layers are distributed on embedded CPUs, such that the CNN workload is balanced among the CPUs, and at every computational step several CNN layers are executed in parallel (pipeline) fashion. At the same time, some of the computations within CNN layers are performed on efficiently-shared embedded GPU devices. Thus, in our methodology, at every computational step all available CPU and GPU resources are efficiently utilized. Therefore, our methodology allows to achieve higher CNN inference throughput, compared to the frameworks, presented in [8–12,15–17].

The frameworks, presented in [7] and [18], exploit task-level parallelism, available among CNN layers, for efficient execution of the CNN inference on an embedded MPSoC. In these frameworks, CNN layers are distributed on the embedded CPUs and executed in parallel (pipeline) fashion, which provides higher CNN throughput than sequential (layer-by-layer) execution of CNN layers. However, these frameworks do not utilize embedded GPUs, available in an MPSoC. As a consequence, these frameworks cannot increase further the CNN inference throughput. In contrast, in our methodology, the throughput, achieved by efficient task-level parallelism exploitation, is further increased by exploitation of data-level parallelism, i.e., by exploitation of embedded GPU devices to accelerate the computations within CNN layers. In our methodology, some computations within CNN layers are offloaded onto embedded GPUs and performed in parallel. Parallel execution of computations within CNN layers allows to reduce the execution time of individual CNN layers and to increase the CNN inference throughput. Therefore, our methodology ensures higher CNN inference throughput, compared to frameworks [7] and [18].

3   Background

In this section, we describe the Convolutional Neural Network (CNN) model, the Synchronous Dataflow (SDF) model, the Cyclo-Static Dataflow (CSDF) model, and specific features of embedded CPUs-GPUs MPSoCs, essential for understanding the proposed methodology.

3.1   CNN Model

The CNN is a computational model [24], commonly represented as a directed acyclic computational graph $CNN(L, E)$ with a set of nodes L, also called layers,

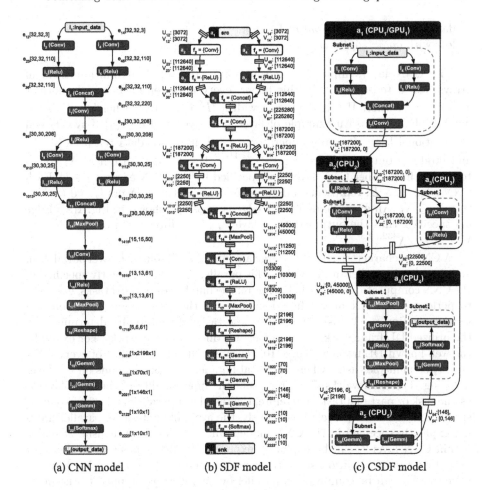

(a) CNN model   (b) SDF model   (c) CSDF model

Fig. 1. CNN, SDF and CSDF computational models

and a set of edges E. An example of a CNN model with $|L| = 23$ layers and $|E| = 24$ edges is given in Fig. 1(a). The CNN model specifies the transformations over the CNN input data, e.g. an image, required to obtain the CNN output data, e.g. an image classification result. Every layer $l_i \in L$ specifies a part of these transformations. It has a layer input data X_i, a layer output data Y_i, and an operator op_i, so that $Y_i = op_i(X_i)$. The operator op_i determines the main difference between the CNN layer types. The most common layer types [1] are:

- convolutional with $op_i = conv$;
- pooling with $op_i \in \{maxpool, avgpool, globalmaxpool, globalavgpool\}$;
- activation with $op_i \in \{relu, thn, sigm\}$;
- Fully Connected (FC) with $op_i \in \{matmul, gemm\}$;
- normalization with $op_i \in \{$Batch Normalization (BN), Local Response Normalization (LRN)$\}$;

- data with $op_i \in \{input, output\}$;
- loss with $op_i = softmax$;

The CNN layers input and output data are stored in multidimensional arrays, called tensors [24]. In this paper, every data tensor T has the format $T^{[W^T, H^T, C^T]}$, where W^T is the tensor width, H^T is the tensor height, C^T is the number of channels. An example of layer l_2 is given in Fig. 1(a). Layer l_2 is a convolutional layer. It applies operator $conv$ to its input data tensor $X_2^{[32,32,3]}$ and produces output data tensor $Y_2^{[32,32,110]}$. The input data tensor X_i comes to layer l_i from other CNN layers, as specified by the CNN edges $e_{ji} \in E$. Each CNN edge $e_{ji} \in E$, represents a data dependency between layers l_j and l_i, such that $Y_j \subseteq X_i$. An example of a CNN edge is edge e_{12}, shown in Fig. 1(a). Edge e_{12} specifies, that the output data of layer l_1 is the input data of layer l_2, i.e., $Y_1^{[32,32,3]} = X_2^{[32,32,3]}$.

A CNN is characterized with a large amount of available task-level parallelism and data-level parallelism. However, this parallelism is not explicitly specified in the CNN computational model. Therefore, the number of parallel tasks, executed to perform the CNN model functionality, and the exact communication and synchronization mechanisms between these tasks are internally determined by the utilized DL framework, and can vary for different frameworks. For example, the well-known DL frameworks [8–10] represent the functionality of every CNN layer l_i as multiple tasks, where the total number of tasks depends on the layer mapping. The frameworks [7,18] represent the functionality of the same layer l_i as one task or part of a task. Therefore, the task-level parallelism is not explicitly specified in the CNN model. Analogously, the available data-level parallelism, is not explicitly specified in the CNN model. The data-level parallelism, available within CNN layer l_i can be explicitly expressed by decomposition of the layer output data tensor Y_i into a set of K output sub-tensors $\{Y_{i1}, Y_{i2}, ..., Y_{iK}\}$, where (1) every Y_{ik} can be computed in parallel by operator op_i, applied to the input data sub-tensor X_{ik}; (2) data elements within every Y_{ik} and every X_{ik} can be processed in parallel. However, the CNN model does not specify the data-level parallelism explicitly, i.e., the number of output data sub-tensors K, the number of elements within sub-tensors X_{ik} and Y_{ik}, and other decomposition parameters are determined by every design framework individually, and can vary for different frameworks. For example, the Caffe2 [9] framework internally represents the $conv$ operator as the $gemm$ operator, so for every Convolutional layer $K = 1$; The TensorFlow framework [10] uses a convolutional operator directly, and computes $K \geq 1$ from the $conv$ operator parameters.

3.2 SDF Model

The SDF model [19] is a well-known dataflow model of computation, widely used in the embedded systems community for efficient mapping of applications on embedded devices [25], including embedded CPUs-GPUs MPSoCs. An application, modeled as a SDF, is a directed graph $G(A, C)$, which consists of a set of nodes A, also called actors, communicating through a set of FIFO channels C. An example of a SDF model with $|A| = 23$ actors and $|C| = 24$ FIFO channels is given in Fig. 1(b). Every actor $a_i \in A$ is a task, which performs certain application functionality, represented as a function f_i. An example of SDF actor a_3 is given in Fig. 1(b). Actor a_3 performs function $f_3 = \{ReLU\}$. Every FIFO channel $c_{ij} \in C$ represents data dependency and transfers data in tokens between actors a_i and a_j. c_{ij} has data production rate U_{ij} and data consumption rate V_{ij}. U_{ij} specifies the production of data tokens into channel c_{ij} by actor a_i. V_{ij} specifies the consumption of data tokens from channel c_{ij} by actor a_j. An example of a communication FIFO channel c_{36} is given in Fig. 1(b). Channel c_{36} transfers data between actors a_3 and a_6. It has production rate $U_{36} = [112640]$, specifying, that, at each firing, actor a_3 produces 112640 data tokens into channel c_{36} and consumption rate $V_{36} = [112640]$, specifying, that, at each firing, actor a_6 consumes 112640 data tokens from channel c_{36}.

3.3 CSDF Model

The CSDF model [21] is a generalization of the SDF model, briefly introduced in Sect. 3.2. Unlike in the SDF model, in the CSDF model, actors have cyclically changing firing rules, and channels have cyclically changing production and consumption rates. An example of a CSDF model with $|A| = 5$ actors and $|C| = 7$ FIFO channels is given in Fig. 1(c). Every actor $a_i \in A$ in the CSDF model performs an execution sequence F_i of length P_i, where $p \in [1, P_i]$ is called a phase of actor a_i. At every phase p, actor a_i executes function $f_i(((p-1)mod P_i) + 1)$. An example of CSDF actor a_2 is given in Fig. 1(c). Actor a_2 performs execution sequence $F_2 = \{Subnet_2^1, Subnet_2^2\}$, where $Subnet_2^1$ and $Subnbet_2^2$ are functions. Actor a_2 has $P_2 = 2$ phases. At phase $p = 1$ actor a_3 performs function $f(1) = Subnet_2^1$, and at phase $p = 2$ actor a_2 performs function $f(2) = Subnet_2^2$.

Instead of fixed production and consumption rates, utilized in the SDF model, in the CSDF model every FIFO channel $c_{ij} \in C$ has data production sequence U_{ij} of length P_i and data consumption sequence V_{ij} of length P_j. Every element $u_{ij}(p) \in U_{ij}$ of the production sequence specifies the amount of tokens, produced by actor a_i into channel c_{ij} at actors phase $p \in [1, P_i]$. Analogously, every element $v_{ij}(p) \in V_{ij}$ of the consumption sequence specifies the amount of tokens, consumed by actor a_j from channel c_{ij} at actors phase $p \in [1, P_j]$. An example of a CSDF communication channel c_{12} is given in Fig. 1(c). Channel c_{12} transfers data between actors a_1 and a_2. It has production sequence $U_{12} = [187200]$, specifying, that actor a_1 produces 187200 tokens into channel c_{12} at its single phase $p = 1$, and consumption sequence $V_{12} = [187200, 0]$, specifying, that actor a_2 consumes 187200 tokens from channel c_{12} at phase $p = 1$ and 0 tokens at phase $p = 2$.

3.4 Embedded CPUs-GPUs MPSoC

We define an embedded MPSoC as a tuple $MPSoC(cpu, gpu)$, where $cpu = \{cpu_1, cpu_2, ..., cpu_n\}$ is a set of all CPU cores, available in the MPSoC; $gpu =$

$\{gpu_1, gpu_2, ..., gpu_m\}$ is a set of all GPU devices, available in the MPSoC, and typically $m \leq n$. An example of an embedded CPUs-GPUs MPSoC with $n = 5$ CPU cores and $m = 1$ GPU device is shown in Fig. 2.

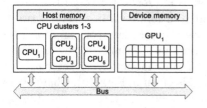

Fig. 2. MPSoC

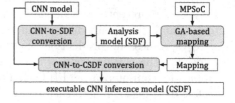

Fig. 3. Our methodology

4   Our Methodology

In this section, we present our three-step methodology for high-throughput execution of a CNN inference on embedded CPUs-GPUs MPSoCs. Our methodology is shown in Fig. 3. In Step 1 (Sect. 4.1), we convert a CNN model into a functionally equivalent SDF model, suitable for efficient mapping of a CNN onto an embedded CPUs-GPUs MPSoC. In Step 2 (Sect. 4.2), we utilize a Genetic Algorithm to find an efficient mapping of the SDF model, obtained in Step 1, onto the MPSoC. In Step 3 (Sect. 4.3), we use the mapping, obtained in Step 2, to convert the CNN model into a CSDF model, representing the final platform-aware executable CNN inference application, which takes full advantage of all CPU and GPU resources, available in an MPSoC for high-throughput execution of the CNN inference on the MPSoC.

Algorithm 1: CNN-to-SDF conversion

   Input: $CNN(L, E)$
   Result: $G(A, C)$
1 $A, C \leftarrow \emptyset$; $G(A, C) \leftarrow$ SDF model (A, C);
2 **for** $l_i \in L$ **do**
3     $f_i = op_i$;
4     $a_i \leftarrow$ actor (f_i);
5     $A \leftarrow A + a_i$;
6 **for** $e_{ij} \in E$ **do**
7     $c_{ij} \leftarrow$ FIFO channel (a_i, a_j);
8     $U_{ij} = W^{Y_i} * H^{Y_i} * C^{Y_i}$;
9     $V_{ij} = W^{X_j} * H^{X_j} * C^{X_j}$;
10    $C \leftarrow C + c_{ij}$;
11 **return** $G(A, C)$

4.1   CNN to SDF Model Conversion

In this section, we show how we automatically convert a CNN model, introduced in Sect. 3.1, into a functionally equivalent SDF model, introduced in Sect. 3.2. The conversion is given in Algorithm 1. It accepts as an input a CNN model $CNN(L, E)$ and generates as an output a functionally equivalent SDF model $G(A, C)$.

In Line 1, Algorithm 1 creates an empty SDF model. In Lines 2–5, Algorithm 1 converts every CNN layer l_i into a functionally equivalent actor a_i. Function f_i, executed by actor a_i, is the operator op_i, performed by layer l_i over its input data tensor X_i to produce its output data tensor Y_i. In Lines 6–10, Algorithm 1 converts every CNN edge e_{ij} into FIFO channel c_{ij}. The production rate U_{ij} of channel c_{ij} is computed in Line 8 of Algorithm 1, and is equal to the number of data elements in tensor Y_i. The consumption rate V_{ij} of channel c_{ij} is computed in Line 9 of Algorithm 1, and is equal to the number of data elements in tensor X_j. An example of the CNN-to-SDF conversion, performed by Algorithm 1, is shown in Fig. 1, where the CNN model, shown in Fig. 1(a), is automatically converted into the SDF model, shown in Fig. 1(b).

Unlike the CNN model $CNN(L, E)$, accepted as an input by Algorithm 1, the functionally equivalent SDF model $G(A, C)$, generated by Algorithm 1, explicitly specifies both task-level and data-level parallelism, which could be exploited during the CNN inference phase, as well as this SDF explicitly specifies the communication and synchronization mechanism between the actors/tasks, needed to execute the CNN inference properly. The task-level parallelism, available among CNN layers, is explicitly specified in the SDF model topology, where every actor $a_i \in A$ is a task, performing the functionality of CNN layer $l_i \in L$, and the total number of tasks, needed to perform the CNN model functionality, is equal to the number of actors in the SDF model. The communication and synchronization between the tasks, are explicitly specified by the SDF FIFO channels, where every channel $c_{ij} \in C$ specifies, that actor $a_i \in A$ communicates with actor $a_j \in A$ through a FIFO buffer, and the production-consumption rates of the channels $c_{ij} \in C$ determine the frequency and the order of the actors firings - for more details see [19]. The data-level parallelism is explicitly specified in the channels production rates. For example, production rate $U_{36} = [112640]$ of FIFO channel c_{36}, shown in Fig. 1(b) and explained in Sect. 3.2, explicitly specifies that, when actor a_3 fires, it produces 112640 data tokens, and each token can be obtained in parallel by executing 112640 parallel $ReLU$ operations within each firing of a_3.

The SDF explicit specification of the tasks, that can be potentially performed during the CNN inference, and the SDF explicit specification of the communication and synchronization between the tasks, allow to perform a search for efficient mappings of the CNN onto an embedded CPUs-GPUs MPSoC.

4.2   Efficient Mapping

In this section, we show how we obtain an efficient mapping of a SDF model $G(A, C)$, generated by Algorithm 1, onto an embedded CPUs-GPUs

Table 1. Mapping example

cpu_1/gpu_1	cpu_2	cpu_3	cpu_4	cpu_5
$a_1, a_2, a_3, a_4, a_5, a_6, a_7$	a_8, a_9, a_{10}, a_{13}	a_{11}, a_{12}	$a_{14}, a_{15}, a_{16}, a_{17}, a_{18}, a_{21}, a_{22}, a_{23}$	a_{19}, a_{20}

a_1	a_2	a_3	a_4	a_5	a_6	a_7	a_8	a_9	a_{10}	a_{11}	a_{12}	a_{13}	a_{14}	a_{15}	a_{16}	a_{17}	a_{18}	a_{19}	a_{20}	a_{21}	a_{22}	a_{23}
cpu_1	cpu_1	cpu_1	cpu_1	cpu_1	cpu_1	cpu_1	cpu_2	cpu_2	cpu_2	cpu_3	cpu_3	cpu_2	cpu_4	cpu_4	cpu_4	cpu_4	cpu_4	cpu_5	cpu_5	cpu_4	cpu_4	cpu_4

Fig. 4. Mapping chromosome example

$MPSoC(cpu, gpu)$, defined in Sect. 3.4. In our methodology, the CNN inference tasks, explicitly specified as SDF actors, are executed on embedded CPU cores, that are able to efficiently handle the task-level parallelism. To efficiently utilize the data-level parallelism, available within the tasks, some of the CPU cores offload computations on the embedded GPUs. Since the number of embedded GPU devices is limited, it may occur, that the efficient exploitation of task-level parallelism, by embedded CPUs, is disrupted due to CPUs competition for the limited embedded GPU devices. To avoid such disruption, for every embedded GPU $gpu_j \in gpu$, we allocate a single CPU core $cpu_i \in cpu$, which offloads computations on gpu_j.

Based on the discussion above, we define a mapping of SDF model $G(A, C)$ onto $MPSoC(cpu, gpu)$, as a partition of actors set A into n subsets, where $n = |cpu|$ is the number of CPU cores, available in the MPSoC. We denote such mapping as $^nA = \{^nA_1, ^nA_2, ..., ^nA_n\}$, where each $^nA_i \in {}^nA$ is a subset of actors, mapped on cpu_i, such that $\cap_{i=1}^{n} {}^nA_i = \emptyset$, and $\cup_{i=1}^{n} {}^nA_i = A$. The first $m = |gpu|$ number of CPU cores in mapping ^nA offload computations on the corresponding embedded GPUs, i.e., the computations within every actor $a_k \in {}^nA_j, j \in [1, m]$ are performed on gpu_j, and the computations within every actor $a_k \in {}^nA_i, i \in [m + 1, n]$ are performed on cpu_i. An example of mapping $^5A = \{^5A_1, ^5A_2, ^5A_3, ^5A_4, ^5A_5\}$ of the SDF model $G(A, C)$, shown in Fig. 1(b) and explained in Sect. 3.2, on the embedded MPSoC, shown in Figure 2 and explained in Sect. 3.4, is given in Table 1. Every Column in Table 1 corresponds to a subset $^5A_i, i \in [1, 5]$. For example, Column 1 in Table 1 corresponds to subset $^5A_1 = \{a_1, a_2, a_3, a_4, a_5, a_6, a_7\}$. The actors within subset $^5A_1$ are mapped on cpu_1, which offloads computations on gpu_1. Column 2 in Table 1 describes subset $^5A_2 = \{a_8, a_9, a_{10}, a_{13}\}$. Every actor $a_i \in {}^5A_2$ is mapped on cpu_2. Since the MPSoC does not have gpu_2, all computations within actors in $^5A_2$ are performed only on cpu_2.

We consider that a mapping is efficient, if it ensures that the workload is balanced [14] among all embedded CPU cores, including those, that offload computations on embedded GPUs. We note, that obtaining such an efficient mapping of an SDF graph onto a CPUs-GPUs MPSoC is a complex Design Space Exploration (DSE) problem. In our methodology, to solve this problem, we propose to use a Genetic Algorithm (GA) [20]: a well-known heuristic approach, widely used for finding optimal solutions for complex DSE problems. We use a simple GA with standard two-parent crossover, a single-gene mutation, and standard user-defined GA parameters, such as initial offspring size, number of epochs, mutation and crossover probabilities [20]. To utilize such a GA for searching of an efficient mapping ^{n}A, we have to specify two problem-specific GA attributes, namely chromosome and fitness function [20]. A chromosome is a representation of a GA solution (in our methodology a solution is a mapping) as a set of parameters (genes), joined into a string [20]. We represent mapping ^{n}A, as a string of length $|A|$, where every gene is a CPU core $cpu_i \in cpu$. An example of the chromosome, corresponding to mapping ^{5}A, shown in Table 1, is given in Fig. 4.

The fitness-function is a special function, which measures the quality of the solutions and guides the GA-based search. During the search, the fitness function should be minimized or maximized. In our methodology, we search for a mapping, in which the workload is balanced among all CPU cores, available in $MPSoC(cpu, gpu)$, i.e., the difference in execution time between every pair of CPU cores $(cpu_i \in cpu, cpu_j \in cpu), i \neq j$, is minimized. Thus, we define a specific fitness-function ϕ to be minimized during the GA-based search as:

$$\phi = \sum_{\forall(cpu_i, cpu_j) \in cpu^2} |\tau_{cpu_i} - \tau_{cpu_j}| \tag{1}$$

where τ_{cpu_i} and τ_{cpu_j} are the total execution time of cpu_i and cpu_j, respectively. For every $cpu_i \in cpu$, τ_{cpu_i} is computed as:

$$\tau_{cpu_i} = \tau_{cpu_i}^t + \tau_{cpu_i}^{com} \tag{2}$$

where $\tau_{cpu_i}^t$ is the time, required by cpu_i to execute all tasks, mapped on cpu_i; $\tau_{cpu_i}^{com}$ is the time, required for communication of cpu_i with other embedded processors. The time $\tau_{cpu_i}^t$ is computed as:

$$\tau_{cpu_i}^t = \sum_{a_k \in {}^{n}A_i} \tau_{(f_k, cpu_i)} \tag{3}$$

where $^{n}A_i$ is the set of all actors, mapped on cpu_i; f_k is the function of actor $a_k \in {}^{n}A_i$; $\tau_{(f_k, cpu_i)}$ is the time, taken by cpu_i to execute f_k, measured on the MPSoC. The time $\tau_{cpu_i}^{com}$ is computed as:

$$\tau_{cpu_i}^{com} = \sum_{a_k \in {}^{n}A_i} \left(\tau_w * \sum_{c_{kj} \in C} U_{kj} + \tau_r * \sum_{c_{jk} \in C} V_{jk}\right) \tag{4}$$

where $^{n}A_i$ is the set of all actors, mapped on cpu_i; $c_{kj} \in C$ is an output channel of actor $a_k \in {}^{n}A_i$, to where, at each firing, actor a_k produces U_{kj} tokens; $c_{jk} \in C$ is an input channel of actor a_k, from where, at each firing, actor a_k consumes V_{jk} tokens; τ_r and τ_w specify the time, needed by a CPU core, to read and write one data token, respectively. τ_r and τ_w are measured on the MPSoC.

4.3   CNN to CSDF Model Conversion

In this section, we show how we automatically convert a CNN model, introduced in Sect. 3.1, into a final executable platform-aware application, represented as a CSDF model, introduced in Sect. 3.3. The conversion is given in Algorithm 2. Algorithm 2 accepts as inputs a CNN model $CNN(L, E)$ and an efficient mapping ^nA, obtained in Sect. 4.2, and generates a CSDF model $G(A, C)$, which performs the functionality of the CNN model $CNN(L, E)$, efficiently mapped on an embedded MPSoC, as specified by mapping ^nA. An example of the CSDF model $G(A, C)$, generated by Algorithm 2, using as inputs the CNN model $CNN(L, E)$, shown in Fig. 1(a) and explained in Sect. 3.1, and mapping ^5A, shown in Table 1 and explained in Sect. 4.2, is given in Fig. 1(c).   In Line 1, Algorithm 2 creates an empty CSDF model. In Lines 3–25, Algorithm 2 generates the set of actors A, such that every actor $a_i \in A$ represents the functionality of all CNN layers, mapped on CPU core cpu_i, as specified in mapping ^nA, where for $\forall l_k \in L$, executed on cpu_i, $\exists a_k \in {}^nA_i$. At every phase $p \in [1, P_i]$ actor a_i executes function $Subnet_i^p$, implemented by means of an existing DL framework. Every $Subnet_i^p$ performs layer-by-layer execution of layers $L_i^p \subseteq L$, mapped on cpu_i, and connected via edges E_i^p. For example, actor a_3, shown in Fig. 1(c), represents the functionality of all CNN layers, mapped on cpu_3. It executes $F_3 = \{Subnet_3^1\}$, where $Subnet_3^1$ performs layer-by-layer execution of layers $L_3^1 = \{l_{11}, l_{12}\}$, connected via edges $E_3^1 = \{e_{1112}\}$, on cpu_3.

Every edge $e_{js} \in E$ between layers l_j and l_s, sequentially executed on the same CPU core, is implemented by means of an existing DL framework, e.g. as device memory, shared by layers l_j and l_s [12]. If layers l_j and l_s, connected via edge $e_{js} \in E$, are executed on different CPU cores, the task-level parallelism is exploited between these layers, and edge e_{js} is converted into a FIFO channel, which explicitly specifies and implements communication and synchronization between actors, executing layers l_j and l_s. For example, edge e_{811}, shown in Fig. 1(a), connects layer l_8, executed by actor a_2 on cpu_2, and layer l_{11}, executed by actor a_3 on cpu_3. Thus, edge e_{811} is converted into a FIFO channel c_{23}, shown in Fig. 1(c), where c_{23} explicitly specifies and implements communication and synchronization between actor a_2, executing layer l_8 and actor a_3, executing layer l_{11}.

Between some actors, cyclic dependencies occur, that may lead to deadlocks in the CSDF model. To avoid the deadlocks, Algorithm 2 specifies the execution of every actor a_i in one or more phases, such that at every phase $p \in [1, P_i]$, actor a_i has no cyclic dependencies. For the example, shown in Fig. 1(c), a cyclic dependency occurs between actors a_2 and a_3. If actor a_2 would execute layers l_8 and l_{13} in one phase, according to the semantics of the CSDF model [21], it would expect 187200 data tokens to be present in channel c_{12} and 22500 data tokens to be present in channel c_{32}, before it can fire. However, data in channel c_{32}, should be produced by actor a_3, which, before it can fire, expects actor a_2 to produce 187200 data tokens in channel c_{23}. Thus, such execution would lead to a deadlock in the CNN inference. To avoid the deadlock, Algorithm 2 specifies the execution of actor a_2 in 2 phases. At phase $p = 1$, actor a_2 executes only layer l_8.

Algorithm 2: CNN-to-CSDF conversion

Input: $CNN(L, E), {}^n A$

Result: $G(A, C)$

1 $A, C \leftarrow \emptyset; G(A, C) \leftarrow$ CSDF model (A, C);

2 $E_{out} = \emptyset$;

3 **for** ${}^n A_i \in {}^n A$ **do**

4      $F_i = \emptyset; p = 1$;

5      $Q = \emptyset; visited = \emptyset$;

6   **for** $l_k : a_k \in {}^n A_i \wedge l_k \notin visited$ **do**

7         $L_i^p, E_i^p \leftarrow \emptyset$;

8         $Q = Q + l_k$;

9   **while** $Q \neq \emptyset$ **do**

10           $l_j = Q.pop()$;

11           $L_i^p = L_i^p + l_j$;

12           $visited = visited + l_j$;

13   **if** $\exists e_{js} \in E : a_s \notin {}^n A_i$ **then**

14   **for** $e_{js} \in E$ **do**

15                 $E_{out} = E_{out} + e_{js}$;

16   break;

17   **else**

18   **for** $e_{js} \in E, l_s \notin visited$ **do**

19                 $Q = Q + l_s$;

20                 $E_i^p = E_i^p + e_{js}$;

21        $Subnet_i^p = $ new Subnet (L_i^p, E_i^p);

22        $F_i = F_i + Subnet_i^p$;

23        $p = p + 1$;

24     $a_i \leftarrow$ actor (F_i);

25     $A = A + a_i$;

26 **for** $e_{ij} \in E_{out}$ **do**

27     $a_k \in A : l_i \in L_k^g; a_r \in A : l_j \in L_r^z$;

28     $c_{kr} \leftarrow$ FIFO channel (a_k, a_r);

29     $u_{kr}(p) = \begin{cases} W^{Y_i} * H^{Y_i} * C^{Y_i}, & \text{if } p = g \\ 0, & \text{otherwise} \end{cases}$

30     $v_{kr}(p) = \begin{cases} W^{X_j} * H^{X_j} * C^{X_j}, & \text{if } p = z \\ 0, & \text{otherwise} \end{cases}$

31 **return** $G(A, C)$

It consumes data only from channel c_{12}, and produces data to channel c_{23}, such that actor a_3 can fire. At phase $p = 2$, actor a_2 consumes data only from channel c_{32}, and executes layers l_9, l_{10} and l_{13}. Thus, at every phase $p = [1, 2]$, actor a_2 has no cyclic dependencies, and no deadlock occurs in the CSDF model execution.

In Lines 5–23, Algorithm 2 performs a mapping-aware Breadth-First Search (BFS) [26] over the CNN model graph and determines functions $Subnet_i^p, p \in [1, P_i]$, executed by actor a_i. In Line 7, for every not-visited layer l_k, mapped on cpu_i, Algorithm 2 creates an empty set of layers L_i^p and an empty set of edges E_i^p. In Line 8, it adds layer l_k to the BFS queue [26] Q, and starts BFS. In Lines 10–12, Algorithm 2 extracts layer l_j from Q and adds l_j to L_i^p. In Line 13, Algorithm 2 checks, if layer l_j, mapped on cpu_i, has at least one child layer l_s, which is not mapped on cpu_i. If the condition in Line 13 is met, to avoid the deadlocks, which can occur in a CSDF model, as discussed above, Algorithm 2 stops adding layers to L_i^p and goes to Lines 14–15, where it adds every output edge of layer l_j to the list of outer edges E_{out}, utilized in Lines 26–30 of Algorithm 2 for CSDF channels generation. If every child layer l_s of layer l_j is mapped on cpu_i (condition in Line 13 of Algorithm 2 is not met), in Lines 18–20, Algorithm 2 adds every connection e_{js} to the set E_i^p, and every layer l_s to Q and continues BFS.

In Line 21, Algorithm 2 creates function $Subnet_i^p$, which performs layer-by-layer execution of layers L_i^p, connected via edges E_i^p. In Line 22, Algorithm 2 adds function $Subnet_i^p$ to execution sequence F_i of actor a_i. When all layers, mapped on cpu_i, are visited, Algorithm 2 adds actor a_i, which executes F_i, to the CSDF model actors set (see Lines 24–25).

In Lines 26–30, Algorithm 2 converts every outer edge $e_{ij} \in E_{out}$ into a CSDF channel c_{kr}, specifying and implementing communication and synchronization between actor $a_k \in A$ executing layer l_i, and actor $a_r \in A$ executing layer l_j. For example, for edge e_{78}, shown in Fig. 1(a), Algorithm 2 creates FIFO channel c_{12}, shown in Fig. 1(c), where actor a_1 executes layer l_7, and actor a_2 executes layer l_8.

5   Experimental Results

In this section, we present our results from an experiment, where real-world CNNs from the ONNX models zoo [22], are mapped and executed on the NVIDIA Jetson TX2 embedded CPUs-GPUs MPSoC [23]. We compare the CNN inference throughput, which we measure, when the CNN is mapped on the NVIDIA Jetson TX2 by: (1) the popular ARM CL framework [27], which, on the NVIDIA Jetson MPSoC, can exploit only task-level parallelism, available in the CNN; (2) the best-known and state-of-the-art for the NVIDIA Jetson TX2 MPSoC, Tensorrt DL framework [12], which exploits only data-level parallelism, available in the CNN; (3) our methodology, explained in Sect. 4, which exploits both task- and data-level parallelism, and uses the ARM CL framework to implement CNN layers on embedded CPUs, and the Tensorrt framework to implement CNN layers on embedded GPUs. For every CNN in the experimental results: (1) The throughput is measured on the platform as an average value over 100 CNN inference executions; (2) original (float32) data precision is utilized, so that the baseline CNN accuracy is preserved; (3) The dataset parameters, such as size and precision of input data samples, as well as the batch size are obtained from the ONNX model representation. (4) The GA, utilized for efficient mapping search (see Sect. 4.2) is executed with initial population size 1000, number of epochs = 500, mutation probability = 5%. If for 50 epochs no improvements are achieved by the GA, the GA stops. The experimental results are given in Table 2.

Column 1 in Table 2 lists the CNNs. Columns 2–4 in Table 2 show the CNN inference throughput in frames per second (fps) for ARM CL, Tensorrt, and our methodology, respectively. Columns 2 and 4 in Table 2 show, that the throughput, achieved by the ARM CL framework is much lower than the throughput, achieved by our methodology. This difference occurs because our methodology exploits both task- and data-level parallelism, available in the CNN, whereas the ARM CL framework, executing the CNN inference on the NVIDIA Jetson MPSoC, does not offload computations on the embedded GPU, available in the MPSoC, and, therefore, does not efficiently exploit the data-level parallelism, available in the CNN. Columns 3 and 4 in Table 2 show, that our methodology achieves up to 20% higher inference throughput, than the Tensorrt framework. This difference occurs because our methodology exploits both task- and data-level parallelism, whereas Tensorrt executes the CNN inference layer-by-layer, and exploits only data-level parallelism, available in the CNN.

Table 2. Experimental results, average over 100 runs

CNN	CNN inference throughput (fps)		
	ARM CL	Tensorrt	Our methodology
bvlc alexnet	3.2	106	112
VGG 19	1.2	13	18
bvlc googlenet	5	115	140
tiny yolo v2	2.6	38	45
inception v1	3.2	115	136
resnet18	7.7	138	143
densenet121	3	52	72
Emotion FER	55	325	401

6 Conclusions

We propose a novel methodology, which exploits both task- and data-level parallelism, available in a CNN, and takes full advantage of all CPU and GPU resources, available in a MPSoC, to achieve high-throughput CNN inference execution. We evaluated our proposed methodology by mapping a set of real-world CNNs on a NVIDIA Jetson embedded CPUs-GPUs MPSoC. The evaluation results show, that taking real-world CNNs from the ONNX models zoo and mapping them on a NVIDIA Jetson MPSoC, a 20% higher throughput is achieved, when the CNN inference is executed with our methodology, compared to the throughput of the CNN inference, executed by the best-known and state-of-the-art Tensorrt DL framework for NVIDIA Jetson MPSoCs.

Acknowledgements. This work has received funding from the European Unions Horizon 2020 Research and Innovation project under grant agreement No. 780788.

References

1. Alom, Md.Z., et al.: The history began from AlexNet: a comprehensive survey on deep learning approaches. CoRR, abs/1803.01164 (2018)
2. Diamant, A., et al.: Deep learning in head and neck cancer outcome prediction. Sci. Rep. **9**, 27–64 (2019)
3. Do, T., et al.: Real-time self-driving car navigation using deep neural network. In: GTSD, pp. 7–12 (2018)
4. Shvets, A., et al.: Automatic instrument segmentation in robot-assisted surgery using deep learning. bioRxiv (2018)
5. Grant, M.: Overview of the MPSoC design challenge. In: DAC (2006)
6. Reinders, J.: Intel Threading Building Blocks. O'Reilly & Associates Inc., Sebastopol (2007)
7. Siqi, W., et al.: High-throughput CNN inference on embedded ARM big. LITTLE multi-core processors. IEEE TCAD **39**, 225–2267 (2019)
8. Abadi, M., et al.: TensorFlow: large-scale machine learning on heterogeneous systems. http://tensorflow.org/ (2015)
9. Jia, Y., et al.: Caffe: convolutional architecture for fast feature embedding. In: MM. ACM (2014)
10. Parvat, A., et al.: A survey of deep-learning frameworks. In: ICISC (2017)
11. Song, L., et al.: HyPar: towards hybrid parallelism for deep learning accelerator array. In: HPCA, pp. 56–68 (2019)
12. NVIDIA TensorRT framework. https://developer.nvidia.com/tensorrt
13. Singh, A., et al.: Energy-efficient run-time mapping and thread partitioning of concurrent OpenCL applications on CPU-GPU MPSoCs. ACM Trans. Embed. Comput. Syst. **16**, 147:1–147:22 (2017)
14. Ando, Y., Shibata, S., Honda, S., Tomiyama, H., Takada, H.: Automated identification of performance bottleneck on embedded systems for design space exploration. In: Schirner, G., Götz, M., Rettberg, A., Zanella, M.C., Rammig, F.J. (eds.) IESS 2013. IAICT, vol. 403, pp. 171–180. Springer, Heidelberg (2013). https://doi.org/10.1007/978-3-642-38853-8_16
15. Kang, D., et al.: C-GOOD: C-code generation framework for optimized on-device deep learning. In: ICCAD (2018)
16. Huynh, L.N., et al.: DeepSense: a GPU-based deep convolutional neural network framework on commodity mobile devices. In: WearSys@MobiSys (2016)
17. Huynh, L., et al.: DeepMon: mobile GPU-based deep learning framework for continuous vision applications. In: MobiSys (2017)
18. Tang, L., et al.: Scheduling computation graphs of deep learning models on many-core CPUs. arXiv:abs/1807.09667 (2018)
19. Lee, E.A., Messerschmitt, D.G.: Synchronous data flow. Proc. IEEE **75**, 1235–1245 (1987)
20. Sastry, K., et al.: Genetic algorithms. In: Burke, E.K., Kendall, G. (eds.) Search Methodologies, pp. 97–125. Springer, Boston (2005). https://doi.org/10.1007/0-387-28356-0_4
21. Bilsen, G., et al.: Cyclo-static dataflow. IEEE Trans. Sig. Process. **44**, 397–408 (1996)
22. ONNX models zoo. https://github.com/onnx/models
23. NVIDIA Jetson TX2. https://www.nvidia.com/en-us/autonomous-machines/embedded-systems/jetson-tx2

24. Abadi, M., et al.: A computational model for TensorFlow: an introduction. In: MAPL. ACM (2017)
25. Ha, S., Teich, J.: Handbook of Hardware/Software Codesign. Springer, Dordrecht (2017). https://doi.org/10.1007/978-94-017-7358-4
26. Even, S.: Graph Algorithms, 2nd edn. Cambridge University Press, Cambridge (2011)
27. ARM compute library. https://github.com/ARM-software/ComputeLibrary

AMAIX: A Generic Analytical Model for Deep Learning Accelerators

Lukas Jünger[1](✉) (iD), Niko Zurstraßen[1] (iD), Tim Kogel[2] (iD), Holger Keding[2] (iD),
and Rainer Leupers[1]

[1] Institute for Communication Technologies and Embedded Systems (ICE), RWTH
Aachen University, Aachen, Germany
`{juenger,zurstrassen,leupers}@ice.rwth-aachen.de`
[2] Synopsys GmbH, Aschheim, Germany
`{tim.kogel,keding}synopsys.com`

Abstract. In recent years the growing popularity of Convolutional Neural Networks (CNNs) has driven the development of specialized hardware, so called Deep Learning Accelerators (DLAs). The large market for DLAs and the huge amount of papers published on DLA design show that there is currently no one-size-fits-all solution. Depending on the given optimization goals such as power consumption or performance, there may be several optimal solutions for each scenario. A commonly used method for finding these solutions as early as possible in the design cycle, is the employment of analytical models which try to describe a design by simple yet insightful and sufficiently accurate formulas. The main contribution of this work is the generic Analytical Model for AI accelerators (AMAIX) for the estimation of CNN inference performance on DLAs. It is based on the popular Roofline model. To show the validity of our approach, AMAIX was applied to the Nvidia Deep Learning Accelerator (NVDLA) as a case study using the AlexNet and LeNet CNNs as workloads. The resulting performance predictions were verified against an RTL emulation of the NVDLA using a Synopsys ZeBu Server-based hybrid prototype. AMAIX predicted the inference time of AlexNet and LeNet on the NVDLA with an accuracy of up to 88% and 98% respectively. Furthermore, this work shows how to use the obtained results for root-cause analysis and as a starting point for design space exploration.

Keywords: Deep Learning Accelerators · Analytical models · Design space exploration · Roofline model

1 Introduction

CNNs have become part of our everyday life in the last years. They can be found in many different applications such as smartphones, data centers, and autonomous driving systems [3,9,11]. These different applications have varying requirements regarding their Key Performance Indicators (KPIs) such as performance, area, power consumption, or cost. Executing CNNs on general purpose

A. Orailoglu et al. (Eds.): SAMOS 2020, LNCS 12471, pp. 36–51, 2020.
https://doi.org/10.1007/978-3-030-60939-9_3

CPUs does often not fulfill these requirements. Therefore, specialized integrated circuits, called Deep Learning Accelerators (DLAs), are developed to mitigate this issue. Designing a DLA is not a trivial task, since a DLA usually consists of different acceleration units for different CNN layers. Each of these units has configuration parameters, leaving the designer with a large design space to explore. For example, the number of Multiply-Accumulate (MAC) units in an accelerator directly influences area, cost, power consumption, and performance. As this work shows, the optimal configuration of a DLA regarding performance strongly depends on the prospective workload, which should therefore also be considered from the very beginning. All these considerations should be included as early as possible in the development process. Although parameters can be altered in later stages as well, small modifications usually entail a series of further changes, especially if the design is already in a more advanced development stage. The more advanced the design is, the higher the costs for the alterations will be.

Common methods to perform early estimates are high-level architecture simulations, also called pre-RTL simulations, and analytical models. Both methods have been applied in DLAs design [2,4,5,10]. However, most approaches focus strongly on the hardware structure to be developed and merely regard the model as a byproduct. These models are usually very specific and therefore cannot be generalized for designing new DLAs. A more generic approach is the *Eyexam* framework proposed in [4]. It shows how a performance evaluation of an arbitrary DLA can be created within seven refinement steps. However, the authors only provide a general overview of how these steps have to be applied and do not mention any formulas or further instructions.

In contrast, this paper presents a novel generic analytical model to estimate the inference performance of an arbitrary DLA. It is based on the popular Roofline model since the assumptions of data/processing parallelism and a small control flow overhead hold valid for most DLA designs [12]. The model still requires characterization regarding the DLA's hardware architecture, but provides a structured and systematic approach to attain it. Other KPIs such as power or area are left for future work. As a case study the model is applied to the Nvidia Deep Learning Accelerator (NVDLA), which was chosen because its open-source RTL implementation and compiler permit to verify the model in great detail. Hence, the estimated inference performance is compared to the results obtained by executing the unmodified NVDLA RTL code in a hybrid prototype using Synopsys ZeBu Server. In addition the estimates are compared to the official Nvidia NVDLA performance sheet [1]. The major contributions of this work are as follows:

- The broadly-applicable AMAIX model for inference performance estimation of DLAs
- Detailed case study on how to apply AMAIX using the NVDLA
- Evaluation of AMAIX's accuracy using hybrid emulation
- Assessment of AMAIX for NVDLA design space exploration

2   The AMAIX Approach

This section deals with the main contribution of this work: AMAIX, a generic analytical model for predicting DLA inference time. When using the Roofline model, which AMAIX is based upon, the designer needs to determine the operational intensity of the application that is modeled. An assumption of the Roofline model is that the operational intensity (the number of operations per byte) during the execution of a task is constant and that the memory and processing resources used do not change. This is depicted in Fig. 1a), where the memory-bound cnn0 task is modeled. If one of these conditions is not fulfilled, a task can be divided into further subtasks, which are mapped to different resources and can have different operational intensities. This is depicted in Fig. 1b). Here the different tasks layer0, layer1, and layer2 are modeled. layer0 is memory bound by the peak bandwidth ceiling memory1, layer1 is compute bound by peak performance ceiling proc1, and layer2 is bound by proc0.

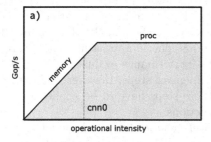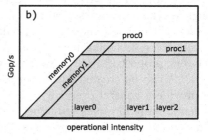

Fig. 1. a) The whole CNN is represented by one task which is mapped to one memory and one processing unit. b) The CNN is described on a layer level. Different layers obtain different operational intensities and can be mapped to different memories and processing units.

Representing an entire CNN as a single task, as for example in [9], was shown to be too simplistic and imprecise [6]. Experiments have shown that operational intensities can be quite different depending on the CNN layer. Therefore, the individual layers that form a CNN must be modeled as individual tasks. In addition, these tasks are usually mapped to different processing units on the DLA. For example on the NVDLA, convolutional layers are executed on the CONV_CORE processing unit, while pooling layers are executed on the PDP processing unit.

In AMAIX we propose that the amount of memory transfers, the number of arithmetic operations and the hardware resources used must be determined per

CNN layer. For this, a mathematical description of CNN layer is introduced as follows:

$$l = \langle i, k, o, map, scale_{ifmap}, scale_{weight}, scale_{ofmap}, scale_{ops} \rangle$$
$$i = \{i_w, i_h, i_c\}, k = \{k_w, k_h, k_c, k_n\}, o = \{o_w, o_h, o_c\}$$
$$map \in \{(proc0, mem0), (proc1, mem1), (proc2, mem1), \ldots\}$$
$$scale_{ifmap} : map \times i \times k \times o \to \mathbb{R}$$
$$scale_{ofmap} : map \times i \times k \times o \to \mathbb{R}$$
$$scale_{weight} : map \times i \times k \times o \to \mathbb{R}$$
$$scale_{ops} : map \times i \times k \times o \to \mathbb{R}$$

Here, i represents the dimensions (width, height, channels) of the input feature map (ifmap), o the dimensions of the output feature map (ofmap) and k the dimensions and number of kernels which are required for a layer's execution. Figure 2 provides an illustration of these parameters. The *map* parameter specifies on which hardware resources a layer is executed. The scaling factors are functions which map a layer's parameters to a real number to incorporate the microarchitectural design of the DLA. They indicate how much the examined data transfers or arithmetic operations deviate from a general model. Since determining the scaling factors correctly is paramount for achieving high modeling accuracy, a more detailed explanation is given in the following subsections.

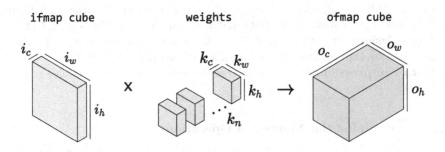

Fig. 2. Visual representation of ifmap, kernel and ofmap parameters

2.1 Determining Data Transfers

The amount of all data transfers (d_{total}) for a CNN's layer is the sum of ifmap data (d_{ifmap}), weight data (d_{weight}), and ofmap data (d_{ofmap}):

$$d_{total} = d_{ifmap} + d_{weight} + d_{ofmap}$$
$$d_{ifmap} = scale_{ifmap} \cdot i_w \cdot i_h \cdot i_c$$
$$d_{weight} = scale_{weight} \cdot k_w \cdot k_h \cdot k_c \cdot k_n$$
$$d_{ofmap} = scale_{ofmap} \cdot o_w \cdot o_h \cdot o_c$$

If $scale_{ifmap} = scale_{weight} = scale_{ofmap} = 1$ is used, the general model is assumed. For example, according to this model the ifmap data is just the number of ifmap elements at one byte per element. This is the volume of the ifmap cuboid shown in Fig. 2. The general model is a good starting point for initial estimates and can be used when there is little information available about the actual hardware.

In practice, there are a number of effects depending on the DLA microarchitecture and executed algorithms causing a scaling smaller or larger than 1. The following list gives an overview of influences on the data scaling factors:

- **Data reload:** On many systems, the size of the on-chip memory is not sufficient to buffer the entire ifmap, kernel and ofmap. This means that the same data has to be fetched/written multiple times from/to the main memory causing an increased scaling factor.
- **Data type:** Frequently used data types are, for example, int8 (1 B) or fp16 (2 B). This must be considered accordingly.
- **Dark bandwidth:** When transferring data via a bus system, the size of the data must be a multiple of the bus width. If this is not the case, dark bandwidth occurs, which results in a larger scaling factor.
- **Zero-padding:** The internal word width of a DLA can cause the data to be padded with zeros increasing the scaling factor.
- **Transformation:** This applies in particular to convolution operations, which can not only be implemented by the standard algorithm. Fourier transform, Winograd convolution, or Toeplitz matrices, can influence the scaling factors.
- **Layer fusion:** Since the output of one layer is usually the input of another, data can be kept locally, which allows a data scaling factor of 0.
- **Data compression**: Data can be compressed resulting in a smaller scaling factor.

2.2   Determining the Number of Operations

Similar to determining data transfers, a formula for the number of arithmetic operations for a CNN's layer is derived:

$$n_{ops} = scale_{ops} \cdot o_w \cdot o_h \cdot o_c \cdot k_w \cdot k_h \cdot k_c$$

For $scale_{ops} = 1$ this formula refers to the number of MAC operations needed for a standard convolution and is also a good first order estimate if no knowledge about the hardware is available. Implementation details of hardware and algorithms can increase or decrease the number of operations scaling factor. Two effects play a particularly important role:

- **Transformation:** Alternative convolution algorithm implementations like Fourier transform or Winograd convolution usually decrease the amount of needed operations.

– **Hardware utilization:** Many DLA designs have fixed processing engine sizes resulting only in a 100% utilization if the data's dimensions comply with these sizes. Chen et al. distinguish between the two cases of *spatial mapping fragmentation* and *temporal mapping fragmentation* leading to underutilized hardware [4]. Since both play an important role in most DLAs, the NVDLA case study section provides an in-depth explanation on how to quantify this effect.

After determining all the scaling factors, a detailed Roofline model can be created. This is covered in the next subsection.

2.3 Applying the Roofline Model

In this subsection the previously presented assumptions and formulas are joined together. As a first step, the Roofline model must be reformulated for each layer l of the CNN L as follows:

$$performance(l) = \min(\ performance_{peak}(l),\ op_{intensity}(l) \cdot memory_{peak}(l)\ )$$

$$op_{intensity}(l) = \frac{n_{ops}(l)}{d_{total}(l)}$$

The inference time of a CNN is the sum over all layer time spans t_{layer}:

$$t_{layer}(l) = n_{ops}(l)/performance(l)$$

$$t_{total}(L) = \sum_{l \in L} t_{layer}(l)$$

Another aspect to be considered is the pipelining of layer operators. Many DLAs like the NVDLA are systolic architectures on layer-level. If one or more layers are pipelined, they must be considered as a whole. The following formulas then apply for a pipeline of layers $pipel = \{l_n, \ldots, l_{n+m}\}$:

$$t_{layer}(pipel) = \max \left(\frac{n_{ops}(l_n)}{performance(l_n)}, \ldots, \frac{n_{ops}(l_{n+m})}{performance(l_{n+m})} \right)$$

$$op_{intensity}(l_{dom}) = \frac{n_{ops}(l_{dom})}{\sum_{k \in pipel} d_{total}(k)}$$

Note, that this model assumes that the overhead for filling and draining a pipeline can be omitted. It can be observed that the slowest unit in a pipeline determines the overall execution time and therefore the performance. A layer l_{dom} which determines a pipeline's executions time is called *dominating*. With all the formulas and descriptions listed above the model is now ready to be applied to an example.

3 Case Study: Nvidia Deep Learning Accelerator

In this section AMAIX, as presented in the preceding section, is applied to the NVDLA. The key challenge here is to determine the different scaling factors.

This is done for bias and convolutional layers as examples in the following. For other layers only the results are presented since a detailed description would go beyond the scope of this paper. With these scaling factors the inference time of the NVDLA is estimated for the widely-used AlexNet and LeNet CNNs [7,8]. These times are then compared with the results of an NVDLA Verilog emulation running in a hybrid prototype based on Synopsys ZeBu Server and Virtualizer. Finally, it is shown how AMAIX can be used to explore the NVDLA's design space.

3.1 Nvidia Deep Learning Accelerator

The NVDLA is an open-source DLA specialised for the inference of CNNs [1]. The project, which exists since 2017, features an open-source SystemC model, a Verilog implementation as well as a corresponding Kernel Mode Driver (KMD) and User Mode Driver (UMD). Executables for the NVDLA can be generated by using the NVDLA compiler. The NVDLA has over 30 configurable hardware parameters. One predefined configuration is the so called NVDLAs full configuration, which is used in this work since it contains all subprocessors and extensions. Figure 3 shows an overview of the NVDLA full configuration.

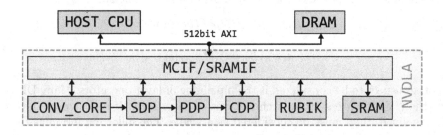

Fig. 3. Overview of the NVDLA full configuration

It can be observed, that the NVDLA is composed of several specialized subprocessors for convolution (CONV_CORE), activation functions (SDP), pooling (PDP), normalization functions (CDP), and memory-to-memory transformations (RUBIK). Also it includes on-chip SRAM and a 512 bit wide AXI bus interface.

3.2 Hybrid Emulation Setup

To verify the results obtained from AMAIX, a hybrid prototype based on Synopsys ZeBu Server and Virtualizer was used for comparison. Here the NVDLA RTL is synthesized for the ZeBu server and then emulated on it, meaning that precise behavioral analysis can be undertaken. In our hybrid emulation setup additional components such as an ARM Cortex A57 CPU cluster and DRAM are added to form an entire embedded system. Since these components only need to be modeled functionally they are part of a Virtualizer SystemC TLM2.0

Virtual Prototype (VP) that is executed on a host computer. This is depicted in Fig. 4. VP and RTL emulation are connected via so-called transactors. Physically a PCIe bus is used for this purpose.

Inside the VP a Linux operating system with the NVDLA drivers is executed on the ARM cluster. To reduce the system's overhead, the simulated ARM cores were clocked at 4 GHz while the NVDLA was clocked at 1 GHz. The DRAM provided in the VP is purely functional and provides no timing annotation. Thus the NVDLA's bandwidth is limited only by its clock speed and bus width, which corresponds to 64 GB/s for the NVDLA full configuration at 1 GHz. This approximation was shown to be valid using a Synopsys Platform Architect Ultra pre-RTL simulation. Using this simulation the DRAM access patterns of the NVDLA were analyzed. It was observed, that nearly 100% of the DRAM bandwidth can be utilized for weight fetching, which dominates the overall data traffic.

Using this setup the execution time for most commonly-used networks like AlexNet or ResNet-18 on the emulated NVDLA is in the range of a few minutes. This allows us to analyze different scenarios quickly.

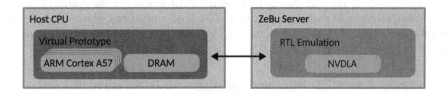

Fig. 4. Hybrid emulation setup.

3.3   Applying AMAIX

As a first example the scaling factors of a convolutional layer shall be derived. These layers are executed on the NVDLA's CONV_CORE which provides a maximum compute power of:

$$performance_{peak} = T_k \cdot T_c \cdot clock$$

With T_k being the width of the NVDLA's MAC unit (which is part of the CONV_CORE) and T_c being the depth of the MAC unit. The MAC unit implements a typical weight-stationary architecture which can also be found in other DLAs. For the NVDLA full configuration with a data type b of fp16, the parameters resolve to $T_k = 16$ and $T_c = 64$.

As a next step the operations scaling factor is derived as:

$$scale_{ops} = \left\lceil \frac{i_c}{Tc} \right\rceil \cdot \left\lceil \frac{k_n}{Tk} \right\rceil \cdot \frac{T_k \cdot T_c}{i_c \cdot k_n}$$

The formula incorporates the previously mentioned cases of *spatial mapping fragmentation* and *temporal mapping fragmentation*. A spatial mapping fragmentation occurs in case of the NVDLA if $i_c < T_c$ and $k_n < T_k$ apply. Temporal mapping fragmentation is similar, but refers to i_c and k_n not being multiples of T_c and T_k. This means that spatial mapping fragmentation never achieves a 100% hardware utilization while temporal mapping fragmentation achieves a 100% hardware utilization only in some cycles of the execution (see Fig. 5).

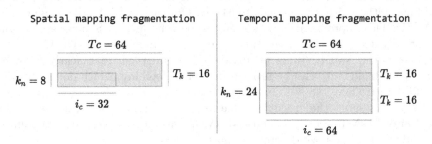

Fig. 5. Depicting temporal and spatial mapping fragmentation. The overall hardware utilization is 0.25 in the first case and 0.75 in the second case. For the spatial mapping fragmentation example each cycle executes 1024 MAC operations. However, only 256 operations contribute to the layer's result. The other 768 operations are dark operations.

To model a lower hardware utilization one can either adjust the computational roof for a given layer or add dark operations. These are operations that are executed but do not contribute to the actual result. In this work the latter approach is used since it combines well with the scaling factor approach and avoids an individual compute roof for each layer.

The next scaling factors discussed are $scale_{ifmap}$ and $scale_{ofmap}$.

The former can be described as follows for the NVDLA full configuration, where $atom_{AXI}/atom_{NVDLA} = 2$, i.e. the AXI bus width is twice the size of the internal NVDLA word width:

$$scale_{ifmap} = pad(i_c, b_i) \cdot \frac{b_i}{i_c} + \frac{d_{darkBW}(i_w, i_h, i_c, b_i)}{i_c \cdot i_w \cdot i_h}$$

$$pad(c, b) = \left\lceil \frac{c \cdot b}{atom_{NVDLA}} \right\rceil \cdot b^{-1} \cdot atom_{NVDLA}$$

$$d_{darkBW}(w, h, c, b) = (w \bmod 2) \cdot h \cdot pad(c, b) \cdot$$

Here four influences on the scaling factor explained in Subsect. 2.1 occur. The first one is scaling due to multi-byte **data types**. The NVDLA uses fp16 as default which results in $b_i = 2$ and linearly scales the amount of data fetc.hed.

Secondly, **zero-padding** occurs. The NVDLA has to work with so-called *atoms* because of its internal word width. In the case of the NVDLA full configuration, an atom must consist of 32 B in the channel direction. This is represented by the parameter $atom_{NVDLA}$. If this is not the case, zero-padding must be applied. For example, for fp16 data types the channels are always padded to be a multiple of 16. So, $i_c = 7$ is padded to 16 channels, $i_c = 17$ to 32 channels and so on.

The third influence on the scaling factor is **dark bandwidth**. Since the $atom_{NVDLA}$ is 32 B while the atom of the bus is 64 B ($atom_{AXI}$) requesting an odd number of atoms will lead to dark bandwidth. Because the NVDLA reads data row-wise, an odd row size will lead to dark bandwidth. So, for every row there are 32 B of dark bandwidth.

Lastly, **data reload** occurs. In the previous formulas it was assumed that ifmap and kernel fit into the 512 KiB convolution buffer of the NVDLA full configuration. However, if this is not the case, the ifmap will be broken into multiple tiles similar to the algorithm proposed by Zhang et al. [5]. These tiles have overlapping areas which result in overall increase of ifmap data. Since the NVDLA treats the individual tiles as separate layers, this should also be done in the analytical model. Otherwise, the scaling factor will quickly become complex.

The last scaling factor to be discussed for convolutional layers is the weight scaling factor $scale_{weight}$. Basically the total amount of weights is the volumes of the kernel cuboids multiplied with the data type and zero-padded to be aligned with the convolutional buffer's width $cbuf_{width}$. This results in the following scaling factor:

$$scale_{weight} = \left\lceil b_k \cdot \frac{k_w \cdot k_h \cdot i_c \cdot k_n}{cbuf_{width}} \right\rceil \cdot \frac{cbuf_{width}}{k_w \cdot k_h \cdot i_c \cdot k_n}$$

Since the amount of weights is often much greater than $cbuf_{width}$ which is 128 B for the NVDLA full configuration, a scaling factor of of $scale_{weight} \approx 2$ is observed for most fp16 cases. The scaling factor for the ofmap is assumed to be 0, since convolutional layers are usually pipelined with a bias layer which will be considered in the following:

$$scale_{ofmap} = 0$$

The next layer to be considered is the bias layer. It always succeeds a convolutional layer and is executed in a pipelined fashion on the NVDLA's SDP. Since it has a fixed throughput of $throughput_X$ ifmap elements per cycle, it is straightforward to determine the operational roof and operation scaling factor as follows:

$$comp_{roof} = throughput_X \cdot clock$$

$$scale_{ops} = \left\lceil \frac{i_w \cdot i_h \cdot pad(i_c, b_i)}{throughput_X} \right\rceil \cdot \frac{throughput_X}{o_w \cdot o_h \cdot o_c \cdot k_w \cdot k_h \cdot k_c}$$

Since a bias layer is always pipelined after a convolutional or an IP layer, there is no ifmap data to fetc.h, so:

$$scale_{ifmap} = 0$$

The ofmap follows the same principles as before:

$$scale_{ofmap} = pad(o_c, b_o) \cdot \frac{b_o}{o_c} + \frac{d_{darkBW}(o_w, o_h, o_c, b_o)}{o_c \cdot o_w \cdot o_h}$$

As the formula shows, the case $o_w = o_h = 1$ is particularly problematic, because here about 50% of the data traffic would consist of dark bandwidth. This is the case after every fully connected layer. Therefore, the NVDLA can be operated in a *compact mode* in which data is read channel-wise rather than row-wise. This reduces the dark bandwidth to a minimum, resulting in the following formula:

$$d_{darkBW}(w, h, c, b) = atom_{NVDLA} \cdot \left(\left\lceil \frac{c \cdot b}{atom_{NVDLA}} \right\rceil mod \, 2 \right)$$

The bias data is transmitted sequentially, therefore the scaling for the weights depends only on the dark bandwidth related to the data type:

$$scale_{weight} = \left\lceil \frac{k_n \cdot b_k}{atom_{AXI}} \right\rceil \cdot atom_{AXI}$$

Since one bias value is needed per output channel, $k_w = k_h = k_c = 1$ and $k_n = o_c$ applies. In addition, a bias has no influence on the dimensions, so $i_w = o_w$, $i_h = o_h$ and $i_c = o_c$ always apply.

Besides bias and convolutional layers there are a number of other layer types for which this methodology was applied. However, these are much less performance-critical and will not be discussed in detail as this would go beyond the scope of this paper.

3.4 Results

In this subsection AMAIX parameterized for the NVDLA as shown in the previous subsection is used to predict inference performance for the AlexNet and LeNet CNNs. The results are compared to the inference performance measured on the hybrid prototype introduced in Subsect. 3.2. The non-cycle accurate SystemC-TLM model was used for measuring the exchanged data amounts with the main memory while the cycle accurate Verilog model was used to measure the time a layer needs for its execution. In addition, the NVDLA performance estimator spreadsheet provided by Nvidia was used for comparison [1].

The standard KMD, UMD and NVDLA compiler in basic mode were used (version: July 2019) to execute the following measurements. As of September 2019 the compiler also supports several optimization options, which were not available for our experiments. All KMD debug output was removed for the RTL measurements, as it turned out to reduce performance significantly.

As a first example the results of LeNet shall be analyzed which are depicted in Table 1. A corresponding roofline graph can be found in Fig. 6. The following parameters are shown in the table: execution time of a layer according to AMAIX ($t_{layer,am}$), the hybrid prototype ($t_{layer,hyb}$) and the NVDLA performance sheet ($t_{layer,ps}$). Furthermore, the boundary (either memory or compute

Table 1. Results of LeNet. In all cases the bias is dominated by the corresponding convolutional/fully connected layer.

Layer	$t_{layer,am}$	$t_{layer,hyb}$	$t_{layer,ps}$	bound	d_{weight}	d_{ifmap}	d_{ofmap}	n_{ops}
Unit	µs	µs	µs	$\{c, m\}$	B	B	B	operations
conv1	28.8	28.9	7.2	c	1,024	25,088	0	29,491,200
(bias)	0	0	0	-	64	0	36,864	18,432
pool1	4.61	4.61	0	c	0	36,864	9,216	18,432
conv2	6.40	6.93	3.2	c	50,048	9,216	0	6,553,600
(bias)	0	0	0	-	128	0	8,192	4,096
pool2	1.02	1.06	0	c	0	8,192	2,048	4,096
fc3	12.5	12.97	15.67	m	800,000	2,048	0	8,388,608
(bias)	0	0	0	-	1,024	0	1,024	512
relu3	0.03	0.08	0	c/m	0	1,024	1,024	128
fc4	0.18	0.37	0.17	m	10,112	1,024	0	131,072
(bias)	0	0	0	-	64	0	64	32
softmax	0	0	0	-	0	0	0	0
idle	0	20.52	0	-	0	0	0	0
Total	53.9	54.92+20.52	26.2	-	862,464	83,712	58,432	44,610,208

bound), data exchanged with main memory (d_{weight}, d_{ifmap}, d_{ofmap}) and number of operations (n_{ops}) are also displayed. The amount of data refers to both simulation and analytical model, since the model predicted this 100% accurately. The number of operations refers only to the analytical model. Layers which are pipelined and not dominant are enclosed in brackets. The execution time of a layer is defined as the time between setting the kick-off register and raising the interrupt flag. The results show that for the total inference time the analytical model predicts the measured inference time of 54.9 µs with 53.9 µs or 98% accuracy. The model deviates from the measurements in some layers, especially in small layers. Several reasons for this were discovered during analysis. Firstly, the individual subprocessors such as the SDP also have internal pipelines which need a certain number of cycles to be filled. Furthermore, a certain amount of data must be available before the execution of operations can be started with. This is a deviation from the perfect parallelism which is assumed by the roofline model. Therefore, the analytical model underestimates the execution time.

The time obtained from the NVDLA performance sheet overestimated the performance of the NVDLA by more than 2x. This is due to the performance sheet assuming optimizations like layer pipelining or Winograd convolution which were not implemented in the NVDLA compiler at the time the performance sheet was released. Due to the lack of configurability, the result given by the performance sheet could not be improved further. Some aspects like ifmap tiling or bias layers are completely omitted, which further deteriorates its accuracy.

Figure 7 shows an activity trace of LeNet on the hybrid prototype. The "idle" parts represents phases in which the NVDLA waits for further instructions from the driver. These times have already been greatly reduced by the previously mentioned modifications of the KMD, but are still significant. One reason for

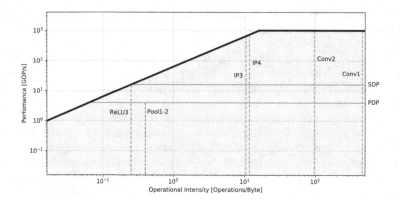

Fig. 6. Applying a roofline graph on the obtained results of LeNet.

this is that LeNet is a very small example for today's standards. As the results show, the NVDLA can process most layers within a few hundred cycles or less. This leads to the hardware being faster than the driver.

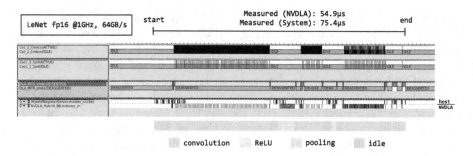

Fig. 7. Activity trace of LeNet running as a Hybrid Emulation.

Therefore, the results of the larger and more recent AlexNet are analyzed. These are shown in Table 2. Again, the analytical model was able to predict the amount of data required 100% accurately. The total inference time of 6.1 ms was accurately predicted to about 88% with an estimate of 5.4 ms. The performance sheet overestimated the performance of the NVDLA again with 2.3 ms by a factor of 2.7x.

The largest deviation of the analytical model is found in layer "fc6". The analysis of this layer showed that the size of the required data causes the compiler to switch the convolution buffer to work in a single buffer mode, so that convolution and memory transfers no longer run in parallel. This effect can also be modeled by dividing a layer into a compute task and a memory task. With this simple extension the analytical model predicts 6005.4 μs which is 98% accurate. However, this results in operational intensities of 0 or infinity which is difficult to represent in the roofline graph.

Table 2. Results of AlexNet. In all cases the bias is dominated by the corresponding convolutional/fully connected layer.

Layer	$t_{layer,am}$	$t_{layer,hyb}$	$t_{layer,ps}$	bound	d_{weight}	d_{ifmap}	d_{ofmap}	n_{ops}
Unit	μs	μs	μs	$\{c, m\}$	B	B	B	operations
conv1-1	479.2	497.2	102.9	c	69,760	423,168	0	490,659,840
(bias)	0	0	0	-	192	0	129,024	63,360
conv1-2	479.2	497.2	0	c	0	423,168	0	490,659,840
(bias)	0	0	0	-	192	0	129,024	63,360
conv1-3	479.2	497.2	0	c	0	423,168	0	490,659,840
(bias)	0	0	0	-	192	0	129,024	63,360
conv1-4	479.2	497.2	0	c	0	423,168	0	490,659,840
(bias)	0	0	0	-	192	0	129,024	63,360
conv1-5	279.5	279.5	0	c	0	255,360	0	286,218,240
(bias)	0	0	0	-	192	0	75,264	36,960
relu1	18.5	18.2	0	c/m	0	591,360	591,360	290,400
norm1	72.6	79.3	0	c	0	654,720	654,720	290,400
pool1	72.6	72.6	0	c	0	591,360	145,152	290,400
conv2	583.2	588	218.7	c	614,400	145,152	0	597,196,800
(bias)	0	0	0	-	512	0	387,072	186,624
relu2	12.1	11.7	0	c/m	0	387,072	387,072	186,624
norm2	46.7	50.8	0	c	0	428,544	897,536	186,624
pool2	46.7	46.7	0	c	0	387,072	93,184	186,624
conv3	146.0	149.6	64.9	c	1,769,472	93,184	0	149,520,384
(bias)	0	0	0	-	768	0	139,776	64,896
relu3	4.4	4.1	0	c/m	0	139,776	139,776	64,896
conv4	219	224.4	48.7	c	1,327,104	139,776	0	224,280,576
(bias)	0	0	0	-	768	0	139,776	64,896
relu4	4.4	4.1	0	c/m	0	139,776	139,776	64,896
conv5	146	151.4	32.4	c	884,736	139,776	0	149,520,384
(bias)	0	0	0	-	512	0	93,184	43,264
relu5	2.9	2.7	0	c/m	0	93,184	93,184	43,264
pool5	10.8	10.8	0	c	0	93,184	18,432	43,264
fc6	1180.2	1792.6	1152.4	m	75,497,472	18,432	0	603,979,776
(bias)	0	0	0	-	8,192	0	8,192	4,096
relu6	0.3	0.3	0	c/m	0	8,192	8,192	4,096
fc7	524.7	525.5	512.3	m	33,554,432	8,192	0	268,435,456
(bias)	0	0	0	-	8,192	0	8,192	4,096
relu7	0.3	0.3	0	c/m	0	8,192	8,192	4,096
fc8	128.2	128.8	125.2	m	8,192,000	8,192	0	66,060,288
(bias)	0	0	0	-	2,048	0	2,048	1,008
softmax	0	0	0	-	0	0	0	0
Total	5415.5	6124.4	2257.4	-	$121{,}9 \cdot 10^6$	$6 \cdot 10^6$	$4.6 \cdot 10^6$	$4.3 \cdot 10^9$

3.5   Design Space Exploration

Since the simulation results have shown that AMAIX allows precise predictions to be made, it will be used to explore the NVDLA's design space in this section. The NVDLA has over 30 different hardware parameters that can be individually set to provide a suitable configuration for each application. Some of these parameters are also found in the analytical model. For example, the width and depth (T_c (depth) and T_k (width)) of CONV_CORE's MAC unit. The performance of AlexNet in frames per second is shown regarding these parameters in Fig. 8. The tuples (width, depth) are chosen such that their product is constant, which corresponds to a constant area. The analysis shows that besides the full configuration of the NVDLA there are other configurations that theoretically allow a faster execution of AlexNet. However, with a convolution buffer size of 512 KiB the design space is limited to the highlighted area of the graphs. Thus the NVDLA full configuration seems to be optimal for AlexNet given the convolution buffer constraint. This result cannot be verified using the NVDLA. Although the hardware synthesis of the NVDLA configurations is possible, the drivers so far only support the full, large and small NVDLA configuration.

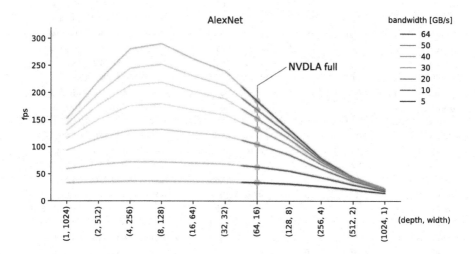

Fig. 8. Design space exploration of the Convolution Core using AlexNet.

4   Conclusions

In this paper the novel AMAIX approach for the inference performance estimation of DLAs was proposed and evaluated. AMAIX's design allows for generic representation of DLAs, due to its configurable scaling factors. Its per layer modeling approach is a reasonable compromise between model complexity and accuracy as shown in the detailed case study. For the NVDLA, the model predicted the inference time with an accuracy of 88% for AlexNet and 98% for LeNet compared to an accurate RTL emulation. In addition it was shown, that AMAIX can be used for design space exploration, especially since it can be evaluated several orders of magnitude faster than a Verilog or SystemC simulation.

In future work, it would be interesting to apply AMAIX to other DLA architectures. Another possible application are compiler optimizations. For example, an analytical model can help to simplify the decision between Winograd convolution and standard convolution. While Winograd convolution can usually be calculated much faster, it still requires more weight data. It should therefore only be used if the system is compute bound. The analytical model can also be used to characterize architecture-level simulation models of DLAs in order to evaluate their impact on the interconnect and memory subsystem.

References

1. NVDLA Github Repository. https://github.com/nvdla. Accessed 27 July 2019
2. Alwani, M., Chen, H., Ferdman, M., Milder, P.: Fused-layer CNN accelerators. In: 49th IEEE/ACM International Symposium on Microarchitecture (MICRO) (2016)
3. Bratt, I.: Arm's first-generation machine learning processor. In: IEEE Hot Chips 30 Symposium (2018)
4. Chen, Y., Emer, J.S., Sze, V.: Eyeriss v2: A Flexible and High-Performance Accelerator for Emerging Deep Neural Networks. CoRR (2018)
5. Zhang, C., Li, P., Guangyu, S.: Optimizing FPGA-based accelerator design for deep convolutional neural networks. In: Proceedings of the 2015 ACM/SIGDA International Symposium on Field-Programmable Gate Arrays (2015)
6. Hill, M.D., Reddi, V.J.: Gables: a roofline model for mobile SoCs. In: IEEE International Symposium on High Performance Computer Architecture (HPCA) (2019)
7. Krizhevsky, A., Sutskever, I., Hinton, G.E.: ImageNet classification with deep convolutional neural networks. In: NIPS'12 Proceedings of the 25th International Conference on Neural Information Processing Systems (2012)
8. LeCun, Y., Bottou, L., Bengio, Y., Haffner, P.: Gradient-based learning applied to document recognition. In: Proceedings of the IEEE, vol. 86 (1998)
9. Jouppi, N.P., Young, C., Patil, N.: In-datacenter performance of a tensor processing unit. In: 44th International Symposium on Computer Architecture (ISCA) (2017)
10. Reagen, B., et al.: Minerva: enabling low-power, highly-accurate deep neural network accelerators. In: 2016 ACM/IEEE 43rd Annual International Symposium on Computer Architecture (ISCA) (2016)
11. Venkataramanan, G.: Compute and redundancy solution for the full self-driving computer. In: IEEE Hot Chips 31 Symposium (2019)
12. Williams, S., Waterman, A., Patterson, D.: Roofline: an insightful visual performance model for multicore architectures. ACM Commun. **52**, 65–76 (2009)

Data Mining in System-Level Design Space Exploration of Embedded Systems

Valentina Richthammer$^{(\boxtimes)}$, Tobias Scheinert, and Michael Glaß

Institute of Embedded Systems/Real-Time Systems, Ulm University, Ulm, Germany
{valentina.richthammer,tobias.scheinert,michael.glass}@uni-ulm.de

Abstract. With increasingly complex applications and architectures, the task of determining Pareto-optimal implementations at the system level becomes a challenge even for state-of-the-art Design Space Exploration (DSE) methodologies. In this field, nature-inspired techniques such as Evolutionary Algorithms (EAs) are frequently employed, since they are well-suited to the multi-objective and hard-constrained nature of the DSE optimization problem. On the other hand, meta-heuristic approaches are problem-agnostic and are often observed to converge relatively quickly. Furthermore, this type of optimization lacks *explainability*, i.e. the way in which the optimization algorithm arrives at improved solutions as well as the individual contributions of design decisions to the resulting quality of a solution are not at all clear - and are consequently not utilized during DSE as of yet. To remedy this, we propose the integration of automated *data-mining* techniques into state-of-the-art DSE flows. Data mining is, thereby, used for (a) the automatic extraction and generation of previously untapped information from the optimization process to be (b) incorporated into the DSE to enhance optimization quality. We present a variety of ways to extract and include relevant knowledge during DSE, as well as (c) several possibilities to gain insight into the interdependence between decision variables and optimization objectives. Experimental results for benchmark systems for large-scale many-cores to networked embedded systems demonstrate the potential of the proposed techniques to improve the quality of the optimized implementations at no DSE-time overhead.

Keywords: Design automation · Knowledge discovery

1 Introduction

Increasingly complex embedded applications and architectures have made the problem of determining high-quality *implementations* mapping an application to an embedded architecture intractable for manual optimization. Instead, Design Space Exploration (DSE) techniques at the Electronic System Level (ESL) are being developed to automatically derive a set of optimized implementation possibilities from a given system specification [30]. This allows to simultaneously optimize a multitude of design objectives, e.g. a system's energy consumption,

A. Orailoglu et al. (Eds.): SAMOS 2020, LNCS 12471, pp. 52–66, 2020.
https://doi.org/10.1007/978-3-030-60939-9_4

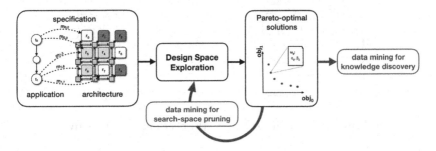

Fig. 1. System-level DSE design flow following the Y-chart approach (black) [15] with proposed incorporation of data-mining techniques (red, bold). (Color figure online)

reliability, or latency. State-of-the-art DSE approaches employ problem-specific heuristics or meta-heuristic optimization techniques to derive a set of *Pareto-optimal* solutions [23] following the established Y-chart approach [15] (cf. Fig 1).

A main challenge that needs to be addressed by any DSE approach is the fact that the feasibility of implementations is typically subject to a number of constraints, e.g. limited area or resource capacities, real-time properties such as execution deadlines, etc. In fact, deriving a single implementation requires the NP-complete steps of deriving a feasible (a) allocation, (b) binding, (c) routing, and (d) scheduling [31] from the system specification that defines the set of *all* implementation possibilities. Therefore, hybrid optimization techniques combining nature-inspired optimization algorithms such as Multi-Objective Evolutionary Algorithms (MOEAs) with automatic symbolic repair strategies have emerged [17,24], offering the advantage of optimizing multiple objectives and solutions in parallel, while guaranteeing feasibility of explored solutions. A problem of these optimization approaches is the fact that the optimization quality converges comparably quickly, as the diversity of explored solutions decreases over time, as illustrated in Fig. 2: After an initial improvement of random starting solutions—indicated by the decreasing ϵ-dominance measuring multi-objective optimization quality (see Sect. 5)—the employed MOEA barely generates any novel solutions that are superior w.r.t. the optimized objectives. Therefore, DSE cannot simply be improved by increasing available exploration time alone.

Furthermore, nature-inspired optimization approaches lack *explainability*, i.e. the relationship between design decisions made by the optimization algorithm and the corresponding quality of a solution is not at all clear. In particular, the combinatorial nature of the DSE problem makes it next to impossible to predict an implementation's quality from the outset, i.e. before actually evaluating it w.r.t. the optimization objectives. This is because the flip of a single optimization variable, i.e. the change of merely one task binding, may drastically alter an implementation's quality (e.g. if a more expensive or less reliable Processing Element (PE) is allocated)—or even render it completely infeasible (if, e.g., communication requirements can no longer be fulfilled). This lack of insight into the optimization also makes it hard to dynamically improve a DSE run in an on-line manner when optimization quality begins to stagnate.

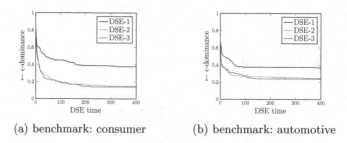

(a) benchmark: consumer   (b) benchmark: automotive

Fig. 2. Stagnating optimization quality of various DSE approaches for benchmark applications from the Embedded Systems Synthesis Benchmark Suite (E3S) [8].

As a remedy, we propose the use of *data-mining techniques* [1] for automatic knowledge discovery during DSE. Originated from the fields of market basket analysis, data mining is concerned with the automated extraction of uncharted information and patterns between the entries of transactional databases. With the growing availability of large-scale data sets and the ensuing interest in automatic analysis techniques, recent years have seen a steady increase in the development and application of data mining techniques to a wide variety of application domains—ranging from medical data analysis to image processing [11].

Typical DSE runs generate vast amounts of data in the form of tens of thousands of feasible, evaluated solutions. Therefore, the integration of data mining into DSE becomes seamlessly possible when treating each explored solution as a database entry containing the corresponding design decisions and quality numbers, so that relationships between the decisions made by the optimizer and their influence on an implementation's quality can easily and automatically be extracted. This information is—for the most part—not utilized in standard iteration-based optimization approaches, where merely a ranking based on qualitative differences between solutions determines whether a solution is selected for further optimization. Novel solutions are, furthermore, generated by generic operators (e.g. random mutation or crossover) that do not take into account which parts of a solution actually contribute to its quality. We, therefore, propose to tap the full potential of the data created during DSE by presenting a variety of mechanisms to integrate data mining into any arbitrary DSE flow. The extracted knowledge is thereby utilized in the following ways (cf. also Fig. 1):

To counteract the problem of converging optimization quality, we present two distinct mechanisms of feeding mined knowledge back into the optimization loop, so that an on-line adjustment of the DSE becomes possible. Both approaches result in a dynamic restriction of the available search space—corresponding to a reduction in problem complexity—to facilitate its exploration. The search-space restriction is achieved by either (a) a tightening of constraints on feasible solutions or (b) a pruning of the input specification to exclude unpromising solutions. Thus, the exploration is guided in the direction of promising solutions.

Secondly, we present a-posteriori DSE analyses that apply data mining to gain insights into the influence of design decisions on an implementation's quality.

This includes approaches for determining (a) a separation between decisions predominantly found in high-quality solutions vs. decisions that have resulted in lower-quality solutions and (b) a discrimination of design decisions based on their influence on *separate* optimization objectives, i.e. to determine which decisions mainly affect the quality of a solution w.r.t. *a single* objective (out of the set of simultaneously optimized objectives). These mechanisms provide novel insights into the DSE process and may help optimization engineers to better understand and utilize the resulting set of implementation possibilities.

In the remainder of the paper, Sect. 2 presents related work on DSE and related applications of data mining, while Sect. 3 introduces the DSE problem and selected data-mining techniques. The integration of data mining to improve DSE and analyse the resulting implementations is presented in Sect. 4 and experimentally evaluated in Sect. 5, before Sect. 6 concludes the paper.

2 Related Work

State-of-the-art DSE approaches are either based on problem-specific heuristics or generic metaheuristic techniques, since an exhaustive evaluation of all implementation possibilities is not feasible for any modern embedded system of real-world complexity [29]. While heuristics require a-priori knowledge about the problem domain and are, thus, limited in their applicability [22], metaheuristics such as *hybrid optimization techniques* [6] are at a disadvantage because of their problem-agnostic nature. One major challenge is the difficulty of balancing the exploration of novel solutions in the search space (global search) with the exploitation of high-quality solutions (local search). Without dynamic adjustments via, e.g., restarts [20] or self-adaptive parameters [2], many metaheuristics converge quickly, resulting in an insufficient exploration of the search space.

In the field of design automation, recent works have demonstrated the unsuitability of such approaches for DSE, and in particular of *monolithic* approaches optimizing the complete system all at once [26], since the complexity of the DSE problem increases exponentially with growing system sizes. Related works in the area of search-space restriction use, again, problem-specific techniques clustering [14] or decomposing the target architecture [5,10,26] or application [21] to reduce DSE complexity. While data mining has been applied to guide metaheuristic search in single-objective optimization via specialized MOEA operators [25,32], its application for search-space decomposition in constrained combinatorial Multi-Objective Optimization Problems (MOPs) such as DSE is, to the best of our knowledge, a novel approach.

Furthermore, system-level DSE is still predominantly evaluated w.r.t. optimization quality and time only. While these metrics give insight into qualitative differences of solutions in terms of the optimization objectives, they provide no information on what actually makes a solution good or bad, i.e. what decisions made during optimization led to high-quality solutions. To gain insight into the relationship between decision variables and optimization objectives, we propose the use of *emerging pattern mining* [9] to determine *discriminative characteristics* between high- and low-quality solutions and between separate objectives. While other data mining [4] and machine learning approaches [13] have been used for knowledge discovery and visualization in other types of MOPs (for an extensive survey see [3]), the presented approach is a novel method to gain insight into the effect of design decisions in combinatorial optimization.

3   Fundamentals

This section introduces DSE as constrained combinatorial MOP together with fundamentals on data mining algorithms that we propose to integrate into DSE.

3.1   System Model

Graph-based system specifications as proposed in [31] are a suitable abstraction for system-level DSE. A system specification (cf. Fig. 1 (left)) consists of *application graph* G_T, *architecture graph* G_R and a set of *mapping edges* E_M between the two to specify implementation possibilities of the application on the architecture. The application is a bipartite directed acyclic graph $G_T(V_T, E_T)$. The set of vertices $V_T = T \cup C$ contains the application's tasks T and messages C that are connected by edges $E_T \subseteq (T \times C) \cup (C \times T)$ to describe data dependencies between the tasks. The architecture is a directed graph $G_R(R, L)$ with vertices R representing PEs connected by communication-link edges L. Mapping edges $E_M \subseteq T \times R$ from tasks T in the application to PEs R in the architecture define the set mapping possibilities. In particular, a mapping edge $m_{t,r} \in E_M$ is part of the specification iff it is possible to feasibly bind task $t \in T$ to resource $r \in R$.

3.2   DSE as Hard-Constrained MOP

During DSE, implementations are derived from the specification by selecting an *allocation*, i.e. a subset of PEs from the architecture, *binding* each application task to an allocated resource, and determining a *routing* of messages and a *schedule* for task execution. At the system level, an implementation is constructed by selecting a subset $E_{M_{\mathrm{act}}} \subseteq E_M$ of available mapping edges to be *activated*. This determines the binding and (implicitly) the allocation and makes DSE a combinatorial optimization problem. Furthermore, *feasible* implementations require that a set of design constraints are fulfilled, e.g. imposed by data dependencies in the application, limitations such as schedulability, physical constraints such as restricted energy budgets or link capacities, etc. DSE, therefore, can formally be defined as a constrained combinatorial MOP [18]:

$$minimize \{\mathbf{f}(\mathbf{x}) \mid A\mathbf{x} \leq \mathbf{b}\} \tag{1}$$

$$\text{with } A \in \mathbb{Z}^{m,n}, \mathbf{b} \in \mathbb{Z}^m, \text{ and } \mathbf{x} \in \{0,1\}^n$$

with a vector of objective functions $\mathbf{f}(\mathbf{x}) = (f_1(\mathbf{x}), \ldots, f_z(\mathbf{x}))$ that can w.l.o.g. be formulated to be minimized. Each implementation, generated by varying decision variables $x_i \in \mathbf{x}$ in the n-dimensional *decision vector* $\mathbf{x} \in \{0,1\}^n$, is evaluated w.r.t. them. Design constraints on feasible solutions are given by $A\mathbf{x} \leq \mathbf{b}$.

Pareto-Optimality for MOPs. Since DSE typically optimizes multiple objectives simultaneously, no single globally optimal solution can be identified. Instead, a *set* of *Pareto-optimal* implementations X_p is derived from the set of feasible solutions X_f, so that an implementation is in X_p iff it is not dominated by any other explored solution [33]. An objective vector $f(\mathbf{x}) = (a_1, \ldots, a_z)$ *dominates* a second objective vector $f(\mathbf{x}') = (b_1, \ldots, b_z)$, iff

$$\forall i : a_i \leq b_i \wedge \exists j : a_j < b_j \tag{2}$$

A dominating solution is, therefore, superior in at least one objective, while it must not be worse for the remaining objectives. The Pareto-front of DSE is usually merely *approximated* by a set of *non-dominated solutions* X_{p^*} called an *archive*, since exhaustive optimization is intractable.

3.3   Fundamentals of Data Mining

Data mining is concerned with the automatic discovery of knowledge from transactional databases [1]. Given a set of possible *items* A, a set $I = \{i_0, i_1, \ldots, i_k\} \subseteq A$ is called an *itemset* and a tuple $T = (id, I)$, with an identifier id is called a *transaction*. A set of transactions form a transactional database D over A. To analyse the occurrence of *frequent* itemsets, i.e. items that commonly occur together in transactions of D, the *support* of an itemset X is defined as the probability of X occurring in D:

$$sup_D(X) = \frac{|\{T | T = (id, I) \in D \wedge X \subseteq I\}|}{|D|} \tag{3}$$

If the support is greater than a given threshold σ_{sup}, i.e. if $sup_D(X) \geq \sigma_{sup}$ with $0 \leq \sigma_{sup} \leq 1$, X is said to be *frequent*.

Association rules $X \Rightarrow Y$ between itemsets X, Y, with $X \cap Y = \emptyset$, model *implication* relationships. The support of an association rule is defined as:

$$sup_D(X \Rightarrow Y) = sup_D(X \cup Y) \tag{4}$$

Furthermore, the *confidence* of an association rule is the conditional probability of Y occurring in transactions given X:

$$conf(X \Rightarrow Y) = P(Y|X) = \frac{sup_D(X \cup Y)}{sup_D(X)} \tag{5}$$

If the support *and* confidence of any such rule $X \Rightarrow Y$ are above given thresholds $\sigma_{sup}, \sigma_{conf}$, it is said to be an *association rule*.

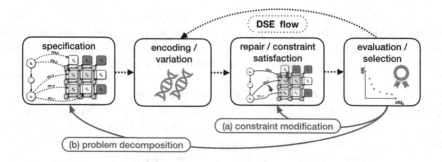

Fig. 3. Data mining in system-level DSE.

In order to determine itemsets whose supports significantly increases between one database D_1 and another D_2, *emerging pattern mining* defines the *growth rate* $gr(X)$ of an itemset X as follows [9]:

$$gr(X) = \begin{cases} 0 & \text{if } sup_{D_1}(X) = 0 \wedge sup_{D_2}(X) = 0 \\ \infty & \text{if } sup_{D_1}(X) = 0 \wedge sup_{D_2}(X) \neq 0 \\ \frac{sup_{D_2}(X)}{sup_{D_1}(X)} & \text{else} \end{cases} \qquad (6)$$

Again, if the growth rate of an itemset X is greater than a predefined threshold, i.e. if $gr(X) \geq \sigma_{gr}$, X is called a σ_{gr}-emerging pattern.

For the determination of frequent itemsets, association rules, and emerging patterns, efficient algorithms have been developed for large-scale data sets [1,9] that can seamlessly be applied to DSE data in the remainder of this work.

4   Data Mining in System-Level DSE

Since DSE is a combinatorial MOP, it is next to impossible to predict the effect of the change in one design decision on an implementation's quality. Furthermore, it is difficult to gain insight into the optimization process of MOEAs, since the design decisions that contribute to optimality and quality of solutions are hard to isolate. This section, therefore, presents automatic ways of knowledge discovery during DSE to dynamically improve the optimization; in particular, the presented data-mining techniques are incorporated into existing DSE flows for (a) on-line, dynamic improvement of the optimization process via search-space pruning and (b) for a-posteriori DSE analysis.

4.1   Data Mining for Search-Space Pruning

Figure 3 gives an overview of a standard DSE flow: The problem description, given by the specification, is suitably encoded for the optimizer that creates random variations of application-to-architecture mappings. Since the feasibility of these implementations cannot be guaranteed by construction, a repair step

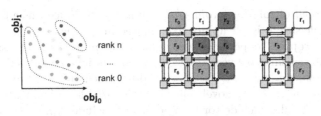

(a) Ranked solutions.   (b) Architecture decomposition.

Fig. 4. Database construction and problem decomposition. (Color figure online)

is typically performed next to ensure that any design constraints on feasible implementations are fulfilled. The corrected solutions are evaluated w.r.t. the design objectives and the best solutions are selected for further optimization.

This offers two possibilities of integrating data mining into system-level DSE: (a) By amending the set of constraints on feasible solutions, a tightening of the search space is automatically achieved, since the repair step will directly exclude and correct any solution violating a constraint. (b) Using the generated knowledge to decompose the specification and, in particular, the target architecture, the complexity of the mapping problem can be dynamically reduced as well.

For both approaches, we define the transactional database D for data mining as a set of evaluated implementations, represented by their decision vectors $\mathbf{x} \in \{0,1\}^n$. An item, therefore, corresponds to a single binary decision variable $x_i \in \mathbf{x}$, so that data mining will return frequently occurring *partial implementations* (itemsets) or association rules between decision variables.

The database is constructed by collecting *all* explored implementations during a *pre-exploration phase* of the DSE and selecting suitable subsets for data mining. In order to identify *promising* areas of the search space, we determine a *ranking* between implementations that is based on non-dominated sorting (cf. Eq. (2)), as, e.g., used in MOEAs [7]. Since a linear comparison of solutions is impossible for MOPs, non-dominated sorting divides the set of solutions into a number of disjoint *ranks* based on their quality numbers, cf. Fig. 4a: Thereby, *rank 0* contains the overall non-dominated solutions generated during DSE (the *archive*), i.e. solutions that dominate any other solution.[1] *rank 1* is constructed by removing all solutions in *rank 0* from the objective space and determining the new non-dominated solutions amongst the remaining solutions. By repeating these steps, all explored solutions of an MOP are ranked according to quality.

Constraint Modification. First, we enhance DSE by amending the constraint set of the repair mechanism to focus the search on promising areas of the search space. To this end, a database D_{hi} of *high-quality* implementations is constructed after pre-exploration. This is achieved by either (a) only selecting solutions from the archive *(rank 0)* or (b) by predetermining a database size and selecting the

---

[1] Solutions within a rank are incomparable, since better energy efficiency might entail higher cost, while a cheaper solution might be less energy efficient.

respective number of solutions from *rank 0, rank 1, etc.* Since this guarantees a sufficient sample size, it is the approach employed in the remainder of this work.

Then, we propose to perform *association rule mining* on D_{hi} to extract implication relationships between decision-variable assignments describing high-quality solutions, e.g. $x_a, x_b, x_c \Rightarrow x_d, x_e$. Adding such rules to the set of constraints will ensure that any novel solution with variable assignments x_a, x_b, x_c will automatically also include (or be modified to include) x_d, x_e as well. Thus, partial task bindings, routings, etc. are directly implanted into the next generation of implementations. This surpasses generic crossover operations that merely recombine randomly selected parts of high-quality solutions—without taking into account whether these parts actually contribute to the solution's quality. In contrast, the patterns determined by data mining are guaranteed to occur in multiple high-quality solutions in order to be selected as association rule, giving an indication that they may actually be related to optimization quality.

We propose to limit the addition of association rules to the constraint set, such as not to constrain the optimization too harshly; instead, information about variable correlations should help guide the local search of the MOEA to promising novel solutions. Therefore, we (a) require the length of either antecedent or precedent of each added association rule to be greater than a parametrizable threshold $l > 1$, since shorter rules may be trivial and lacking impact. Furthermore, we exclude *redundant* association rules [12] (e.g. $x_a, x_b, x_c \Rightarrow x_d$ for the example above), since they contribute no additional information and will be implicitly enforced by non-redundant rules. Finally, varying support and confidence thresholds allows to control the actual number of association rules generated.

Problem Decomposition. For problem decomposition, we propose to decompose the specification at architecture level as, e.g., in [10,28]. By reducing the number of available target PEs and, thus, mapping possibilities, DSE complexity is quickly and significantly reduced, resulting in higher optimization quality as well as shorter DSE times. To determine a suitable decomposition, we propose the use of *emerging pattern mining* to differentiate between the allocations in high- and low-quality solutions, cf. Fig. 4b: First, we define two databases D_1 containing low-quality solutions (i.e. from *ranks n, (n-1), (n-2), ...*) and D_2 containing high-quality solutions (*ranks 0, 1, 2...*). Using emerging pattern mining, we determine decision-variable combinations whose support significantly increases from D_1 to D_2, i.e. that frequently occur together in high-quality solutions, but not in low-quality ones. Reversing this process allows to analogously find variable combinations present in low-quality, but less likely in high-quality solutions.

For a decomposition of the target architecture, information about allocated PEs for task binding and message routing needs to be extracted from the decision variables (that define the binding of tasks) and is extracted in a subsequent step. Consolidating this information allows to determine areas of the target architecture that predominantly used in high-quality solutions (green in Fig. 4b(left)) or low-quality solutions (red). Areas that are neither part of high- nor low-quality solutions remain neutral, similarly to areas that are part of high-quality *as well as* low-quality solutions, since no definite assessment is possible in theses cases. The architecture graph is decomposed by removing the identified low-quality PE nodes and respective communication links. Neutral areas are removed (randomly) as well until a sufficiently small sub-architecture of parametrizable size is generated. Mapping edges ending in pruned PEs are, additionally, removed from the set of available mapping edges E_M, so that the DSE can be continued using a less complex system specification as novel input.

4.2   A-Posteriori DSE Analysis

In order to gather information about the impact of design decisions made by the optimizer during DSE, we furthermore propose an a-posteriori DSE analysis using *emerging pattern mining*. Since most DSE approaches merely result in a Pareto front of non-dominated implementations, optimization engineers have, as of yet, few indicators on which design decisions contribute to a solution's quality or have an influence on the separate design objectives. In this sense, DSE lacks explainability, since it remains unclear how the optimization arrives at the set of high-quality solutions. On the other hand, knowing what design decisions distinguish high- and low-quality solutions, or what variable assignments mainly affect separate design objectives may be of interest to, e.g., further enhance future designs, help better explain resulting designs to engineers, managers, or customers, or utilize in manual optimization or further DSE runs.

Qualitative Differences. To better explain qualitative differences between DSE solutions, we propose to form two databases $D_{hi} = D_2$ with high-quality solutions (*ranks 0, 1, 2...*) and $D_{lo} = D_1$ with *all* other explored solutions. Whether D_{hi} only contains the resulting Pareto-optimal solutions from *rank 0* or solutions from multiple high-quality ranks is a trade-off between quality and sufficient sample size. Emerging patterns between D_{lo} and D_{hi} represent variable assignments predominantly found in high-quality solutions and not in low-quality ones, indicating partial implementations contributing to high optimization quality.

Differentiating Optimization Objectives. Identifying variable combinations that predominantly contribute to *one specific* optimization objective *obj* requires a different mechanism for database generation. First, a number of high-quality solutions needs to be selected by unifying *ranks 0, 1, 2, ...* until a sufficiently large database D is created. This database is then split into two by extracting all solutions from D whose objective value for *obj* is lower than a predefined threshold. Alternatively, D can be halved depending on *obj*. Solutions with high quality in *obj* then form D_{hi}, while the remaining solutions represent D_{lo}. Thus, emerging pattern mining can identify exactly those design decisions that are predominantly found in solutions with best *obj*-values, and not in solutions that are superior in other objectives. Repeating this process for any other design objectives allows a similar analysis for each dimension of the objective space.

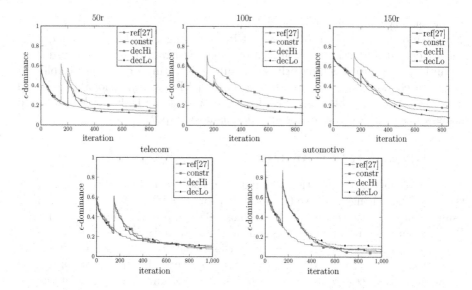

Fig. 5. Optimization quality in ϵ-dominance over number of iterations.

5   Experimental Evaluation

To evaluate the effect of data mining in system-level DSE, we present an experimental evaluation using many-core as well as networked systems as found in, e.g., the automotive domain.

5.1   Experimental Setup

All approaches, as well as a state-of-the-art reference DSE [27] were implemented in the open-source optimization framework OPT4J [19] and use a hybrid MOEA [7,17]. The evaluated benchmarks range from large-scale many-core systems from the Embedded Systems Synthesis Benchmarks Suite (E3S) [8] (*telecom, automotive*) to synthetic networked embedded systems (*50r, 100r, 150r*). These benchmarks cover a wide variety of typical application scenarios and system complexities—with application sizes of 48–155 tasks and architecture sizes of 64–75 PEs, resulting in 2^{262}–$2^{3,072}$ possible implementations. We simultaneously optimize for 3 objectives: execution latency, energy consumption, and implementation cost. All results are the average over 10 DSE runs per benchmark with 850/1000 iterations of the MOEA and a population size of 100 solutions.

DSE Quality. To evaluate the optimization quality of multi-objective DSE, we employ ϵ-dominance [16] to measure the *distance* of the implementations generated by the novel approaches to a reference of the overall best solutions. Lower values ($\rightarrow 0$), therefore, correspond to *higher* quality.

5.2   Experimental Results

DSE Quality and Time. Figure 5 presents optimization quality over the number of EA iterations, since the run time of the data-mining module is negligible compared to the total DSE time. We compare a state-of-the-art reference DSE without data mining *ref* [27] with the best parametrizations of the novel constraint-based (*constr*) as well as decomposition-based (*dec**) applications of data mining. The number of database entries was set to 100 in each case to allow for a sufficient differentiation of solution quality (if applicable). Support and confidence thresholds were experimentally set to $\sigma_{sup} = \sigma_{conf} = 0.4$.

For decomposition, we present the proposed approach of retaining high-quality PEs in the architecture while excluding low-quality PEs (*decHi*); For validation, we also demonstrate the effect of a reverse decomposition, i.e. *pruning high-quality PEs* (*decLow*). This allows to analyse whether data mining can actually differentiate between high- and low-quality parts of the specification, or whether the simple restriction of the search space improves DSE quality (as [26]).

Looking at the data, this does not seem to be the case; In the majority of the examined benchmarks, optimization quality is significantly lower for *decLo* (dotted, black diamonds) than for the proposed *decHi* (solid, blue triangles), while both decompositions result in comparable quality for the exceptions (*100r, telecom*). In most cases, *decLo* even deteriorates optimization quality compared to the reference DSE *ref* [27]. In contrast, *decHi* improves optimization quality for all benchmarks by up to ≈51%, especially for the more complex benchmarks *100r, 150r,* and *automotive*. Thus, the proposed application of data mining for problem decomposition demonstrates its potential to differentiate between low- and high-quality areas of the search space.

Constraint-based decomposition (solid, light-blue squares), on the other hand, only improves the many-core benchmarks (by $\approx 21 - 48\%$), where it is the overall most successful application of generated knowledge for the most complex *automotive* benchmark. On the other hand, it results in deteriorated quality for all networking benchmarks. This may be due to the fact that the many-core benchmarks only contain few constraints on feasible solutions, since, e.g., communication is possible between any two PEs via a Network-on-Chip (NoC) infrastructure and the architecture contains multiple instances of each PE type. In contrast, the networking benchmarks have a greater number and more complex constraints to begin with, e.g. on feasible message routings and a required use of specialized PEs available only once, so that the addition of data-mining constraints to guide the search may actually hinder successful exploration.

A-Posteriori DSE Analysis. To illustrate potential insights generated from a-posteriori DSE analysis, Fig. 6 presents emerging patterns differentiating between high- and low-quality solutions (top) and patterns correlated with selected objectives (bottom). Each pattern represents a partial implementation, given by the combination of items, i.e. mapping variables $m_i \in E_M$, it consists of. To give an indication of the dependability of the results, respective *support values* (above a required support threshold of $\sigma_{sup} = 0.4$) are presented as well.

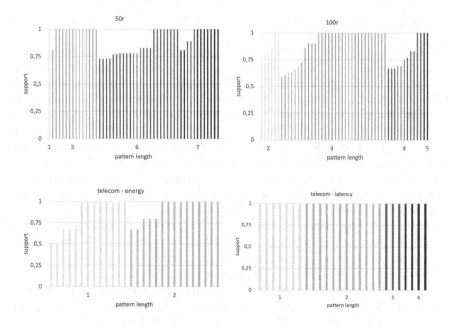

Fig. 6. Emerging patterns for qualitative differentiation (top) and design-objective differentiation (bottom).

In the high- vs. low-quality case, on average ≈51 emerging patterns were generated with a length of 1–7 items. Average support for each pattern was ≈86,5%, so that the proposed approach provides a variety of partial implementations that is well-supported amongst the high-quality solutions.

When differentiating between separate objectives, as presented for energy consumption and latency of benchmark *telecom*, 3–28 patterns were found, ranging from 1–4 items. Interestingly, non-linear objectives such as latency resulted in longer and better supported patterns for most examined benchmarks, compared to linear objectives such as energy consumption or implementation cost. This may indicate that (a) low latency is correlated with recurring, absolutely necessary design decisions or (b) that all explored low-latency implementations were, in fact, discovered in a confined local neighbourhood, so that further exploration to increase the diversity of solutions would be required.

Insights such as these may help to better understand and explore complex search spaces as posed by DSE and open up a range of further research directions.

6   Conclusion

This paper presents novel ways of integrating data-mining techniques to improve and analyse DSE at the system level. Using automatically extracted knowledge from the DSE process to reduce problem complexity, optimization quality of benchmark applications was improved by up to ≈51%. Furthermore, applying data mining for an a-posteriori analysis of solution quality presents novel insights into previously untapped information on the relationship between design decisions and optimization quality in combinatorial MOEAs.

References

1. Agrawal, R., Imielinski, T., Swami, A.: Mining association rules between sets of items in large databases. In: SIGMOD Conference, vol. 22, p. 207 (1993)
2. Bäck, T.: An overview of parameter control methods by self-adaptation in evolutionary algorithms **35**, 51–66 (1998)
3. Bandaru, S., Ng, A., Deb, K.: Data mining methods for knowledge discovery in multi-objective optimization: Part a - survey. Expert Syst. Appl. **70**, 119–138 (2017)
4. Bandaru, S., Ng, A., Deb, K.: Data mining methods for knowledge discovery in multi-objective optimization: Part b - new developments and applications. Expert Syst. Appl. **70**, 139–159 (2017)
5. Benhaoua, M.K., Singh, A.K.: Heuristic for accelerating run-time task mapping in NoC-based heterogeneous MPSoCs. J. Digit. Inf. Manage. **12**(5), 293 (2014)
6. Blum, C., Puchinger, J., Raidl, G.R., Roli, A.: Hybrid metaheuristics in combinatorial optimization: a survey. Appl. Soft Comput. **11**(6), 4135–4151 (2011)
7. Deb, K., Pratap, A., Agarwal, S., Meyarivan, T.: A fast and elitist multiobjective genetic algorithm: NSGA-II. IEEE Trans. Evol. Comput. **6**(2), 182–197 (2002)
8. Dick, R.: Embedded System Synthesis Benchmarks Suite (E3S) (2018). http://ziyang.eecs.umich.edu/~dickrp/e3s/
9. Dong, G., Li, J.: Efficient mining of emerging patterns: discovering trends and differences. In: Proceedings of the 5th ACM SIGKDD International Conference on Knowledge Discovery and Data Mining, pp. 43–52 (1999)
10. Faruque, M.A.A., Krist, R., Henkel, J.: ADAM: run-time agent-based distributed application mapping for on-chip communication. In: 2008 45th ACM/IEEE Design Automation Conference, pp. 760–765 (2008)
11. Fournier Viger, P., Lin, C.W., Vo, B., Truong, T., Zhang, J., Le, B.: A survey of itemset mining. Wiley Interdisciplinary Reviews: Data Mining and Knowledge Discovery (2017)
12. Fournier-Viger, P., Tseng, V.S.: Mining top-k non-redundant association rules. In: Chen, L., Felfernig, A., Liu, J., Raś, Z.W. (eds.) Foundations of Intelligent Systems, pp. 31–40. Springer, Heidelberg (2012)
13. Joardar, B.K., Kim, R.G., Doppa, J.R., Pande, P.P., Marculescu, D., Marculescu, R.: Learning-based Application-Agnostic 3D NoC Design for Heterogeneous Manycore Systems (2018). http://arxiv.org/abs/1810.08869
14. Kang, S., Yang, H., Schor, L., Bacivarov, I., Ha, S., Thiele, L.: Multi-objective mapping optimization via problem decomposition for many-core systems. In: 10th Symposium on Embedded Systems for Real-time Multimedia, pp. 28–37 (2012)
15. Kienhuis, B., Deprettere, E.F., van der Wolf, P., Vissers, K.: A methodology to design programmable embedded systems - the Y-chart approach, pp. 18–37 (2002)
16. Laumanns, M., Thiele, L., Deb, K., Zitzler, E.: Combining convergence and diversity in evolutionary multiobjective optimization. Evol. Comput. **10**(3), 263–282 (2002)
17. Lukasiewycz, M., Glaß, M., Haubelt, C., Teich, J.: SAT-decoding in evolutionary algorithms for discrete constrained optimization problems. In: IEEE Congress on Evolutionary Computing (2007)

18. Lukasiewycz, M., Glaß, M., Haubelt, C., Teich, J.: Solving multi-objective Pseudo-Boolean problems. In: Marques-Silva, J., Sakallah, K.A. (eds.) SAT 2007. LNCS, vol. 4501, pp. 56–69. Springer, Heidelberg (2007). https://doi.org/10.1007/978-3-540-72788-0_9

19. Lukasiewycz, M., Glaß, M., Reimann, F., Teich, J.: Opt4J: a modular framework for meta-heuristic optimization. In: Proceedings of the 13th Annual Conference on Genetic and Evolutionary Computing, pp. 1723–1730. ACM, New York (2011)

20. Luke, S.: When short runs beat long runs. In: Proceedings of the 3rd Annual Conference on Genetic and Evolutionary Computation, pp. 74–90 (2001)

21. Neubauer, K., Haubelt, C., Glaß, M.: Supporting composition in symbolic system synthesis. In: 2016 International Conference on Embedded Computer Systems: Architectures, Modeling and Simulation (SAMOS), pp. 132–139 (2016)

22. Padmanabhan, S., Chen, Y., Chamberlain, R.D.: decomposition techniques for optimal design-space exploration of streaming applications. In: Proceedings of the 18th ACM SIGPLAN Symposium on Principles and Practice of Parallel Programming, PPoPP 2013, pp. 285–286. ACM, New York (2013)

23. Panerati, J., Sciuto, D., Beltrame, G.: Optimization strategies in design space exploration. In: Ha, S., Teich, J. (eds.) Handbook of Hardware/Software Codesign, pp. 189–216. Springer, Dordrecht (2017). https://doi.org/10.1007/978-94-017-7267-9_7

24. Puchinger, J., Raidl, G.R.: Combining metaheuristics and exact algorithms in combinatorial optimization: a survey and classification. In: Mira, J., Álvarez, J.R. (eds.) IWINAC 2005. LNCS, vol. 3562, pp. 41–53. Springer, Heidelberg (2005). https://doi.org/10.1007/11499305_5

25. Raschip, M.: Guiding Evolutionary Search with Association Rules for Solving Weighted CSPs (2015)

26. Richthammer, V., Glaß, M.: On search-space restriction for design space exploration of multi-/many-core systems. In: Workshop "Methoden und Beschreigungssprachen zur Modellierung und Verifikation von Schaltungen und Systemen" (MBMV) (2018)

27. Richthammer, V., Glaß, M.: Efficient search-space encoding for system-level design space exploration of embedded systems. In: 2019 IEEE 13th International Symposium on Embedded Multicore/Many-core Systems-on-Chip (MCSoC), pp. 273–280 (2019)

28. Richthammer, V., Fassnacht, F., Glaß, M.: Search-space decomposition for system-level design space exploration of embedded systems. ACM Trans. Des. Autom. Electron. Syst. 25(2), 14 (2020)

29. Singh, A.K., Shafique, M., Kumar, A., Henkel, J.: Mapping on multi/many-core systems: survey of current and emerging trends. In: 2013 50th ACM/EDAC/IEEE Design Automation Conference (DAC), pp. 1–10 (2013)

30. Srinivasan, V.P., Shanthi, A.P.: A survey of research and practices in multiprocessor system on chip design space exploration. J. Theoret. Appl. Inf. Technol. 64, 1 (2014)

31. Blickle, T., Teich, J., Thiele, L.: System-level synthesis using evolutionary algorithms. Des. Autom. Embedded Syst. 3(1), 23–58 (1998)

32. Wang, S., Yin, Y.: Performance assessment of multiobjective optimizers: an analysis and review. Front. Comput. Sci. 12(5), 950–965 (2018). https://doi.org/10.1007/s11704-016-6104-3

33. Zitzler, E., Thiele, L., Laumanns, M., Fonseca, C.M., da Fonseca, V.G.: Performance assessment of multiobjective optimizers: an analysis and review. IEEE Trans. Evol. Comput. 7(2), 117–132 (2003)

CoPTA: Contiguous Pattern Speculating TLB Architecture

Yichen Yang[✉], Haojie Ye, Yuhan Chen, Xueyang Liu, Nishil Talati, Xin He, Trevor Mudge, and Ronald Dreslinski

University of Michigan, Ann Arbor, MI 48109, USA
{yangych,yehaojie,chenyh,marliu,talatin,xinhe,tnm,rdreslin}@umich.edu

Abstract. With the growing size of real-world datasets running on CPUs, address translation has become a significant performance bottleneck. To translate virtual addresses into physical addresses, modern operating systems perform several levels of page table walks (PTWs) in memory. Translation look-aside buffers (TLBs) are used as caches to keep recently used translation information. However, as datasets increase in size, both the TLB miss rate and the overhead of PTWs worsen, causing severe performance bottlenecks. Using a diverse set of workloads, we show the PTW overhead consumes an average of 20% application execution time.

In this paper, we propose CoPTA, a technique to speculate the memory address translation upon a TLB miss to hide the PTW latency. Specifically, we show that the operating system has a tendency to map contiguous virtual memory pages to contiguous physical pages. Using a real machine, we show that the Linux kernel can automatically defragment physical memory and create larger chunks for contiguous mapping, particularly when transparent huge page support is enabled. Based on this observation, we devise a speculation mechanism that finds nearby entries present in the TLB upon a miss and predicts the address translation of the missed address assuming contiguous address allocation. This allows CoPTAto speculatively execute instructions without waiting for the PTW to complete. We run the PTW in parallel, compare the speculated and the translated physical addresses, and flush the pipeline upon a wrong speculation with similar techniques used for handling branch mispredictions.

We comprehensively evaluate our proposal using benchmarks from three suites: SPEC CPU 2006 for server-grade applications, GraphBIG for graph applications, and the NAS benchmark suite for scientific applications. Using a trace-based simulation, we show an average address prediction accuracy of 82% across these workloads resulting in a 16% performance improvement.

Keywords: Virtual memory · Page table walk · TLB · Speculative execution

© Springer Nature Switzerland AG 2020
A. Orailoglu et al. (Eds.): SAMOS 2020, LNCS 12471, pp. 67–83, 2020.
https://doi.org/10.1007/978-3-030-60939-9_5

1   Introduction

Virtual memory is widely used in modern computing systems because it offers an abstraction for different applications to own a large, exclusive memory space along with some security guarantees. Supporting virtual memory requires a processor to translate a vir-

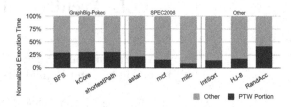

Fig. 1. Processor time breakdown for different benchmarks.

tual address to a physical memory address before requesting the data from the memory hierarchy. The Translation Look-aside Buffer (TLB) serves as a dedicated cache for storing address translation information. A miss in the TLB triggers a Page Table Walk (PTW), which incurs several serialized memory accesses. The core has to wait to receive the translated address before servicing the memory request, therefore, PTW can cause a serious performance bottleneck upon frequent TLB misses.

Modern big-data workloads use large volumes of data that can easily stress the TLB both due to limited TLB size and complex PTW procedure. TLBs employ a fully-associative structure with limited capacity (e.g., 64-entries for L1 TLBs in modern CPUs) in order to keep a reasonable lookup latency. To illustrate this bottleneck, we profiled several graph processing, server, and scientific workloads from GraphBIG [26] and SPEC CPU2006 [18] and elsewhere on an x86-based host machine. Figure 1 shows the fraction of execution time spent on the PTW, which shows that a significant portion (more than 25% in some benchmarks) is spent on translating addresses upon TLB misses. Prior endeavors to mitigate this issue adopt superpages to increase TLB reach [34]. However, this approach suffers from internal fragmentation, wastes space, and stresses memory bandwidth.

The goal of this work is to reduce the overhead of PTW by speculating the physical address upon a TLB miss. To this end, we propose CoPTA, a Contiguous Pattern Speculating TLB Architecture, which speculates the address translation of a TLB misses using a nearby entry present the TLB. CoPTAexploits the opportunities that contiguous virtual addresses are likely to be mapped to contiguous physical addresses. This is supported by characterization experiments performed on workloads running in a real machine running Linux. By predicting a memory address translation, CoPTAallows the execution to speculatively proceed while performing the PTW in parallel. The benefit of such a scheme is that the core can execute dependent instructions without waiting for the translation. Given most contiguous virtual pages are mapped to contiguous physical pages, this speculation yields correct translation most of the time. In the event of miss-speculation, we use a technique similar to what is used for a branch misprediction to flush the speculatively executed instructions from the re-order buffer (ROB).

To evaluate the performance benefits of CoPTA, we use a trace-based simulation methodology. A variety of real-world big-data workloads from graph analytics, server applications, and scientific computing domains are used to evaluate CoPTA. We show that using a negligible 0.4 KB of storage, CoPTAcan achieve an average address translation prediction accuracy of 82%, which can potentially result in an average performance by 16%.

2   Background and Motivation

2.1   Virtual Address Translation

To achieve process isolation, each process issues instructions with virtual addresses [25]. This is an abstraction provided by the operating system (OS) that can (a) hide physical memory fragmentation, (b) leave the burden of managing the memory hierarchy to the kernel, and (c) create the illusion of an infinite address space for each process.

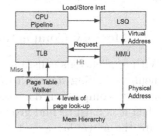

The translation of virtual addresses to physical addresses is enforced by the Memory Management Unit (MMU) (Fig. 2). Memory is typically split into 4 KB pages, and a page table keeps track of all the mappings between a virtual page number (VPN)

Fig. 2. Overview of address translation.

and a physical page number (PPN). To avoid storing all the translations in a monolithic large mapping table, MMU usually uses a hierarchical page table. For example, the x86 architecture uses 4 levels of page tables [3,5]. Even with this design, the overall size of the page table is too large to fit in any on-chip cache structure entirely. A PTW for address translation in an x86 system will incur 4 levels of page table lookup, which leads to a significant performance overhead. To alleviate the PTW latency, a dedicated cache called the translation look-aside buffer (TLB) is used to cache the recently used translations.

Each time an address translation is requested, the MMU will look up a corresponding entry in the TLB for faster access. Thus the TLB plays a very important role in the performance of address translation [15,24]. Upon a TLB hit, the matched PPN combined with the offset will be used for the data access. If the TLB misses a request, it invokes a PTW that looks up the corresponding PPN in the memory hierarchy, and caches it into the TLB for future references.

Each level of the page table needs to be fetched from the main memory, so in the worst case, a single PTW can incur 4 times the memory latency before the MMU can access the physical address. Note that the PTW can be done in hardware (i.e., there is a dedicated controller to lookup the page tables) or in software (i.e., an interrupt subroutine is called to service the address translation lookup). When virtualization is involved, the nested page table lookup can take up to 24 memory access, increasing the latency to get the final page translation, which becomes a huge overhead [6,17].

2.2   Physical Page Allocation

When a process requests a new page, the OS allocates a physical page to be mapped to the virtual page, either by allocating an unused page or by evicting a used page. Linux uses a buddy allocator that operates as follows: when an application makes a `malloc` call and asks for multiple pages, the OS will try to allocate continuous physical page frames whenever possible [2,29]. In detail, when the process requests N pages at a time, the OS will look for N contiguous physical pages in the memory or break larger contiguous chunks to create N contiguous physical pages. Our experiment shows that the OS tends to map contiguous physical pages to virtual pages, which opens up an opportunity for our TLB speculation mechanism.

2.3   Memory Compaction and Transparent Hugepage Support

With applications constantly allocating and freeing pages, memory will be fragmented, making it hard to find a large contiguous region. Many OS provide a memory compaction daemon. Linux, for example, invokes memory compaction when it is hard to find groups of physically-contiguous pages. The OS will relocate the movable pages to the free pages, filling up the holes in memory and reducing fragmentation, also known as defragmentation.

Linux has a Transparent Hugepage Support (THS) mechanism, that allows the memory allocator attempting to find a free 2 MB block of memory [2]. In the 2 MB memory chunk, if the VPNs and PPNs are aligned, the OS will construct a 2 MB superpage with 512 consecutive 4 KB pages. Memory compaction and THS provide a better memory mapping that favors CoPTA.

3   Related Work

Previous works mainly focused on reducing the TLB miss rate and reducing page walk overhead.

Reduce TLB Miss Rate. CoLT [29] exploits and takes advantage of contiguous page allocation by coalescing contiguous page translations into one TLB entry, and therefore increasing the TLB reach. However, the maximum number of pages coalesced in CoLT is limited by the size of a cache line. Hybrid TLB coalescing [28] relaxes this limitation with the help of software. Our work has no limit to the range that the contiguous pattern can be searched, thus allowing a more flexible contiguous mapping range, not limited by the size of a cache line.

Superpages [9,34] increase the TLB coverage and therefore reduces miss rate. Works have shown efforts to exploit support for superpages by using either split TLB hardware [29] or unified TLB hardware for all page sizes [16]. Other works also explored ways to accelerate multiprocessor TLB access [8,11]. CoPTAinstead uses speculation and can be applied orthogonally to superpages, CoLT, and multiprocessors.

Hiding the Page Walk Latency. SpecTLB [6] utilizes a reservation-based physical memory allocator. When allocating memory, the handler will reserve large chunks if a superpage is appropriate, and any future allocation in the reserved superpage will be aligned [27,33]. SpecTLB requires the OS to support superpage reservation [27,33], and can only provide speculation if the miss request is part of the superpage. Our work requires minor changes to the TLB, and can potentially provide speculations for any virtual page number because the searching range can be customized.

Prefetched Address Translation [23] modifies the OS to force contiguous page allocation. Therefore it is faster to locate the page table and faster to prefetch the translation, reducing the page walk latency.

4   CoPTA: TLB Speculation Architecture

In this section, we detail the proposed CoPTAarchitecture. We modify the TLB and load store queue (LSQ) to support the TLB speculation scheme, as shown in Fig. 3. The modified TLB architecture relaxes the exact matching requirement of address translation. Instead of searching for a single, exact match of the query in the TLB by a CAM circuit, CoPTAwill return a hit entry upon matching a predefined number of most significant bits in the tag array. In this way, the *approximate* search will find a "close-neighbor" of the virtual address query, even if the exact match is missing in the TLB. The proposed speculation-supported LSQ adds a physical address column and 1 additional bit to each entry, totalling in 0.4 KB additional storage for a 48 entry LSQ. The physical address column is used to indicate the value of the speculative physical address translation that has not been verified yet. The additional bit is used to indicate whether data in each LSQ entry is generated by a speculative translation.

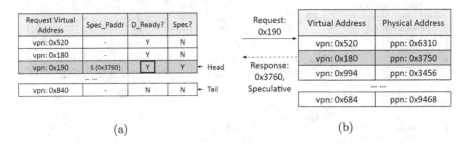

(a)   (b)

Fig. 3. (a) Speculation supported Load Store Queue (Data for VPN 0x190 may arrive earlier than the translation response from walker, the data remain speculative in LSQ before translation is resolved, **D_ready** indicates Data is ready to commit from LSQ). (b) Speculation supported Translation Lookaside Buffer (Incoming request VPN 0x190 will incur a miss but find the close neighbor (0x180) in the TLB, a speculative translation response 0x3760=0x3750+(0x190-0x180) is returned within Hit latency.)

With these modifications, CoPTAcan parallelize the data request sent to the memory hierarchy and the hierarchical PTW process. The processor can then send data requests without stalling for the translation response to complete. The pipeline is illustrated in Fig. 4. When encountering a TLB miss, conventional architectures will block the data request until the address translation is resolved. These events happen in the order of A1 → B1 → C1 → C2 → B2 → D1 → D2 → A2. By contrast, with CoPTA, the augmented L1 TLB is able to predict the physical address and issue a data request with the predicted physical address, along with sending the translation request to the page table walker, thus overlapping with the time interval during which the page table walker serves the translation miss. The speculated physical address translation will have a copy saved in the corresponding LSQ entry, with the marked speculation bit. The CPU pipeline can speculatively execute based on the predicted physical address. In Fig. 4, event A1 triggers event B1 with speculative response b2. Then C1 → C2 happens in parallel with D1 → D2 to hide the PTW latency, and event a2 send the speculated result to the LSQ. When the translation is resolved from the PTW, the verification signal is sent to the LSQ (C2 → a2). The returned (accurate) physical address is compared against the prediction (saved in the LSQ) to verify its correctness. If the result matches the speculation, the speculation bit is cleared and the PTW latency can be hidden from the execution. If the speculation is incorrect, the CPU pipeline will be flushed similar to a branch miss-prediction, and the pipeline will roll back to the state before the request with the accurate physical address being issued. Given a high prediction accuracy, speculative execution can hide the PTW latency and improve TLB performance.

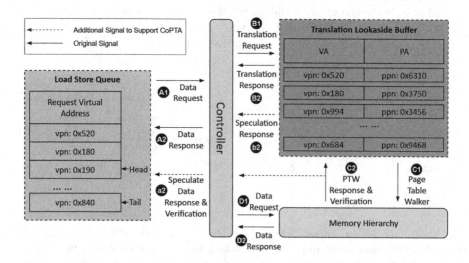

Fig. 4. Overview of TLB speculation architecture.

Regardless of whether an exact match/miss is obtained, CoPTAexecutes the same procedures as the original TLB design. The only difference is when the translation misses an exact match but hits a neighborhood match. The conventional design will block the data request for this LSQ entry until the translation is resolved, while the CoPTAwill match a close-neighbor in the TLB, as shown in Fig. 3(b). In the close-neighbor match scenario, the TLB returns the speculative physical address based on the distance of virtual addresses between the request and its close-neighbor (in Fig. 3(b), the close-neighbor of requesting VPN = 0×190 is VPN = 0x180, the speculative PPN = $0 \times 3750 + (0 \times 190 - 0 \times 180) = 0 \times 3760$). The speculative address is returned to LSQ and attached with a speculation bit to the LSQ.

The data request is sent to the memory hierarchy in parallel with launching a PTW to fetch the accurate physical address translation. In this situation, the data may be returned to the corresponding LSQ entry earlier than the accurate translation and will be marked as a speculative data value, because the verified translation has not arrived to clear the speculation bit of the entry (Fig. 3(a)). The current register states will be check-pointed (e.g. using register renaming) and the commits beyond this speculation point will be saved in a write buffer to protect the memory state. When the accurate translation returns to the TLB, a verification signal will be set and the LSQ will be notified (Fig. 4). If the speculative translation matches with the accurate translation from the page walker, the speculation bit is cleared, and the registers and memory states can be safely committed. If the speculative translation does not match with the walker, the pipeline is flushed as if there is a misprediction. The speculative register state and the write buffer are cleared, and the CPU pipeline will restore to the point before issuing the mispredicted load/store request in the LSQ.

Note that pipeline flushes are relatively rare events. Flushes are only necessary when both the data arrives earlier than the page table walker in a TLB miss and a misprediction happens because the incorrect data has been retrieved and used. We discuss the overhead of misprediction in Sect. 8. When the accurate translation returns earlier than the outstanding data request, the address verification happens before the data is used. If the speculative translation matches the translation result from the page table walker, no further action needs to be performed. If the speculative translation does not match the accurate result, a second LSQ request is sent to the memory hierarchy and the previously speculative data request is discarded. Therefore, the data response of the previous LSQ request with an incorrect physical address is ignored.

5   Methodology

5.1   Real Machine Memory Allocation Characterization

The proposed CoPTAarchitecture relies on the contiguity of the system memory mapping. With a longer contiguous virtual memory address to physical memory address mapping region, this architecture will achieve higher prediction accuracy and better performance improvement. To characterize the contiguity of memory mapping on a real machine, we modified DynamoRio [1,14] to dump the trace of the virtual to physical mappings from a real machine and then analyze the contiguity. The configuration of our modeled real machine is shown in Table 1.

Similar to the prior works [29] that study the effect of memory compaction, we manually invoke memory compaction in the Linux kernel and characterize the memory contiguity. With memory compaction, the system will defragment the memory and create a larger chunk in the memory to map the following address allocation requests. By setting the Linux `defrag` flag, the system triggers the memory compaction for different situations. We also enable and disable the Linux transparent hugepage support (THS) to investigate how the system built-in memory defragmentation functions and how supperpage support helps our proposed architecture. The experimental machine has been running for a month to mimic typical memory fragmentation as compared to a clean boot. We study the memory contiguity under different configurations. Due to space constraints, we present the result of the following configurations: (a) before and after manually invoking memory compaction, (b) THS disabled, normal memory compaction (current default setting for Linux), (c) THS enabled, normal memory compaction, and (d) THS enabled, low memory compaction.

5.2   Simulation Based Speculation Evaluation

Similar to the previous works [5,6,8,10,29] that evaluate the performance of CoPTA, we use a trace-based approach. Performing an online prediction evaluation with a full-system out-of-order processor simulator is infeasible due to inordinate simulation time. Also, it is not possible to evaluate the performance on a real machine because CoPTAneeds hardware modifications that cannot be emulated on the host machine. To collect the translation trace, we apply a simulation-based approach instead of using real machine traces to avoid interference from DynamoRio [1,14]. We run the benchmarks on the gem5 simulator [12] in full system mode and modify the simulator to collect the virtual to physical address translation trace. The trace is then fed into a customized TLB simulator. Prior works on TLBs [5,6,8,32] mainly focus on measuring the TLB miss rate. In addition, we estimate the overall performance improvement by assuming the number of L1 TLB misses is directly propotional to the time spent on the PTW, following the methodology used by Basu et $al.$ [7]. We run Linux `perf` on a real machine, using hardware counters to collect the average and total number of cycles spent on PTWs. The performance improvement metric is defined in Eq. 1, which is calculated by multiplying the portion of time spent on the PTWs (T_{PTW}) with the TLB predictor hit rate ($A_{CoPTA\_prediction}$). This is an upper-bound estimation of CoPTAbecause we make several assumptions, including an optimal misprediction penalty and collecting the translation trace under the best memory conditions, detailed in Sect. 8.

$$Performance\_Improvement = T_{PTW} \times A_{CoPTA\_prediction} \qquad (1)$$

Table 1 shows the specification of the real machine and gem5 simulator setup. Both run a similar Linux kernel on x86 ISA processors to ensure a similar page assignment strategy. The customized TLB simulator has a 64-entry, fully-associative L1 TLB and no L2 TLB, adopting the least recently used (LRU) replacement policy. When the TLB simulator matches multiple close-neighbors (based on the higher order bits of the virtual addresses), it selects the first hit and calculates the result based on its physical address.

5.3 Benchmarks

We study the memory map-ping contiguity on the graph workloads from GraphBig [26] with the SlashDot dataset [20], and later measure the per-formance on GraphBig [26], SPEC CPU2006 benchmark suite [18], NAS [4], Hash Join [13] and the HPC Challenge Benchmark [22]. For graph workloads, two differ-ent datasets are used. Slash-Dot and Pokec are real-world social network graphs from SNAP [20]. They have 0.08M nodes, 0.95M edges and 1.6M nodes, 30M edges, respectively. For the SPEC CPU2006 benchmark suite, the largest inputs are used. Detailed information about the benchmarks is listed in Table 2.

Table 1. Experiment setup specifications.

	Host Machine	gem5 Simulator
Processor	Intel i7-6700K	X86 single-core atomic
Linux Kernel	4.15.0	4.8.13
L1 Cache	32kB	32kB
L2 Cache	256kB	256kB
L3 Cache	2MB	No
RAM	16GB	16GB
L1 TLB	64 entries	64 entries
L2 TLB	1536 entries	No

Table 2. Summary of the benchmarks evaluated.

Benchmark	Source	Input	
BFS	GraphBig [26]	SlashDot & Pokec [20]	
ConnectedComp	GraphBig [26]	SlashDot & Pokec [20]	
kCore	GraphBig [26]	SlashDot & Pokec [20]	
PageRank	GraphBig [26]	SlashDot & Pokec [20]	
ShortestPath	GraphBig [26]	SlashDot & Pokec [20]	
TriangleCount	GraphBig [26]	SlashDot & Pokec [20]	
astar	SPEC [18]	ref input	
lbm	SPEC [18]	ref input	
mcf	SPEC [18]	ref input	
milc	SPEC [18]	ref input	
IntSort	NAS [4]	/	
ConjGrad	NAS [4]	/	
HJ-8	Hash Join [13]	-r 12800000 -s 12800000	
RandAcc	HPCC [22]	100000000	

6 Memory Allocation Contiguity Characterization

We qualitatively analyze the effect of the Linux buddy allocator, memory com-paction and THS on the memory contiguity on a real machine. Here we define the address mapping contiguity as follows: if contiguous virtual pages VP, VP + 1, VP + 2 are mapped to contiguous physical pages PP, PP + 1, PP + 2 for page walkers. , the contiguity is 3. Therefore, a contiguity of 1 means this address mapping is not contiguous with any other. We use a cumulative density func-tion (CDF) to show the contiguity of the memory allocation for some graph workloads (Fig. 5a to 6c). Note that the x-axis is in a log scale. A steep line to the right indicates that the memory mapping is more contiguous, thus bene-fiting CoPTAmore. To illustrate these we present graph workloads and use the moderately sized SlashDot dataset as an input.

6.1   Memory Compaction Effect

We first characterize the effect of memory compaction. Figure 5 shows the memory contiguity before and after manually invoking memory compaction. Before memory compaction (Fig. 5a), some benchmarks reflect a certain level of contiguity. But when manually invoking the memory compaction before launching each benchmark (Fig. 5b), all the benchmarks show better memory contiguity, as a result of the Linux buddy allocator. As long as there are unused contiguous memory spaces in physical memory, the buddy allocator will assign these contiguous physical addresses to contiguous virtual addresses. Thus, memory compaction along with the buddy allocator provides the prerequisite for CoPTA.

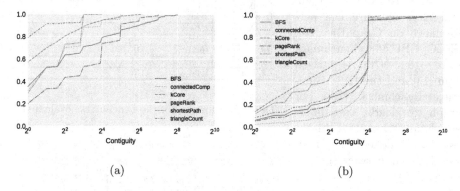

(a)   (b)

Fig. 5. (a) CDF for memory contiguity before memory compaction. (b) CDF for memory contiguity after memory compaction.

6.2   Effect of Transparent Hugepage Support

Figure 6 shows the memory contiguity under different Linux kernel configurations. Here, we first manually invoke memory compaction and launch BFS six times sequentially. BFS-1 stands for the first run, BFS-2 stands for the second run, etc. In Fig. 6a, the memory contiguity decreases over time, as the memory is not defragmented by the Linux kernel. When THS is disabled, the system doesn't need to reserve larger memory fragments for hugepages, so the Linux kernel compaction is not triggered after 6 runs of BFS. A similar situation is observed in Fig. 6c. As we disabled the `defrag` flag in the kernel, the system does not trigger memory compaction automatically, thus resulting in decreased memory contiguity. When THS is enabled with the normal `defrag` flag (Fig. 6b), the memory contiguity decreases for the first five runs and returns to a good condition during the sixth run. The memory compaction is automatically triggered during that time, resulting in memory defragmentation.

With auto-triggered memory compaction, the memory mapping contiguity is bounded within a certain range. When the memory is highly fragmented, the kernel will trigger memory compaction to defragment the memory mapping.

This bounds the performance benefit from CoPTA. High memory fragmentation will lead to performance degradation on the CoPTAarchitecture. To correct this, the system will thus trigger memory compaction automatically and CoPTAcan continue offering high performance improvements.

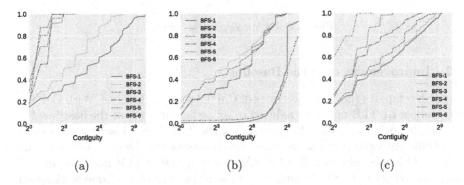

(a)   (b)   (c)

Fig. 6. (a) CDF for memory contiguity with normal `defrag`, THS disabled. (b) CDF for memory contiguity with normal `defrag`, THS enabled. (c) CDF for memory contiguity disable `defrag`, THS enabled.

7   CoPTAPerformance Evaluation

In this section, we quantitatively evaluate the performance improvements of our proposed CoPTAarchitecture and justify it by presenting a reduced TLB miss rate compared to the baseline.

7.1   CoPTAPrediction Accuracy

Figure 7 shows the address translation prediction accuracy of CoPTA. The gem5 full-system simulator is set to disable THS and normal `defrag` to mimic the default setting in Linux. The benchmarks begin execution in a state of minimal memory fragmentation after the simulator has booted up. This state is similar to the memory condition after the memory compaction is triggered in a real machine. Note that these conditions estimate the upper bound of the performance benefits from CoPTA. For the graph workloads, the CoPTAachieves a higher prediction accuracy with a smaller dataset. The accuracy of a smaller dataset SlashDot is 80% compared to 55% for a larger dataset Pokec. For other workloads, the prediction accuracy is higher than irregular graph workloads. The overall average prediction accuracy is 82%.

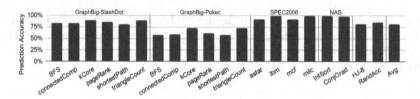

Fig. 7. CoPTAprediction accuracy.

7.2 Improvement over the Baseline

Figure 8 compares the TLB miss rates of CoPTAwith the baseline. With CoPTA, the average L1 TLB miss rate reduced to 2%, where it is 8% at the baseline. For the graph workloads with a larger dataset, the TLB size is insufficient to cover the whole data range in the baseline, which results in a higher TLB miss rate of 11%. Other benchmarks like RandAcc incur a higher TLB miss rate of 21% that is also caused by the irregular data access pattern over a large working set size. CoPTApredicts address translations well in these cases, reducing the TLB miss rate by 82% on average.

Figure 9 compares the percentage of time spent on the PTWs by CoPTAand the baseline. For the baseline, this is collected on a real machine with hardware counters. For CoPTA, we only scale the fraction of PTW time spent by the CPU using CoPTAprediction estimations. Graph workloads with a larger dataset show a higher portion of the execution time spent on the PTWs. The performance loss due to time spent on PTWs becomes a serious bottleneck for some workloads (e.g., RandAcc) and can be as high as 40%. Although some of this 40% can be overlapped with out-of-order execution, the pipeline will quickly fill the instruction buffer with dependent instructions and stall. By predicting the address translations, CoPTAis able to reduce an average fraction of the application execution time spent on the PTW to 4% compared to 20% in the baseline.

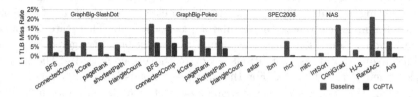

Fig. 8. L1 TLB miss rate for baseline and CoPTA.

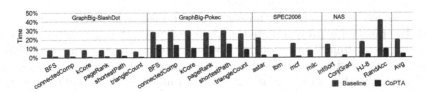

Fig. 9. Percentage of time spent on PTWs for baseline and CoPTA.

7.3 Overall Performance Improvement

Figure 10 shows that CoPTAimproves the performance of the baseline by 16% on average (up to 35%). To evaluate this, we used the performance improvement rule defined in Eq. 1. For graph workloads, even though the address translation prediction accuracy is relatively low on larger datasets, the percentage of time spent on PTWs is dominant enough to gain a significant performance boost. CoPTAimproves the performance of irregular workloads with larger data sets better than others. With `defrag` flag enabled in Linux, the system will automatically defragment the memory when the system is too fragmented (Fig. 6b) and create as large of a contiguous region as possible. This is similar to the optimal memory condition in our full-system simulation-based experiments.

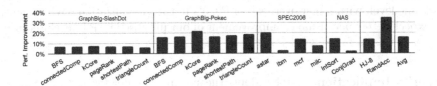

Fig. 10. Performance improvement estimation with CoPTA.

8 Discussion

Performance Improvement Metric. The performance improvement metric we defined in Eq. 1 is based on several assumptions and limitations. First, the portion of time spent on the PTWs is directly propotional to the L1 TLB miss rate. Ideally, executing the PTW in parallel with the following instructions will remove the PTW portion from the critical path, but this may incur structural stalls in the pipeline. This effect is difficult to quantitatively analyze. Second, we ignore the overhead of miss-speculation recovery. Even if miss-speculation happens, the data should respond earlier than the page table walker, and the CPU pipeline should be flushed and start over. This may also pollute the cache with data from miss-speculated addresses. Based on our experiments, pipeline flushes will rarely occur because of the high prediction accuracy. Furthermore the cost of flushing the pipeline is as small as branch miss-speculation. For these reasons, we consider the miss-speculation cost is negligible. Finally, we used the translation trace collected in the gem5 full-system simulator and use the `perf` result from a real machine. Because the benchmark starts execution right after the system is booted up and there are no other processes running simultaneously, the memory is not fragmented and the Linux buddy allocator can assign the contiguous physical pages to the memory allocation requests, which is the optimal condition for CoPTAto achieve the best performance.

Software vs. Hardware Page Walker. Different architectures use different mechanisms for page walkers. With a software page walker, CoPTAwill have limited benefits since the instructions for a PTW will be executed by the core, preventing the translation results from being actually used. However, the hardware page walker will execute the PTW in the background and let the pipeline continue executing the proceeding instructions.

Virtualization. PTW takes as many as 4 memory accesses on a host machine. But with virtualization involved, a CPU will have a nested page table where the host and guest OS manage their own set of page tables, shown in previous works [6,17,23,30,31]. In this case, 4 memory accesses will be needed in the host OS to find the next level hierarchy page table of the guest OS, thus resulting in as many as 24 memory accesses [17]. If the prediction accuracy can maintain at the same level, with larger overhead of PTWs in the virtualization environment, we expect better performance improvement of our proposed CoPTAarchitecture. We leave this as future works.

Security Implication. CoPTAadopts the speculation idea for address translation, similar to branch prediction and speculatively reading data from the store queue. Attacks such as Spectre [19] and Meltdown [21] can exploit this feature to steal information from the system by accessing cache when doing speculative execution. CoPTAdoes not introduce any new types of security vulnerabilities in addition to what already exists for speculation.

9   Conclusion

TLB misses introduce a non-trivial overhead as page table walks require several slow main memory accesses. This can especially be problematic for workloads with large data footprints and irregular memory accesses with insignificant data locality (e.g. graph processing workloads). Our experiments show that the overhead caused by the page table walks can take up to 40% of total execution time. We also demonstrate that the built-in Linux buddy allocator and defragmentation mechanism tend to map contiguous virtual pages to contiguous physical pages. Motivated by this observation, we propose the CoPTAarchitecture that leverages this mechanism to predict the address translations upon TLB misses and speculatively execute proceeding instructions while concurrently performing the page table walk. With a negligible storage requirement of 0.4 KB, CoPTAachieves an average address prediction accurate of 82% while improving end-to-end performance by 16%.

References

1. Dynamic instrumentation tool platform. https://dynamorio.org/
2. Linux kernel documentation. https://www.kernel.org/doc/
3. Advanced micro devices. AMD x86–64 architecture programmer's manual (2002)
4. Bailey, D.H., et al.: The NAS parallel benchmarks summary and preliminary results. In: Supercomputing 1991: Proceedings of the 1991 ACM/IEEE Conference on Supercomputing, pp. 158–165. IEEE (1991)
5. Barr, T.W., Cox, A.L., Rixner, S.: Translation caching: skip, don't walk (the page table). In: ACM SIGARCH Computer Architecture News, vol. 38, pp. 48–59. ACM (2010)
6. Barr, T.W., Cox, A.L., Rixner, S.: SpecTLB: a mechanism for speculative address translation. In: ACM SIGARCH Computer Architecture News, vol. 39, pp. 307–318. ACM (2011)
7. Basu, A., Gandhi, J., Chang, J., Hill, M.D., Swift, M.M.: Efficient virtual memory for big memory servers. In: Proceedings of the 40th Annual International Symposium on Computer Architecture, ISCA 2013, pp. 237–248. ACM, New York (2013). https://doi.org/10.1145/2485922.2485943. http://doi.acm.org/10.1145/2485922.2485943
8. Bhattacharjee, A., Lustig, D., Martonosi, M.: Shared last-level TLBS for chip multiprocessors. In: 2011 IEEE 17th International Symposium on High Performance Computer Architecture, pp. 62–63, February 2011. https://doi.org/10.1109/HPCA.2011.5749717
9. Bhattacharjee, A., Lustig, D.: Architectural and Operating System Support for Virtual Memory. Synthesis Lectures on Computer Architecture 12(5), pp. 1–175 (2017)
10. Bhattacharjee, A., Martonosi, M.: Characterizing the TLB behavior of emerging parallel workloads on chip multiprocessors. In: 2009 18th International Conference on Parallel Architectures and Compilation Techniques, pp. 29–40. IEEE (2009)
11. Bhattacharjee, A., Martonosi, M.: Inter-core cooperative TLB for chip multiprocessors. SIGARCH Comput. Archit. News 38(1), 359–370 (2010). https://doi.org/10.1145/1735970.1736060
12. Binkert, N., et al.: The gem5 simulator. SIGARCH Comput. Archit. News 39(2), 1–7 (2011). https://doi.org/10.1145/2024716.2024718. http://doi.acm.org/10.1145/2024716.2024718
13. Blanas, S., Li, Y., Patel, J.M.: Design and evaluation of main memory hash join algorithms for multi-core CPUs. In: Proceedings of the 2011 ACM SIGMOD International Conference on Management of Data, pp. 37–48 (2011)
14. Bruening, D.L.: Efficient, transparent, and comprehensive runtime code manipulation. Ph.D. thesis, Cambridge, MA, USA (2004). aAI0807735
15. Chen, J.B., Borg, A., Jouppi, N.P.: A simulation based study of TLB performance. In: Proceedings of the 19th Annual International Symposium on Computer Architecture, ISCA 1992, pp. 114–123. Association for Computing Machinery, New York (1992). https://doi.org/10.1145/139669.139708

16. Cox, G., Bhattacharjee, A.: Efficient address translation for architectures with multiple page sizes. ACM SIGOPS Oper. Syst. Rev. **51**(2), 435–448 (2017)
17. Gandhi, J., Basu, A., Hill, M.D., Swift, M.M.: Efficient memory virtualization: reducing dimensionality of nested page walks. In: 2014 47th Annual IEEE/ACM International Symposium on Microarchitecture, pp. 178–189, December 2014. https://doi.org/10.1109/MICRO.2014.37
18. Henning, J.L.: SPEC CPU2006 benchmark descriptions. ACM SIGARCH Comput. Archit. News **34**(4), 1–17 (2006)
19. Kocher, P., et al.: Spectre attacks: exploiting speculative execution. In: 2019 IEEE Symposium on Security and Privacy (SP), pp. 1–19 (2018)
20. Leskovec, J., Krevl, A.: SNAP Datasets: Stanford large network dataset collection, June 2014. http://snap.stanford.edu/data
21. Lipp, M., et al.: Meltdown: reading kernel memory from user space. In: 27th USENIX Security Symposium (USENIX Security 2018), pp. 973–990. USENIX Association, Baltimore, August 2018. https://www.usenix.org/conference/usenixsecurity18/presentation/lipp
22. Luszczek, P.R., et al.: The HPC challenge (HPCC) benchmark suite. In: Proceedings of the 2006 ACM/IEEE Conference on Supercomputing, vol. 213, pp. 1188455–1188677. Citeseer (2006)
23. Margaritov, A., Ustiugov, D., Bugnion, E., Grot, B.: Prefetched address translation. In: Proceedings of the 52nd Annual IEEE/ACM International Symposium on Microarchitecture, pp. 1023–1036. ACM (2019)
24. McCurdy, C., Cox, A., Vetter, J.: Investigating the TLB behavior of high-end scientific applications on commodity microprocessors, pp. 95–104, May 2008. https://doi.org/10.1109/ISPASS.2008.4510742
25. Mittal, S.: A survey of techniques for architecting TLBs. Concurr. Comput. Pract. Experience **29**(10), e4061 (2017)
26. Nai, L., Xia, Y., Tanase, I.G., Kim, H., Lin, C.: GraphBIG: understanding graph computing in the context of industrial solutions. In: SC 2015: Proceedings of the International Conference for High Performance Computing, Networking, Storage and Analysis, pp. 1–12, November 2015. https://doi.org/10.1145/2807591.2807626
27. Navarro, J., Iyer, S., Druschel, P., Cox, A.: Practical, transparent operating system support for superpages. SIGOPS Oper. Syst. Rev. **36**(SI), 89–104 (2003). https://doi.org/10.1145/844128.844138
28. Park, C.H., Heo, T., Jeong, J., Huh, J.: Hybrid TLB coalescing: improving TLB translation coverage under diverse fragmented memory allocations. In: Proceedings of the 44th Annual International Symposium on Computer Architecture, pp. 444–456 (2017)
29. Pham, B., Vaidyanathan, V., Jaleel, A., Bhattacharjee, A.: CoLT: coalesced large-reach TLBs. In: Proceedings of the 2012 45th Annual IEEE/ACM International Symposium on Microarchitecture, pp. 258–269. IEEE Computer Society (2012)
30. Pham, B., Veselý, J., Loh, G.H., Bhattacharjee, A.: Large pages and lightweight memory management in virtualized environments: can you have it both ways? In: Proceedings of the 48th International Symposium on Microarchitecture, pp. 1–12 (2015)
31. Ryoo, J.H., Gulur, N., Song, S., John, L.K.: Rethinking TLB designs in virtualized environments: a very large part-of-memory TLB. ACM SIGARCH Comput. Archit. News **45**(2), 469–480 (2017)
32. Saulsbury, A., Dahlgren, F., Stenström, P.: Recency-based TLB preloading. In: Proceedings of the 27th Annual International Symposium on Computer Architecture, pp. 117–127 (2000)

33. Talluri, M., Hill, M.D.: Surpassing the TLB performance of superpages with less operating system support. SIGOPS Oper. Syst. Rev. **28**(5), 171–182 (1994). https://doi.org/10.1145/381792.195531
34. Fang, Z., Zhang, L., Carter, J.B., Hsieh, W.C., McKee, S.A.: Reevaluating online superpage promotion with hardware support. In: Proceedings HPCA Seventh International Symposium on High-Performance Computer Architecture, pp. 63–72, January 2001. https://doi.org/10.1109/HPCA.2001.903252

A Fine-Granularity Image Pyramid Accelerator for Embedded Processors

Chun-Jen Tsai[(⊠)] and Chiang-Yi Wang

Department of Computer Science, National Chiao-Tung University, Hsinchu, Taiwan
cjtsai@cs.nctu.edu.tw

Abstract. Image-pyramid generator is an important component for many computer vision applications. Due to the complexity of image scaling operations, embedded application processors usually generate three- or four-level image pyramids for vision applications. In this paper, we present an image pyramid accelerator for embedded processors that generates image pyramids of up to 24-levels of down-sampled resolutions for the input image. Since image pyramids are crucial for the coarse-to-fine analysis of many computer vision problems, more resolution levels in the image pyramid can improve the parameter-estimation accuracy. Furthermore, the down-sampling filters used in the proposed design is based on a long-tap Sine-windowed Sinc function filter. Therefore, it preserves more image details than other low-complexity filters such as the bilinear or the bicubic interpolation filter. The proposed circuit is verified on an FPGA development board with a Xilinx Kintex-7 device and will be made open-source. The experimental results show that the design is very promising for real-time computer vision applications.

Keywords: Image pyramid · Down-sampling filter · Computer vision · Coarse-to-fine processing · Hardware-software codesign

1 Introduction

Coarse-to-fine processing is a typical technique for computer vision and image recognition applications [1–3]. For example, for optical flow estimations, one of the most popular methods is to solve the optical flow constraint equation proposed by Horn and Schunck [4]. However, the optical flow equation is a first-order approximation to the spatiotemporal differential change of the image intensity of a moving pixel. The approximation is valid when the motion magnitudes of all objects between two video frames are less than a pixel. However, in practice, this is only true if the frame rate of the video sequence is extremely high, or if the motions are extremely slow. Since most videos are acquired at a frame rate of 30 or 60, to validate the optical flow equation, image pyramids are used to diagonally down-scale an image in the spatial domain, which effectively downscales the temporal differences between two consecutive frames. Therefore, the motions at low-resolution levels become very small, which can be used as the initial guesses for estimating the motions at higher resolution levels. Most state-of-the-art optical flow estimation techniques are based on the non-linear estimation of motion vectors under

© Springer Nature Switzerland AG 2020
A. Orailoglu et al. (Eds.): SAMOS 2020, LNCS 12471, pp. 84–95, 2020.
https://doi.org/10.1007/978-3-030-60939-9_6

the optical flow constraint in the image pyramid data [5]. The optimization complexity and accuracy of such algorithms depend on the resolution levels and the quality of the image pyramid used. Using more levels of the image pyramids and better down-scalers can simplify the non-linear estimation problem.

Another example of the image pyramid application is for visual recognition. The most successful approaches today for visual object recognition are based on the deep learning convolutional neural networks (CNN). However, when one trains the CNN to recognize the features of some objects, the training data are usually set around a fixed range of resolution scales. Although one can increase the range to train a CNN to capture scale-independent features, for the same amount of training data, increasing the resolution scales of the training data usually means decreasing the training data for other image features. With an image pyramid structure, a CNN can perform better in locating the trained objects with drastic scale differences in an image [6].

In this paper, we present the design and implementation of a HW-SW codesigned image pyramid generator. The main contribution of this paper is that this is the first open-source[1] circuit implementation of a 24-level image pyramid generator that is based on the Sine-windowed Sinc-function (SWS) filters [7]. The SWS filter was adopted in the scalable extension of the H.264/AVC video standard since it preserves image details better than other filter kernels.

The top-level controller of the pyramid generator is a piece of software executed by an embedded processor. A hardwired fine-granularity down-sampling AXI-bus master circuit is responsible for the image scaling task. The processor core is responsible for specifying the input image address, the output image address, and the decimation level(s) to the scaling circuit for image pyramid generation. The proposed system can be flexibly used for various multi-resolution vision applications. The scaling circuit can generate 24 different levels of down-scaled resolutions from an input image. The paper is organized as follows. In Sect. 2, we describe the problem of image pyramids generation and its challenges for hardware architecture design. Section 3 presents the proposed HW-SW codesign architecture. Implementation results and the analysis of the proposed design are presented in Sect. 4. Finally, some conclusions and future work are described in Sect. 5.

2 Problem Formulation

An image pyramid is illustrated in Fig. 1. The input to a pyramid generator is an image with the highest resolution. A down-sampler is used to scale the first level of the image to smaller resolutions. To avoid propagation of sub-sampling errors, low resolution images are always subsampled directly from the original input image. Therefore, multiple down-sampling filters with different decimation rates must be used for a high-quality pyramid generator.

There are two main design decisions to make for an image pyramid generator. The first one is about the image filter used for scaling. The second one is about the memory architecture (the on-chip buffering mechanism) for the scaler circuit. We will present brief discussions on each issue in the following two subsections.

---

[1] See https://github.com/eisl-nctu/pyramid.

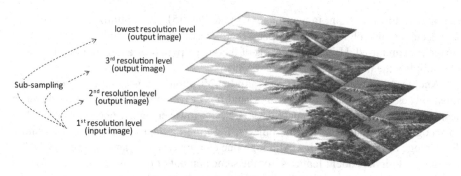

Fig. 1. Image pyramid generation.

2.1 Mathematical Model of the Down-Scaler

An image pyramid allows us to manipulate a digital image at multiple scales. Ideally, given a digital input image, it can be mathematically modelled as a continuous 2-D waveform using a 2-D Sinc filter, and then resampled to different scales. In practice, such operations are often replaced by a 2D convolutional kernel that combines low-pass filtering and down-sampling operations. Popular filters used for this purpose are short-tap Gaussian, bilinear, or bi-cubic filters [9]. However, when the filter tap is short, it can result in loss of detail (high frequency) information. Therefore, more complex filters have been proposed to construct an image pyramid [8].

In this paper, we use a long-tap 2D filtering kernel to design the down-sampling filter. We have chosen to use the SWS filter as the kernel of the proposed image pyramid. The SWS filter was adopted in the scalable extension of the H.264/AVC video coding standard to support spatial scalability of coded video sequences [7]. The mathematical model of the filter kernel is defined in Eq. (1):

$$f(x) = \begin{cases} \frac{\sin\frac{\pi x}{D}}{\pi x/D} \times \sin\left(\frac{\pi}{2}\left(1 + \frac{x}{N \times D}\right)\right), & |x| < N \times D \\ 0, & otherwise \end{cases} \tag{1}$$

where N is the number of Sinc filter lobes on each side (fixed to 3 here) and D is a decaying parameter that produces different frequency responses of the filter. D is dependent on the decimation rate of the down-scaler. The one-dimensional digital FIR filter derived from Eq. (1) is a set of 12-tap filters. For 2D image scaling operations, this set of 1D filters can be applied as a set of separable 2D filters. That is, two passes of 1D filtering operations, one in horizontal direction and one in vertical direction, can be used to scale a 2D image.

The SWS filter is an adaptive filter such that the filter weights are adaptive to different scales. The original SWS filter used in the H.264/AVC scalable coding standard only requires three to four levels of kernel coefficients for scalable video coding applications. In this paper, we have designed 24 levels of kernel coefficients based on Eq. (1) for fine-granularity image pyramid generation.

2.2 Related Work

There have been a few papers on the design of image pyramid generators for FPGAs. Lee [3] proposes an SoC architecture for image pyramid generation that is similar to the one presented in this paper. However, the design was for a low-complexity Gaussian pyramid generator using a 3-tap filter. The implementation was based on a simple AMBA AHB bus for on-chip communications. Agrawwal and Chowdhury [8] present a Laplacian pyramid circuit for image fusion applications, a 5-tap Gaussian filter is used for scaling operations. The design constrains the number of image levels to 4 to serve the needs of the target application. Nuno-Maganda and Arias-Estrada [9] propose a 4-tap bicubic hardware scaler for FPGAs. However, bicubic interpolator tends to overshoot around the sharp edges of an image. Such filters may not be suitable for vision applications that require the preservation of fine image features at different scales. A high-level synthesis (HLS) approach for automatic generation of image pyramid circuits for FPGAs is presented in Schmid et al. [14]. It is known that HLS can generate high performance circuits for image and vision applications at the cost of using more hardware resources. It is difficult to make a direct comparison between the circuit in [14] and the one presented in this paper because different filters are implemented. Nonlinear bilateral filters are used in [14], while we have implemented 12-tap SWS filters for 24 different scales. For 3×3 bilateral filters, the proposed circuit in [14] requires 56,978 LUTs while the scaler in this paper used 4,557 LUTs, both on Xilinx 7th generation FPGAs.

2.3 Buffering and Pipeline Considerations of the Pyramid Generators

The main challenges of an image pyramid generation circuit come from the fact that the image data are usually too big to fit in the on-chip memory. Therefore, an efficient buffering scheme must be used to increase the performance of 2-D filtering, otherwise, the data transfer overhead between the main memory (DRAM) and the on-chip memory can be much higher than the processing speed of the circuit. If short-tap filters are used, on-the-fly data transfer and processing can be achieved without using large on-chip buffers [9]. However, the resulting down-scaled images may lose some high frequency details. There are some approaches trying to adopt a short-tap filter (e.g., the bilinear filter) to perform the scaling operations while using the edge detectors and the sharpening filters to recover some of the details [12]. Such scalers may be appropriate for multimedia applications, but not suitable for computer vision applications.

On the other hand, if long-tap filters (e.g., the SWS filters), or adaptive filers (e.g., the Newton filter [11]) are applied in the system, two passes of separable 1-D filtering operations can be used to implement the 2-D filters to maintain burst transfer of data from DRAM to the on-chip buffer [10]. In the proposed design, we chose to use the long-tap SWS filters since they have been verified thoroughly by the MPEG organization.

Another memory-related decision to make is about the generation order of the image pixels in the pyramid. There are two types of pyramid generation pipelines, the segment pipelines and the linear pipelines [13]. For the segment pipeline, one complete level of down-scaled image is generated after another (as the illustration in Fig. 1 shows). For the linear pipeline, the generator works on the down-scaling operations for all levels of images in parallel (or in a time-sharing manner, as proposed in [13]). Theoretically, the linear pipeline design is more memory bandwidth-efficient than the segment pipeline since an area of the input image can be cached in an on-chip buffer and used to generate the co-located areas in all levels of scaled images before the circuit needs to read in another area. However, the proposed design in this paper chooses the segment buffer approach due to its application flexibility. The proposed design allows for 24 levels of output resolution. Nevertheless, not all vision applications require all 24 levels of scales for processing. In addition, many coarse-to-fine analysis algorithms are iterative across different resolution scales. With the segment pipeline design, it would be possible to adaptively determine the resolution scale for the next level of analysis based on the outcome of the current level. As a result, a segment pipeline may be more memory- and computation-efficient than a linear pipeline in the end.

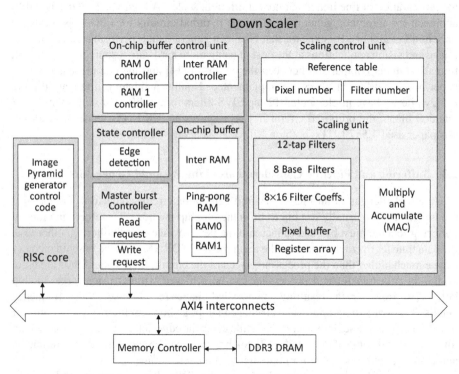

Fig. 2. The overall system architecture of the image pyramid generator.

3   Architecture Design of the Pyramid Circuit

To generate a fine-granularity image pyramid, the key component would be a set of down-scaler filters with controllable scaling factors that preserve image features as much as possible. In this paper, we present a hardware design of the SWS filters with 24 resolution scales. The filter can generate output images of scaling ratios of $k/32$, where $k = 8, 9, \ldots,$

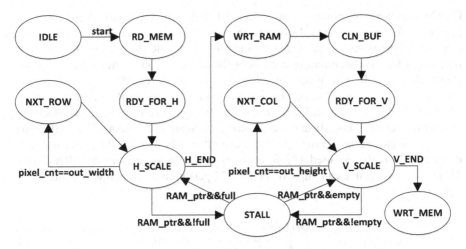

Fig. 3. The main controller of the down-scaler circuit architecture.

31. The complete pyramid generator architecture is composed of a RISC core, a down-scaler circuit, and a DDR3 DRAM shared between the RISC core and the down-scaler through an ARM AXI4 bus interconnect, as shown in Fig. 2.

The RISC core is responsible for executing the top-level control code for pyramid generation. It specifies the input/output DRAM addresses of the image pyramid and triggers the execution of the down-scaler with different resolution scales. The down-scaler circuit is a bus-master IP that, once triggered, reads an input image from the DRAM memory and output the down-scaled image back to the DRAM memory. Although it is easy to replace the RISC core with a hardwired controller to create a fully hardwired image pyramid circuit, there will be no performance advantage for such design. We opt for a small RISC core in the proposed design due to its application flexibility. As mentioned in Sect. 2.2, some coarse-to-fine vision algorithms may adaptively determine the resolution scales it needs for analysis. It would be much easier to implement such algorithms if the pyramid generation controller is done in software.

3.1 Controller Design of the Down-Scaler

The finite-state machine of the main controller is shown in Fig. 3. Two separable 1-D horizontal and vertical filters are used to construct the 2-D down-sampler. The horizontal scaling is performed before the vertical scaling. The image pixels stored in DRAM will be fetched into an on-chip buffer for the filtering operations. As soon as there are enough data in the buffer for horizontal scaling, the filtering operations will begin. The output from the horizontal scaling filters will be stored in a second on-chip buffer waiting for vertical scaling. The output from the vertical scaler will be written back to the first buffer for burst output to DRAM.

To save computational resources, the horizontal and the vertical scaling operations share the same processing elements. Thus, the 1-D horizontal and vertical scalers do not operate concurrently. On the other hand, the scaling operations do overlap with the

DRAM read/write operations to save time. Since the DRAM bandwidth is often the bottleneck for many embedded systems, there is no point wasting logic resources on concurrent horizontal/vertical scaling operations if the DRAM bandwidth is limited. If one opts for the concurrent operations of the horizontal and vertical filters, the on-chip buffers as well as the processing elements must be increased to maintain efficient operations, which may not be cost effective. The timing diagram of various tasks of the proposed design is shown in Fig. 4. From this diagram, one can see that the memory read/write operations take about the same time as the scaling operations. The overlapping of the memory and the scaling operations can efficiently increase the performance of the circuit. Note that we used a 32-bit memory controller to accesses the DRAM data. There are methods that can improve the DRAM performance, which will be discussed in Sect. 4.

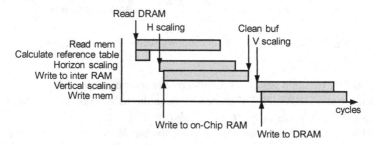

Fig. 4. The timing diagram of the scaler tasks.

3.2 The Memory Architecture of the Down-Sampler

The down-sampling architecture is composed of two parts: the on-chip memory architecture and the datapath of the down-scaling filters. Figure 5 illustrates the on-chip memory architecture while Fig. 6 shows the datapath of the scaler.

There are two SRAM buffers in the proposed architecture. The first one contains two SRAM blocks that form a ping-pong SRAM pair. This buffer, referred to as the ping-pong RAM, is used as the input pixel source for the horizon scaling operation. Since it takes a long time to read data from the DRAM, the scaling operation will begin as soon as one of the ping-pong SRAM blocks is filled with data. When the circuit is scaling the pixels in the first SRAM block, the DRAM reading circuit will be filling the second SRAM block of the ping-pong buffer simultaneously. The other SRAM buffer, called the Inter RAM, is used to store the output data for the horizontal scaler as well as the input data for the vertical scaler. Note that the two scalers share the same datapath circuit and do not operate concurrently.

At the vertical scaling stage, the ping-pong RAM is also used to store the output pixels and to overlap the scaling operations with the DRAM write-back operations. In Fig. 5, there is a 32 × 9-bit reference table that is implemented as a register array. The table is used to select the pixels and the filter coefficients for computing an output pixel. The input to the table is the "down_level" parameter (ranges from 8 to 31, representing the down-scaling rates of 8/32 to 31/32, respectively) and the "pixel_counter" parameter. The outputs are the "filter_number" and the "pixel_number" parameters (to be explained in Sect. 3.3) for the filtering operations. The initialization of the reference table requires 16-bit integer divisions. It is initialized once before the first DRAM read operation and does not impose extra overhead to the scaling operations.

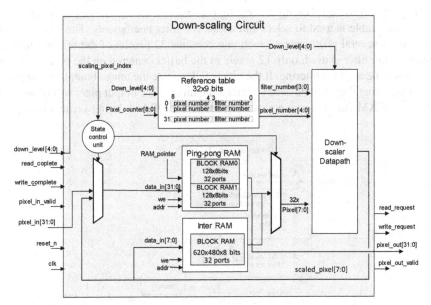

Fig. 5. The on-chip memory architecture of the down-scaler.

3.3 The Datapath of the Down-Sampler

The proposed 2D down-scaler circuit implements a two-pass separable 1D SWS filter based on Eq. (1). However, only integer arithmetic is used to approximate the SWS filter. As discussed in Sect. 2, each of the resulting 1D filters has a 12-tap convolutional kernel. The center of the filter is located at the filter coefficient position number 6 (the position index starting at 0). The input image is divided into pixel groups. Each pixel group contains 32 pixels. Once the decimation rate is determined, some pixels in each pixel group will be selected as the center for each filtering operation. For example, if the decimation rate is 11/32, then 11 pixels in each pixel group will be selected as the center of 11 filtering operations. Each operation computes the normalized convolution between the 12 filter coefficients and the 12 pixels around the center pixel (six to the left and five to the right). The filter weights are computed based on Eq. (1), the decimation rate, and the position of the center pixels.

In the proposed design, we do not compute the filter weights on-the-fly. Instead, the filter weights are pre-computed and stored in on-chip ROMs. The ROM contains eight filter set (for eight different D values) and each filter set contains 16 different 12-tap filter coefficients. Each coefficient is stored as a 9-bit signed integer number. A filter selection logic is used to select the correct filter to use. After each convolution operation, the output must be divided by 128 (7-bit right shift) for normalization purpose.

Figure 6 is the datapath of the down-scaler architecture. Both the horizontal and the vertical 1-D scalers share the same datapath. The down-level parameter (i.e., the decimation rate) and the filter number parameter are used to select the base filter when the datapath is activated. During the scaling process, the filter_number parameter from the reference table is used to select and adjust the filter coefficients. The source pixel buffer stores several pixel groups (each one contains 32 pixels) of the original image. Since a 12-tap filter is used, only 12 pixels in the buffer centered on the pixel_number position will be used for filtering. If the pixels fall outside the image boundary, the pixel at the image boundary will be used to extend the image. The output pixel will be written to the Inter RAM during horizontal scaling and to the DRAM during vertical scaling.

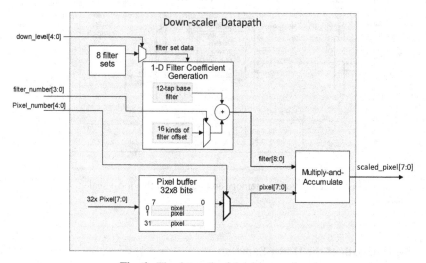

Fig. 6. The datapath of the down-scaler.

4 Implementation and Experimental Results on FPGA

The proposed architecture has been implemented on a Xilinx KC705 platform with a Kintex-7 XC7K325T-2FFG900C FPGA device. The RTL model of the down-scaler circuit is written using Verilog and synthesized at 100 MHz using the Xilinx Vivado 2018.2 EDA tool. AXI-4 bus with a 32-word burst length is used for DRAM accesses. The logic utilization on the Kintex-7 FPGA is shown in Table 1. Table 2 presents a list of the on-chip memory blocks used in the design. Finally, Fig. 8 shows the number of execution cycles of the proposed down-scaler to generate output images at each resolution scale when the input image is 640 × 480.

Current design of the hardware-software system adopts a 32-bit memory controller with the logic running at 100 MHz. With these parameters, the image pyramid generator

Table 1. Logic usage on a Xilinx Kintex-7 FPGA DEVICE. The full system contains a Microblaze RISC core, the down-scaler, and all AXI4 infrastructure logics in Fig. 2.

Logic	#LUT6	# flip-flops	#BRAMs (4 KB)
Down-scaler	4557	2490	128
Full system	27814 (13.65%)	27173 (6.67%)	136 (30.56%)

Table 2. On-chip memory usage (for 640×480 input images).

Memory type	Size	Function
Ping-pong RAM	$2 \times 128 \times 8$ bits	Composed of two SRAM units. Each unit contains 128×8-bit memory. That is, each SRAM block can be filled up by one burst of AXI4 DRAM access
Inter RAM	$465 \times 680 \times 8$ bits	Stores the output pixels. This buffer is not optimized. The size can be further reduced to $12 \times 640 \times 8$ bits in the future
Pixel buffer	32×8 bits	The buffer is synthesized using registers
12-tap base filters	$8 \times 12 \times 9$ bits	Stores the base filter coefficients in each filter set (per each D value)
All filter coefficients	$8 \times 16 \times 12 \times 9$ bits	Stores the coefficient differences between all other filters and the base filter of each D value
Reference table	31×9 bits	Stores the mapping between the decimation rate and the filter set number and the center pixel position

can generate eleven 24-level pyramids per second. This number can be derived from the performance chart shown in Fig. 7, which was measured using a hardware counter register on the real platform. The main bottleneck of the design is in the DRAM bandwidth. The data path design is fine-tuned to match the DRAM bandwidth such that the memory read/write time and the logic computation time have maximal overlaps. As illustrated in Fig. 4, the scaler pipeline does strike a good balance between the computation time and the memory access time.

For the KC705 platform used in this paper, the DRAM chips are connected to the FPGA using 64 bits wires. The DDR3 DRAM clock can run at 800 MHz. Therefore, the FPGA platform can be theoretically used to emulate a 512-bit DRAM bus at 100 MHz (or a 256-bit DRAM bus at 200 MHz). In this case, we can hardwire the pyramid generator to pump out thirty 24-level pyramids per second for real-time applications. However, this also means that we need bus wrappers to adapt the 32-bit logics (e.g., the RISC core) to the 512-bit DRAM bus. We will leave this work for future research.

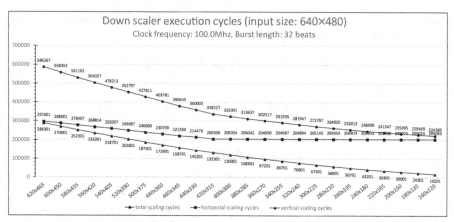

Fig. 7. The number of cycles it takes for the proposed down-scaler to generate images at different scales on the Xilinx KC705 platform.

5 Conclusions and Future Work

In this paper, we have presented the design of a fine-granularity down-sampler for image pyramid generation. The circuit has been implemented and verified on a Xilinx Kintex-7 FPGA. The proposed design adopts a sophisticated 12-tap Sine-windowed Sinc filter to produce high quality down-scaled images. The current design uses only a single scaling pipeline to reduce the quantity of circuit resources while maintaining high performance.

Based on the measurements on a real FPGA platform, the proposed architecture can generate eleven 24-level pyramids per second from a 640×480 input image at 100 MHz with a 32-bit DDR3 DRAM bus. It is possible to increase the performance further by introducing a wider DRAM bus and extra parallel pipelines, as discussed in Sect. 4. For future work, we will look into the optimization of the architecture to support 30-fps real-time applications. We will also investigate the reduction of on-chip memory requirement by optimizing the buffering architecture.

In addition to the refinement of the image pyramid generator, we will also apply the system to construct a dense optical flow estimator. The state-of-the-art in optical flow estimators use coarse-to-fine approaches with complex non-linear iterative optimizers that make real-time application impractical. With a 24-level image pyramid generator, it is possible to adopt a fast total least-squares estimator to iterate through each level of the image pyramid to obtain accurate optical flow estimates. In summary, the proposed HW-SW system is very promising for computer vision applications.

References

1. Adelson, E.H., Anderson, C.H., Bergen, J.R., Burt, P.J., Ogden, J.M.: Pyramid methods in image processing. RCA Eng. **29–6**, 33–41 (1984)
2. Nuno-Maganda, M.A., Arias-Estrada, M.O., Feregrino-Uribe, C.: Three video applications using an FPGA-based pyramid implementation: tracking, mosaics and stabilization. In Proceedings of IEEE International Conference on Field Programmable Technology (FPT), Tokyo, Japan (2003)

3. Lee, B.: Design and implementation of image-pyramid. J. Korea Multimedia Soc., 19–7 (2016)
4. Horn, B., Schunck, B.: Determining optical flow. Artif. Intell. **17**, 185–203 (1981)
5. Deqing, S., Roth, S., Black, M.J.: Secrets of optical flow estimation and their principles. In: IEEE International Conference on Computer Vision and Pattern Recognition (CVPR'10) 13–18 2010, San Francisco, pp. 2432-2439 (2010)
6. Farabet, C., Poulet, C., Han, J.Y., LeCun, Y.: CNP: an FPGA-based processor for convolutional networks. In: Proceedings of 2009 International Conference on Field Programmable Logic and Applications, Prague, pp. 32–37 (2009)
7. Sun, S., Reichel, J.: AHG Report on Spatial Scalability Resampling, JVT-R006. The 18th Meeting of the Joint Video Team. Bangkok, Thailand (2006)
8. Agrawal, K., Chowdhury, S.R.: Real-time multisensor Laplacian fusion on FPGA. In: Proceedings of the 19th International Symposium on VLSI Design and Test (2015)
9. Nuno-Maganda, M.A., Arias-Estrada, M.O.: Real-time FPGA-based architecture for bicubic interpolation: an application for digital image scaling. In: Proceedings of International Conference on Reconfigurable Computing and FPGAs (ReConFig'05), Puebla City, Mexico, pp. 28–30 (2005)
10. Ramachandran, S., Srinivasan, S.: Design and FPGA implementation of an MPEG based video scalar with reduced on-chip memory utilization. J. Syst. Architect. **51**, 435–450 (2005). Elsevier
11. Xiao, J., Zou, X., Liu, Z., Guo, X.: Adaptive interpolation algorithm for real-time image resizing. In: Proceedings of the 1st International Conference on Innovative Computing, Information and Control - Volume I (ICICIC'06). Beijin, China (2006)
12. Suryavanshi, R.A., Sheelvant, S.: Review of implementation of image scaling algorithm on FPGA. Int. J. Innov. Adv. Comput. Sci. **4–7**, 96-99 (2015). Academic Science
13. Zhu, Q., Garg, N., Tsai, Y.-T., Pulli, K.: An energy efficient time-sharing pyramid pipeline for multi-resolution computer vision. In: Proceeedings of IFIP/IEEE 21st International Conference on Very Large Scale Integration (VLSI-SoC), Istanbul, Turkey, pp. 278–281 (2013)
14. Schmid, M., Reiche, O., Schmitt, C., Hanning, F., Teich, J.: Code generation for high-level synthesis of multiresolution applications on FPGAs (2014). arXiv:1408.4721

Rec2Poly: Converting Recursions to Polyhedral Optimized Loops Using an Inspector-Executor Strategy

Salwa Kobeissi, Alain Ketterlin, and Philippe Clauss$^{(\boxtimes)}$

Inria Camus, ICube Lab., CNRS University of Strasbourg, Strasbourg, France
`philippe.clauss@inria.fr`

Abstract. In this paper, we propose Rec2Poly, a framework which detects automatically if recursive programs may be transformed into affine loops that are compliant with the polyhedral model. If successful, the replacing loops can then take advantage of advanced loop optimizing and parallelizing transformations as tiling or skewing.

Rec2Poly is made of two main phases: an offline profiling phase and an inspector-executor phase. In the profiling phase, the original recursive program, which has been instrumented, is run. Whenever possible, the trace of collected information is used to build equivalent affine loops from the runtime behavior. Then, an inspector-executor program is automatically generated, where the inspector is made of a light version of the original recursive program, whose aim is reduced to the generation and verification of the information which is essential to ensure the correctness of the equivalent affine loop program. The collected information is mainly related to the touched memory addresses and the control flow of the so-called "impacting" basic blocks of instructions. Moreover, in order to exhibit the lowest possible time-overhead, the inspector is implemented as a parallel process where several memory buffers of information are verified simultaneously. Finally, the executor is made of the equivalent affine loops that have been optimized and parallelized.

Keywords: Polyhedral model · Recursive functions · Automatic program parallelization and optimization

1 Introduction

From code development to final execution on a hardware platform, a software goes through many transformation phases, making the final executable code significantly different from the initial source code. The final goal is obviously to generate an executable which is semantically equivalent to the input source code, but whose runtime behavior is satisfactory regarding execution time, code size, energy consumption, or security. Compilers apply many optimization passes on the input source code that often modify or even remove instructions, control structures, or data structures. Such code transformations may apply from the

A. Orailoglu et al. (Eds.): SAMOS 2020, LNCS 12471, pp. 96–109, 2020.
https://doi.org/10.1007/978-3-030-60939-9_7

instruction level until the global code structure. A clear example of the latter kind of transformations, performed by mainstream compilers, is the transformation of tail-recursive calls into loops. Indeed, recursive programs generally suffer from not being as easily handled as other code structures like loops, for automatic optimization and parallelization. In the literature dealing with recursion optimization, either recursive functions are handled directly ≪as they are≫ [5,10], or are firstly transformed into loops [1]. Although such approaches may provide significant performance improvements, they do not capture cases where recursive codes can be rewritten as *affine* loops, which are the most convenient loops for efficient data locality and parallelization optimizations. Affine loops are compliant with the polyhedral model [3,4], which is a well-known mathematical framework unifying all the most important loop optimizing transformations as loop interchange, skewing or tiling.

Being a static (source-level) framework, the polyhedral model places stringent conditions on the programs that it can handle. Many programs do not directly fit the model, either because of superficial languages idiosyncrasies, or because of radical language differences (as in the case of recursive functions). It often turns out that source programs that seem not to fit the model actually have a matching behavior at runtime, at least for significant portions of their execution. The APOLLO speculative optimizer [9,13] aims at capturing these transient polyhedral behaviors and leverage polyhedral tools to optimize them at runtime.

We present Rec2Poly, a framework devoted to the transformation of recursive codes into affine loops. Rec2Poly detects a polyhedral-compliant behavior of a target recursive code at runtime, using an offline profiling phase. When successful, it builds a semantically equivalent code where all the execution flow related to recursive functions is replaced with affine loops. Moreover, the so-generated loops are parallelized and optimized thanks to polyhedral transformations. Since this transformation is based on a runtime profiling, its validity is not ensured whatever the input data. Thus, it is speculative and a fast runtime verification mechanism is also generated, which follows an inspector-executor scheme [11,12]. At runtime, the inspector verifies that the affine loops are valid regarding the current execution context. If the inspector does not detect an unpredicted behavior, the executor launches the optimized parallel loops. Note that the original recursive code is launched in parallel with the inspector, in order to save the time-overhead of Rec2Poly if the affine loops are not valid in the current context. We firstly presented our proof of concept of Rec2Poly's analysis, profiling and recursion to optimized loops transformation phases in a previous work [8]. In this paper, we extend these phases in addition to introducing the new embedded verification feature based on an inspector-executor strategy.

The originality of our approach is twofold: (1) Seeking a polyhedral-compliant runtime behavior in recursions; and (2) using an inspector-executor scheme not only verifying memory access patterns, as it is usually done when using this scheme, but also verifying the control flow as being compatible with affine loops. Note that our approach can also be seen as dynamic code rewriting.

The paper is organized as follows. Next Section presents an overview of the Rec2Poly framework, while the following sections provide more details on its phases. Section 3 explains how important functions involved in the recursions are automatically identified, as well as the important instructions of these functions. It also presents essential aspects regarding memory instructions. In Sect. 4, it is explained how variables which are local to functions are globalized for code instrumentation, in order to promote memory accesses following affine functions of loop indices. Rec2Poly mostly relies on a software tool called NLR (Nested Loop Recognition) whose main features are recalled in Sect. 5. Generation of the inspector program is presented in Sect. 6, while the generation of the optimized affine loops is presented in Sect. 7. Experiments are presented in Sect. 8 and related work in Sect. 9. Conclusions are given in Sect. 10.

2 Overview of the Rec2Poly Framework

The main phases of Rec2Poly are depicted in Fig. 1. Every analysis, transformation and code generation phase has been implemented as passes of the mainstream compiler Clang-LLVM.[1]

A target recursive code is first deeply analyzed in order to identify the recursive functions as well as the functions that may be invoked by, or that may invoke, the recursive ones. We call these identified functions as *impacting functions*. Then, the Backward Static Slice (BSS) of every memory store instruction in these functions is built, by collecting the identifiers of every Basic Block (BB) that contains at least one instruction involved in the computation of the target memory address or in the computation of the stored value. We characterize such basic blocks as *impacting basic blocks*.

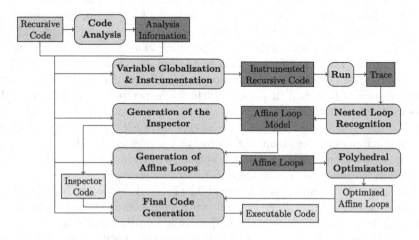

Fig. 1. Rec2Poly

---

[1] http://www.llvm.org.

An instrumented version of the target recursive code is then generated by using the so-collected information. In this code, an invocation counter is added to each impacting function, and each data structure which is local to an impacting function is transformed into a global data structure indexed using this counter (this is called Variable Globalization). Moreover, every impacting function is augmented with instructions for generating the output trace, which is composed of impacting basic block identifiers, invocation counter values and memory addresses referenced in the impacting basic blocks, through load and store instructions.

After having run the instrumented code, the generated code is given as input to the Nested Loop Recognition software tool NLR [7]. NLR generates a representation of the whole trace made of affine loops computing affine expressions. Then, the so-generated affine loop model is used to build a fast parallel inspector code and a code made of optimized and parallelized loops, which is dedicated to replace the impacting functions in the original recursive code. Since the replacing loops are based on the modeling of one execution of the target recursive code, their validity for further executions must be ensured at runtime. This is achieved by the inspector code whose role is to verify that the original recursive code still behaves in compliance with the replacing loops.

Since the replacing loops are made of affine loops, they can benefit from polyhedral optimization and parallelization transformations. For this purpose, we use the state-of-the-art polyhedral compiler Pluto [3]. Finally, the executable code is made of the inspector code and the transformed code made of optimized loops. More details on the main phases of Rec2Poly are given in the following subsections.

3 Code Analysis

First of all, Rec2Poly, our LLVM-Clang based tool, takes as an input a target recursive source code and transforms it into its intermediate representation (IR) that will be analyzed and transformed in the following steps. We do not activate the tail call elimination LLVM pass which transforms tail recursive calls into loops for two reasons: (1) the way the target recursive function is transformed may not result in an affine loop and (2) if there are several nested recursive calls in the target code, only one tail call may be eliminated.

Rec2Poly checks if the program involves any recursions, and, if so, it identifies these recursions and the functions participating in them. In order to detect recursions, it uses the call graph extracted from the LLVM IR of the program. Figure 2 shows an example of a call graph of a program made up of nine functions: *main*, A, B, C, D, E, F, G and H where: function *main* calls A which calls B which calls C; C invokes itself, E and D; E calls back C, and calls F and G; G calls H. In this example, note that function C exhibits a direct recursion with itself and an indirect recursion through function E.

From the call graph, Rec2Poly seeks strongly connected components (SCC), which are sub-graphs where every node is reachable from every other node. In

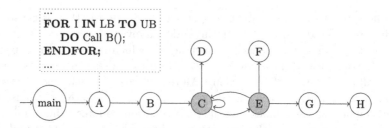

Fig. 2. Example of a call graph of an arbitrary recursive program

this context, a cycle in a SCC means that a recursion occurs among the functions associated to the nodes involved in this cycle. If the cycle is made up of only one node, *i.e.* a loop, then it is a direct recursion. Otherwise, it is indirect. For the example in Fig. 2, there are two SCC's: one loop over C showing a direct recursion, and a cycle from C to E and E back to C, showing an indirect recursion between C and E.

Recursion Reachability Recognition: We are interested in tracking impacting basic blocks, whether they are executed directly or indirectly by the recursive functions. For this reason, in addition to the recursive functions themselves, our framework also determines their reachability in the program. Reachability means all the functions that can be reached by a sequence of calls initiated by the recursive functions themselves. In Fig. 2, the reachability of the recursive functions C and E includes: D (directly called by C), F and G (directly called by E) and H (indirectly called by E through G).

Recursion Source Recognition: Not only do we track functions constituting a recursion and their reachabilities in a program, but also the source of recursions. The initial source function may be a function invoking, from within a loop, a recursive function, either directly or indirectly, through a chain of invoked functions. In addition, in case of indirect invocation of the recursion from a loop, all other functions participating in the sequence of calls from the initial source function to the recursion are considered as taking part of this source.

Analyzing source functions is necessary since otherwise, the profiling phase would be incomplete. A looping behavior detected afterwards and associated to the recursion itself would be incorrect when the recursion is invoked from within a loop. Furthermore, it helps in understanding how a recursion behaves relatively to its iterative invocations, and obviously to build affine loops which are equivalent to this whole part of the original program.

For instance, the set of source functions of the recursion in Fig. 2 includes A and B because A calls B from the body of a for-loop, and B, in turn, calls the recursive function C. The loop in A cannot benefit from efficient loop polyhedral optimizations, due to the existence of the embedded recursive call. If it is possible to replace it with equivalent affine loops, the loop may eventually be able to take advantage of sophisticated optimizations.

Impacting Basic Blocks: Such basic blocks are identified in the following way. In the LLVM intermediate representation of the program, our framework marks the stores to the *main data structure*. The *main data structure* is defined as being the final output data structure of the recursion and its corresponding reachable functions. Then, for every store instruction of this kind, it also marks every instruction leading and contributing to it, i.e., its *backward static slice* (BSS). A backward static slice is the set of instructions existing in the code of a program that may affect a certain value, *i.e.*, in our case, a value stored in the data structure which is the final output of the recursion.

Intra-Function and Inter-Function Memory Behavior Analysis: Additionally to the identification of a looping behavior of the targeted recursion, the sequence of memory addresses touched by each memory instruction, inside the impacting basic blocks, must be successfully modeled by affine functions of the surrounding loop indices.

However, among different execution instances of the same target recursive code, with exactly the same input data and the same hardware platform, the touched memory addresses are obviously not the same, since data structures are not always allocated at the same memory addresses. Nevertheless, the memory behavior relatively to the base addresses of the data structures may still be identical among the execution instances. Moreover, we are interested in cases where the relative memory behavior can be modeled by affine functions of surrounding loop indices. Thus, the memory offsets that are relative to the base addresses are collected from instrumentation.

When handling data structures which are local to functions, the analysis phase requires two steps:

- Intra-Function Analysis: Each memory access is associated to its corresponding base address visible in the scope of the current function i.e., the parameters of the function are the farthest analysis point.
- Inter-Function Analysis: If the accessed data structures are function parameters, intra-function analysis is not enough. Memory analysis propagates further outside the function to trace arguments fed to the function. Inter-function analysis associates each access to its actual base address in the program.

On the other hand, when handling global data structures, the accessed memory addresses can be directly associated to their base addresses.

4   Local Variable Globalization and Code Instrumentation

The first goal of Rec2Poly is to detect an affine behavior of the impacting functions, regarding their control flow, and also their memory accesses: for each memory instruction, the sequence of touched memory addresses must potentially be represented as affine expressions of surrounding loop indices. However, at each invocation of an impacting function , its local data structures are obviously allocated on the call stack. Thus, accesses to these local structures can never exhibit any affine memory accesses across all invocations of the function. Moreover, in the affine loops that are expected to replace the impacting functions, these data structures must obviously still be referenced. This is why in the instrumented code, all data structures that are local to an impacting function are transformed into global arrays, which are indexed by the function invocation counter. In this way, references to these globalized data may exhibit affine behaviors whether the related functions are invoked following an affine control flow.

5 Nested Loop Recognition

Rec2Poly instruments the target recursive program in order to generate an execution trace. This trace is made of tuples composed by:

- the impacting basic block ID;
- for each memory instruction in the current basic block: the relative offset of the touched memory address.

After having been generated by running the instrumented recursive program, the trace is analyzed by NLR. The NLR software tool, originally presented in [7], takes as input a trace of a program execution and constructs a sequence of loop nests that produce the same original trace when run. The applications of this algorithm include: (1) program behavior modeling for any measured quantity such as memory accesses, (2) execution trace compressing and (3) value prediction, i.e., extrapolating loops under construction (while reading input) to predict incoming values.

In our tool, not only do we use NLR to model memory accesses, which is one of its original goals, but also to model sequences of basic blocks IDs, which is more singular. Given our trace of a target recursive program, if NLR builds affine loop nests including the interesting basic blocks IDs and memory addresses interpolated by the constructed loop indices, then the generation of equivalent affine loops may be performed.

Two examples of NLR outputs are shown in Figs. 3a and 3b. The generated loops exhibit the way basic blocks (BB1, BB2, BB3, BB4) inside functions (F1, F2) are invoked by following an affine looping behavior, and how memory is referenced through relative addresses that can be modeled as affine functions of the loop indices.

Note that in Fig. 3b, NLR uses one of its more advanced features which detects that the affine modeling of a trace may be subject to some basic unknown values. NLR discovers these values and exhibits a memory behavior which is actually not fully affine: some coefficients in the affine functions may be lists of values. In the showed example, each list contains 10 integer values which are successively used to compute the referenced memory address. For example, [10:3,5,...,1][i0] means that:

```
for i0 = 0 to 99                      for i0 = 0 to 99
  val F1::BB1                           val F1::BB1
  for i1 = 0 to 49                      for i1 = 0 to 49
    val F2::BB1                           val F2::BB1
    , 0                                  , 0
    for i2 = 0 to 24                     for i2 = 0 to 24
      val F2::BB2                           val F2::BB2
      , 1*i0                               , 1*i0
      , 4*i0 + 2*i1 + 1*i2                 , [10:3,5,...,1][i0] + 2*i1 + 1*i2
      , 4*i0 + 1*i1 + 1*i2                 , [10:7,1,...,6][i0] + 1*i1 + 1*i2
    val F2:BB3                            val F2:BB3
  val F2::BB4                           val F2::BB4
```

(a) NLR Model for Linear Control and (b) NLR Model for Linear Control
Memory Behavior   and Non-Linear Memory Behavior

Fig. 3. NLR models

$$[10:3,5,...,1][i_0] = \begin{cases} 3 & \text{if } i_0 \ modulo \ 10 = 0 \\ 5 & \text{if } i_0 \ modulo \ 10 = 1 \\ ... \\ 1 & \text{if } i_0 \ modulo \ 10 = 9 \end{cases}$$

6   Generation of a Fast Parallel Inspector

The affine loop model generated by NLR is then used by Rec2Poly to generate the inspector. Its role will be to verify that the optimized and parallelized
affine loops, which replace the recursive program, are still correct in the current
execution context. It is made of three main kinds of components:

1. *Trace generators*, which are minimal versions of the original recursive program, devoted to producing the same kind of execution traces as the one
   which was generated at the profiling phase, *i.e.*, tuples made of functions and
   basic blocks IDs, and referenced memory addresses;
2. *Verifiers*, whose role is to check if the generated traces are still compliant
   with the NLR affine loop model;
3. *A parameter saver*, whose role is to collect function input values which are
   used by instructions of the impacting basic blocks.

We illustrate their functionality and how Rec2Poly modifies the IR of a given
recursive code to build its suitable inspector.

Trace Generators: A trace generator is made up of light minimal clones of the
impacting functions, *i.e.*, source, recursive and reachable functions. Its role is to
generate a trace representing the actual control flow or the sequence of touched
memory addresses.

After cloning impacting functions and their basic blocks, Rec2Poly removes
instructions that involve access to memory such as stores and loads. Instructions
that are fundamental to preserve a correct control behavior of these functions

must be preserved such as branches, conditions, loop related instructions and calls. We assume for this study that conditional branches do not depend on any memory access. Moreover, in the clones, the referenced impacting functions in call instructions must be replaced by their proper clones.

A trace generator is expected to output a trace so the latter can be verified against the NLR affine loop model. For this sake, global memory buffers or arrays are added to the IR.

The Inspector must be significantly slower than the original recursive program, such that the final couple Inspector-Executor provides significant speedups. Generating one complete trace of full tuples of values, similar to the trace generated at the profiling phase, would be too costly. Thus, in order to guarantee a fast trace generation process, an inspector, created by Rec2Poly, is composed of multiple trace generators, *i.e.*, multiple clones of impacting functions, that are executed in parallel each by a distinct parallel thread. Each of these generators is responsible for generating one sub-part of the trace, *e.g..*, one generates the whole control flow IDs, and the others generate sequences of touched memory addresses. Accordingly, Rec2poly is expected to tackle a load balancing issue among threads by deciding how many and which memory accesses a single trace generator must handle.

Verifiers: For every trace generator, Rec2Poly creates a corresponding trace verifier based on the NLR affine loop model. Each verifier is generated as a new function that implements the NLR loops and minimal versions of their enclosed basic blocks. At runtime, the trace verifiers are also launched in parallel threads.

Parameter Saver: Some input arguments of impacting functions may be values transmitted by the calling function and used directly by instructions. Such parameters have to be collected specifically in order to instantiate the replacing loops. Like trace generators, a parameter saver is made up of a minimal light version of the code part involving impacting functions. It saves function input values in a global buffer array at the entry of every impacting function. Parameter savers are also executed simultaneously with trace generators and verifiers.

Further Inspector Optimizations: In some cases, the inspector does not need to handle every memory access inside an impacting basic block. For instance, in cases of array accesses, if the same array is accessed several times through indices computed using the same induction variable, then only one of these accesses is worth being handled and verified by the inspector.

Figure 4 shows the call graph of an example of inspector based on the arbitrary example of recursive program of Fig. 2. It shows that the main function launches $M + 2$ parallel threads. There are one parameter saver and $M/2$ trace generators, which require $M/2+1$ minimal light clones of the impacting functions which are the source functions A and B; the recursive functions C and E; and the reachable functions D, F, G and H. For every thread that initiates a trace generator, there is a thread initiating a verifier function. Each trace generator and its verifier have their own set of buffers to process on, and they synchronize using two semaphores. For instance, Thread 1 and Thread 2 synchronize using Semaphores sem 0 and sem 1. Each trace generator saves its traces in its dedicated $N+1$ buffers to be verified by its corresponding verifier.

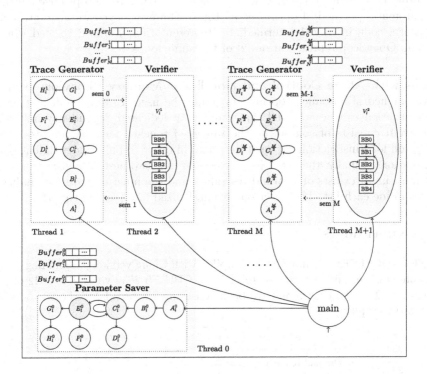

Fig. 4. Detailed inspector call graph example

7   Generation of Optimized Affine Loops as Executor

This last phase of code generation takes as input the recursive program after variable globalization, and the corresponding NLR affine loop model obtained at the profiling phase. Rec2Poly builds the replacing affine loop program by: (1) cloning the impacting basic blocks; (2) replacing the referenced memory addresses by the corresponding NLR affine functions added to the related base addresses collected at runtime; and (3) replacing the use of function input values by the values collected at runtime by the Inspector. Finally, the function called in the original program to initiate the recursion is replaced by the newly created function made up of the iterative code constructed from NLR affine loop model.

As mentioned in Sect. 5, NLR may produce two types of loop models: (1) affine control and memory behavior and (2) affine control and non-linear memory behavior. We use different approaches for optimizing each of these types of affine loops, as it is explained below.

Loops with Affine Control and Memory Behavior: This is the most favorable case with pure affine loops which are ready to be optimized using an automatic polyhedral optimizer as Pluto. However, since we generate and transform code in LLVM Intermediate Representation, we need to feed Pluto with an OpenScop representation [2] of the affine loops.

Loops with Affine Control and Non-linear Memory Behavior: In this case, polyhedral automatic optimizers cannot be used. However, efficient loop parallelization can be achieved that requires a dedicated dependency analysis process. It consists of computing the ranges of touched memory addresses by store and load instructions at each iteration, in order to build independent sets of iterations. Finally, the outer loop is broken into two nested loops: the outer one iterating over lists of loop indices values and the inner one over the indices values inside each list. The outer one is parallelized into parallel threads.

8   Experiments

The following programs have been compiled with Clang version 6.0 and flags -O3 -march=native, and run on two Intel Xeon CPU E5-2650 v3 @ 2.30 GHz of 10 cores each. Parallel programs have been run using 20 threads on the 20 cores of the hardware platform.

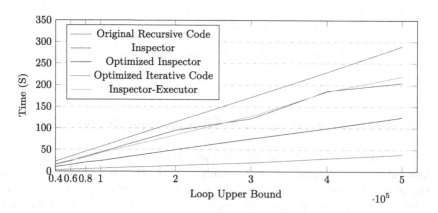

Fig. 5. Program heat experimental results

Our first experiment has been conducted on program Heat which is a recursive C implementation of a stencil computation. It involves a direct recursion invoked from within a loop. Its reachable functions also include for-loops accessing memory numerous times. In such an example, the recursion distorts the existence of loops, and it is interesting to test how much time performance can be gained by removing the recursion and applying polyhedral optimizations to the recursion-free loop nest. Both control and memory behavior are linear. Hence, an affine loop code can be reconstructed automatically from the NLR affine loop model. The affine iterative code equivalent to this recursive program is optimized using Pluto. Two versions of the inspector have been experimented here: (1) the original inspector and (2) the optimized inspector. In the original inspector, we verify all memory addresses referenced by impacting functions besides the control. Thus, 10 trace generators and 10 verifiers are launched. On the other hand, in the optimized version, half of the time overhead is eliminated by not verifying redundant memory accesses, thus only 5 trace generators and 5 verifiers are generated. Figure 5 shows the obtained execution times (vertical axis), relatively to an increasing value of the upper bound of the loop invoking the recursion (horizontal axis). The inspector version of the code, given that the loop bound equals 500000, has about 29% better performance than the original recursive code that can be optimized more deeply to perform 56.8% faster. The equivalent optimized iterative code executes about 86.5% faster than the original code. Overall, by executing both of the optimized inspector and executor together instead of the recursive code, the gain is about 24%.

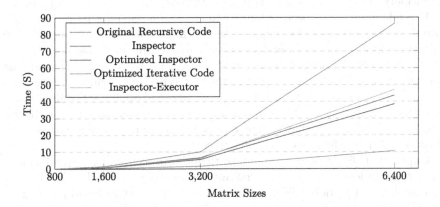

Fig. 6. Program GEMM experimental results

Our second experiment was conducted on a C implementation of the recursive matrix-matrix multiplication (GEMM) handling sub-matrices by successive dichotomy until a given threshold. It involves an indirect recursion among four functions. There is one reachable function from this recursion that includes a sequence of affine loops accessing memory. The recursion in this program has a linear control, but a non-linear memory behavior. Thus, the iterative code handles independent lists of iterations that are executed in parallel. Note that the original inspector is composed of 7 trace generators and 7 verifiers where the optimized version includes only 4 trace generators in addition to 4 verifiers. Figure 6 shows the obtained execution times. For matrix size 6400 × 6400, the inspector version executes about 49.5% faster than the original recursive code while the optimized inspector executes 55.5% faster. The equivalent optimized iterative code executes about 87.8% faster than the original code. Overall, by executing both the optimized inspector and executor together instead of the recursive code, the gain is about 45.6%.

9   Related Work

Our study has been inspired by the automatic speculative polyhedral loop optimizer APOLLO [9,13]. APOLLO applies automatic, speculative and dynamic loop optimizing and parallelizing transformations. It addresses loop nests that do not have an affine structure, yet adopt an affine memory behavior at run-time discovered by dynamic profiling. Also, APOLLO's verification of speculative loop transformations is partially based on the inspector-executor paradigm. In comparison, Rec2Poly goes further by handling recursive codes and making use of a profiling technique not only to discover the memory behavior, but also the control behavior. Finally, Rec2Poly applies the Inspector-Executor paradigm to verify recursions against a loop model, which requires the verification of both control and memory behaviors, while APOLLO uses this paradigm only to verify the memory behavior of loop nests against the one of a predictive loop model.

Multiple works have been published to transform recursive codes and optimize them. Nevertheless, the proposed approaches are mainly static and involve task parallelization where several recursive calls are run simultaneously.

PolyRec [14] optimizes nested recursive programs by polyhedral scheduling transformations. To allow such optimizations, PolyRec represents recursive function instances and their dependences as polyhedra, and applies scheduling transformations. Nevertheless, their approach is exclusively committed to particular forms of recursions such that recursive invocations are nested and data is organized in two trees, the inner and outer trees.

Gupta *et al.* [6] propose an approach to optimize recursive task parallel programs through lessening task creation and termination overhead. Adriadne [10] is a compiler that retrieves, from recursive functions, directive-based parallelism. It applies either: (1) recursion elimination, (2) parallel-reduction removing recursion such that workload is distributed to independent tasks, or (3) thread-safe recursive functions parallelization involving independent recursive calls. Adriadne is solely devoted to recursive functions whose parameters remain unchanged among recursive calls except for one integer parameter.

10   Conclusion

To our knowledge, Rec2Poly is the first attempt of speculative program optimization involving the rewriting of the target code. We have shown that using such an approach, some recursive programs may take advantage of efficient affine loops optimizations, and even take advantage of advanced transformations of the polyhedral model.

However, while the inspector-executor mechanism is adapted to such speculative optimizations, the final performance is mostly relying on the performance of the inspector. We have shown that the inspector must also be deeply optimized and parallelized to lower its time overhead. In the near future, we will still investigate strategies to lower even further the inspector time-overhead.

References

1. Arsac, J., Kodratoff, Y.: Some techniques for recursion removal from recursive functions. ACM Trans. Program. Lang. Syst. **4**(2), 295–322 (1982)
2. Bastoul, C.: Openscop: a specification and a library for data exchange in polyhedral compilation tools. University of Paris-Sud, France, Technical report, September 2011
3. Bondhugula, U., Hartono, A., Ramanujam, J., Sadayappan, P.: A practical automatic polyhedral parallelizer and locality optimizer. In: PLDI 2008, pp. 101–113. ACM (2008)
4. Feautrier, P., Lengauer, C.: Polyhedron model. In: Padua, D. (ed.) Encyclopedia of Parallel Computing, pp. 1581–1592. Springer, Boston (2011)
5. Gupta, M., Mukhopadhyay, S., Sinha, N.: Automatic parallelization of recursive procedures. Int. J. Parallel Prog. **28**(6), 537–562 (2000)
6. Gupta, S., Shrivastava, R., Nandivada, V.K.: Optimizing recursive task parallel programs. In: Proceedings of the International Conference on Supercomputing, ICS 2017, pp. 11:1–11:11. ACM, New York (2017)
7. Ketterlin, A., Clauss, P.: Prediction and trace compression of data access addresses through nested loop recognition. In: Proceedings of the 6th IEEE/ACM International Symposium on Code Generation and Optimization, CGO 2008, pp. 94–103. ACM, New York (2008)
8. Kobeissi, S., Clauss, P.: The polyhedral model beyond loops recursion optimization and parallelization through polyhedral modeling. In: IMPACT 2019–9th International Workshop on Polyhedral Compilation Techniques, In conjunction with HiPEAC 2019, Valencia, Spain, January 2019
9. Martinez Caamaño, J.M., Selva, M., Clauss, P., Baloian, A., Wolff, W.: Full runtime polyhedral optimizing loop transformations with the generation, instantiation, and scheduling of code-bones. Concurr. Comput. Pract. Exp. **29**(15), June 2017
10. Mastoras, A., Manis, G.: Ariadne - directive-based parallelism extraction from recursive functions. J. Parallel Distrib. Comput. **86**(C), 16–28 (2015)
11. Rauchwerger, L., Padua, D.A.: The LRPD test: speculative run-time parallelization of loops with privatization and reduction parallelization. IEEE Trans. Parallel Distrib. Syst. **10**(2), 160–180 (1999)
12. Saltz, J.H., Mirchandaney, R., Crowley, K.: Run-time parallelization and scheduling of loops. IEEE Trans. Comput. **40**(5), 603–612 (1991)
13. Sukumaran-Rajam, A., Clauss, P.: The polyhedral model of nonlinear loops. ACM Trans. Archit. Code Optim. **12**(4), 48:1–48:27 (2015)
14. Sundararajah, K., Kulkarni, M.: Scheduling transformation and dependence tests for recursive programs (2018)

DRAMSys4.0: A Fast and Cycle-Accurate SystemC/TLM-Based DRAM Simulator

Lukas Steiner[1(✉)], Matthias Jung[2], Felipe S. Prado[1], Kirill Bykov[1], and Norbert Wehn[1]

[1] Technische Universität Kaiserslautern, Kaiserslautern, Germany
{lsteiner,wehn}@eit.uni-kl.de
[2] Fraunhofer IESE, Kaiserslautern, Germany
matthias.jung@iese.fraunhofer.de

Abstract. The simulation of DRAMs (Dynamic Random Access Memories) on system level requires highly accurate models due to their complex timing and power behavior. However, conventional cycle-accurate DRAM models often become the bottleneck for the overall simulation speed. A promising alternative are DRAM simulation models based on Transaction Level Modeling, which can be fast and accurate at the same time. In this paper we present DRAMSys4.0, which is, to the best of our knowledge, the fastest cycle-accurate open-source DRAM simulator and has a large range of functionalities. DRAMSys4.0 includes a novel simulator architecture that enables a fast adaptation to new DRAM standards using a Domain Specific Language. We present optimization techniques to achieve a high simulation speed while maintaining full temporal accuracy. Finally, we provide a detailed survey and comparison of the most prominent cycle-accurate open-source DRAM simulators with regard to their supported features, analysis capabilities and simulation speed.

Keywords: DRAM · Simulation · SystemC · TLM

1 Introduction

Since today's applications become more and more data-centric, the role of *Dynamic Random Access Memory* (DRAM) in compute platforms grows in importance due to its large impact on the whole system performance and power consumption. Over the last two decades, the number of DRAM standards specified by the *JEDEC Solid State Technology Association* has been growing rapidly. Because of the large variety of standards, system designers have to face the difficult task of choosing devices that match system requirements for performance, size, power consumption and costs best. A short time to market aggravates this choice and creates the need for DRAM simulation models that allow both fast and truthful design space exploration.

DRAM subsystems are composed of a DRAM controller and one or several DRAM devices. Although the DRAM standards define a framework of rules

© Springer Nature Switzerland AG 2020
A. Orailoglu et al. (Eds.): SAMOS 2020, LNCS 12471, pp. 110–126, 2020.
https://doi.org/10.1007/978-3-030-60939-9_8

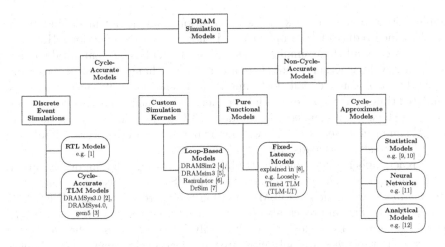

Fig. 1. Different DRAM simulation models

for the sequence and minimum time distance between DRAM commands, the controller still has some freedom on their placement and the scheduling of incoming requests. Different controller implementations exploit this freedom in order to optimize for different metrics (e.g., latency, bandwidth, power). Therefore, a DRAM subsystem simulation represents (1) one specific DRAM controller implementation and (2) one specific DRAM standard. It can be performed on different levels of abstraction, each offering a certain trade-off between speed and accuracy. Figure 1 provides an overview of different models for DRAM subsystem simulations.

Non-cycle-accurate DRAM simulation models (right side) allow high simulation speeds but lack in accuracy. The simplest, pure functional model for a DRAM subsystem is a fixed-latency model [8]. Within this approach all request experience the same constant amount of latency and all subsystem internals are omitted. However in reality, the latencies of DRAM accesses vary between a dozen and several hundred cycles due to the complex device architecture. Therefore, a pure functional model is not useful for design space exploration and performance estimations. Cycle-approximate models try to mimic the latency behavior of real DRAM subsystems by utilizing e.g. statistical methods [9,10] or neural networks [11]. Unfortunately, their accuracy can change from simulation to simulation, which makes them unsuitable for reliable performance estimations and design space exploration, too.

Cycle-accurate DRAM simulation models (left side) provide full temporal accuracy for truthful investigations, but usually take a lot more time to execute. RTL models of real DRAM controllers [1] can be simulated with the help of a *Discrete Event Simulation* (DES) kernel to represent a clock signal, trigger the execution of processes and model the hardware's concurrency. Most state-of-the-art cycle-accurate DRAM simulators, namely DRAMSim2 [4], DRAMsim3 [5], Ramulator [6] and DrSim [7], avoid the overhead of a DES kernel and use a simple loop to represent clock cycles. In addition, they do not model individual signals, which reduces the complexity and allows faster modifications. However, the processes of all these simulators as well as the RTL models are evaluated in each clock cycle, whether or not there are any state changes in the system. Consequently, the consumed wall clock time for a simulation grows linearly with the simulated time and is more or less independent of the memory access density (see Sect. 3). Thus, when coupled with modern CPU simulators, the cycle-accurate DRAM simulation even starts to become the bottleneck of the overall simulation speed for realistic workloads [13].

To reach higher simulation speeds while still providing full temporal accuracy, the design space exploration framework DRAMSys3.0 [2] uses the concept of *Transaction Level Modeling* (TLM) based on the SystemC/TLM2.0 IEEE 1666 Standard [14]. This approach also relies on a DES kernel, however, new events are not generated by a clock signal but only by the processes themselves. In this way the processes are only evaluated in clock cycles where state changes occur (see Subsect. 2.1). As a result the simulation speed is heavily dependent on the memory access density and can be significantly higher than the speed of the abovementioned simulators. Up until now DRAMSys3.0 is not open sourced and does not support the latest DRAM standards. gem5 [3], an open-source full-system simulator, uses a similar TLM concept to speed up simulations. Major drawback of its provided cycle-accurate DRAM model [15] is a close link to the DDR3/4 standards, which leads to a reduced accuracy for simulations with other DRAM standards as shown in [13].

To the best of our knowledge, there exists no cycle-accurate open-source DRAM simulator that fully supports the latest DRAM standards, performs simulations in a speed that enables fast design space exploration, allows a direct coupling to other system components based on the state-of-the-art system-level modeling language SystemC or to the full-system simulator gem5, and offers enough capabilities for a holistic performance analysis.

In this paper we present DRAMSys4.0, a completely revised version of DRAMSys3.0 [2]. It supports the latest JEDEC DRAM standards (e.g., DDR4, LPDDR4, GDDR6 and HBM2), is optimized to achieve between 10× to 20× higher simulation speeds compared to its predecessor, and offers a large toolbox for analysis and validation. The framework will be open sourced on GitHub.[1]

In summary, this paper makes the following contributions:

- We present DRAMSys4.0, which is, to the best of our knowledge, the fastest open-source DRAM simulator with cycle accuracy. We present a novel simulator architecture that enables a fast adaptation to new DRAM standards and different DRAM controller implementations.
- We present a sophisticated approach to automatically generate the source code of this simulator for new standards from formal descriptions based on a Petri Net model. The same approach is used to validate the functional behavior of state-of-the-art simulators.

---

[1] https://github.com/tukl-msd/DRAMSys.

- We demonstrate how RTL descriptions of real DRAM controllers can be validated with DRAMSys4.0 by embedding them into the framework and by exploiting our analysis tools. To speed up the RTL simulation of the DRAM controller, we suppress unnecessary events by disabling the clock signal during idle phases.
- We provide a detailed survey and a fair comparison of the most prominent cycle-accurate open-source DRAM simulators with regard to their supported features and analysis capabilities (see Table 2). We also compare their simulation speed.

The remaining paper is structured as follows: In Sect. 2 DRAMSys4.0 is presented, including all its functionalities for fast adaptation, result analysis and validation. Section 3 discusses related cycle-accurate simulators, provides a detailed comparison among them, and presents cycle-approximate approaches for a fast and accurate DRAM simulation. Section 4 concludes the work.

2 DRAMSys4.0

In this chapter we present DRAMSys4.0, which supports the latest JEDEC DRAM standards and is optimized to achieve much higher simulation speeds than the predecessor. More precisely, we present its architecture and functionality, discuss our optimizations to increase the simulation speed, and give an overview of the framework's unique features. Among them are the *Trace Analyzer* for visual and metric-based result analysis, the possibility for the co-simulation with RTL controllers, and the Petri-Net-based code generation and validation.

2.1 Functionality and Architecture

As mentioned in the introduction, DRAMSys[2] uses the concept of TLM based on the SystemC/TLM2.0 IEEE 1666 Standard [14] for a fast and fully cycle-accurate simulation. In accordance with the standard, all components are designed as SystemC modules (sc_module) and connected by TLM sockets. The simulator utilizes the *Approximately Timed* (AT) coding style, which defines a non-blocking four-phase handshake protocol.[3] A four-phase handshake is required to model the DRAM subsystem's pipelined behavior and out-of-order responses to the initiators. However, since a single memory access can cause the issuance of multiple DRAM commands depending on the device's current state (e.g., precharge (PRE) - activate (ACT) - read (RD)/write (WR) for a row miss), four phases are still not sufficient to model the communication between controller and device with full temporal accuracy. To close this gap, a custom TLM protocol (called DRAM-AT) that defines application-specific phases for all DRAM commands

---

[2] DRAMSys without a version number refers both to DRAMSys3.0 and DRAMSys4.0.

[3] The TLM-AT base protocol consists of the phases BEGIN_REQ, END_REQ, BEGIN_RESP and END_RESP.

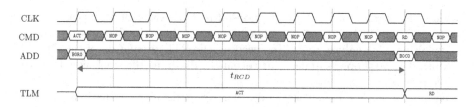

Fig. 2. TLM implementation of the ACT command [16]

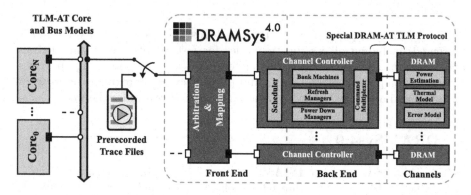

Fig. 3. Architecture of DRAMSys4.0

was introduced in [16]. These phases allow a projection of the cycle-accurate DRAM protocol to TLM.

The rule of thumb for making cycle-accurate simulations fast is to reduce the number of simulated clock cycles or events, respectively, and the control flow overhead that is executed. Therefore, DRAMSys only simulates the clock cycles in which state changes occur. Figure 2 shows an example for an ACT command and its timing dependency[4] t_{RCD} to a following RD command. While all loop-based simulators would simulate ten clock cycles to issue both commands, DRAMSys only simulates the first clock cycle, notifies an event after t_{RCD}, and directly simulates the tenth clock cycle to issue the RD command. All clock cycles in between are skipped and the simulation time is fast-forwarded. Especially in scenarios where the memory access density is low, this approach can lead to an enormous event reduction and a resulting simulation speedup of several orders of magnitude (see Table 1 and Sect. 3) while still yielding fully cycle-accurate results.

From an architectural point of view, DRAMSys4.0 consists like its predecessor of an arbitration & mapping unit (short arbiter) as well as independent channel controllers and DRAM devices for each memory channel, shown in Fig. 3. The arbiter cross-couples multiple initiators and DRAM channels on the basis of

---

[4] Timing dependencies are temporal constraints that must be satisfied between issued DRAM commands.

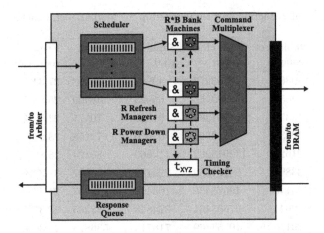

Fig. 4. Channel controller architecture

a predefined address mapping. It is followed by independent channel controllers for each DRAM channel. Their task is to issue the requests to the DRAMs by sending required commands according to the devices' current states. The connected DRAM devices then manage the storage of transferred data and enable a coupling to power estimation tools (DRAMPower [17]), thermal models (3D-ICE [18]) and retention time error models.

The architectural difference between DRAMSys4.0 and its predecessor is in the simulator's core component, the channel controller. DRAMSys4.0's channel controller architecture is inspired by advanced hardware DRAM controllers (e.g., [1]). As shown in Fig. 4, it is composed of a scheduler, $R \cdot B$ bank machines where R is the number of ranks the channel is composed of and B the number of banks per rank, R refresh managers, R power down managers, a command multiplexer, a response queue and a timing checker. Since SystemC is based on the object-oriented C++ programming language, all components can be designed polymorphically, which allows different policies to be selected during runtime. This is used to specify different DRAM standards and channel controller implementations without requiring a recompilation of the tool or creating additional control flow that results in a slowdown (see also Subsect. 2.2). In addition, the predefined interfaces simplify and speed up the integration of new features. An overview of all supported policies and DRAM standards will be provided in Table 2 in Sect. 3.

The scheduler buffers incoming requests and reorders them with respect to bandwidth or latency improvements based on a scheduling policy. After selecting one request, it is forwarded to a bank machine, which keeps track of the associated bank's current state and issues a sequence of commands to serve this request. Similar to the scheduler, the bank machines support various page policies [15] to improve the bandwidth or latency of different workloads by automatically precharging the bank's opened row in some cases. Since DRAMSys4.0 models the timing, power, thermal and error behavior of DRAM devices in full detail,

Table 1. Event reduction and total speedup for MediaBench benchmarks [19]

Benchmark	Number of requests	Total clock cycles	Simulated v3.0	Events v4.0	Event reduction	Total speedup
h263decode	9867	142185273	49904	36258	27.34%	9.22
g721encode	14655	152283166	65528	48900	25.38%	8.98
g721decode	19350	171781365	91828	70171	23.58%	9.73
gsmdecode	19734	42213726	93520	71158	23.91%	9.07
c-ray-1.1	21627	132918262	119660	85124	28.86%	10.12
fractal	33895	64184959	228184	156697	31.33%	11.15
jpegdecode	43143	19675438	196408	148407	24.44%	9.23
mpeg2decode	72043	97603461	374848	272235	27.37%	10.01
unepic	129145	10557869	718716	536878	25.30%	10.02
jpegencode	173995	39209690	769872	580929	24.54%	9.35
epic	182957	55148722	940708	698595	25.74%	9.80
mpeg2encode	616935	798646158	3457084	2522754	27.03%	9.98
h263encode	858099	526757549	4312932	3148787	26.99%	9.35

the channel controller also has to regularly issue refresh commands and has to trigger power down operation during idle phases. These tasks are taken over by the rank-wise refresh managers and power down managers. Both components are designed polymorphically as well to represent different refresh and power down policies. To find the earliest possible time for issuing a command to the DRAM while satisfying all timing dependencies, bank machines, refresh managers and power down managers invoke the timing checker. On the basis of the whole command history and required information extracted from the DRAM standards, the timing checker calculates this point in time. Since the timing dependencies slightly differ from standard to standard, DRAMSys4.0 uses a separate checker for each of them. If more than one bank machine, refresh manager or power down manager wants to issue a command in the same clock cycle, a conflict arises because of the shared command bus. The command multiplexer resolves this conflict by prioritizing one command (e.g., round robin among ranks/banks). As last component, the channel controller includes a response queue. It buffers the read responses for a transport back to the arbiter and can also reorder them.

2.2   Optimizations for Simulation Speed

To further increase the simulation speed of DRAMSys while maintaining its cycle accuracy, several optimizations have been performed during the revision. As stated earlier, simulations can be sped up by reducing the number of simulated clock cycles or events, respectively, and the executed control flow overhead. Although the used TLM concept ensures a minimum of simulated clock cycles, multiple events may still be fired in the same clock cycle that trigger separate processes or the same process several times. This mechanism is usually needed to model the hardware's concurrency. While DRAMSys3.0's channel controller internally used three event-triggered processes, the new channel controller only needs a single event-triggered process to represent all functionality. It manages the communication and transfer of data between the internals. If, however, multiple events the process is sensitive to are still notified for the same clock cycle, the SystemC simulation kernel performs only a single execution. That way the numbers of simulated events and simulated clock cycles in DRAMSys4.0's channel controller are identical.

Table 1 shows the event reduction in the channel controller for memory traces of the MediaBench benchmarks [19] simulated with a DDR3 DRAM (1 GB DDR3-1600, single channel, single rank, row-bank-column address mapping, FR-FCFS scheduler, open-page policy, run on an Intel Core i9 with 5 GHz). The simulations were performed with a disabled refresh mechanism to see the correlation between the number of requests and events. The table also shows the large difference between the total number of clock cycles and simulated events.

By means of the polymorphic software architecture, DRAMSys4.0 is capable of modeling different DRAM standards and channel controller implementations without introducing any additional control flow that has to be executed frequently during the simulation and, thus, slows it down. For illustration let us assume that the channel controller should be capable of modeling both the open- and closed-page policy.[5] Instead of checking the page policy each time a read or

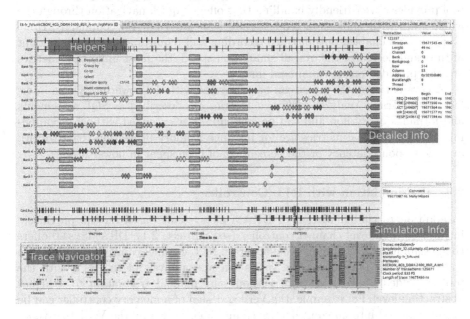

Fig. 5. Program interface of the Trace Analyzer [2]

---

[5] Controllers that implement the open-page policy keep the corresponding row open after a read or write access, while controllers that implement the closed-page policy automatically precharge the corresponding row after a read or write access.

write command is issued, DRAMSys4.0 instantiates bank machines that implement the selected policy once at the start of the simulation and implicitly issues the right commands for the remaining simulation.

Time-consuming string manipulations for the creation of debug messages or log files can be completely removed in the revised version if they are not required. The gained simulation speedup with disabled refresh mechanism for the MediaBench benchmarks is also shown in Table 1, more speedup results will be presented in Fig. 8 in Subsect. 3.1.

2.3 Trace Analyzer

To provide better analysis capabilities for DRAM subsystem design space exploration than the usual performance-related outputs to the console or a text file, DRAMSys4.0 provides the Trace Analyzer just like its predecessor. After having recorded all TLM transactions of the channel controller in an output trace SQLite database during a simulation, the data can be evaluated using the Trace Analyzer. It illustrates a time window of requests, DRAM commands and the utilization of all banks as shown in Fig. 5, which can help system designers to understand the subsystem's internal behavior and to find limiting issues. Exploiting the power of SQL, the data aggregation happens quickly and the tool provides a user-friendly handling that offers a quick navigation through the whole trace with millions of requests and associated DRAM commands. However, since an enabled output trace recording still requires a reasonable amount of time and decreases the overall simulation speed, the most important metrics are also provided on the command line.

An evaluation of the traces can be performed with the powerful Python interface of the Trace Analyzer. Different metrics are described as SQL statements and formulas in Python and can be customized or extended without recompiling the tool. Typical metrics are for instance memory utilization (bandwidth), average response latency or the percentage of time spent in power down.

2.4 Co-simulation with RTL Controller

In addition to the simulation of DRAM subsystems based on the previously introduced high-level channel controller (see Subsect. 2.1), DRAMSys4.0 offers the possibility of embedding cycle-accurate RTL channel controller models into the framework. This allows the validation and analysis of the RTL with the tools provided by DRAMSys4.0 without any manual translation to a higher abstraction level. For example, the Verilog design of a memory controller can be auto-translated into an equivalent SystemC RTL model by the Verilator[6] tool.

To convert the TLM transports into associated RTL signals (including a clock signal, which is not present in DRAMSys) and vice versa, a special transactor module has to be wrapped around the RTL design as shown in Fig. 6. Such a

---

[6] https://www.veripool.org/projects/verilator/.

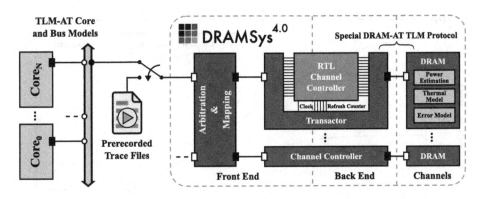

Fig. 6. Architecture of DRAMSys4.0 with embedded RTL channel controller

transactor was developed for the DDR3 channel controller presented in [1] and exhaustively tested with DRAMSys4.0.

An RTL simulation can also be accelerated by suppressing unnecessary events, see, e.g., [20]. Similar to the idea of clock gating in real circuits for power saving, turning off the clock signal during idle phases of an RTL simulation saves a lot of simulation events since clock signals have high event generation rates. Thus, the so-called clock suppression can tremendously speed up a simulation without changing its results. We adopted this technique for the RTL co-simulation. However, since the internal refresh counter of the RTL channel controller is not incremented by the suspended clock, the transactor saves the refresh counter state externally before suspending the clock and notifies an event at the time the next refresh command should be executed. When this event is fired or a new request arrives, the internal refresh counter is updated to the proper value and the clock is resumed.

Figure 7 shows the speedups of DRAMSys4.0 and the clock-suppressed RTL for artificial traces with random access patterns and varying access densities (accesses per clock cycle) normalized to the plain RTL model (1 GB DDR3-1600, single channel, single rank, row-bank-column address mapping, FCFS scheduler, open-page policy, run on an Intel Core i9 with 5 GHz). For high densities the clock suppression mechanism does not bring an advantage because the controller never turns idle. Instead, it creates a very small computational overhead. With decreasing densities the idle time increases and the speedup rises until it saturates to a factor of 40 because of the refresh commands that also have to be issued regularly during idle phases (self refresh operation is not supported by the RTL controller). The TLM model achieves an even higher speedup across the entire range, which is of factor 3 for high densities and rises to a factor of 4000 for low densities (self refresh operation of the TLM model was disabled for a fair comparison). This is mainly a result of the higher abstraction level that does not model individual signals and thus saves lots of events.

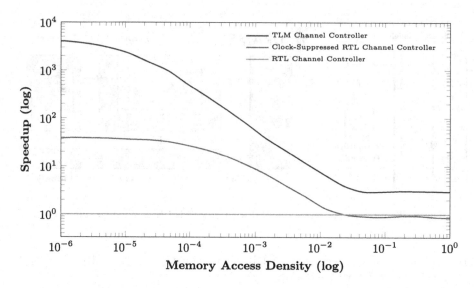

Fig. 7. Simulation speedups normalized to RTL channel controller

2.5   Code Generation and Validation

As stated in the introduction, an increasing number of different DRAM standards
have been presented by the JEDEC in recent years. Since each new standard
comes with slight changes in the DRAM protocol compared to previous ones,
the memory simulation models as well as the RTL models must be modified
and validated repeatedly. In order to keep pace with these frequent changes and
the large variety of standards, a robust and error-free methodology for a fast
adaptation must be established.

In [21] we presented a comprehensive and formal *Domain Specific Language*
(DSL) based on Petri Nets [22] to describe the entire memory functionality of a
DRAM standard including all timing dependencies in just a few lines of code.
Using the formal description of a corresponding Petri Net, different simulation
and validation models are generated in this work:

- **TLM Model Generation:** The source code of the channel controller's
  standard-specific timing checkers (see Subsect. 2.1) can be generated automatically and correct by construction from these DSL descriptions, replacing
  the error-prone handwritten SystemC implementation of a new memory standard by the fast generation of SystemC code from a high-level description.
- **RTL Controller Validation Model:** As shown in Subsect. 2.4 and Subsect. 2.3, DRAMSys4.0 offers functionalities for embedding an RTL model of a
  memory controller into the framework and for recording the executed DRAM
  commands in an output trace database. Using the formal DSL descriptions,
  a standard-specific executable C++ validation model can be created, which
  analyzes a recorded DRAM command trace for standard compliance. This
  approach provides fast feedback to an RTL developer if a change in the RTL
  description led to a protocol violation.

– **DRAM Simulator Validation Model:** The same validation model is used to analyze recorded command traces of other state-of-the-art DRAM simulators. In Subsect. 3.1 we reveal errors in DRAMsim3, Ramulator and in the gem5 DRAM model using our validation model.

3   Related Work and Results

This section provides a comparison between the most prominent open-source cycle-accurate DRAM simulators and introduces approaches for the cycle-approximate modeling of DRAM subsystems.

3.1   Cycle-Accurate Simulators

As stated in the introduction, there are several publicly-available cycle-accurate DRAM simulators. Table 2 provides a comprehensive comparison that also includes both DRAMSys3.0 and DRAMSys4.0. For simplicity, we only focus on DRAM standards and features specified by the JEDEC since they are best qualified for real system developments.

DRAMSys3.0, DRAMSim2 and DrSim were already developed several years ago but never updated over time, leading to an exclusive support of older standards and making them unsuitable for most current system developments. DRAMSys4.0, DRAMsim3, Ramulator and the gem5 DRAM model are all updated from time to time, however, only DRAMSys4.0 and DRAMsim3 currently support the latest standards like GDDR6 or HBM2. For request initiation all simulators provide trace players and a coupling to gem5. In addition, DRAMsim3 supports a coupling to the simulation frameworks SST [27] and ZSim [28]. DRAMSys3.0 and DRAMSys4.0 can be coupled to any TLM-AT-compliant core model. While all simulators seem to be cycle accurate at first view, some of them do not model the full set of timing dependencies for all standards they support. Using our Petri-Net-based validation model of Subsect. 2.5, we were able to find missing timing dependencies in DRAMsim3, Ramulator and in the gem5 DRAM model (e.g., missing command bus dependencies for multi-cycle commands of LPDDR4 or HBM1/2).[7] Besides the performance perspective, for most of today's system developments the power consumption and thermal behavior is of great importance, especially in the field of embedded systems. All simulators except DrSim offer a functionality for power estimation. DRAMSys3.0, DRAMSys4.0 and DRAMsim3 can also model the thermal behavior of devices. For performance evaluation, all simulators output bandwidth-, latency- and power-related statistics. Moreover, DRAMSim2 supplies DRAMVis [4], a tool that can visualize the bandwidth, latency and power over time. Similarly, DRAMSys3.0 and DRAMSys4.0 provide the Trace Analyzer for visual result analysis (see Sect. 2.3).

---

[7] We will report the missing timing dependencies to the developers of the other simulators.

Table 2. Overview of the most prominent open-source DRAM simulators

Feature	DRAMSys 4.0 (this work)	DRAMSys 3.0 [2]	DRAMSim2 [4]	DRAMsim3 [5]	Ramulator [6]	DrSim [7]	gem5 DRAM model [15]
DRAM standards	DDR3/4, LPDDR4, Wide I/O 1/2, GDDR5/5X/6, HBM1/2	DDR3/4, Wide I/O 1	DDR2/3	DDR3/4, LPDDR3/4, GDDR5/5X/6, HBM1/2	DDR3/4, LPDDR3/4, GDDR5, Wide I/O 1/2, HBM1	DDR2/3, LPDDR2	DDR3/4, LPDDR2/3, Wide I/O 1, GDDR5, HBM1
Refresh modes	All-bank refresh, per-bank refresh	All-bank refresh	All-bank refresh	All-bank refresh, per-bank refresh	All-bank refresh, per-bank refresh	All-bank refresh	All-bank refresh
Power down modes	Active & precharge power down, self refresh	Active & precharge power down, self refresh	Precharge power down	Self refresh	Active & precharge power down, self refresh	Active & precharge power down	Active & precharge power down, self refresh
Address mappings	Any bijective boolean function [23]	Any bijective boolean function [23]	7 different mappings	Mappings with hierarchy granularity	Mappings with hierarchy granularity	Fixed mapping with optional interleavings	3 different mappings
Schedulers	FCFS, FR-FCFS [24], FR-FCFS Grouping	FCFS, FR-FCFS [24], FR-FCFS Grouping, Par-BS [25], SMS [26]	Issue requests ASAP	Issue requests ASAP	FCFS, FR-FCFS [24], FR-FCFS Cap, FR-FCFS PriorHit	FCFS, FR-FCFS [24]	FCFS, FR-FCFS [24]
Page policies	Open, open adaptive, closed, closed adaptive [15]	Open, closed	Open, closed	Open, closed	Open, closed, closed with auto precharge, timeout	Open, closed	Open, open adaptive, closed, closed adaptive [15]
Configuration	Controller policies, address mapping, DRAM standard, organization, timings & currents (JSON file)	Controller policies, address mapping, DRAM standard, organization, timings & currents (XML file)	Controller policies, address mapping, DRAM organization, timings & currents	Controller policies, address mapping, DRAM standard, organization, timings & currents	Address mapping, DRAM standard, speed bin & size	Controller policies, address interleaving, DRAM organization & timings	Controller policies, address mapping, DRAM organization, timings & currents (Python file)
Request initiators	Trace players (fixed & elastic memory traces), SystemC-based core models, gem5 core models	Trace players (fixed & elastic memory traces), SystemC-based core models, gem5 core models	Trace player (fixed memory traces), gem5 core models	Trace player (fixed memory traces), gem5 core models, SST [27], ZSim [28]	Trace player (fixed, untimed memory traces, timed CPU traces), gem5 core models	Trace player (fixed memory traces), gem5 core models	Trace players (fixed & elastic memory traces), gem5 core models
Power estimation	DRAMPower [17]	DRAMPower [17]	Micron power model	Micron power model & DRAMPower [17]	DRAMPower [17] & Vampire [29]		DRAMPower [17]
Thermal modeling	3D-ICE [18] (only Wide I/O 1)	3D-ICE [18] (only Wide I/O 1)					
Error modeling	Custom model (only Wide I/O 1)	Custom model (only Wide I/O 1)		Custom model (all standards)			
Validation method	Petri-Net-based code generation & result checking [21], result visualization	Testing script, result visualization	DDR2/3 command traces fed into Micron Verilog model	DDR3/4 command traces fed into Micron Verilog model	DDR3 command trace fed into Micron Verilog model	Comparison to DRAMSim2	Comparison to DRAMSim2
Outputs/metrics	Average bandwidth & power consumption, metrics for SQLite command trace	Average bandwidth & power consumption, metrics for SQLite command trace	Average bandwidth & power consumption, metrics power per epoch	Bandwidth, latency & power per epoch	Metrics in output file, command trace	Metrics in console	Metrics in output file
Result visualization	Trace analyzer	Trace analyzer	DRAMVis [4]	Plot of metrics			
Considered timing dependencies	All	No inter-rank dependencies	All	No multi-cycle-command dependencies	No multi-cycle-command dependencies	All	Only DDR3/4 timing dependencies
Simulation model	TLM-based (IEEE 1666 SystemC/TLM2.0 [14])	TLM-based (IEEE 1666 SystemC/TLM2.0 [14])	Loop-based	Loop-based	Loop-based	Loop-based	TLM-based (gem5 [31])

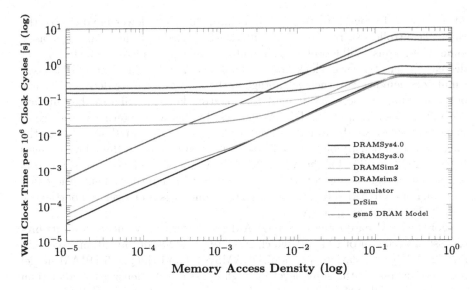

Fig. 8. Simulation speeds of state-of-the-art DRAM simulators

All simulators are also compared with regard to their simulation speed. As stated earlier, the wall clock time that a simulation requires does not only depend on the amount of simulated time, but also on the memory access density (accesses per clock cycle). This can especially be observed for the TLM-based simulators. For that reason, we investigate the simulation speed for a large range of densities using artificial traces. To minimize the impact of the simulators' different controller implementations (e.g., queuing mechanisms, scheduling policies, further bandwidth-improving techniques like read snooping[8]), the memory traces exclusively provoke read misses and utilize all banks uniformly. Different densities are created by increasing the gaps between accesses. Apart from that, all simulators are configured as similar as possible (1 GB DDR3-1600 since DDR3 is the only standard supported by all of them, single channel, single rank, row-bank-column address mapping, open-page policy, run on an Intel Core i9 with 5 GHz), built as release version, and run with a minimum of generated outputs. Using these traces, the achieved performance and total simulated time of all simulators except Ramulator are very similar (maximum deviations of 2% because all simulators implement a different power down operation). Ramulator did not model the bank parallelism properly at the time of our testing and therefore achieved much lower bandwidths. Meanwhile the bug has been fixed.

The simulation speeds of all simulators are shown in Fig. 8. For high trace densities the speeds of the fastest loop-based and TLM-based simulators (DRAMSim2, Ramulator, DRAMSys4.0 and the gem5 DRAM model) do not differ much from each other because state changes occur in almost all clock cycles.

---

[8] Using read snooping a read request can be served directly within the controller if an earlier write request to the same address is still pending.

At a density of around 0.2 (0.1 for Ramulator due to its lower bandwidth), the channel controllers start to turn idle and the consumed wall clock time decreases. While the graphs of all loop-based simulators converge to a fixed value for further decreasing densities (wall clock time to simulate pure idle cycles), the TLM-based simulators demonstrate their advantage in the form of a steady decrease, clearly outperforming all loop-based simulators. During long idle phases they initiate self refresh operation of the DRAM devices. In this way external refresh commands can be omitted and no clock cycles have to be simulated at all. Since the memory access density of real applications is often located in these lower ranges (e.g., $7 \cdot 10^{-5}$–$1 \cdot 10^{-2}$ for the MediaBench benchmarks), TLM-based simulators can speed up the simulation by several orders of magnitude. Thus, the exact modeling of a DRAM subsystem in a system context is no longer the bottleneck from a simulation perspective.

For the TLM-based simulators, DRAMSys4.0 constantly outperforms its predecessor by a factor of 10 to 20, which is the result of our optimizations (see Subsect. 2.2). The simulation speeds of DRAMSys4.0 and the gem5 DRAM model are more or less on the same level for high densities. At densities smaller than 10^{-3} the gem5 DRAM model starts to become slightly slower than DRAMSys4.0 because the switching to self refresh operation is implemented less efficiently.

As mentioned in Sect. 1, a DRAM subsystem simulation consists of a specific controller model and the model of a specific DRAM standard. Since each simulator represents a different controller implementation (scheduling policy, power down operation, request buffer etc.), a fair comparison of accuracy is not possible; all simulators might yield different results for the same inputs while still being cycle accurate and standard compliant.

3.2   Cycle-Approximate DRAM Models

Beside the cycle-accurate DRAM simulators, further approaches that approximate the behavior exist (see Fig. 1). In [12] the authors propose an analytical DRAM performance model that uses traces to predict the efficiency of the DRAM subsystem. Todorov et al. [9] presented a statistical approach for the construction of a cycle-approximate TLM model of a DRAM controller based on a decision tree. However, these approaches suffer from a significant loss in accuracy. More promising approaches based on machine learning techniques have been presented recently. The paper [10] presents the modeling of DRAM behavior using decision trees. In [11] the authors present a performance-optimized DRAM model that is based on a neural network.

4   Conclusion

In this paper we presented DRAMSys4.0, a SystemC/TLM-based open-source DRAM simulation framework. Due to the optimized architecture it reaches very high simulation speeds compared to state-of-the-art simulators while ensuring full cycle accuracy and standard compliance. DRAMSys4.0 supports a large collection of controller features and DRAM standards and offers unique functionalities for adaptation and result analysis, making it perfectly suitable for both fast and truthful design space exploration. In addition, the framework can be used to validate RTL descriptions of real hardware memory controllers. In the future we plan to extend DRAMSys4.0 by further emerging DRAM standards (e.g., LPDDR5 and DDR5) and associated new features.

Acknowledgements. This work was supported within the Fraunhofer and DFG cooperation programme (Grant no. WE2442/14-1) and supported by the *Fraunhofer High Performance Center* for *Simulation- and Software-based Innovation*. Furthermore, we thank Synopsys and the anonymous reviewers for their support.

References

1. Sudarshan, C., et al.: A lean, low power, low latency DRAM memory controller for transprecision computing. In: Pnevmatikatos, D.N., Pelcat, M., Jung, M. (eds.) SAMOS 2019. LNCS, vol. 11733, pp. 429–441. Springer, Cham (2019). https://doi.org/10.1007/978-3-030-27562-4_31

2. Jung, M., et al.: DRAMSys: a flexible DRAM subsystem design space exploration framework. IPSJ Trans. Syst. LSI Des. Methodol. **8**, 63–74 (2015)

3. Binkert, N., et al.: The gem5 simulator. SIGARCH Comput. Archit. News **39**(2), 1–7 (2011)

4. Rosenfeld, P., et al.: DRAMSim2: a cycle accurate memory system simulator. Comput. Archit. Lett. **10**(1), 16–19 (2011)

5. Li, S., et al.: DRAMsim3: a cycle-accurate, thermal-capable DRAM simulator. IEEE Comput. Archit. Lett. **19**(2), 106–109 (2020)

6. Kim, Y., et al.: Ramulator: a fast and extensible DRAM simulator. IEEE Comput. Archit. Lett. **15**(1), 45–49 (2015)

7. Jeong, M.K., et al.: DrSim: a platform for flexible DRAM system research. http://lph.ece.utexas.edu/public/DrSim. Accessed 15 Aug 2019

8. Jacob, B.: The Memory System: You Can'T Avoid It, You Can'T Ignore It, You Can'T Fake It. Morgan and Claypool Publishers, San Rafael (2009)

9. Todorov, V., et al.: Automated construction of a cycle-approximate transaction level model of a memory controller. In: Proceedings of the Conference on Design, Automation and Test in Europe, DATE 2012, pp. 1066–1071. EDA Consortium, San Jose (2012)

10. Li, S., et al.: Statistical DRAM modeling. In: Proceedings of the International Symposium on Memory Systems, MEMSYS 2019, pp. 521–530. Association for Computing Machinery, New York (2019)

11. Jung, M., et al.: Fast and accurate DRAM simulation: can we further accelerate it? In: Proceedings of the Conference on Design, Automation and Test in Europe, DATE 2020, Grenoble, pp. 364–369 (2020)

12. Yuan, G.L., et al.: A hybrid analytical DRAM performance model (2009)

13. Li, S., et al.: Rethinking cycle accurate DRAM simulation. In: Proceedings of the International Symposium on Memory Systems, MEMSYS 2019, pp. 184–191. Association for Computing Machinery, New York (2019)

14. IEEE Computer Society: IEEE Standard for Standard SystemC Language Reference Manual. IEEE Std 1666–2011 (2012)

15. Hansson, A., et al.: Simulating DRAM controllers for future system architecture exploration. In: 2014 IEEE International Symposium on Performance Analysis of Systems and Software (ISPASS), pp. 201–210 (2014)
16. Jung, M., et al.: TLM modelling of 3D stacked wide I/O DRAM subsystems: a virtual platform for memory controller design space exploration. In: Proceedings of the 2013 Workshop on Rapid Simulation and Performance Evaluation: Methods and Tools, RAPIDO 2013, pp. 5:1–5:6. ACM, New York (2013)
17. Chandrasekar, K., et al.: DRAMPower: Open-source DRAM power & energy estimation tool. http://www.drampower.info. Accessed 15 Aug 2019
18. Sridhar, A., et al.: 3D-ICE: fast compact transient thermal modeling for 3D ICs with inter-tier liquid cooling. In: Proceedings of ICCAD 2010 (2010)
19. MediaBench Consortium. Mediabench (2015). http://euler.slu.edu/~fritts/mediabench/. Accessed 28 Aug 2015
20. Muhr, H., et al.: Accelerating RTL simulation by several orders of magnitude using clock suppression. In: 2006 International Conference on Embedded Computer Systems: Architectures, Modeling and Simulation, pp. 123–128 (2006)
21. Jung, M., et al.: Fast validation of DRAM protocols with timed petri nets. In: Proceedings of the International Symposium on Memory Systems, MEMSYS 2019, pp. 133–147. ACM, New York (2019)
22. Petri, C.A.: Kommunikation mit Automaten. PhD thesis, Universität Hamburg (1962)
23. Jung, M., et al.: ConGen: an application specific DRAM memory controller generator. In: Proceedings of the Second International Symposium on Memory Systems, MEMSYS 2016, pp. 257–267. ACM, New York (2016)
24. Rixner, S., et al.: Memory access scheduling. In: Proceedings of the 27th Annual International Symposium on Computer Architecture, ISCA 2000, pp. 128–138. ACM, New York (2000)
25. Mutlu, O., et al.: Parallelism-aware Batch-scheduling: enhancing both performance and fairness of shared DRAM systems. In: 35th International Symposium on Computer Architecture (ISCA). Association for Computing Machinery Inc. (2008)
26. Ausavarungnirun, R., et al.: Staged memory scheduling: achieving high performance and scalability in heterogeneous systems. In: Proceedings of the 39th Annual International Symposium on Computer Architecture, ISCA 2012, pp. 416–427. IEEE Computer Society, Washington, DC (2012)
27. Rodrigues, A.F., et al.: The structural simulation toolkit. SIGMETRICS Perform. Eval. Rev. **38**(4), 37–42 (2011)
28. Sanchez, D., et al.: ZSim: fast and accurate microarchitectural simulation of thousand-core systems. ACM SIGARCH Comput. Archit. News **41**, 475 (2013)
29. Ghose, S., et al.: What your DRAM power models are not telling you: lessons from a detailed experimental study. Proc. ACM Meas. Anal. Comput. Syst. **2**(3), 1–41 (2018)

Transpiling Python to Rust for Optimized Performance

Henri Lunnikivi[✉] ⓘ, Kai Jylkkä ⓘ, and Timo Hämäläinen ⓘ

Tampere University, Tampere, Finland
{henri.lunnikivi,tau,kai.jylkka,timo.hamalainen}@tuni.fi
http://tuni.fi

Abstract. PYTHON has become the de facto programming language in machine learning and scientific computing, but high performance implementations are challenging to create especially for embedded systems with limited resources. We address the challenge of compiling and optimizing PYTHON source code for a low-level target by introducing RUST as an intermediate source code step. We show that pre-existing PYTHON implementations that depend on optimized libraries, such as NumPy, can be transpiled to RUST semi-automatically, with potential for further automation. We use two representative test cases, Black–Scholes for financial options pricing and robot trajectory optimization. The results show up to 12× speedup and 1.5× less memory use on PC, and the same performance but 4× less memory use on an ARM processor on PYNQ SoC FPGA. We also present a comprehensive list of factors for the process, to show the potential for fully automated transpilation. Our findings are generally applicable and can improve the performance of many PYTHON applications while keeping their easy programmability.

Keywords: Python · Rust · Embedded computing · Transpilation

1 Introduction

PYTHON is the most popular language in Machine Learning (ML) and is rapidly replacing others in signal processing and scientific computing. Yet, its execution time and memory consumption are not workable in constrained systems. Additionally, energy awareness in ML computing in general is becoming a big concern. Because of the wide adoption of PYTHON, an improvement in process will have multiplied effects in the large scale, which makes the issue important. This paper addresses the challenge of how a pre-existing PYTHON implementation could be automatically compiled to a high performance and low energy implementation while retaining easy programmability.

In a typical use case, a high-level language like PYTHON is used to write domain-specific steering code that then relies on optimized libraries. Key challenges of optimizing to a target are cross-library memory optimization, platform specific optimization, and parallelization. Cross-library optimization is required

© Springer Nature Switzerland AG 2020
A. Orailoglu et al. (Eds.): SAMOS 2020, LNCS 12471, pp. 127–138, 2020.
https://doi.org/10.1007/978-3-030-60939-9_9

because there is a risk of needless data movement at function and library bound-aries of which a typical user is not aware. Platform specific optimization is required to take advantage of the particular capabilities of the platform, and for many platforms, extracting parallelism out of the programming model is a necessary part of that.

Many of the approaches towards compiling PYTHON into low-level machine code work better for cloud-like computer infrastructure. However, large runtime systems and current end-to-end optimization technologies do not work as well for embedded devices. Runtime systems are computationally unaffordable and end-to-end optimization technologies create additional challenges for understanding application performance [14] or require changes to used libraries (eg. [3,5,9,10, 15–17]).

Our proposal is based on RUST[1] as an intermediate source code step. PYTHON and RUST are both high-level languages that allow problems to be modelled using domain-specific idioms. Expressions of idioms in PYTHON can be converted to expressions in RUST at least semi-automatically, and at least one open-source implementation [8] exists. The benefit is that source-to-source transpiled code retains readability, which allows for further changes, experimentation, and opti-mization.

To our best knowledge, this is the first publicly available, reproducible, and systematic study on translation and transpilation of PYTHON to RUST for opti-mized implementations. We have two research questions: 1) How much speedup can be gained by transpiling? 2) How automatable is the process? Our contri-butions are as follows:

1. A workflow for quick optimization of a high-level description of an algorithm for a low-end target with support for parallel execution
2. A measurement on how functionally equivalent high-level implementations in PYTHON and RUST might perform with respect to each other
3. Evaluation of feasibility of `pyrs` [8] for transpilation
4. Propositions for further automation of transpilation
5. Two use cases for performance analysis: Financial data analytics and motion trajectory optimization for robots

This paper is organized as follows. We will introduce related work in Sect. 2, and our approach in Sect. 3. We will describe the two use cases in Sect. 4 and results in Sect. 5. We will give our conclusions and future work in Sect. 6.

2   Related Work

Most software is built from layers upon layers of other software. An application is described in an expressive, high-level language, using domain-specific idioms and libraries relevant to the problem being solved. The application and its libraries must then be translated to a hardware-specific stream of instructions by compil-ers, interpreters, or both. A popular workflow involves writing domain-specific

---

[1] RUST. https://www.rust-lang.org/.

steering code in PYTHON and then relying on one of a myriad of techniques to ensure that the program performs at the required level on the target platform. Techniques include use of optimized libraries [1,12,13,21], optimizing compilers [2–5,9,10,15–17], and runtimes with just-in-time (JIT) compilation [3,5,9–11,15–18].

Our approach is based on compiled RUST, which allows optimization of the code as a whole including the libraries. RUST is a recent, high-level alternative for performance-oriented programming, which allows a path from a high level of abstraction to optimized machine code. The approach is similar to that taken by the developers of Cython[2] and MicroPython[3]. Cython allows an improvement in performance by using a static compiler via C, while MicroPython is a Python runtime, optimized for microcontrollers. Our approach differs in that the transpiled code is compiled to a runtimeless, fully optimizable native executable without reliance on an interpreter. Our method also resembles that of the C2Rust tool[4], which translates C into semantically matching RUST. Our approach differs in both the source language and the fact that C2Rust generates RUST code using the *unsafe* subset of the RUST language, while our approach is focused on *safe* RUST, preserving the memory safety of the PYTHON implementation. We use an experimental open-source PYTHON tool called pyrs [8] to convert PYTHON syntax into RUST.

Compared to optimized PYTHON, RUST offers similar capabilities but with a smaller degree of separation between high-level development processes and native tooling. RUST seems to allow combining optimization processes, such as use of domain specific, optimized, native libraries and cross-platform algorithm development, with low-level native tooling such as standard Linux tools perf[5], valgrind[6], and the LLVM debugger[7]. As an LLVM-compiled language, RUST allows similar performance enhancements as an end-to-end optimizer, a staple in deployment of PYTHON. This similar optimization is achieved with compiler enforced pointer aliasing rules[8]. Additionally, RUST allows extended utilities for embedded development, such as the no_std[9] feature that allows the compiler to not assume the existence of heap memory, networking support or threads.

3   Methods

We summarize first the environment for conducting this work. The tools used in transpilation are pyrs [8], MonkeyType [6], and IntelliJ IDEA [7]. RUST 1.31 is used to compile the resultant RUST program using the package manager cargo[10]

---

[2] Cython. https://github.com/cython/cython.

[3] MicroPython. https://github.com/micropython/micropython.

[4] C2Rust. https://github.com/immunant/c2rust.

[5] perf. https://perf.wiki.kernel.org/.

[6] valgrind. https://valgrind.org/.

[7] The LLDB Debugger. https://lldb.llvm.org/.

[8] Aliasing in Rust. https://doc.rust-lang.org/nomicon/aliasing.html.

[9] RUST: No stdlib. https://doc.rust-lang.org/1.7.0/book/no-stdlib.html.

[10] cargo the RUST package manager. https://doc.rust-lang.org/cargo/.

and the `rustc` compiler. The two chosen use cases are a simple Black–Scholes model and an advanced algorithm for trajectory optimization [20] abbreviated as Motion Planning. The performance was tested on a Windows PC with an AMD Ryzen 7 3700X processor and PYNQ Z1 All Programmable System-on-Chip (APSoC)[11]. Additionally, as proof-of-concept, the transpiled programs were cross-compiled to Snapdragon 835 mobile Hardware Development Kit[12], which to our best knowledge does not natively support PYTHON.

The PYNQ processing system includes a 650 MHz dual-core Cortex-A9 processor and 512 MB DDR3 memory. The device was running a Ubuntu 18.04 PYNQ Linux OS including a PYTHON 3.6 interpreter. We installed the RUST toolchain[13] on the device and compiled the source code used for the tests on the device. We also successfully verified our transpiling method on Snapdragon 835 development kit running with Android 7.1.2 OS. We cross-compiled RUST source code on Ubuntu 16.04 host PC and used `Android Debug Bridge` to run compiled binaries on the device.

3.1 Transpilation Workflow

PYTHON source code is transpiled to RUST. The general outline of the transpilation process is depicted in Fig. 1.

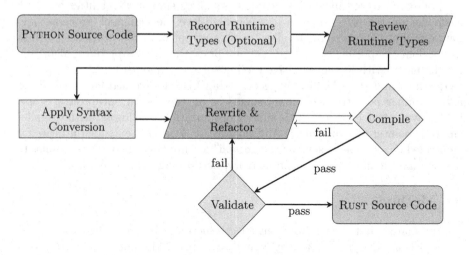

Fig. 1. Transpiling Python to Rust.

Transpilation comprises the following phases: optional application of runtime types, syntax conversion, manual refactoring, and validation testing.

---

[11] PYNQ Z1.https://reference.digilentinc.com/reference/programmable-logic/pynq-z1/start.

[12] Snapdragon 835 HDK. https://developer.qualcomm.com/hardware/snapdragon-835-hdk.

[13] `rustup` the RUST toolchain installer. https://github.com/rust-lang/rustup.

Before syntax conversion, the PYTHON program can be run against a tool[14] to obtain information about the concrete types used by the application. Types recorded this way allow for more information to be available in the later steps of transpilation, but may be unnecessarily constraining.

Next, the syntax conversion is applied using a publicly available automatic syntax converter that creates a PYTHON Abstract Syntax Tree (AST) from the PYTHON source code. The PYTHON AST is automatically made into RUST source code by visiting each AST node using the visitor pattern[15] and outputting the equivalent RUST code. Syntax conversion allows for rough, automatic transformation of PYTHON syntax to almost equivalent RUST. After syntax conversion, the program is unlikely to immediately compile using the RUST compiler and must be manually edited with help from the RUST compiler. Once the compiler accepts the source code, it must be further tested to validate that the code is functionally equivalent to the original. Once the program is validated, the program source code can be further edited, optimized, and compiled as a RUST program.

The performance of the compiled RUST code can be measured either by native RUST benchmarks or by dispatching library functions via its C foreign function interface (CFFI) via a PYTHON 3.8.1 interpreter. Execution on PC is measured using the CFFI and the PYTHON interpreter for a fair comparison against the original SciPy and BLAS optimized PYTHON code. Deployability on embedded targets is verified by natively compiling the program on PYNQ and by cross-compiling to Snapdragon using the cross-compilation framework cross[16].

4   Use Cases

Two distinct use cases were chosen for examining the difficulty and outcomes of transpiling and its feasibility for embedded implementations. The first use case is a simple Black–Scholes model for options pricing in financial markets. The second is a recent, complex algorithm for motion planning in robotics [20]. Black–Scholes is a collection of established small benchmark methods that can each be represented in around 5 lines of PYTHON with SciPy. Motion Planning, on the other hand, is a novel and experimental algorithm in robotics, spanning 437 lines of PYTHON with NumPy as formatted by autopep8, omitting blank lines and comments. We transpiled it *as is* from the developers during development of the algorithm.

4.1   Black–Scholes Model

Black–Scholes is a well-known model for the dynamics of financial markets. It was selected for its readability, compact source code size and good coverage of

---

[14] MonkeyType. https://github.com/Instagram/MonkeyType.

[15] Visitor Pattern. https://en.wikipedia.org/wiki/Visitor_pattern.

[16] cross. https://github.com/rust-embedded/cross.

results in other studies [9,15,16,18]. We implemented[17] the model in PYTHON using NumPy based on an online source [19], and added validation tests. A notable feature of the implementation is that because of NumPy, it works the same for both scalar and array inputs. Our transpiled sources are publicly available[18].

The transpilation was conducted as explained earlier in Sect. 3. After automatic syntax conversion, compiler-assisted library mapping was straightforward. NumPy functions generally mapped to RUST standard library functions of similar names and signatures. The more complex SciPy-call to a cumulative distribution function required a manual implementation using statrs, though a direct expression-to-expression mapping was found to exist. Automatic syntax conversion introduced an incorrect calculation order issue that was captured by validation tests and corrected. Potential, automatic solutions to the described issues are discussed in Sect. 5.

The transpiled RUST source code and its dependencies were compiled natively on PC and PYNQ, and cross-compiled to Qualcomm Snapdragon using cross. Fixed inputs produce same results on all platforms.

4.2 Motion Planning

Multi-convex path constrained trajectory optimization for mobile manipulators [20], or Motion Planning, is a recent proposition for an algorithm in robotics, written in PYTHON and NumPy. Motion Planning allows a robot, such as a mobile manipulator, to find a path through space while respecting kinematic constraints and avoiding collisions [20]. Key qualities of the algorithm are its parallel nature and the suitability for experimentation in the physical world. The physical aspect makes it a good candidate for optimizing and deploying on an embedded target. Singh et al. note that prototyping the algorithm in a low-level language might improve computation time [20].

The original Motion Planning implementation uses Basic Linear Algebra Subprograms (BLAS) specification to prescribe optimizations via NumPy. Our transpiled implementation maps NumPy functions to RUST community library ndarray[19]. In our experiments, the BLAS optimizations are implemented by linking to Intel MKL on PC and to OpenBLAS[20] on PYNQ. The total runtime of the original implementation is a couple of seconds on a multicore desktop PC when allowed to run for 100 iterations. In the experiments, the parameters to the algorithm are built-into the library, which reduces reliability of the measurements for both the PYTHON and the transpiled RUST implementations. Measurements were taken with careful examination of allocations and verification of produced outputs.

After automatic syntax conversion, we used regular expressions extensively to fix remaining errors and library references. Multiple manual implementations

---

[17] Black–Scholes based on [19]. https://github.com/hegza/black-scholes-py.

[18] Transpiled Black–Scholes. https://github.com/hegza/black-scholes-transpiled-rs.

[19] ndarray. https://github.com/rust-ndarray/ndarray.

[20] OpenBLAS. https://www.openblas.net/.

of expressions (<1% of all expressions) were required though each was straight-forward with output from the RUST compiler. Validation tests revealed that the original PYTHON implementation converged slightly faster than the RUST implementation. This is possibly due to different linear algebra implementations in the respective libraries. Slower convergence was not taken into account in performance measurements.

The transpiled RUST source code and its dependencies were compiled natively on PC and PYNQ, and cross-compiled to Qualcomm Snapdragon using `cross`. Results converge on the same values with fixed inputs on all platforms.

5   Results and Analysis

We consider the results of transpilation in wall clock time, memory consumption, and complexity in terms of issues encountered and regularity for potential automation. We also consider what processes transpiled sources now allow. Lines of code is not considered a feasible measure because the number of lines is almost the same, with differences being due to the differing formatters of each language.

5.1   Performance

The performance of PYTHON implementations on PC is measured with `timeit` library, which avoids the overhead from PYTHON garbage collection. RUST implementations are measured with `criterion.rs`[21], a community library for RUST benchmarks. Memory use is measured with `valgrind --tool=massif`. Intel `MKL` and `OpenBLAS` are dynamically linked to the runtimes where applicable. The Black–Scholes model was calculated for 72 million *put options*[22], which were loaded from a file for the RUST implementation to prevent excessive LLVM optimizations. Motion Planning was run for 100 iterations. The performance of the Black–Scholes model is as follows:

Table 1. Execution profile of Black–Scholes on PC (allocations included).

Black–Scholes	Python (MKL)	Rust (native)
Execution time	27.29 s	11.70 s
Peak memory consumption	9.372 GB	3.456 GB

Table 1 shows that the native RUST implementation uses less memory and runs faster. Output from Valgrind's `massif` seems to suggest that the PYTHON implementation reserves the input and output arrays arrays 2–3 times. Memory use of both measurements seems realistic, as the theoretical memory consumption of the Black–Scholes algorithm for this use case is

---

[21] `criterion.rs`. https://github.com/bheisler/criterion.rs.
[22] https://en.wikipedia.org/wiki/Put_option.

$$\text{floating\_point\_width} \times \text{number\_of\_options}$$
$$\times (\text{number\_of\_inputs} + \text{number\_of\_outputs})$$
$$= 8 \text{ bytes} \times 72 \text{ million} \times (5 + 1)$$
$$= 3.456 \ GB \text{ (decimal)}.$$

The result presented in Table 1 shows that a naively transpiled PYTHON / NumPy implementation may perform equally well as – or better than – the original implementation in memory limited scenarios. Further investigation reveals that the RUST implementation links statically into `matrixmultiply`[23], which is a native RUST implementation of matrix multiplication. This enables full memory optimization via LLVM. Static linking of `Intel MKL` is possible for both implementations, but this is not the default behavior of either of the toolchains and requires manual work that is not portable across implementations on our chosen devices.

The performance results for Motion Planning are presented in Tables 2, 3, and 4.

Table 2. Execution profile of Motion Planning on PC using `Intel MKL`.

Motion Planning	Python	Rust (`CFFI`)	Rust
Execution time	6.44 s	0.671 s	0.532 s
Peak memory consumption	9.40 MB	8.45 MB	6.47 MB

Table 3. Execution profile of Motion Planning on PC using `OpenBLAS`.

Motion Planning	Python	Rust
Execution time	4.10 s	2.80 s
Peak memory consumption	8.85 MB	1.93 MB

Table 2 shows that the transpiled version of the `Intel MKL` accelerated implementation speeds up 12.1×. All `Intel MKL` implementations are parallel and speedup is likely to be mainly gained by LLVM optimizations, which are better at considering all of the code compared to PYTHON steered calls to functions. Dispatching the transpiled Motion Planning algorithm from a PYTHON interpreter via `CFFI` shows increased memory use due to the interpreter but runs faster than accelerated PYTHON. Memory use improves by a factor of 1.45×. Table 3 shows that the transpiled version speeds up 1.46× when linked against `OpenBLAS`, with a 4.2× improvement in memory consumption. Further investigation with PYTHON tooling[24] reveals that most of the memory used by the

---

[23] `matrixmultiply`. https://github.com/bluss/matrixmultiply.
[24] `tracemalloc`. https://docs.python.org/3/library/tracemalloc.html.

PYTHON implementations is due to the loaded PYTHON runtime and libraries, while runtime workload allocates 1.99 MB of memory. The RUST implementation slightly improves in peak memory consumption for runtime data with 1.93 MB allocated.

Table 4. Execution profile of Motion Planning on PYNQ using `OpenBLAS`.

Motion Planning	Python	Rust (`CFFI`)	Rust
Execution time	70.5 s	70.3 s	69.0 s
Peak memory consumption	6.9 MB	2.7 MB	1.7 MB

Table 4 shows that the `OpenBLAS` accelerated implementation runs equally fast on PYNQ when executed via either language. The higher memory consumption of the PYTHON implementation is partially explained by the included interpreter. The transpiled native RUST implementations can also be cross-compiled to Qualcomm Snapdragon. All implementations use more memory than what is necessary due to the benefits caching can provide in some circumstances. However, the right trade-off between execution time and memory consumption is important. RUST implementations generally both run as fast or faster as PYTHON implementations and consume less memory.

5.2 Transpilation Regularity and Automation

The introduced method was applicable as-is and numerous automatable conversions were identified. The used automatic syntax conversion tool (`pyrs`) introduced a calculation order error in the Black–Scholes use case. The calculation order could be more accurately traced between the languages by introducing a step for converting the PYTHON AST to a RUST AST, as shown in Fig. 2.

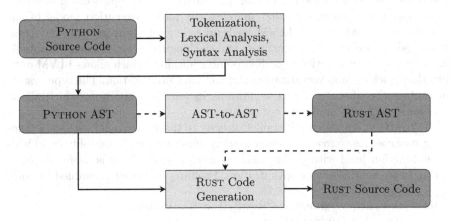

Fig. 2. Proposed AST-to-AST transpilation step (dashed arrows).

Creating such an AST-to-AST transpiler would require an implementation of a transformation from each source AST node to each target AST node. A PYTHON AST implementation in RUST is available via community library RustPython[25] and a RUST AST implementation in RUST is available via community library syn[26].

In our use cases, PYTHON library references could be converted to RUST library references in a highly regular fashion using a regex. A more sophisticated approach would be to use an AST aware transpiler to correctly map the method calls from source to target. Method calls can be mapped from a function body expression in PYTHON into a RUST path segment, and the parameters can be mapped expression-by-expression. In developed domain-specific libraries, a single declarative mapping for functions in· source language to functions in target language may exist, and could be maintained via tooling to create a persistent mapping if desirable.

Issues arising from syntactic differences between the languages were all found to be automated, or automatable. However, in addition to syntax translation, conversion from PYTHON to RUST requires accounting for semantic differences. RUST ownership semantics can be at least partially accounted for by preferring use-by-reference for read-only bindings and by rebinding variable data for each use, trusting the compiler to optimize. PYTHON and RUST variable scopes do not match 1:1 and need to be corrected by hand, though these issues were found to be rare in our use cases with one semantic scope issue in Black–Scholes and none in Motion Planning. All found issues were detectable at compile-time with associated error messages, apart from the singular incorrect calculation order error in Black–Scholes. All problems were solvable via human intervention, as demonstrated by the use cases. The vast majority of issues were automated via pyrs, or could have been automatable.

5.3   Implications of Transpiled Source

The transpiled source code is easily programmable and compiles down to a high performance implementation that matches the native execution model of the platform, provided that an LLVM backend exists for the platform. The transpiled code adheres to RUST semantics and the language's type system. A notable example is RUST semantics regarding pointer aliasing, which allows LLVM optimizations such as loop vectorization and constant propagation. The type system guarantees the absence of race conditions in parallel execution, which allows additional paths for multicore optimization.

As the RUST source code compiles directly to target assembly without a managing runtime, its source code can be easily annotated with assembly or LLVM-IR at function level with tooling such as cargo-asm[27]. This is useful for comparing implementations for optimization. Profiling on target is enabled by tools

---

[25] RustPython. https://github.com/RustPython/RustPython.

[26] syn. https://docs.rs/syn/1.0.16/syn/.

[27] cargo-asm. https://github.com/gnzlbg/cargo-asm.

such as `perf`, that allows the programmer to determine where in the code the processor spends most time. For instance, in combination with `FlameGraph`[28], profiling information generated and annotated with `perf` can be used to determine if the main workload spends time allocating heap memory that could be pre-allocated, or if the time is spent in an optimized library like `Intel MKL`. Direct access to profiling information like this allows the programmer to identify bottlenecks and make informed decisions about what to optimize next.

In addition to hardware oriented tooling, use of RUST allows the programmer to rely on type system guarantees when producing parallel implementations. In fact, the inner loop of Motion Planning is trivially convertible to a data-parallel implementation by rewriting the loop expression in terms of a parallel iterator as provided by the community library `rayon`[29], though this seems to provide no significant advantage over `Intel MKL` enabled data-parallelism in this workload.

6   Conclusions

Transpiled implementations are generally faster than accelerated PYTHON implementations up to an order of magnitude for the more complex use case. Transpilation seems automatable and generally applicable. An almost 1:1 syntactic mapping from expression to expression exists between PYTHON and RUST, and could be applied with an AST-to-AST transpiler. Library references can be mapped out and applied in a highly regular fashion. Issues arising from differing type systems and borrow checking semantics cannot be solved at the level of syntax conversion and another approach is required.

Transpiled implementations can be further developed and optimized. The implementation of the Black–Scholes model can be further accelerated by linking to `Intel MKL` statically, and bottlenecks in the motion planning algorithm can be investigated. The motion planning algorithm could also be made more portable and lighter on memory by using native RUST matrix solvers in place of `BLAS`, or faster by linking statically to `Intel MKL`.

Our future work focuses on comparing transpiled implementations to end-to-end optimized implementations, and improving the automation of transpilation. Further advancements in the transpilation process for such applications are certainly available. AST-to-AST transpilation allows improved control over syntax transformation. Library mappings can be defined declaratively and automated.

References

1. Abadi, M., et al.: Tensorflow: a system for large-scale machine learning. In: 12th {USENIX} Symposium on Operating Systems Design and Implementation ({OSDI} 16), pp. 265–283 (2016)
2. Behnel, S., et al.: Cython: C-Extensions for Python (2008)

---

[28] FlameGraph. https://github.com/brendangregg/FlameGraph.
[29] `rayon`. https://github.com/rayon-rs/rayon.

3. Bradbury, J., et al.: JAX: Composable Transformations of Python+NumPy programs (2018). http://github.com/google/jax
4. Chen, T., et al.: {TVM}: An automated end-to-end optimizing compiler for deep learning. In: 13th {USENIX} Symposium on Operating Systems Design and Implementation ({OSDI} 18), pp. 578–594 (2018)
5. Frostig, R., Johnson, M.J., Leary, C.: Compiling machine learning programs via high-level tracing. In: Systems for Machine Learning (2018)
6. Instagram: (2020). https://github.com/Instagram/MonkeyType
7. JetBrains: (2020). https://www.jetbrains.com/idea/
8. Konchunas, J.: Python to rust transpiler (2020). http://www.github.com/konchunas/pyrs
9. Kristensen, M.R., Lund, S.A., Blum, T., Skovhede, K., Vinter, B.: Bohrium: unmodified numpy code on cpu, gpu, and cluster. In: 4th Workshop on Python for High Performance and Scientific Computing (PyHPC'13) (2013)
10. Kristensen, M.R., Lund, S.A., Blum, T., Skovhede, K., Vinter, B.: Bohrium: a virtual machine approach to portable parallelism. In: 2014 IEEE International Parallel & Distributed Processing Symposium Workshops, pp. 312–321. IEEE (2014)
11. Leary, C., Wang, T.: Xla: Tensorflow, compiled. TensorFlow Dev Summit (2017)
12. Maclaurin, D., Duvenaud, D., Adams, R.P.: Autograd: Effortless gradients in numpy. In: ICML 2015 AutoML Workshop, vol. 238 (2015)
13. Oliphant, T., Peterson, P., Eric, J.: Scipy.org (2001). https://www.scipy.org/
14. Ousterhout, K., Rasti, R., Ratnasamy, S., Shenker, S., Chun, B.G.: Making sense of performance in data analytics frameworks. In: 12th {USENIX} Symposium on Networked Systems Design and Implementation ({NSDI} 15), pp. 293–307 (2015)
15. Palkar, S., et al.: Weld: rethinking the interface between data-intensive applications. arXiv preprint arXiv:1709.06416 (2017)
16. Palkar, S., et al.: Evaluating end-to-end optimization for data analytics applications in weld. Proc. VLDB Endow. 11(9), 1002–1015 (2018)
17. Palkar, S., et al.: Weld: A common runtime for high performance data analytics. In: Conference on Innovative Data Systems Research (CIDR) (2017)
18. Palkar, S., Zaharia, M.: Optimizing data-intensive computations in existing libraries with split annotations. In: Proceedings of the 27th ACM Symposium on Operating Systems Principles, pp. 291–305 (2019)
19. Schlegel, A.: Black-scholes formula and python implementation (2018). https://aaronschlegel.me/black-scholes-formula-python.html
20. Singh, A.K., Ahonen, A., Ghabcheloo, R., Muller, A.: Inducing multi-convexity in path constrained trajectory optimization for mobile manipulators. arXiv preprint arXiv:1904.09780 (2019)
21. van der Walt, S., Colbert, S.C., Varoquaux, G.: The numpy array: a structure for efficient numerical computation. Comput. Sci. Eng. 13(2), 22–30 (2011)

A Fast Heuristic to Pipeline SDF Graphs

Alexandre Honorat$^{(\boxtimes)}$, Karol Desnos, Mickaël Dardaillon,
and Jean-François Nezan

Univ Rennes, INSA Rennes, CNRS, IETR - UMR 6164, 35000 Rennes, France
{alexandre.honorat,karol.desnos,
mickael.dardaillon,jean-francois.nezan}@insa-rennes.fr

Abstract. A common optimization of signal and image processing applications is the *pipelining* on multiple Processing Elements (PE) available on multicore or manycore architectures. Pipelining an application often increases the throughput at the price of a higher memory footprint. Evaluating different pipeline configurations to select the best one is time consuming: for some applications, there are billions of different possible pipelines. This paper proposes a fast heuristic to pipeline signal and image processing applications modelled with the Synchronous DataFlow (SDF) Model of Computation (MoC). The heuristic automatically adds pipeline stages in the SDF graph in the form of delays, given the Execution Time (ET) of the actors and the number of PEs. The heuristic decreases the time spent by the developer to pipeline its application from hours to seconds. The efficiency of the approach is illustrated with the optimisation of a set of signal and image processing applications executed on multiple PEs. On average, when adding one pipeline stage, our heuristic selects a stage resulting in a better throughput than 90% of all possible stage emplacements.

Keywords: SDF · Pipeline · Parallelism · Throughput

1 Introduction

Synchronous DataFlow (SDF) [10] is widely used to model signal and image processing applications and to optimize them on multicore embedded systems. Pipelining is made possible in SDF by adding *delays*. Delays represent initial data in buffers, which break data dependencies. This method has already been proved to be efficient on SDF applications [9] but usually requires to add the delays manually in the SDF graph or to call heuristics [7]. Indeed, computing the optimal throughput of an application is a problem of high complexity that also requires computing the scheduling, the mapping and the pipelining.

This project has received funding from the European Union's Horizon 2020 research and innovation programme under grant agreement No 732105 (project CERBERO) and from the Région Bretagne (France) under grant ARED 2017 ADAMS. We would like to thank Michael Masin for his help to generate all admissible graph cuts.

A. Orailoglu et al. (Eds.): SAMOS 2020, LNCS 12471, pp. 139–151, 2020.
https://doi.org/10.1007/978-3-030-60939-9_10

In this paper we propose a fast heuristic to automatically pipeline an application modelled with an SDF graph. This heuristic is performed before mapping and scheduling the application, and is thus suboptimal but fast and scalable. It automatically adds delays in the SDF graph, given the number of Processing Elements (PEs) and application profiling information. The heuristic is parametric: the user can choose the number of pipeline stages that he wants to add. Various experiments demonstrate that our heuristic increases the throughput of the majority of the tested applications. When adding one pipeline, the heuristic finds the solution ensuring optimal throughput for 19 applications out of 24 tested.

The paper is organized as follows. Section 2 presents the main properties of the SDF Model of Computation (MoC). Section 3 specifies the notion of pipeline for SDF graphs and outlines necessary conditions for their validity. The main contribution, automatic pipelining of SDF graphs, is developed in Sect. 4. Extensive experiments follow in Sect. 5 with both theoretical evaluation of the throughput gain and real measurements on hardware. The main drawback of pipelining, memory footprint increase, is also quantified. Related work is presented in Sect. 6. Finally, Sect. 7 concludes this paper.

2 Background

SDF [10] graphs are directed multi-graphs annotated with data communication *rates*. The vertices are called *actors*, and the edges are called *buffers*. Actors correspond to the processing of the application, while buffers contain the data sent from an actor to another. Data stored in a buffer are called *tokens*. Two rates are specified per buffer b: a production rate $\text{prod}(b) \in \mathbb{N}^*$ on the sending side of b, and a consumption rate $\text{cons}(b) \in \mathbb{N}^*$ on the receiving side. Hence, each time an actor is *fired*, which means its computations are executed, it consumes and produces a fixed number of tokens on each input and output buffers, respectively.

Only *consistent* SDF graphs are considered in this paper. An SDF graph is consistent when there exists a finite number of firings of each actor bringing back all buffers with the exact same number of tokens as initially. Such minimal number of firings is called a *repetition vector* and denoted r. It is computed from the buffers production and consumption rates.

To avoid deadlocks, cycles of the graph need initial tokens in at least one of their buffers. These initial tokens are called *delays*. The size of a delay on a buffer b, that is the number of initial tokens that b contains, is denoted $d_0(b)$. In this paper, it is assumed that the user already set delays in cycles, ensuring no deadlock. Delays are not restricted to cycles though; when placed correctly and outside cycles, delays cut some data dependencies and create pipeline stages. This point will be discussed and illustrated in the next section.

The contribution of this paper is a heuristic for automating the placement of pipeline delays in any SDF graph. Following the semantics introduced in [2], we assume all delays being permanent, which means that their token values are transmitted from one graph iteration to the next.

3   Admissible Graph Cuts for Pipelining

Admissible graph cuts for pipelining correspond to *feed-forward* graph cuts as defined for the design of integrated circuits [14]. A graph cut is a set of edges which, if removed, disconnects the graph in two or more components. In a feed-forward graph cut, all edges of the cut are going in the same direction. Hence, such cut cannot contain an edge from a cycle. The direction of an edge is deduced from the topological ranks of the actors. An example of actor ranks of As Soon As Possible (ASAP) and As Late As Possible (ALAP) topological orderings is presented in Fig. 1a. Lowest actor rank 1 correspond to actors without input buffers, and the highest actor rank correspond to actors without output buffers.

A pipeline is created by adding delays on all buffers of a feed-forward graph cut, in order to break the data dependencies. For example, the feed-forward graph cut (dashed line) between topological ranks 1 and 2 of the graph in Fig. 1a breaks the data dependencies between actors A and B, and A and Δ. The pipeline increases the throughput of the graph, as depicted in Fig. 1b. In Fig. 1a as in all SDF graphs presented in this section, rates are all equal to 1 for simplification. The throughput is defined by the inverse of the *Initiation Interval (II)* duration, that is the duration to periodically execute a graph *iteration*. A graph iteration contains as many firings as in the repetition vector r. We assume that there is a synchronization barrier at the end of each graph *iteration*. On the left part of Fig. 1b, without pipeline, the II duration is 3, whereas on the right part, the II duration is only 2 with the pipeline. Note that, depending on the topological ordering, the graph cuts may not be identical.

To create a pipeline on an SDF graph, the size of a delay on a buffer b must be equal to $d_0(b) = \text{prod}(b) \times r[\text{src}(b)] = \text{cons}(b) \times r[\text{dst}(b)]$. Thus, dependencies between all firings of producer actor $\text{src}(b)$ and receiver actor $\text{dst}(b)$ are broken. If multiple feed-forward graph cuts contains the same buffer, the delay sizes are summed. In this paper, the number of pipelines n correspond to n different feed-forward graph cuts, dividing the execution of the application in $n+1$ *stages*.

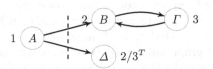

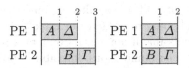

(a) Graph example annotated with ASAP and ALAP topological orderings. ALAP ordering is specified with ^{T}, only if different from ASAP.

(b) Two schedule examples of graph 1a on two PEs: on the left without pipeline, on the right with one pipeline between ranks 1 and 2.

Fig. 1. Topological ordering and schedule example without and with pipeline.

Unfortunately, the number of admissible graph cuts may be large. An example is given with a commonly used split-join graph topology [17], which is a subcategory of SDF graph. Although the graph represented in Fig. 2 only contains 4 parallel paths with 3 buffers each, $3^4 = 81$ cuts are admissible. Indeed, if l paths connect a split actor to a join actor, each path having m buffers, the total number of feed-forward graph cuts is equal to m^l. Because the number of admissible graph cuts may grow exponentially with the number of edges of the graph, exploring them all is not feasible. For this reason, our heuristic algorithm will only explore a subset of the admissible cuts. For example, our heuristic considers at most 3 admissible cuts for the graph in Fig. 2. Those admissible cuts are detailed in the next section.

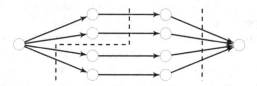

Fig. 2. Split-join graph with four parallel branches. 2 admissible cuts are represented with a dashed line, among 81 possible.

4   Automatic Pipelining of SDF Graphs

The automatic pipelining heuristic has two main steps: (1) generation of topological graph cuts, (2) selection of topological graph cuts. The first step, described in Sect. 4.1, computes a subset of admissible cuts. The second step, detailed in Sect. 4.2, selects a few cuts among the cuts computed in step (1).

4.1   Computing Topological Graph Cuts

The heuristic selects a subset of admissible graph cuts: *topological* graph cuts according to the ASAP and ALAP topological orderings. A topological graph cut of rank c contains all buffers coming from an actor of rank lower than c and going to an actor of rank higher than or equal to c. Such topological cut is admissible if none of its buffers is part of a directed cycle of the graph.

The number of admissible topological graph cuts is upper bounded by the diameter of the graph, that is the number of buffers on the longest path. For example, the graph depicted in Fig. 2 admits only 3 topological cuts according to ASAP graph ordering, whereas this graph admits 81 admissible cuts in total. Moreover, in the case of Fig. 2, ASAP and ALAP graph orderings are identical so the same 3 graph cuts are considered for both topological orderings.

In order to build the ASAP and ALAP topological orderings, a cycle analysis of the graph is run first: the Johnson's algorithm [6] computes all simple cycles of a directed graph. Johnson's algorithm upper bounds the complexity of the whole heuristic. The buffers being part of cycles are recorded to later filter the admissible cuts. For example, the topological cut of rank 3 in the SDF graph depicted in Fig. 1a is invalid since there is a cycle between actors B and Γ.

Note that it is assumed that the user sets enough delays on at least one buffer of any cycle, so that this buffer breaks the data dependency of the cycle. Thanks to this assumption, ASAP and ALAP orderings are computed by a mere breadth first search on the graph, not visiting the buffer breaking each cycle.

The number of admissible topological graph cuts is small and upper bounded by the graph diameter, enabling our heuristic to be fast. The admissible topological graph cuts naturally include all cuts located at sequential bottlenecks of the application, so they are the best candidates to increase the application performances by pipelining. Formally, sequential bottlenecks are located on single paths of the graph: when two successive actors of ranks $c - 1$ and c are the only actors having these ranks. Selecting such cuts particularly benefits the applications having single paths and their repetition vector equal to $\mathbf{1}$.

4.2   Selecting Best Topological Graph Cuts

To select the best topological graph cuts, the presented heuristic relies on a map linking topological ranks to an estimate of the Execution Time (ET) of all their actors. By definition, all actors having the same topological rank can be executed in parallel. We introduce a few notations to formalize the computation of this map. $T(a)$ denotes the Execution Time (ET) of an actor a. The number of firings of a is $r[a]$. The rank of a is $\mathrm{rank}(a)$. The number of PEs is $\#\mathrm{PE}$. The ET estimate of rank c, denoted $\mathrm{rankLoad}(c)$, is computed as follows in Eq. (1).

$$\mathrm{rankLoad}(c) = \frac{\sum_{\mathrm{rank}(a)=c} \left\lceil \frac{r[a]}{\#\mathrm{PE}} \right\rceil \times T(a)}{\#\{a | \mathrm{rank}(a) = c\}} \tag{1}$$

The main purpose of Eq. (1) is to provide a metric indicating if cutting before actors of rank c improves the throughput, that is to balance the computation before and after the cut. To do so, we actually compare the estimated ET of all ranks before the cut of rank c, $\sum_{1 \leq i < c} \mathrm{rankLoad}(i)$, with the estimated ET of all ranks after the cut of rank c, $\sum_{c \leq i} \mathrm{rankLoad}(i)$. However, it is needed to weight the ranks according to the amount of parallelism that they contain, so that the graph is cut where it matters most: on single paths for example. Thus, Eq. (1) contains two divisions in order to reduce the weight of already parallel ranks: the repetition factor is divided by $\#\mathrm{PE}$, and the whole sum is divided by the number or actors in the considered rank. The rankLoad is averaged for both ASAP and ALAP topological orderings.

The selection of cuts is parameterized by two integers: the number of cuts wanted by the user x, selected among the number of balanced cuts to consider y (denoted D x, y in Sect. 5). We always have x lower than or equal to y, and y lower than the highest actor rank. y helps to define a first set of equally distributed topological graph cuts. To do so, the sum of all rankLoad(i) is divided by y, giving an average stage load avgStageLoad. Then we enumerate ASAP cuts by increasing order of their rank, and select the closest ones to a multiple of avgStageLoad. The same operation is performed on ALAP cuts sorted by decreasing order of their rank. At most, $2 \times y$ balanced cuts are selected, since cuts selected with ASAP and ALAP orderings may not be identical. Both orderings are considered in order to avoid selecting 0 cuts because of unbalanced ETs.

The last step of the heuristic is to select x cuts among the $2 \times y$ balanced cuts. This is done by two means: removing cuts that are too close from each other, and then selecting the one using less delays. Two topological cuts of rank c_1 and c_2 are considered too close from each other if the sum of their intermediate estimated ET is lower than avgStageLoad, as formalized in Eq. (2).

$$avgStageLoad > \sum_{c_1 \leq i < c_2} rankLoad(i) \qquad (2)$$

5   Evaluation

The presented heuristic is evaluated on various applications coming from the StreamIt [18] benchmark, the examples provided with the SDF3 [16] tool, and the applications provided with the PREESM [15] tool. These applications represent a panel of basic state of the art signal and image processing algorithms, as well as more complex telecommunications, video coding and computer vision applications. The heuristic results are compared by gain in throughput, relative to the sequential non-pipelined throughput on a single Processing Element (PE).

Three different evaluations are performed. In Sect. 5.1, the theoretical throughput gain is computed based on the schedule length obtained after adding the pipelines selected by the heuristic. A comparison is made with the optimal throughput gain among all admissible cuts, for applications amenable to an exhaustive exploration, while large applications are detailed in Sect. 5.2. Finally in Sect. 5.3, the throughput and memory increases are measured on real executions of applications running on hardware.

All experiments have been run with the open-source PREESM tool (https://preesm.github.io/), on a laptop with an Intel processor i7-7820HQ. For all selected applications, the execution time of the proposed heuristic is between 1 and 18 ms (maximum reached for SIFT). Note that the StreamIt/SDF3 applications are all stateless, except h263decoder (noAC) having self-loops. Self-loops disable auto-concurrency of an actor: multiple firings are serialized.

Main characteristics of the applications are presented in the results tables. In the second column, MAP is the Maximum number of Actors in Parallel in the SDF graph; MAP equals the maximum number of parallel paths in the graph. When known, the total number of admissible graph cuts is specified in the column labeled #Cuts. Note that multiple versions of SIFT and sobel-morpho applications are considered: their graph is identical but they do not have the same amount of firings. Some of their actors are fired a number of times equal to a multiple of a parameter p. Only SIFT and stereo contain directed cycles in their SDF graph. In all results tables, the columns labeled by D x, y contain the throughput gain obtained by the heuristic selecting x pipelines among y balanced pipelines. Columns labeled by C x contain the optimal throughput gain, over all admissible cuts, for x pipelines. Lines of results tables without any value printed in bold means that the throughput gain is similar for all setups; otherwise, the value in bold corresponds to the best gain among the line.

5.1   Theoretical Throughput Gain: Regular Applications

Theoretical throughput gain obtained with the heuristic is presented in Table 1, for three setups: no pipeline, one pipeline among one, three pipelines among three. Most applications have a repetition vector r equal to 1, except Chain4.2noAC (which contains self-loops), cd2dat, h263decoder, modem, mp3decoder, samplerate and satellite. Chain4.2noAC and Chain4.1 are toy examples made to fit the best cases of the heuristic; they correspond to the graph depicted in Fig. 2, with only one path instead of four.

In Table 1, the best throughput gain is obtained by the heuristic with 3 cuts (D 3,3) for 11 of the 17 applications. More importantly, the heuristic finds a close to the optimal throughput with 1 cut for all applications except mp3decoder. The number of admissible cuts generating a throughput gain lower than or equal to D 1,1 is reported as a percentage of the total number of admissible cuts, in column %. In average, D 1,1 reaches a better throughput gain than 91% of the admissible cuts. Note that two applications are not compared with the optimal gain, FMRadio and Vocoder, because they admit too many cuts. These applications, and three others, are discussed in Sect. 5.2.

On DCT and h263decoder, the throughput gain is less than 2.0, even with 3 pipelines: this comes from too few actors in the original graphs (respectively 8 and 4), having unbalanced ETs. This configuration leads the heuristic to find only 2 graph cuts for DCT and h263decoder, even if 3 pipelines were asked by the user. The number of effectively selected cuts is specified as an exponent. The same behavior happens for modem and mp3decoder applications: only 2 cuts are selected whereas 3 pipelines were asked. To avoid this problem, only 2 pipelines among 3 are requested for the PREESM applications, see Table 2 Indeed, in these applications the ETs are greatly unbalanced and the ET of the longest actor represents up to 47% of the sequential ET of sobel-morpho (p1).

For the PREESM applications evaluated in Table 2, the heuristic reaches the best throughput in 7 cases out of 9. SIFT application is a difficult case: its SDF graph is widely parallel (up to 30 parallel paths) and contains multiple cycles. Moreover, its parallel paths have unbalanced ET. In this situation, selecting topological cuts is not the best option and 1 optimal cut (C 1) even reaches a better throughput than 2 cuts from the heuristic (D 2,3): for SIFT (p1) and SIFT (p2). However, when more balanced parallelism is expressed, for SIFT (p4), the heuristic configuration D 2,3 once again is better than the other setups.

Table 1. Characteristics and throughput gain with delays (D) of SDF benchmark applications, on four PEs. D 0 corresponds to no pipeline. D 1,1 corresponds to one pipeline selected among one. C 1 corresponds to the optimal single stage pipeline. % is the percentage of cuts worst than or equal to the heuristic. D 3,3 corresponds to three pipelines selected among three.

Name	MAP	#Actors	#Cuts	D 0	D 1,1	C 1	%	D 3,3
Chain4.1	1	4	3	1.0	2.0	2.0	100	**3.9**
Chain4.2noAC	1	4	3	1.4	2.3	2.3	100	**3.4**
BitonicSort	4	40	141	1.6	2.9	2.9	100	**3.6**
cd2dat	1	6	5	4.0	4.0	4.0	80	4.0
DCT	1	8	7	1.0	1.8	1.8	100	1.8^2
DES	3	53	128	1.2	2.2	2.2	96	**2.4**
FFT	1	17	16	1.0	2.0	2.0	100	**3.7**
FMRadio	12	43	—	3.1	**3.3**	—	—	**3.3**
h263decoder (noAC)	1	4	3	1.8	1.8	1.9	100	2.0^2
modem	1	6	5	2.0	**3.3**	3.3	100	3.3^2
mp3decoder	2	14	33	3.7	3.7	**3.8**	66	3.7^2
MPEG2noparser	3	23	140	1.1	2.2	2.2	100	**2.7**
samplerate	1	6	5	4.0	4.0	4.0	60	4.0
SAR	2	44	63	1.0	1.8	1.8	100	**2.3**
satellite	3	22	90	4.0	4.0	4.0	68	4.0
TDE	1	29	28	1.0	1.9	1.9	100	**3.4**
Vocoder	17	114	—	1.2	2.1	—	—	**2.6**

Table 2. Throughput gain with delays (D) of SDF benchmark applications, on four PEs. D 0 corresponds to no pipeline. D 1,1 corresponds to one pipeline selected among one. C 1 corresponds to the optimal single stage pipeline. % is the percentage of cuts worst than or equal to the heuristic. D 2,3 corresponds to two pipelines selected among three possibilities.

Name	MAP	#Actors	#Cuts	D 0	D 1,1	C 1	%	D 2,3
SIFT (p1)	30	54	868	1.2	1.6	**2.2**	92	1.6
SIFT (p2)	30	54	868	2.3	2.8	**3.7**	91	3.0
SIFT (p4)	30	54	868	3.5	3.5	3.6	80	**3.7**
sobel-morpho (p1)	1	6	5	1.0	**2.0**	2.0	100	2.0
sobel-morpho (p2) *	1	6	5	1.7	2.4	2.4	100	**2.6**
sobel-morpho (p3) *	1	6	5	2.3	**3.5**	3.5	100	3.4
sobel-morpho (p4)	1	6	5	2.3	2.8	**3.3**	40	3.3
stereo	3	28	3631	3.3	3.9	**3.9**	99	3.9
lane-detection *	3	11	24	1.0	1.7	1.7	100	**2.5**

5.2   Theoretical Throughput Gain: Widely Parallel Applications

This subsection evaluates the applications revealing the main advantage of the presented heuristic: no explosion of the number of cuts to test when the SDF graph is already parallel. Indeed, all evaluated applications in Table 3 admit between 10^5 and 10^{10} cuts, which makes it impossible to evaluate the throughput of each cut by performing scheduling and mapping. Moreover, the number of possibilities also explodes with the number of pipelines asked: it is equal to the number of cut combinations without repetition (binomial coefficient): $\binom{\#Cuts}{\#Stages-1}$.

Table 3 presents results for the applications already having parallelism expressed in their graph: MAP is between 12 and 17 for all of them. In this experiment, the throughput is evaluated on 64 PEs for the heuristic setup D 3,3 selecting 3 pipelines. Having 64 PEs ensures to observe the effect of the pipelines instead of the inherent task parallelism. Indeed, the maximum number of actors in parallel MAP (17) is almost 4 times smaller than the number of PEs. The maximum theoretical throughput gain with unlimited PEs, Max Θ, is given as a reference. All applications in Table 3 are acyclic, so Max Θ is computed by dividing the sequential ET of the application by the ET of its longest actor, as if each buffer had a pipeline delay. Adding 3 pipelines increases the throughput gain from a factor 2 (for FMRadio) to 3 (for ChannelVocoder).

Table 3. Throughput gain with delays (D) of SDF benchmark applications, on sixty-four PEs. D 0 corresponds to no pipeline. D 3,3 corresponds to three pipelines selected among three possibilities. Max Θ corresponds to the maximum possible throughput gain, with unlimited PEs.

Name	MAP	#Actors	#Cuts	D 0	D 3,3	Max Θ
Beamformer	12	57	1.7×10^7	8.9	19.0	25.6
ChannelVocoder	17	55	1.3×10^{10}	11.1	33.2	33.4
Filterbank	16	85	4.3×10^8	10.5	30.5	32.2
FMRadio	12	43	2.6×10^5	6.0	12.7	13.1
Vocoder	17	114	3.0×10^{10}	1.2	2.7	2.8

5.3   Practical Experimentation

In this subsection, the throughput and memory measurements come from real executions on hardware, on the same laptop used for all experiments, having 4 PEs. Note that the scheduler used in this practical experimentation differs from the one used in the theoretical experimentation. Both schedulers are a variant of list scheduling [8]. Memory is allocated after the scheduling process, with buffer merging [4] optimizations activated. The memory needed is computed by PREESM, and compared with the sequential version on 1 PE for reference.

Results are provided in Table 4, for an average of 100 executions for SIFT and stereo, and 10000 executions for sobel-morpho and lane-detection. The heuristic especially improves the throughput of SIFT and sobel-morpho with $p = 1$ and $p = 2$, that is, when the application is not parallel enough. Yet, for lane-detection which has $r = 1$, the heuristic only slightly increases the throughput, while increasing the memory by a factor 1.9. The theoretical throughput gain of lane-detection is 2.5, that is two times higher than reality. We explain this gap by the variability of the ET of the display actor, representing 28% of the application sequential execution time. Also, synchronization points added by PREESM may be non-negligible. None of the applications reaches the throughput expected in the theoretical evaluation.

An interesting point is that selecting 1 cut among 2 (D 1,2) gives better results than 1 among 1 for half of the cases. Such heuristic setups may compensate the case of unbalanced ETs or cycles, especially for SIFT (p2). Moreover for SIFT (p2) the D 1,2 setup greatly reduces the memory footprint compared to D 1,1: from a factor 3.0 to 1.1. Finally, the heuristic offers a trade-off between memory footprint and throughput. This trade-off is especially needed for memory bounded application as SIFT requiring 197 MBytes (reference). At worst, for sobel-morpho (p4), adding one pipeline decreases the throughput while greatly increasing the memory (3.3 times). The memory increase is due to the graph cut location: between buffers transmitting numerous data, and thus it causes additional time for memory copies and synchronizations.

Table 4. Throughput and memory increases with delays (D), on four PEs, for different parallelism parameters (p). Specific mapping constraints are enforced for applications marked with *: read and display actors are alone on their core if there is a pipeline.

Name	D 0		D 1,1		D 1,2		D 2,3	
	Sp.	Mem.	Sp.	Mem.	Sp.	Mem.	Sp.	Mem.
SIFT (p1)	1.2	1.1	**1.6**	2.1	1.4	1.3	1.3	1.8
SIFT (p2)	1.8	1.1	1.9	3.0	**2.4**	1.2	2.2	2.3
SIFT (p4)	**2.5**	1.2	2.2	1.1	2.2	1.1	2.5	1.8
sobel-morpho (p1)	0.9	1.0	1.3	2.2	1.3	2.6	**1.6**	3.8
sobel-morpho (p2)	1.7	1.6	2.3	2.1	**2.5**	2.4	2.1	3.4
sobel-morpho (p3) *	2.3	2.1	2.4	2.8	**2.5**	2.6	2.5	3.2
sobel-morpho (p4)	**2.5**	2.0	1.9	2.6	2.2	2.3	2.4	3.3
stereo	2.2	1.1	2.3	1.1	2.3	1.1	**2.4**	1.1
lane-detection *	1.0	1.0	1.1	1.8	1.1	1.7	**1.2**	1.9

6   Related Work

Pipelining and more generally retiming has been extensively studied in the context of VLSI circuit design [11,14]. Pipelining legality was formally defined by

Parhi [14] for a subset of SDF graphs: Homogeneous Synchronous DataFlow (HSDF) graphs, which always have their repetition vector equal to **1**. It was also studied for software pipelining [1], with retiming methods used in this context [3]. Our work focus on pipelining SDF graphs, avoiding the costly conversion to HSDF and thus reducing the analysis complexity.

Pipelining of SDF graphs was originally proposed by Lee [9] as an optimization. Gordon et al. [5] proposed an heuristic to pipeline a partially unfolded SDF graph, as well as Kudlur et al. [7]. The heuristic presented by Kudlur et al. requires the Initiation Interval (II) length as an input of their algorithm; on the contrary, our heuristic requires a maximum number of pipelines as an input, and tries to minimize the II accordingly. Also, the heuristic presented by Gordon et al. relies on a first transformation of the original actors, in order to balance the ETs and to adapt the amount of parallelism.

Multiple works [12,21] addressed the optimal finding of a retiming to reduce the makespan of a graph. Additionally, [21] accepts a constraint on the maximum number of processors, at the cost of non-optimality. Both use symbolic execution of a partially unfolded SDF graph to find a retiming. In this paper we focus on the pipelining of an SDF graph in its reduced original form to provide a fast heuristic. We do not perform any execution, symbolic or not.

Scheduling has been largely explored in optimal and heuristic forms [8,13]. A few works look at combining pipelining with scheduling, restricted to HSDF graphs [19] or acyclic SDF graphs [20]. Our work separates pipelining from scheduling. Scheduling is computed afterwards on the pipelined graph, taking advantage of original data and task parallelism, as well as temporal parallelism.

7   Conclusion

A fast heuristic to automatically pipeline SDF applications at coarse grain has been presented and actually improves the throughput of the evaluated applications. The heuristic is able to quickly pipeline applications containing up to billions of admissible cuts. Our algorithm limits its exploration to a few cuts to reduce analysis time, and experiments show this method is close to the optimal solution. The last experiment have shown a gap between the theoretical throughput gain and the practical gain, always lower than expected. This gap is observed for both our heuristic and the theoretical optimal solution.

The presented heuristic is especially useful when considering a large amount of PEs. However, our method can still be improved for complex applications, especially if containing cycles, for examples by adding smaller delays to break the dependencies between only a certain amount of firings instead of all.

Finally, this heuristic is only one optimization method among various others, as the most related to this work: retiming. Combination of our pipelining heuristic and classic retiming techniques is kept for future work.

References

1. Allan, V.H., Jones, R.B., Lee, R.M., Allan, S.J.: Software pipelining. ACM Comput. Surv. **27**(3), 367–432 (1995)
2. Arrestier, F., Desnos, K., Pelcat, M., Heulot, J., Juarez, E., Menard, D.: Delays and states in dataflow models of computation. In: SAMOS XVIII (2018)
3. Calland, P.Y., Darte, A., Robert, Y.: Circuit retiming applied to decomposed software pipelining. IEEE Trans. Parallel Distributed Syst. **9**(1), 24–35 (1998)
4. Desnos, K., Pelcat, M., Nezan, J.F., Aridhi, S.: On memory reuse between inputs and outputs of dataflow actors. ACM Trans. Embedded Comput. Syst. (TECS) **15**(2), 30 (2016)
5. Gordon, M.I., Thies, W., Amarasinghe, S.: Exploiting coarse-grained task, data, and pipeline parallelism in stream programs. SIGPLAN Not. **41**(11), 151–162 (2006)
6. Johnson, D.B.: Finding all the elementary circuits of a directed graph. SIAM J. Comput. **4**(1), 77–84 (1975)
7. Kudlur, M., Mahlke, S.: Orchestrating the execution of stream programs on multicore platforms. ACM SIGPLAN Notices **43**(6), 114–124 (2008)
8. Kwok, Y.K., Ahmad, I.: Static scheduling algorithms for allocating directed task graphs to multiprocessors. ACM Comput. Surv. **31**(4), 406–471 (1999)
9. Lee, E., Messerschmitt, D.: Pipeline interleaved programmable dsp's: synchronous data flow programming. IEEE Trans. Acoustics, Speech, Signal Process. **35**(9), 1334–1345 (1987)
10. Lee, E.A., Messerschmitt, D.G.: Synchronous data flow. Proc. IEEE **75**(9), 1235–1245 (1987)
11. Leiserson, C.E., Saxe, J.B.: Retiming synchronous circuitry. Algorithmica **6**(1), 5–35 (1991)
12. Liveris, N., Lin, C., Wang, J., Zhou, H., Banerjee, P.: Retiming for synchronous data flow graphs. In: 2007 Asia and South Pacific Design Automation Conference, pp. 480–485 (2007)
13. Malik, A., Gregg, D.: Orchestrating stream graphs using model checking. ACM Trans. Archit. Code Optim. **10**(3), 19:1–19:25 (2013)
14. Parhi, K.K.: VLSI digital signal processing systems : design and implementation (2007)
15. Pelcat, M., Desnos, K., Heulot, J., Guy, C., Nezan, J.F., Aridhi, S.: PREESM: a dataflow-based rapid prototyping framework for simplifying multicore DSP programming. In: EDERC, p. 36 (2014)
16. Stuijk, S., Geilen, M., Basten, T.: SDF^3: SDF for free. In: Application of Concurrency to System Design, 6th International Conference, ACSD 2006, Proceedings, pp. 276–278 (2006)
17. Tendulkar, P., Poplavko, P., Maler, O.: Symmetry breaking for multi-criteria mapping and scheduling on multicores. In: Braberman, V., Fribourg, L. (eds.) Formal Modeling and Analysis of Timed Systems, pp. 228–242 (2013)
18. Thies, W., Karczmarek, M., Amarasinghe, S.P.: Streamit: a language for streaming applications. In: Proceedings of the 11th International Conference on Compiler Construction, pp. 179–196. CC 2002 (2002)
19. Yang, H., Ha, S.: Pipelined data parallel task mapping/scheduling technique for MPSOC. In: 2009 Design, Automation, Test in Europe Conference Exhibition, pp. 69–74 (2009)

20. Chen, Y., Hai, Z.: Buffer minimization in pipelined SDF scheduling on multi-core platforms. In: 17th Asia and South Pacific Design Automation Conference, pp. 127–132 (2012)
21. Zhu, X., Geilen, M., Basten, T., Stuijk, S.: Multiconstraint static scheduling of synchronous dataflow graphs via retiming and unfolding. IEEE Trans. Comput.-Aided Des. Integrated Circ. Syst. 35(6), 905–918 (2016)

System Simulation of Memristor Based Computation in Memory Platforms

Ali BanaGozar[1]([✉]), Kanishkan Vadivel[1], Joonas Multanen[2],
Pekka Jääskeläinen[2], Sander Stuijk[1], and Henk Corporaal[1]

[1] Eindhoven University of Technology, Eindhoven, The Netherlands
{a.banagozar,k.vadivel,s.stuijk,h.corporaal}@tue.nl
[2] Tampere University, Tampere, Finland
{joonas.multanen,pekka.jaaskelainen}@tuni.fi

Abstract. Processors based on the von Neumann architecture show inefficient performance on many emerging data-intensive workloads. Computation in-memory (CIM) tries to address this challenge by performing the computation on the data location. To realize CIM, memristors, that are deployed in a crossbar structure, are a promising candidate. Even though extensive research has been carried out on memristors at device/circuit-level, the implications of their integration as accelerators (CIM units) in a full-blown system are not studied extensively. To study that, we developed a simulator for memristor crossbar and its analog peripheries. This paper evaluates a complete system consisting of a Transport Triggered Architecture (TTA) based host core integrating one or more CIM units. This evaluation is based on a cycle-accurate simulation. For this purpose we designed a simulator which a) includes the memristor crossbar operations as well as its surrounding analog drivers, b) provides the required interface to the co-processing digital elements, and c) presents a micro-instruction set architecture (micro-ISA) that controls and operates both analog and digital components. It is used to assess the effectiveness of the CIM unit in terms of performance, energy, and area in a full-blown system. It is shown, for example, that the EDAP for the deep learning application, LeNet, is reduced by 84% in a full-blown system deploying memristor based crossbars.

Keywords: Computation in memory · Memristor · Simulator · Non-von neumann architectures · Transport Triggered Architecture

1 Introduction

Optimization of speed and power consumption in conventional processor architectures, i.e. von Neumann based processors, is difficult due to the fundamental design choice to place the memory unit apart from the processing unit (Fig. 1(a)). For this configuration to operate, data is required to be transferred between the two units back and forth many times. These data movements not only elongate the process-time but also consume a significant amount of energy. Adding levels to the memory hierarchy and introducing small-sized caches, close to the processing unit, have alleviated the problem (Fig. 1(b)). Nonetheless, such techniques

A. Orailoglu et al. (Eds.): SAMOS 2020, LNCS 12471, pp. 152–168, 2020.
https://doi.org/10.1007/978-3-030-60939-9_11

fail to meet ever-increasing performance and energy requirements of emerging data-intensive applications, e.g. deep learning networks.

Computation in-memory, on the other hand, suggests processing the data in the very same site where it resides [15,17,19]. Eliminating a huge part of the data transfers, CIM reduces the data bandwidth constraints, decreases energy budget requirements, and improves performance. Reference [17] realizes CIM by placing complex computational elements on the logic layer below the 3D memory stack (Fig. 1(c)). Reference [19] proposes exploiting the analog attribute of DRAM technology to perform bulk bitwise operations right inside a DRAM. Doing so a DRAM is used at its full internal bandwidth.

Another approach to realize CIM is to exploit emerging non-volatile memories, e.g., resistive random access memory (ReRAM), phase change memory (PCM), and spin-transfer torque magnetic random access memory (STT-MRAM) [22] (Fig. 1(d)). These devices offer promising features like compact realizations, ultra-low static power –hardly any leakage, and non-volatility – eliminating the required energy to refresh cells– which makes them favorable candidates to realize CIM. Being organized in a crossbar structure, they can operate as extremely dense memory units. Employing the very same structure, several operations such as vector matrix multiplication (VMM), and bulk Boolean bitwise operation (BBB), can be executed on them exploiting their analog behavior. These operations are explained in more details in Sect. 2. To enjoy data locality and reuse, CIM is connected to the DRAM and not directly to the DISK. Although memristor based CIM is considered one of the most promising options for the next generation of processors, the implications associated with their deployment at the computer architecture level are rarely studied. The number of studies that are exploring memristors at the device level, as well as the required driving mixed-signal circuitry, are quite considerable, however. The contributions of this paper are as follows:

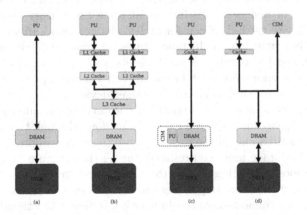

Fig. 1. a) Early computers, b) Multi-processor with multi-level caches, c) computation in memory (DRAM), d) computation in memory (memristor) [21]

○ An in depth system level analysis of the efficacy of deploying memristor cross-bar based CIM accelerators at system-level. Based on the study, using memristor crossbars the EDAP is reduced by 84% for the LeNet kernel (Sect. 5).
○ A novel C++ based CIM unit simulator that includes the memristor cross-bar, its surrounding analog drivers, and the required interface to communicate to the co-processing digital part. Furthermore, a micro-instruction set architecture (micro-ISA) for memristor crossbar based platforms, which is independent of technology and capable of execution various memristor crossbar operations, is presented (Sect. 3).
○ Integration of CIM unit(s) into a TTA, a class of exposed data path architectures. Using TTA-based Co-design Environment (TCE), an open-source tool-set that enables the designer to freely customize the TTA, energy, area, and performance figures at system-level are calculated (Sect. 4).

2   Background and Related Work

For a good understanding a proper background is needed. This section presents the basics of non-volatile memories, their organization in a crossbar structure, and memristor crossbar based CIM processors are presented.

2.1   Memristors and Memristor Crossbars

Device engineers have been seeking for alternative technology for the post-CMOS era since the device scaling is reaching the atomic realm. Non-volatile memories, e.g. phase change memories (PCM), resistive RAMs (ReRAM), are considered a promising instance of such devices. Information maps to the conductance states of a device. The device retains its value until it is (RE)SET by a voltage higher than its threshold voltage.

Being organized in an area-efficient crossbar structure, they can be exploited as dense blocks of memories. To further increase the density –bits per area– multi-level cells are used. The non-linear I-V characteristics of the memristors allow them to hold multiple conductance states. In multi-level cells, multiple bits of information can be stored on a single device with multi-conductance states. To fine-tune the conductance level, in a write-verify scheme, pulses with different width (amplitude) are applied across the target device.

However, the non-linear characteristics of the device itself, and the sneak path current in a crossbar –an undesired current that flows through the memory cells parallel to the desired one– make it hard to use the device in practice. To make the programming stage more controllable, the 1T1R structure (1-Transistor 1-Resistor) is proposed [27] (Fig. 2a). In the 1T1R structure, a transistor is placed in series with a memristor. Depending on the direction in which the gates of the transistors are connected, row/column-wise, different functionalities can be achieved. For instance, if the gates are connected horizontally, bulk Boolean bit-wise operations (BBB) can be executed, but not hyper-dimensional computation (HDC) [9]. Whereas, if the gates are connected vertically, the platform is suitable for HDC and not BBB.

2.2   Memristor Crossbars Functions

Memristors, both individually or in a crossbar layout, have been employed for various use cases. They have been used as physically unclonable functions [11], radio frequency switches [18], dot product engines [10], and memory blocks [8]. In this section, we focus on the memristor crossbar based use-cases.

The most appealing feature of memristors is that they can perform vector-matrix multiplication (VMM), which is the core operation of many applications especially neural networks, in a single shot. To perform a VMM ($Y_{1 \times n} = X_{1 \times m} \times W_{m \times n}$), where W, X, and Y are weight matrix, input vector, and output vector, respectively, several measures should be taken. First, the elements of the weight matrix are mapped to the conductance states of the crossbar cells. Then, elements of the input vector are encoded to the amplitude or the length of pulses to be applied to the rows. Note that the amplitude of the input voltages should not exceed the threshold voltage of the device, as this destructs the stored information. Next is to drive the input voltages into the word-lines while the bit-lines are virtually grounded. According to Ohm's law, a current equal to the product of input voltage and the cell conductance flows through the device ($I_{ij} = V_i \times G_{ij}; 0 \leq i < m, 0 \leq j < n$). The currents, that are resulted of all element-by-element multiplications, are accumulated and sensed simultaneously at the end of active columns. Thanks to this attribute, memristor crossbars are considered one of the most promising platforms to realize neuromorphic computing architectures [3,10,20,23]. It is worth mentioning that if the required analog peripheries –which drive the crossbar in the reverse direction– are available, it is possible to do VMM on the transpose matrix using the same crossbar [6].

The other use-case, in which memristor crossbars have shown promising results, is in-memory bulk Boolean bit-wise operations [14]. BBB is frequently performed in database queries and DNA sequence alignment [19]. To perform a bit-wise operation, reference [25] programs every single bit of an operand to cells in a row. Then, by applying a read voltage to two desired rows, where targeted operands are stored, currents flow in bit-lines. Currents are sensed using scouting logic. The reference current of the sense amplifier is determined based on the operation, i.e. AND, OR, XOR to be performed. Comparing the sensed current with the reference current(s), different Boolean operations can be realized.

2.3   Architectures and Simulators

Although memristors are broadly examined at the device and circuit levels higher abstraction levels are barely studied. Architectural simulators like [7,8,20,24] present designs that put memristor crossbar models into practice at the architecture abstraction level. In [20], for example, the memristor crossbars are arranged in a pipelined structure that targets the efficient execution of convolutional neural networks (CNNs). Similarly, in [8] and [24] architectural simulators that are designed for performing neural network implementation are presented.

Ankit et al. propose a "programmable ultra-efficient memristor-based accelerator" (PUMA) that adds general-purpose execution units to enhance memristor crossbars for machine learning purposes [2]. PUMA presents a specialized ISA that offers programmability without degrading the efficiency of in-memory computing. The instructions, however, are considerably long which performs inefficiently if subtle changes are required to be made. PUMA also is an accelearator which again bears the above mentioned problem.

Zidan et al. propose a "field programmable crossbar array" (FPCA) which unites various combinations of memristor crossbar use cases, namely memory, digital and analog computing in one basic core that can be reconfigured dynamically [28]. The low write endurance of the memristors, however, limits the number of times a unit can be reprogrammed [26]. Consequently, the reconfiguration, which was the core idea of FPCA, seems impractical.

To the best of our knowledge, our work is the first system level analysis of memristor based CIMs integration into a fully programmable architecture. Our research in some aspects is inline with PUMA, i.e. enhancing the memristor crossbars by adding general-purpose execution units. While PUMA focuses on presenting an accelerator we integrate our CIM unit into a fully programmable architecture. Doing so, we investigate and address the possible challenges such an integration brings. Additionally, by introducing a configuration register file, we significantly simplify our instruction set architecture. Hence, it can easily be expanded if new operations are developed for memristor crossbars.

3   CIM Unit

As memristor technologies are hardly available, to develop an architecture for processors based on memristor crossbars we designed a simulator that replicates the functional behavior of memristor crossbars. The simulator also covers the operation of the peripheral mixed-signal circuitry. We call this mixed-signal part "Calculator" (see Fig. 2b). For the Calculator to communicate with other processing elements, we have expanded the simulator, by adding the necessary digital components, e.g. buffers, register files, controller. The added digital components all together comprise the "Micro-engine". In the remainder of this section, first, the architecture of the CIM unit is illustrated; then, the proposed micro-ISA is introduced; and in the end, the tasks of the controller are described.

3.1   CIM Architecture

CIM tile, a cycle-accurate simulator that is developed in C++, replicates the function of a memristor crossbar, the driving mixed-signal circuits, and necessary digital elements. The tile includes two different domains, mixed-signal, the Calculator, and digital, the Micro-engine (Fig. 2b).

In the Calculator, various modules are defined to imitate the behavior of every single analog component, i.e. the crossbar, analog/digital converters (ADC), digital input modulators (DIM), sample and holds (S&H). This modular design

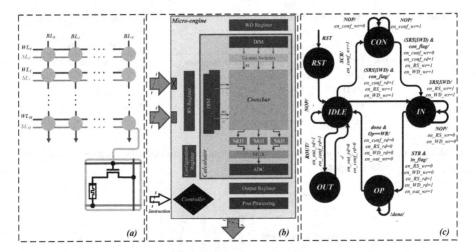

Fig. 2. Overall look of the CIM unit. a) 1T1R non-volatile memory crossbar , b) the tile structure, c) The controller. (only memory units enable/disable signals are presented in the FSM)

enables a designer to change the configuration of the Calculator, e.g. crossbar size, number of ADC/DIMs, or add new modules with a negligible effort.

DIMs and ADCs, at the edges of the Calculator, are connected to digital buffers, i.e. RS/WD/Output. DIMs convert the raw data into amplitude/width of pulses that are to drive the crossbar. Crossbar results, if operation produces any, are converted to digital values by ADCs and stored in the output buffer. Simple digital logics, present inside the Micro-engine, carry out simple operations like weighted sum if desired. To instruct the CIM unit to carry out different operations, we propose a micro-instruction set architecture (Table 1). The micro-instructions promote the nano-instructions that are presented in [5]. Although the nano-instructions offer full control over the tile, there is quite some room to enhance them. For example, the process of fetching raw data into buffers requires the whole buffer to be overwritten, even if only a few entries are supposed to change. The full control offered by nano-architecture is not desirable as it comes with many dependencies between instructions. This not only make the compilation complex, long, and inefficient but may lead to unreliable code. Therefore we designed a micro-ISA to void interfering with any pre/post-processing stage inside the CIM unit, thus eliminating the chance of external error. The controller reads the operation parameters that are written into the configuration register via SCR instruction and manage the whole operation based on these registers.

3.2 Micro-ISA and Micro-Engine

To avoid very long instructions, that include several execution parameters, a configuration register is introduced to hold these parameters (Table 2). The controller, a mealy machine (FSM), ensures the correct execution of instructions,

Table 1. Micro instructions. Simplified instruction set that can easily be extended.

Class	Mnemonic	Description	Operands
Initialization	SCR	Set Configuration Register	Address, data
	SRS	Set Row Select Buffer	Data
	SWD	Set Write Data Buffer	Data
Compute	STR	Start operation, e.g. Write, VMM, BBB	-
Read	ROUT	Read result Out	-

Table 2. Configuration Registers. Controller conducts an operation based on the content of configuration register

Register index	0	1	2	3	4	5	6	7	8	9-15
Register content	Start Row	Start Col	Number of Rows	Number of Cols	Input Precision	Weight Precision	Output Precision	Truncate Bits	Operation	Reserved

e.g. filling buffers, enabling/disabling the analog elements, etc. (Table 1). To carry out an operation, first, the configuration register should be filled using the set configuration register (SCR) instructions. Based on the contents of the configuration register, the FSM calculates the address of the buffers, aligns the data, triggers the operation, collects the crossbar output, and post-processes the output (if needed). In the end, the FSM controls the process of sending the final results out. As mentioned, the controller is a mealy machine that issues the control signal based on the received micro-instructions, configuration register contents, the state of the FSM, and the internal flags (Fig. 2c). The digital buffers, the configuration registers, and the controller, all together, constitute the Micro-engine.

Without loss of generality, we use PCM technology to demonstrate our work. According to a prototype developed by IBM [13], to write a phase change memory (PCM), or to perform a VMM takes respectively 2.5 μs and 1 μs. Considering that these delays are considerable, we attempted to schedule some tasks into these very long time slots. The data that must be processed on the CIM unit is a vector. Therefore we propose to add an extra set of buffers in the CIM unit (double buffering (DB)) to fetch the $(n + 1)^{th}$ vector while vector n^{th} is being processed (Fig. 3b). To ensure that no data is lost, we add an extra level to the controller that supervises the correct redirection of the control signals. This approach of having a top-layer in the controller enables us to perform the operations that are targeted in [9].

4   TTA-CIM

We integrate our CIM unit into *Low-power TTA* (LoTTA) –a processor design based on Transport Triggered Architecture (TTA)– developed for energy-efficient execution of always-on application [16]. This section start with introducing TTAs. It is followed by a description of the TTA Co-design Environment (TCE), an open-source tool-set that allows adding special functional units like the CIM unit to the architecture. Lastly, the details of the CIM special functional unit (CIM-SFU) integration into TTA architecture are explained.

4.1 TTA and TCE

Transport Triggered Architectures are a class of Exposed Data Path Architectures (EDPAs), where the data path of the processor is exposed to the programmer. Fine-grain control over the data path allows compile-time bypassing of data between processing-elements, i.e. software bypassing, without dependency checking hardware circuitry, which improves energy-efficiency. Furthermore, static scheduling of instructions on EDPAs opens up new optimization possibilities on the software as well as on the hardware side. Compared to traditional operation triggered architectures, where operation triggers data-path activity, the TTA instruction represents the data transports (TTA data-move) and the computations are triggered as a side effect of the data-move. Functional Units of TTA comprise one or more operand ports and optional result ports that can communicate data over the interconnect network. In TTAs, one of the operation ports of FUs is designated as a special port named "trigger-port". A data move to the trigger port starts the execution of an operation on FUs. Figure 4 (bottom) depicts an example of a TTA processor instance with three communication resources (bus network) and one CIM unit as an added special functional unit (CIM-SFU). The trigger port of the FUs are marked with a cross mark. The CIM-SFU is the functional model of the CIM unit with CIM-ISA defined in Sect. 3. The Fig. 4 (top) shows a TTA program for simple increment operation (i.e. $a = a + 5$) on the processor instance [16] to illustrate a programming model of the TTAs. Three buses in the instance imply that three data transports can happen in parallel during each clock cycle. Therefore, both operands move (a and 4) can happen in parallel for the considered example and the whole operation takes two cycles in total as shown by the highlighted data moves. The data move $4 \rightarrow ALU1.add.in1t$ triggers execution of an add operation in the ALU unit with operands on input ports $in1t$ and $in2$ at cycle-1. At cycle-2, the result of the add operation (assuming add latency is one cycle) is written back to RF.

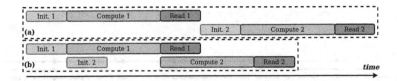

Fig. 3. CIM unit execution flow, a) without DB, b) with DB (Init., Compute and read are three classes of micro instructions in Table 1)

A mature open-source tool-set, TTA Co-design Environment (TCE), enables users to design and freely customize TTAs for their purpose. It includes a re-targetable instruction-set compiler, cycle-accurate ISA simulator, RTL genera-tor, and support for adding special compute units for dedicated functions. TTAs are an ideal candidate for energy-efficient application-specific instruction-set pro-cessors (ASIPs), and a sensible choice for prototyping experimental platforms such as our CIM unit.

The core used for evaluations in this paper is a variant of the original Low-power TTA (LoTTA). Functional units of the core and its interconnection net-work are presented in Fig. 4 (top). Considering that LoTTA is specifically opti-mized for energy efficiency it is a suitable core to start with.

4.2   CIM Unit Integration (CIM-SFU)

As pointed out in Sect. 3, the latency of the CIM computations (VMM, Write, etc.) is much higher than the regular operations on the traditional FUs such as ALU, MUL, etc. This gives rise to two main requirements for the CIM-SFU design, 1) A multi-cycle FU model to hide the latency of the CIM-SFU from other units, and 2) Pipelined FU model to separate the CIM compute unit (Calculator) from the TTA interface (operand and result ports) to hide data-latency with the double-buffering concept (Fig. 3b). The semi-virtual time latching model of the FUs in the TCE allows for a multi-cycle, pipelined TTA-SFU model in the TCE tool-set. Figure 2b depicts the designed CIM-SFU. The CIM-SFU is modelled as a three-stage pipeline with the first-stage fetching the input data, the second stage covering the core CIM mixed-signal computation logic (*Calculator*), and the third stage sending the results out (Fig. 3a). The pipeline of the SFU is controlled by a trigger move. i.e. when the trigger move happens, the operands ($input_{1t}$ and optional $input_{2-n}$) are latched to the Micro-engine and the opcode is issued to the controller of the Micro-engine. The FSM, then, issues necessary

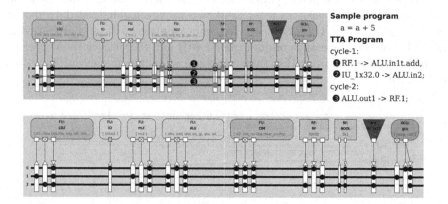

Fig. 4. TTA based processors overview. LoTTA(Top). LoTTA+1 × CIM(Bottom)

Table 3. CIM unit characteristics

Crossbar parameters	Value	
Memristor Technology	PCM (from IBM)	
Cell precision	8-bit (implemented by 2×(4-bit) PCMs)	
Compute and Write Latency/8-bit	1 µs and 2.5 µs	
Compute Energy/8-bit	200 fJ (2×100 fJ/4-bit PCM)	
Write Energy/8-bit	200 pJ (2×100 pJ/4-bit PCM)	
Area (128 × 128)	50 µm^2	
Peripheral Circuitry	**Energy**	**Area**
Mixed signal	2.1 nJ/cycle (@1.2 GHz)	1252 µm^2
Micro-engine (Digital)	64.8 pJ/byte	865 µm^2

control signals for the rest of the components. The Calculator, which is modeled cycle-accurately, produces the result on the output buffer once the operation latency is elapsed for the triggered operation. The data on the output buffer is then serialized to the output port via an explicit trigger commands to controller. The architecture template of the TCE requires that each operation in the FU to have a deterministic latency such that the resulting read for the operation can be scheduled at compile time.

5   Experiments

In this section, we present the effects of adding the CIM unit in a quantitative manner. To do so, we employ LoTTA, without a CIM-SFU, as a base setup. Then, CIM-SFU(s) added to LoTTA to explore its effect on various parameters such as performance, energy, and area. For evaluation, we used gemm as well as deep learning LeNet kernels.

5.1   Experimental Setup

The energy and area estimates for the LoTTA core are obtained after synthesis with Synopsys Design Compiler, version 2016.12. A 28 nm process is used at 0.95 V operating voltage and 25 °C temperature process corner. For power consumption analysis, switching activity information files (SAIFs) are generated with ModelSim 10.5. The weights to be mapped on the memristor crossbar are 8-bit values (8-bit precision is enough to obtain a reasonable accuracy) which are mapped on IBM's 4-bit PCM [12], as it has shown promising results [12]. To mimic an 8-bit weight with 4-bit cells, two columns are used, one for four MSBs and the other for four LSBs. The final result is computed by a weighted sum of MSB and LSB columns in the Micro-engine. The models for the CIM unit components are from [12] and [20].

5.2   Evaluation

As mentioned earlier, we evaluated gemm and LeNet kernels. For gemm, we studied the impact of different input and matrix sizes. For LeNet, we evaluated performance, accuracy, energy, as well as area for different crossbar sizes.

Gemm: To evaluate how memristor crossbars perform on VMM, we implemented the gemm kernel on a crossbar of size 256×256. Figure 5a shows that by increasing the number of input vectors the speedup increases from 1.2X to 3.9X for basic CIM unit without double buffering. This was expected since the computation dominates the initial overhead of programming the crossbar. Increasing the number of the rows of the weight matrix, i.e. the columns of the input matrix, it is observed that although the speed-up increases, the improvement rate is less significant compared to the previous case (Fig. 5b). This happens as the number of cycles required to program the crossbar dominates the overall execution time. Considering these two experiments, and the fact that memristors still suffer from low endurance, the read/write ratio shall be taken into account to assess if it is reasonable to use a memristor crossbar or not. Lastly, in Fig. 5c we observe that increasing the number of weight matrix columns increases the speed-up rate of LoTTA+CIM over LoTTA since the size of the vector to be programmed grows while the required time for programming the crossbar just slightly increases.

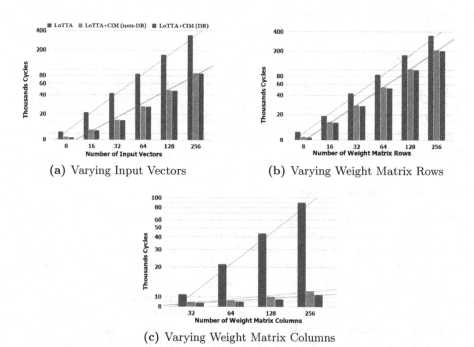

(a) Varying Input Vectors

(b) Varying Weight Matrix Rows

(c) Varying Weight Matrix Columns

Fig. 5. Performance for gemm kernel (in thousands cycles).

Double Buffering: Figure 5a shows that although by deploying double buffering performance improves compared to non-DB, the relative speedup goes down from 1.02X to 1.01X. This happens since the size of input vector is too small, thus, a limited number of instructions can be scheduled to a VMM execution period (Compute stage in Fig. 3.) However, in Fig. 5c we observe that as the number of columns of weight matrix increases the relative speedup caused by deployment of DB goes from 1.02X to 1.10X. This happens since the size of the vector to be loaded and programmed on the crossbar grows; therefore, more instructions can be scheduled to a write execution period.

LeNet: To assess the suitability of memristor based CIMs for deep learning applications, we implemented the LeNet architecture on LoTTA and LoTTA+CIM unit(s). The LeNet architecture comprises both convolutional as well as fully connected neural network layers that makes it a perfect data-intensive application instance to study with respect to implications associated with deploying memristor crossbars in a full-blown system. One of the challenges that memristor crossbars should address is the possibility that the weight matrix exceeds the memristor crossbar in size, i.e., either in the number of columns or rows. If the number of columns of the weight matrix is bigger than that of the actual memristor crossbar, the only measure that should be taken is to divide the weight matrix over M CIM units, where M = $\lceil \frac{WeighMatrix_{col}}{MemristorCrossbar_{col}} \rceil$, or to divide the task over time and use a CIM unit M times. The second solution is not quite desirable due to the low endurance of memristors. Obviously the RS buffer in each and every CIM unit has to hold the exact same data. Since columns results are independent they can be handled without any dependency. In case the number of rows of the weight matrix is bigger than that of the actual memristor crossbar, like in the previous case, either N CIM units are required, where N = $\lceil \frac{WeighMatrix_{row}}{MemristorCrossbar_{row}} \rceil$, or the operation should be carried out in N time steps with one CIM unit. Unlike the previous case the results of each part are only partial results and should be accumulated to produce the final result. To study this, we assume various sizes for the memristor crossbar. The biggest memristor crossbar has 512 rows and the smallest has 128. The number of columns of all the layers of LeNet are always smaller than the matrix

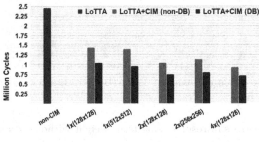

Fig. 6. Performance comparison of architectures for LeNet deep neural network

size. Considering that the weight matrix of the second and the third layers of LeNet after unrolling are 150 and 400 rows, respectively, these layers should be either distributed temporally, if the resources are limited, or spatially, if enough CIM units are available. Figure 6 shows the results of various implementations. Using only one CIM unit, even one that is big enough to map a whole layer to the crossbar, performance is worse than any other implementation with multiple CIM units due to parallelism. Distributing weights matrix amongst several CIM units saves quite a few cycles while programming the crossbar, since this is the most time consuming step of performing an operation on a memristor crossbar. The reason that the implementation with two units of size 256×256 yields worse results, in terms of speed and energy, compared to the one with two crossbars of size 128×128 is that we map a whole layer to one crossbar if it was possible. This is important as splitting weight degrades the accuracy (Fig. 7). As can be seen in Fig. 6, we have mapped the architecture for the DB version as well. The best performance is achieved when the four CIM units that are deployed in the design, do the calculation in parallel.

Accuracy: The error sources that we have spotted are two folds; 1) MSB and LSB columns are truncated by the DC offset of the ADC before being summed up together; therefore, the expected carry bit from the addition of the lower bits is lost, 2) The saturation voltage of ADC clips the high/low voltages. In case a crossbar is distributed amongst several CIM units or it is multiplexed in time, a partial sum may exceed the saturation voltage while other partial sums do not reach the saturation voltage. If all parts were together this would be a saturated result while in the distributed case partial sums produce a different result. In a mathematical terminology $\Sigma F(x_i^j) \neq F(\Sigma x_i^j)$, where F is a non-linear function – characteristics of ADC – and x_i^j is the output of ith column of jth CIM tile. Looking at Fig. 7, we observe that splitting the weight matrix in different manners results in different errors. As an instance, for crossbar(s) of

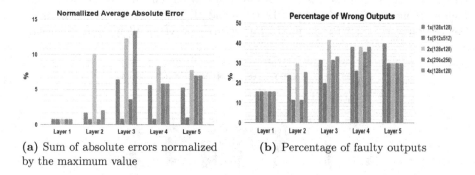

(a) Sum of absolute errors normalized by the maximum value

(b) Percentage of faulty outputs

Fig. 7. Errors in results using basic weight without retraining

size 128 × 128, although the inputs are the same, just by splitting the second layer weight differently different number of faulty errors with different averages are reported (see blue, yellow, and orange bars in the figure). Although these error degrades the final result, due to the resilient nature of LeNet the input images are still classified correctly. To address the degradation of the results, it is required to retrain the network with crossbar size being taken into account. The retraining process is out of the scope of this paper.

Energy and Area: One of the most important concerns in the deployment of CIM units is their analog nature which requires data conversion that can be costly. Although digital/analog converters (DACs) are relatively cheap in terms of energy/area, analog/digital converters (ADCs) can be extremely costly – more than 500× more power hungry and more than 7000× bulkier compared to DACs [20]. One of the techniques that is commonly used to reduce the energy/area overhead is to share an ADC amongst several columns. To do so, sample and hold circuits (S&Hs) are introduced between the ADC and crossbar. With such modifications the required energy budget falls into a reasonable scale. Table 4 shows that in the best case up to 69% energy reduction can be achieved, while area is increased by 80%. Looking at EDAP –energy, delay, area, product– we observe that in almost all cases, except for a crossbar of size 512 × 512, the double buffered version performs better than all other implementation in the basic CIM unit. Also, it is spotted that in the DB version the 2 × (128 × 128) yields the best EDAP, while in the basic version the best EDAP is obtained by 4 × (128 × 128). The reason why the DB version consumes less energy compared to the non-DB version is that the total energy consumed by other FUs reduces as the number of total required cycles declines.

Table 4. Energy and area results for different CIM unit configurations

Core	LoTTA	1 × (128 × 128)		1 × (512 × 512)		2 × (128 × 128)		2 × (256 × 256)		4 × (128 × 128)	
		non-DB	DB	non-DB	DB	non-DB	DB	non-DB	DB	non-DB	DB
Energy (mJ)	1.54	0.92	0.68	0.89	0.62	0.68	0.49	0.74	0.52	0.61	0.48
Area (μm^2)	10009	12175	12460	17534	18674	13761	14331	16934	18074	16934	18074
EDAP (10^9)	13.25	5.66	7.61	3.43	4.97	3.36	3.07	3.88	1.86	2.65	2.18

6 Conclusion

In this paper, we proposed a cycle-accurate simulator for memristor based CIM accelerators to scrutinize its challenges. The simulator offers a micro-ISA that allows a memristor crossbar to be integrated into a transport triggered architecture. The integration not only enhances the crossbar with general-purpose functional units to execute complex kernels but also enables us to study the challenges that are associated with a memristor crossbar deployment in a full-blown system.

Deploying CIM unit(s) shows huge improvements in terms of performance and energy, up to 3.9X speedup and 69% energy reduction. However, including CIM units has a price. The extra units increase the overall area. In our examples, the area increases between 21% and 86%. In addition, accuracy of the results may degrade since the architecture is not taken into account while the networks are trained. Hence, training should take the architecture properties into account. Of course it would elongate the training process [4]. The huge reduction of EDAP (up to 84%) is an extremely motivating point, though.

To follow up on this research, first, one can improve the CIM unit model by introducing non-ideal characteristics of both the memristor crossbars, such as IR drop, and noise, as well as the surrounding driving circuits, like process variation. This would certainly affect the final result and should be compensated by CIM unit characteristics aware training. Another interesting topic is to study the data reuse and local memory size on reducing the number of accesses to the global memory, which can further improve the energy and performance figures.

Acknowledgment. This research is supported by EC Horizon 2020 Research and Innovation Program through MNEMOSENE project under Grant 780215. The work also recevied support from the FitOptiVis project [1] funded by the ECSEL Joint Undertaking under grant number H2020-ECSEL-2017-2-783162.

References

1. Al-Ars, Z., et al.: The FitOptiVis ECSEL project: highly efficient distributed embedded image/video processing in cyber-physical systems. In: Proceedings of the 16th ACM International Conference on Computing Frontiers, CF 2019, pp. 333–338. (2019)
2. Ankit, A., et al.: Puma: a programmable ultra-efficient memristor-based accelerator for machine learning inference. In: Proceedings of the 24th International Conference on Architectural Support for Programming Languages and Operating Systems, ASPLOS 2019, pp. 715–731. Association for Computing Machinery, New York (2019)
3. Ansari, M., et al.: PHAX: Physical characteristics aware ex-situtraining framework for inverter-based memristive neuromorphic circuits. IEEE Trans. Comput. Aided Des. Integr. Circuits Syst. **37**(8), 1602–1613 (2017)
4. BanaGozar, A., Maleki, M.A., Kamal, M., Afzali-Kusha, A., Pedram, M.: Robust neuromorphic computing in the presence of process variation. In: Design, Automation Test in Europe Conference Exhibition (DATE), pp. 440–445 (2017)
5. BanaGozar, A., et al.: Cim-sim: computation in memory SIMulator. In: Proceedings of the 22nd International Workshop on Software and Compilers for Embedded Systems, pp. 1–4. ACM (2019)
6. Cai, F., et al.: A fully integrated reprogrammable memristor-CMOS system for efficient multiply-accumulate operations. Nat. Electron. **2**(7), 290–299 (2019)
7. Chen, P.Y., Peng, X., Yu, S.: NeuroSim+: an integrated device-to-algorithm framework for benchmarking synaptic devices and array architectures. In: 2017 IEEE International Electron Devices Meeting (IEDM), pp. 6–1. IEEE (2017)

8. Chi, P., et al..: Prime: a novel processing-in-memory architecture for neural network computation in ReRam-based main memory. In: Proceedings of the 43rd International Symposium on Computer Architecture, ISCA 2016, pp. 27–39. IEEE Press, Piscataway (2016)

9. Hamdioui, S., et al.: Applications of computation-in-memory architectures based on Memristive devices. In: 2019 Design, Automation Test in Europe Conference Exhibition (DATE), pp. 486–491 (2019)

10. Hu, M., Strachan, J.P., Li, Z., Stanley, R., et al.: Dot-product engine as computing memory to accelerate machine learning algorithms. In: 2016 17th International Symposium on Quality Electronic Design (ISQED). pp. 374–379. IEEE (2016)

11. Jiang, H., et al.: A novel true random number generator based on a stochastic diffusive memristor. Nat. Commun. 8(1), 882 (2017)

12. Le Gallo, M., Sebastian, A., Cherubini, G., Giefers, H., Eleftheriou, E.: Compressed sensing with approximate message passing using in-memory computing. IEEE Trans. Electron Devices 65(10), 4304–4312 (2018)

13. Le Gallo, M., et al.: Mixed-precision in-memory computing. Nat. Electron. 1(4), 246 (2018)

14. Li, S., Xu, C., Zou, Q., Zhao, J., Lu, Y., Xie, Y.: Pinatubo: a processing-in-memory architecture for bulk bitwise operations in emerging non-volatile memories. In: 2016 53nd ACM/EDAC/IEEE Design Automation Conference (DAC), pp. 1–6 June 2016

15. Mittal, S.: A survey of ReRAM-based architectures for processing-in-memory and neural networks. Mach. Learn. Knowl. Extr. 1(1), 75–114 (2018)

16. Multanen, J., Kultala, H., Jääskeläinen, P., Viitanen, T., Tervo, A., Takala, J.: Lotta: energy-efficient processor for always-on applications. In: 2018 IEEE International Workshop on Signal Processing Systems (SiPS), pp. 193–198. IEEE (2018)

17. Nair, R., et al.: Active memory cube: A processing-in-memory architecture for exascale systems. IBM J. Res. Dev. 59(2/3), 1–17 (2015)

18. Pi, S., Ghadiri-Sadrabadi, M., Bardin, J.C., Xia, Q.: Nanoscale memristive radiofrequency switches. Nat. Commun. 6, 7519 (2015)

19. Seshadri, V., et al.: Ambit: in-memory accelerator for bulk bitwise operations using commodity dram technology. In: Proceedings of the 50th Annual IEEE/ACM International Symposium on Microarchitecture, pp. 273–287. ACM (2017)

20. Shafiee, A., et al.: Isaac: a convolutional neural network accelerator with in-situ analog arithmetic in crossbars. In: Proceedings of the 43rd International Symposium on Computer Architecture, pp. 14–26. IEEE Press, Piscataway (2016)

21. Singh, G., et al.: A review of near-memory computing architectures: Opportunities and challenges. In: 2018 21st Euromicro Conference on Digital System Design (DSD), pp. 608–617. IEEE (2018)

22. Upadhyay, N.K., Jiang, H., Wang, Z., Asapu, S., Xia, Q., Joshua Yang, J.: Emerging memory devices for neuromorphic computing. Adv. Mater. Technol. 4(4), 1800589 (2019)

23. Wang, Z., et al.: Fully memristive neural networks for pattern classification with unsupervised learning. Nat. Electron. 1(2), 137 (2018)

24. Xia, L., et al.: MNSIM: simulation platform for memristor-based neuromorphic computing system. In: 2016 Design, Automation Test in Europe Conference Exhibition (DATE), pp. 469–474 (2016)

25. Xie, L., et al.: Scouting logic: a novel memristor-based logic design for resistive computing. In: 2017 IEEE Computer Society Annual Symposium on VLSI (ISVLSI), pp. 176–181. IEEE (2017)

26. Yang, J.J., Strukov, D.B., Stewart, D.R.: Memristive devices for computing. Nat. Nanotechnol. **8**(1), 13 (2013)
27. Zangeneh, M., Joshi, A.: Performance and energy models for memristor-based 1T1R RRAM cell. In: Proceedings of the Great Lakes Symposium on VLSI, GLSVLSI 2012, pp. 9–14. Association for Computing Machinery, New York (2012)
28. Zidan, M.A., Jeong, Y., Shin, J.H., Du, C., Zhang, Z., Lu, W.D.: Field-programmable crossbar array (FPCA) for reconfigurable computing. IEEE Trans. Multi-Scale Comput. Syst. **4**(4), 698–710 (2018)

Compiler Optimizations for Safe Insertion of Checkpoints in Intermittently Powered Systems

Bahram Yarahmadi[✉] and Erven Rohou[iD]

Univ Rennes, Inria, CNRS, IRISA, Rennes, France
{bahram.yarahmadi,erven.rohou}@inria.fr

Abstract. A large and increasing number of Internet-of-Things devices are not equipped with batteries and harvest energy from their environment. Many of them cannot be physically accessed once they are deployed (embedded in civil engineering structures, sent in the atmosphere or deep in the oceans). When they run out of energy, they stop executing and wait until the energy level reaches a threshold. Programming such devices is challenging in terms of ensuring memory consistency and guaranteeing forward progress. Previous work has proposed to insert checkpoints in the program so that execution can resume from well-defined locations. In this work, we propose to define these checkpoint locations based on statically-computed worst-case energy consumption of code sections. We also apply classical compiler optimizations in order to decrease the required number of checkpoints at runtime. As our method is based upon worst-case energy consumption, we can guarantee memory consistency and forward progress.

Keywords: Worst-case energy consumption · Static analysis · Energy harvesting · Checkpoint

1 Introduction

We live in the era of Internet of things (IoT) where the world around us is surrounded with a large number of tiny objects sensing, communicating and processing data in our environment. For these tiny objects, energy provision and consumption are challenging: it is not economically viable, or even physically possible to configure them with large, heavy, and high maintenance batteries. Recently, using energy harvesting techniques as an alternative way to supply energy without resorting to batteries has been proposed. In these techniques, energy is extracted from different sources in the environment (e.g., sun light or wind) and stored in a buffer such as a capacitor. However, one problem with harvested energy sources is that they are all unstable. This instability of energy sources and the small amount of energy a capacitor can store make the execution of programs interrupted by power failures. As a result, tasks with long running

© Springer Nature Switzerland AG 2020
A. Orailoglu et al. (Eds.): SAMOS 2020, LNCS 12471, pp. 169–185, 2020.
https://doi.org/10.1007/978-3-030-60939-9_12

processing time cannot be completed with a single charge of the capacitor. One way to guarantee forward progress to completion of tasks is by leveraging the idea of taking checkpoints. That is, storing all necessary volatile data such as processor state, program stack and heap into a persistent memory before energy depletion. When the energy becomes available again, all the volatile state will be copied back and the program can continue its execution.

On one hand, checkpointing volatile state of the program into the non-volatile memory available in embedded systems seems to be promising, as a program can have intermittent execution to completion. On the other hand, incautious taking of checkpoints either makes the system not to have forward progress or to suffer from performance and energy degradation. For instance, fewer number of checkpoints than what is needed, called the optimal number of checkpoints, causes at least a section of code to consume more energy than the maximum amount of energy in the capacitor. As a result, it makes the section to be executed repeatedly without any forward progress. This is a unique bug in intermittent computation jargon which is also called facing non-termination. On the contrary, taking more checkpoints that the optimal number one, wastes the system energy for doing unnecessary work, since taking checkpoint is not without cost. Also, Ransford and Lucia [21] pinpointed that checkpointing and resuming execution may lead to program correctness violations when the program performs side-effects, such as changing non-volatile data. For example, consider a case that a checkpoint is taken and then the program reads and modifies some data in non-volatile memory. If a power failure happens before reaching the following checkpoint, the system must rollback to the previous checkpoint and re-execute the same instructions. However, the second time, the data in non-volatile memory are not correct.

The contribution of this paper is the following:

- we propose a static, automatic, compiler-based technique for insertion of checkpoints that guarantees correctness and termination of a program on an intermittently powered system;
- we leverage compiler optimizations to reduce the number of checkpoints;
- we limit the burden on programmers to a negligible additional effort;
- we provide a portable solution not requiring any extra hardware support.

Section 2 is an overview of related work. Section 3 presents our method. We evaluate it in Sect. 4. We conclude in Sect. 5.

2   Related Work

Researchers have proposed software-only, joint hardware/software as well as fully hardware solutions for having forward progress as well as program correctness in energy harvesting systems. In this section, we will discuss them briefly.

To the best of our knowledge, Mementos [22] was the first solution addressing forward progress on a harvesting MCU. At compile-time, it inserts trigger points at different program locations such as loop-latches (aka tail of back-edges), and function returns. These trigger points are calls to a function that estimates the available energy at run-time by comparing the capacitor's voltage with a predefined threshold with the help of an analog-to-digital converter (ADC). If the voltage is below the threshold, Mementos checkpoints volatile state of the system onto non-volatile memory. Mementos cannot always guarantee forward progress. For instance when one iteration of the loop body consumes more energy than maximum energy in the capacitor. A driving principle of Mementos was to "reason minimally about energy at compile time, maximally at run time", because even expert programmers are not reliable when reasoning about energy. Conversely, we propose to do all the work at compile time, but also keep programmers out of the loop and rely only on automatic static analysis tools. Also, Mementos probes ADC at run-time regularly which is costly.

Ratchet [23] inserts checkpoints at compile-time. It exploits the notion of idempotency[1] for creating restartable code sections. It places checkpoints at idempotent region boundaries. However, because of limitations in alias analysis, the number of checkpoints might be more than needed. Ratchet only works with systems with one unified non-volatile memory. In contrast, our work is portable and works with any hardware regardless of the type of the memory.

Researchers have also presented task based programming models [8,19,20], where a programmer is responsible for decomposing the program into tasks that execute atomically. However, in these models, the programmer must be sure that a task's energy consumption does not exceed the maximum available energy in capacitor. Otherwise, the system would face the forward progress problem and would execute the same task repeatedly. To make sure that the application have forward progress, the programmer can act conservatively and place more task boundaries into the code results in wasting more time and energy. In summary, reasoning about the number and the size of tasks is painful and error-prone for programmers. The burden will be worst when it comes to changing the code or some features of the hardware such as capacitors as the programmer must reconstruct the whole process again.

A few prior works [2,5,9] also consider checkpoint placement by estimating energy. However, at some point in their work, they estimate energy by profiling or measurement techniques or they did not insert checkpoints based on WCEC (worst-case energy consumption). As a result, in both cases, their approaches are not safe. In contrast, our work proposes safety by leveraging WCEC. In addition, our work does not require any extra hardware feature. As far as we know, there exists only one work [25] which proposed checkpointing based on WCEC. The work is a runtime kernel which schedules tasks based on the estimated WCEC. Our work differs from it in a way that it is based on the WCEC of program sections and the control-flow graph of the program. Also, our work applies classical compiler optimization in order to decrease the number of checkpoints.

Recently, a series of solutions [3,4,14] requiring extra hardware support try to improve the whole process of taking checkpoint. Although these approaches

---

[1] A piece of code is *idempotent* if repeated subsequent invocations do not modify the state of the machine.

perform well as they take checkpoint when it is needed, they do not have the portability of software solutions. In addition, adding or using a hardware feature increases the energy consumption of the MCU.

3   WCEC Aware Checkpoint Placement

3.1   Technical Background

Determining checkpoint locations is based on the control flow graph (CFG) of the program. It is similar to the computation on worst-case execution time (WCET) estimates in the real-time domain [26].

The goal is to have a safe as well as tight estimation of the energy consumption of a program executing on the hardware. Safety means that the actual consumption must be less than, or equal to, the estimate, regardless of program input and dynamic events. Tightness means that the estimation must be as close as possible to actual WCEC. Herein, the safety property of WCEC guarantees forward progress and program correctness.

For the forward progress, safety guarantees that the energy consumption for reaching the next checkpoint is less than or equal to the energy a capacitor can provide, since checkpoints are placed based on WCEC with the distance of capacitor's maximum energy. We restrict the system to resume execution after a checkpoint only when the capacitor is full (it may enter a low-power mode for better efficiency). This way, we ensure that when the system wakes up from a checkpoint, it reaches the next one, where it waits for the capacitor the recharge.

This property also helps coping with the aforementioned memory consistency issue:

As re-execution do not occur, we avoid problems related to memory inconsistency or replaying side effects [21]. With the exception of the checkpoints and resuming code, the application follows its normal control flow.

Also, herein, the tightness of WCEC relates to the number of checkpoints relative to the optimal number. The tighter the WCEC, the lower the number of unnecessary checkpoints.

Estimating WCEC statically necessitates to have a representation of the program as well as an energy model which reflects the energy consumption of the system. For the former, the CFG of the program represents complex structures such as loops, conditions and function calls. For the latter, energy models at the lower levels of the software such as ISA are more accurate as they are closer to the hardware [10]. Figure 2 (a) shows a sub CFG of a program generated from the binary representation of the program. It contains eight basic blocks. The number besides each block indicates the worst-case amount of energy that the basic block consumes, computed based on the energy model (e.g. for simple architectures, by adding the amount of energy each instruction of the block consumes). In this CFG, the estimated worst-case consumption is 209 pJ.

For real-life applications, CFGs are large and the overall estimated WCEC is always much larger than the maximum energy a capacitor can provide.

Also, due to the branches and loops, the number of paths from the start node to the end node is large. For instance, in the above mentioned simple CFG, the number of paths from node A to node H is three. This number increases as the CFG gets larger and more complex with branches and loops.

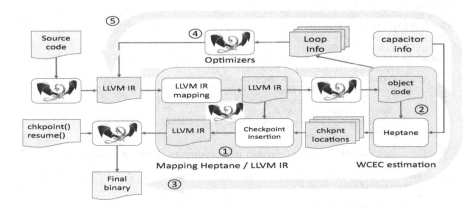

Fig. 1. Overview of our flow

As typical in the real-time domain, interrupts and preemption cannot be handled at this level. If present, they should be handled in a distinct part of the system runtime.

3.2   Approach

Problem Statement. For any given capacitor size (i.e. energy amount), our approach consists in inserting checkpoints at various places in the program such that, from any checkpoint, another checkpoint can be reached, regardless of the dynamic path taken by the application.

Solution. To make the problem tractable, we adopted an algorithm based on Single-Entry-Single-Exit (SESE) regions [15]. SESE regions may be complex, but they have a single well-defined entry as well as a single well-defined exit node. As such, they provide convenient placeholders for checkpoints. Also, these regions can be nested, sequentially composed or disjoint (see Fig. 2 (b)). The largest SESE region is the CFG itself as it has one start node and one end node[2]. The smallest SESE regions are basic blocks and instructions. In our work, since our granularity for checkpoint placement is basic blocks, we chose the basic block as the smallest SESE region.

The input of the algorithm (see Algorithm 1) is the CFG of the program with its corresponding SESE regions, and the capacitor size. The algorithm starts by

---

[2] Even in the presence of multiple return statements in, a function, a compiler can easily create a new block and add edges to it to guarantee a single exit node.

estimating the WCEC of the outermost region and if the estimated WCEC is bigger than the available energy, it recursively analyzes the nested regions.

Algorithm 1. Checkpoint Locating Algorithm

Data: CFG with Identified SESE Regions
Result: Checkpoint Locations
C is the energy of capacitor
CheckpointLocations is a vector of line numbers
r is the outermost region
IdentifyChKLocations(r,C)
  function IDENTIFYCHKLOCATIONS(*SESERegion R, AvailableEnergy E*)
     $e \leftarrow \delta$-WCEC(*Entry node of R,Exit node of R*)
     if $e > E$ **then**
        if *R has nesting regions* **then**
           $E \leftarrow E$ - *(Energy consumption of Entry node of R)*
           for *All Region N_i Nested in R* **do**
              $remainingEnergy \leftarrow min_i$ *(IDENTIFYCHKLOCATIONS(N_i,E))*
           end
        else
           remainingEnergy $\leftarrow$ C - e, Add this Location to CheckpointLocations
        end
     else
        remainingEnergy $\leftarrow$ E - e
     end
     return *remainingEnergy*
  end function

For estimating the energy of a region, we rely on partial WCET estimation (δ-WCET) proposed by Bouziane et al. [6,7]. However, for the sake of clarity in Algorithm 1, we used energy consumption in lieu of execution time wherever relevant. For instance, consider the CFG of Fig. 2 (b), and assume the capacitor can store 80 pJ. The algorithm first estimates the energy of region R1. Since the estimated value exceeds 80 pJ, it recursively estimates the energy of R2 and R3 after subtracting the cost of block A (remaining energy of 32 pJ = 80 pJ − 48 pJ). It continues until it reaches the innermost SESE regions (basic block) and it places a checkpoint at the beginning of that basic block. The algorithm returns the amount of remaining energy. When it places a checkpoint, the return value will be the maximum amount of energy in the capacitor subtracted by the energy consumption of the basic block Fig. 2 (c) shows the CFG with inserted checkpoints.

As shown, the input of the proposed toolchain is the capacitor size and high-level C code annotated with maximum loop bound information. It is worth noting that specifying this information is the only supplementary effort requested from the programmer, and it is typical of embedded real-time systems. The output of our tool-chain is a binary code enriched with checkpoint trigger calls. Each checkpoint trigger is a call to a run-time library which is responsible for checkpointing the volatile state of the program into the non-volatile memory. The overhead and the energy cost of checkpointing itself is highly dependent on the underlying architecture. For architecture with non-volatile memory as unified memory, the cost of checkpointing is almost constant since only CPU registers must be copied. However, for systems configured with a volatile memory such as SRAM as well as a type of non-volatile memory, the cost of checkpointing is

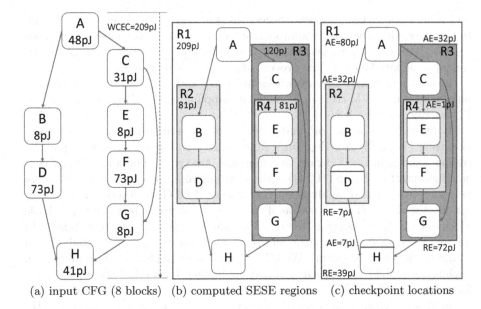

(a) input CFG (8 blocks)   (b) computed SESE regions   (c) checkpoint locations

Fig. 2. Input CFG, computed single-entry single-exit regions, and selected checkpoint locations (red lines, AE = available energy, RE = remaining energy) (Color figure online)

variable and dependent on program state such as the size of stack and heap, as well as the amount of live data at the time of checkpointing. In the latter case, we need to guarantee we have enough energy to perform the checkpointing in the worst case, and the location of the checkpoint matters. In the worst case the system must have enough energy to checkpoint all volatile memory.

Our solution can deal with both types of architectures. However, in this work, we assume that there is always enough energy available for checkpointing a constant number of CPU registers in the former case or all volatile memory in the latter case, and we focus on the placement of checkpoints that guarantees correctness, and forward progress.

3.3   WCEC Estimation

Our implementation consists of a component for estimating the WCEC (Heptane [13], see Sect. 3.3), augmented with a checkpoint insertion algorithm.

Figure 1 shows the overview of our flow. The first component (box ① in the figure) is LLVM augmented by a few passes. It first builds a mapping between LLVM IR and binary code (see Sect. 3.4), compiles the code and invokes our WCEC estimation tool. This tool, called Heptane (box ② in the figure) determines where checkpoints should be located based on information about the capacitor and a power model of the architecture. This information is fed back to LLVM for actual insertion of the checkpoints and production of the binary. This process is highlighted by the arrow designated as ③. We also explored how loop optimizations can be leveraged to decrease the cost of checkpoints (Sect. 3.6). In this case, Heptane selects appropriate loop optimizations that are forwarded to LLVM (box ④). This results in a new version of the program in LLVM IR (arrow designated as ⑤). The process of arrow ③ is repeated.

In addition, since Heptane works in binary code and our final checkpoint placement is in LLVM IR [16], we added a mapping between Heptane and LLVM IR described in Sect. 3.4.

Heptane [13] is a tool originally developed for estimating worst-case execution time (WCET) [26]. Heptane's functionality is divided into two separated components: **Heptane Extract** and **Heptane Analysis**. The former is for generating control-flow graph (CFG) of the program from the object code. The latter performs two types of analysis on the generated CFG: high-level analysis and low-level analysis. The low-level analysis compute an upper-bound for each basic block in CFG by considering the cost of instructions as well as features related to micro-architecture such as cache and pipeline. Then, the high-level analysis can compute the whole program's WCET by performing Implicit Path Enumeration Technique (IPET) [18] which is based on Integer Linear Programming (ILP) formulation of the WCET calculation problem.

In this work, since our concern is energy, inspired by Wägemann et al. [24], an energy cost for each instruction is specified instead of cycle cost that Heptane normally considers. Due to the simplicity of the processors in the domain, that is processors without caches and branch prediction, applying complex analysis in Heptane is not necessary. However, our approach is general and can include more complex architectures as long as an accurate (and safe) energy model is provided by manufacturer. Also, herein, the goal of work is not the WCEC of the whole program; instead we want to fragment the program into code sections which can be executed in one life cycle when the capacitor is fully charged. These code sections are bounded by checkpoint trigger calls. As a result, the location of these checkpoint trigger calls in the program must be identified.

3.4 Mapping Between Heptane and LLVM IR

Since the analysis part is performed on binary code, and placing checkpoint trigger calls is applied at LLVM IR level, we need a mapping between the two. To achieve this, inspired from Grech et al. [11], we "hijacked" the debug information mechanism that propagates source-location information into a binary: at LLVM-level, we replace source location by the line number in the LLVM representation. The regular toolchain processes it as usual, carrying our information instead of traditional source line numbers.

We created two LLVM passes. *Source Line to LLVM IR* traverses the LLVM IR and replaces source location information with LLVM IR location information. After this pass, the binary code is generated and given to Heptane. As mentioned, the output of Heptane is a series of line numbers which specify where to place checkpoint triggers in LLVM IR. The *Checkpoint placement* is responsible to place checkpoint triggers based on the line numbers that Heptane produces.

After this pass, the final binary code is generated and the program is ready to be executed on energy harvesting device.

3.5   Coping with Non-termination

In our work, coping with non-termination and guaranteeing forward progress through the execution of programs is straightforward. In the WCEC analysis part, Heptane checks for every basic block whether its energy consumption exceeds the capacitor energy when it is fully charged. If a basic block consumes more energy than the maximum amount of energy in the capacitor, that basic block can easily be broken into smaller ones by the compiler. For that, Heptane reports the line numbers of the basic blocks that are too long. LLVM subsequently splits these blocks and applies LLVM IR mapping pass again. It is worth noting that this process could also be done at assembly level. However, herein for the sake of simplicity we preferred to do at LLVM IR level.

3.6   WCEC-Aware Compiler Transformations and Optimizations

Compiler optimizations heavily modify the structure of programs, hence the locations of checkpoints. As shown in the experimental section, optimizations are vital to decrease the amount of checkpointing at runtime. Our objective here is not to provide an exhaustive study of the impact of every optimizations, but rather to demonstrate the benefit of selected optimizations to the energy management of intermittently powered systems. As loops are the most time and energy consuming part of programs, we have chosen optimizations on loops. Also, placing checkpoints in loops can increase the energy consumption of the execution, making it critical to process loops with care.

Clearly, not all optimizations can be applied to all loops, since data dependences must be checked to guarantee program semantics is preserved. In this section, we briefly introduce the optimizations that we have selected. An exhaustive survey of compiler optimizations, their applicability and advantages can be found in Bacon et al. [1].

Conditional checkpoints is the simplest optimization that our toolchain applies, making checkpoints conditional on the loop iteration number. This is advantageous when a full charge of the capacitor is not enough to execute the entire loop, but we can prove that it can execute several iterations. Checkpointing at each iteration would be inefficient. This is illustrated on Fig. 3 (a) and (b) respectively for the original loop, and the transformation, assuming we can execute three iterations of the loop with a single charge. This is always correct. Note that the same effect would be achieved by unrolling the loop three times and inserting a single checkpoint. Unrolling, however, increases code size and it is rarely applied on small systems with limited amount of memory.

Loop splitting divides the iteration space in two pieces (or more) with the same loop body. An example is given in Fig. 3 (c). The effect is similar to conditional checkpoints, but it saves the cost of the condition, at the expense of duplicating the loop body.

Each generated loop can be executed in one charge of capacitor. Splitting is always legal.

Loop fission (aka loop distribution) also divides a loop into pieces, but takes statements apart. See the example on Fig. 3 (d). Depending on the energy cost of the statements (S1 and S2 in the figure) and the value of n, it may offer more interesting tradeoffs. In this optimization new loops have less energy consumption and can be processed in one charge of capacitor. The checkpoint trigger call is also between two loops. Fission is not always legal, and depends on the type of dependence between S1 and S2, if any.

Loop interchange consists in swapping two loops in a loop nest (see Fig. 3 (e) and (f) respectively for original and transformed loop nests). This is profitable when $n < m$ and the body of the nested loop can be executed m times with a single charge. This reduces the number of taken checkpoints from m to n. Interchange is not always legal, depending on dependences. It also impacts locality, however small intermittently powered devices typically do not feature a data cache. In case they do, the reduction in the number of checkpoints should be balanced with the overhead in cache misses.

Optimizations are not hindered by checkpoint insertion which is applied later in the compilation flow. It is worth noting that each optimization affects the estimated WCEC. For instance, in conditional checkpoints, a few instructions are being added which alter the WCEC. For preserving the safety of the WCEC, we run Heptane for the second time after each optimization. Also, one complication derives from the fact that loop bounds must be statically known for the tools to estimate a worst-case execution time/energy consumption. This is typically done by manually adding annotations to loops in source code, and disabling compiler optimizations to guarantee that the CFGs at source and binary levels match. Tracing loop bounds through the entire compilation flow is complex. We address a simpler problem, focusing particular loops and applying a limited repertoire of transformations. For example, the bounds of a split loop are obtained by dividing the original bound by two. Fission creates a new loop with the same bound. In the case of interchange, bounds must be interchanged as well. For a larger set of optimization, careful tracking of annotations must be enforced. However, previous work by Li et al. [17] has shown the feasibility.

To preserve the safety of the WCEC estimation, after each optimization, the WCEC estimation part of our tool-chain checks that with the insertion of the checkpoint and the transformation the new WCEC provides safety. When the safety is approved with the WCEC part, the generated binary code can be executed on the device.

`for(i=0; i < n; i++) {`
  `S1;`
  `S2;`
`}`
 	
(a) original loop
	`for(i=0; i < n; i++) {`
	  `if (i % 3 == 0)`
	    `checkpoint();`
	  `S1;`
	  `S2;`
	`}`
	(b) conditional checkpoint
		`for(i=0; i < m; i++) {`
		  `for(j=0; j < n; j++) {`
		    `S1;`
		  `}`
		`}`
		(e) original loop nest

`for(i=0; i < n/2; i++) {`
  `S1;`
  `S2;`
`}`
`checkpoint();`
`for( ; i < n; i++) {`
  `S1;`
  `S2;`
`}`
(c) loop splitting
	`for(i=0; i < n; i++) {`
	  `S1;`
	`}`
	`checkpoint();`
	`for(i=0; i < n; i++) {`
	  `S2;`
	`}`
	(d) loop fission
		`for(j=0; j < n; j++) {`
		  `checkpoint();`
		  `for(i=0; i < m; i++) {`
		    `S1;`
		  `}`
		`}`
		(f) loop interchange

Fig. 3. Loop optimizations

Table 1. Benchmarks used for the evaluation

Benchmark	Description
bs	Binary search for the array of 15 integer elements
bsort100	Bubblesort program
crc	Cyclic redundancy check computation on 40 bytes of data
edn	Finite Impulse Response (FIR) filter calculations
fdct	Fast Discrete Cosine Transform
fibcall	Iterative Fibonacci, used to calculate fib(30)
insertsort	Insertion sort on a reversed array of size 10
minmax	Simple program with infeasible paths and without loops
ndes	Complex embedded code. Bit manipulation, shifts, array and matrix calculations
mm	rectangular matrix multiplication

4 Evaluation

Settings. We assigned an energy cost to each instruction for ARMv6-m ISA, derived from an actual core synthesized in 28 nm ST FDSOI. This ISA is used for a number of processors such as ARM Cortex-M0+ in low-power domains. We run the final executable generated by our tool-chain in a modified version of a cycle-accurate simulator for the mentioned ISA [23].

Benchmarks. We selected nine benchmarks (Table 1) from the Mälardalen suite [12]. They are highly used in research publications on embedded systems and sensors. In addition, in terms of CFG complexity, they contain loops, inner-loops and function calls. Therefore, they can show the effectiveness and correctness of the proposed checkpoint placement strategy. Also, they perform a significant amount of computation in the main MCU core, as this work is only

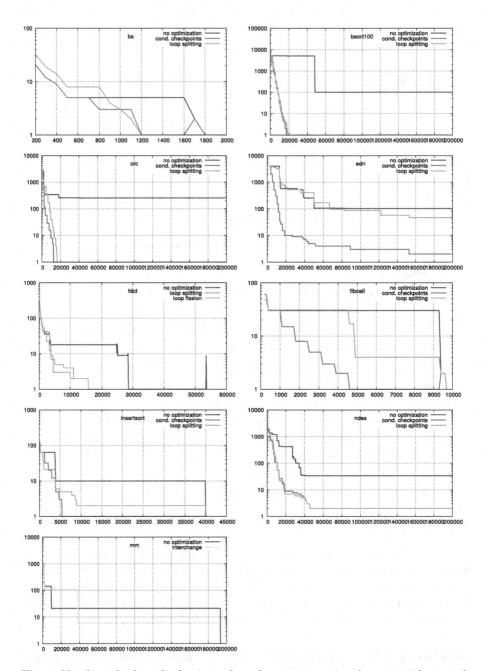

Fig. 4. Number of taken checkpoints when the capacitor size changes, without and with optimizations. The x-axis represents the capacitor size in picojoules (pJ). The y-axis represents the number of checkpoints taken at runtime (logscale) (Color figure online).

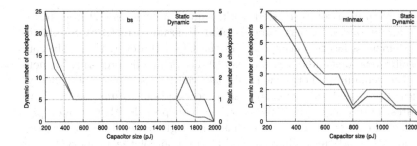

Fig. 5. Evolution of the dynamic (left axis) and static (right axis) numbers of checkpoints. No optimization is applied.

focusing on the main CPU computation. We added a matrix multiplication we developed ourselves to experiment with cases not covered in the suite.

Experiments. To show the sensitivity of our approach, we tested several benchmarks with a wide range of capacitor sizes, selected with respect to the overall WCEC of the benchmark. We apply our algorithm to insert checkpoints, run the program in the simulator, and report the number of checkpoints taken during execution. On Fig. 4, the bold purple line shows the number of checkpoints in the absence of optimizations, while other lines show the impact of individual optimizations. minmax is not reported here because it contains no loop, we discuss is below.

We explored with very small capacitor sizes, such as 200 pJ, which may not be realistic for deployed IoT systems[3]. The reasons are: 1) the Mälardalen benchmarks have rather small execution times and we still wanted to experiment with a wide range of values; 2) we wanted to test the scalability of our approach towards small as well as large values.

Number of Executed Checkpoints. As expected, our strategy is sensitive to capacitor size, and the number of taken checkpoints decreases when the capacitor size increases. However, we also observe long plateaus where the number of checkpoints remains constant for a wide range of capacitor sizes (e.g. bs between 500 pJ and 1600 pJ). The main reason for that is the presence of loops. As long as the execution of the entire loop (with worst-case trip count) requires more energy than the capacitor can provide, a checkpoint must be placed inside the loop body. In some cases, it also happens that our toolchain cannot place the checkpoints exactly where Heptane suggested (i.e. just outside the loop) because LLVM IR instructions are sometimes slightly coarser than assembly instructions. This explains the occasional peaks of the curves.

---

[3] The available energy can be related to the capacitance C through the formula $E = \frac{1}{2}C(V_{start}^2 - V_{stop}^2)$, where V_{start} and V_{stop} represent voltages when the capacitor is full, and when the system is forced to stop because the voltage is too low.

Our work in comparison to related work, namely Mementos [22] from Ransford et al. can guarantee forward progress and program correctness. Similar to our work, Mementos inserts checkpoints in the CFG. However, they only considered specific locations and opted for loop latches or function returns. Mementos checks the remaining energy (actually the voltage as a proxy for energy) only at these predefined locations. In case a loop body or a function (without loop) requires more energy than the capacitor can provide, they cannot prevent unprotected energy depletion, and thus cannot guarantee forward progress. Also, if Mementos had the ability to modify the non-volatile memory by the program semantic, a failure may corrupt the memory and cause the program to be incorrect. In comparison to Ratchet [23], which checkpoints between every WAR dependence, our work is more efficient in terms of number of both static and dynamic checkpoints. For instance, Ratchet is forced to insert checkpoints in the example provided in this paper [2] no matter how much energy is in the capacitor size. But, as our checkpoint placement is sensitive to the capacitor size, it can place checkpoints outside the loop whenever it is possible to process a loop with one full charge of capacitor.

Impact of Optimizations. Our results show that optimizations have the capability to reduce the number of necessary checkpoints.

First, making checkpoints conditional is always beneficial, and this can have dramatic impact. For example, unoptimized fibcall requires 30 checkpoints to complete execution, whereas conditional checkpoints can progressively reduce this number down to 15, then 8, and so on. The same behavior is visible in all benchmarks.

Loop splitting is also very effective, and in most cases similar to conditional checkpointing. When they differ, splitting is usually underperforming. This is visible in bs for small capacitor sizes, as well as fibcall and crc. Yet, in some occasions, splitting slightly outperforms conditional checkpointing: particular values in bs, or ndes between 20,000 pJ and 40,000 pJ.

Fission was applicable to fdct. It is similar in effect to splitting, slightly better or slightly worse, depending on values.

Interchange was not successfully applied to our set of benchmarks. This is why we added a simple matrix multiplication example. Our results show that interchange can reduce significantly the number of checkpoints for 141 to 111 for small sizes, and from 21 to 6 for larger sizes. For intermediate values, interchange degrades performance.

In some cases, optimizations produce worse results than unoptimized code. This can be observed with splitting in bs for small values, edn, and marginally in fibcall (31 vs. 30), as well as interchange as discussed. This behavior is not different from optimizing for performance that is tuned for average case and occasionally results in poor performance.

So far, we only experimented with applying a single optimization at a time, in order to show the potential. It is well known that optimizations interact in complex. A promising direction consists in combining many optimizations to decrease the number of checkpoints. Iterative compilation can certainly be applied to explore a region of interest of the optimization search space, and heuristics be developed in a way similar to compiling for performance.

Number of Static Checkpoints. Figure 5 shows the static number of checkpoints inserted along with the number of times they are taken at runtime (dynamic number on the left axis, static on the right). We only report a limited number of benchmarks, as they all exhibit the same behavior.

Overall, the number of static checkpoints is decreasing as the number of dynamic checkpoints, as expected. However, there are exceptions, as in bs. The reason for that is when it is possible to process the whole loop with a full charge of capacitor size, our algorithm places two checkpoints right before and after loop instead of placing the checkpoint inside the loop. The first checkpoint is to have energy for processing loop and the second checkpoint is to have energy for continuing the rest of the code. The number of static checkpoints only impacts on the code size. However, each checkpoint that it is taken at run-time consumes time and energy. So, it is worthy to increase the number of static checkpoints whenever it is possible to decrease the number of dynamic ones. For minmax, when the capacitor size is increased from 800 pJ, an increase in the number of static and dynamic checkpoint is observed. This is because our algorithm is biased to place checkpoints before a function call as a function might have more than one context (call site). However, minmax is a very simple program, all functions have only one context. It is better to process the function and place the checkpoint when it is necessary. In the future we will consider the number of contexts of a function and improve the number of checkpoints. Also, minmax is a benchmark without loop and it has infeasible paths which are never taken at runtime. This is the reason that the number of static checkpoints for some capacitor sizes is larger than the number of dynamic checkpoints.

5 Conclusion

We propose a compile-time checkpoint insertion strategy for intermittently powered system. Our approach simultaneously guarantees program correctness and forward progress. It does not require any additional hardware. To achieve this, our toolchain inserts checkpoint trigger calls based on worst-case energy consumption of program sections. The called function saves the state of the program to non-volatile memory before the energy depletes. In addition, we show that classical compiler optimizations can be exploited to reduce the number of checkpoints, hence the overhead.

References

1. Bacon, D.F., Graham, S.L., Sharp, O.J.: Compiler transformations for high-performance computing. ACM Comput. Surv. **26**(4), 345–420 (1994)
2. Baghsorkhi, S.S., Margiolas, C.: Automating efficient variable-grained resiliency for low-power IoT systems. In: CGO, pp. 38–49. ACM (2018)

3. Balsamo, D., et al.: Hibernus++: a self-calibrating and adaptive system for transiently-powered embedded devices. IEEE TCAD **35**(12), 1968–1980 (2016)
4. Balsamo, D., Weddell, A.S., Merrett, G.V., Al-Hashimi, B.M., Brunelli, D., Benini, L.: Hibernus: sustaining computation during intermittent supply for energy-harvesting systems. IEEE Embed. Syst. Lett. **7**(1), 15–18 (2015)
5. Bhatti, N.A., Mottola, L.: HarvOS: efficient code instrumentation for transiently-powered embedded sensing. In: IPSN. IEEE (2017)
6. Bouziane, R., Rohou, E., Gamatié, A.: Energy-efficient memory mappings based on partial WCET analysis and multi-retention time STT-RAM. In: RTNS (2018)
7. Bouziane, R., Rohou, E., Gamatié, A.: Partial worst-case execution time analysis. In: Conférence d'informatique en Parallélisme, Architecture et Système (2018)
8. Colin, A., Lucia, B.: Chain: tasks and channels for reliable intermittent programs. In: ACM SIGPLAN Notices, vol. 51, pp. 514–530. ACM (2016)
9. Colin, A., Lucia, B.: Termination checking and task decomposition for task-based intermittent programs. In: International Conference on Compiler Construction. ACM (2018)
10. Georgiou, K., Xavier-de Souza, S., Eder, K.: The IoT energy challenge: a software perspective. IEEE Embedded Syst. Lett. **10**(3), 53–56 (2018)
11. Grech, N., Georgiou, K., Pallister, J., Kerrison, S., Eder, K.: Static energy consumption analysis of LLVM IR programs. arXiv (2014)
12. Gustafsson, J., Betts, A., Ermedahl, A., Lisper, B.: The mälardalen WCET benchmarks: past, present and future. In: International Workshop on Worst-Case Execution Time Analysis (2010)
13. Hardy, D., Rouxel, B., Puaut, I.: The Heptane static worst-case execution time estimation tool. In: International Workshop on Worst-Case Execution Time Analysis (2017)
14. Jayakumar, H., Raha, A., Raghunathan, V.: QuickRecall: a low overhead HW/SW approach for enabling computations across power cycles in transiently powered computers. In: 27th International Conference on VLSI Design and 13th International Conference on Embedded Systems. IEEE (2014)
15. Johnson, R., Pearson, D., Pingali, K.: The program structure tree: computing control regions in linear time. In: ACM SigPlan Notices, vol. 29. ACM (1994)
16. Lattner, C., Adve, V.: LLVM: A compilation framework for lifelong program analysis & transformation. In: CGO. IEEE Computer Society (2004)
17. Li, H., Puaut, I., Rohou, E.: Tracing flow information for tighter WCET estimation: application to vectorization. In: RTCSA. IEEE (2015)
18. Li, Y.T.S., Malik, S.: Performance analysis of embedded software using implicit path enumeration. In: ACM SIGPLAN Notices, vol. 30. ACM (1995)
19. Lucia, B., Ransford, B.: A simpler, safer programming and execution model for intermittent systems. ACM SIGPLAN Not. **50**(6), 575–585 (2015)
20. Maeng, K., Colin, A., Lucia, B.: Alpaca: intermittent execution without checkpoints. Oopsla **1** (2017)
21. Ransford, B., Lucia, B.: Nonvolatile memory is a broken time machine. In: Workshop on Memory Systems Performance and Correctness. ACM (2014)
22. Ransford, B., Sorber, J., Fu, K.: Mementos: system support for long-running computation on RFID-scale devices. In: ACM SIGARCH Computer Architecture News, vol. 39. ACM (2011)
23. Van Der Woude, J., Hicks, M.: Intermittent computation without hardware support or programmer intervention. In: USENIX OSDI (2016)

24. Wägemann, P., Distler, T., Hönig, T., Janker, H., Kapitza, R., Schröder-Preikschat, W.: Worst-case energy consumption analysis for energy-constrained embedded systems. In: ECRTS. IEEE (2015)
25. Wägemann, P., Distler, T., Janker, H., Raffeck, P., Sieh, V.: A kernel for energy-neutral real-time systems with mixed criticalities. In: RTAS. IEEE (2016)
26. Wilhelm, R., et al.: The worst-case execution-time problem–overview of methods and survey of tools. ACM TECS **7**(3), 1–53 (2008)

Fine-Grained Power Modeling
of Multicore Processors Using FFNNs

Mark Sagi$^{(\boxtimes)}$, Nguyen Anh Vu Doan, Nael Fasfous, Thomas Wild,
and Andreas Herkersdorf

Technical University of Munich, Munich, Germany
{mark.sagi,anhvu.doan,nael.fasfous,thomas.wild,herkersdorf}@tum.de

Abstract. To minimize power consumption while maximizing performance, today's multicore processors rely on fine-grained run-time
dynamic power information – both in the time domain, e.g. μs to ms,
and space domain, e.g. core-level. The state-of-the-art for deriving such
power information is mainly based on predetermined power models which
use linear modeling techniques to determine the core-performance/core-
power relationship. However, with multicore processors becoming ever
more complex, linear modeling techniques cannot capture all possible
core-performance related power states anymore. Although, artificial neural networks (ANN) have been proposed for coarse-grained power modeling of servers with time resolutions in the range of seconds, no work has
yet investigated fine-grained ANN-based power modeling. In this paper,
we explore feed-forward neural networks (FFNNs) for core-level power
modeling with estimation rates in the range of 10 kHz. To achieve a high
estimation accuracy, we determine optimized neural network architectures and train FFNNs on performance counter and power data from
a complex-out-of-order processor architecture. We show that, relative
power estimation error decreases on average by 7.5% compared to a
state-of-the-art linear power modeling approach and decreases by 5.5%
compared to a multivariate polynomial regression model. Furthermore,
we propose an implementation for run-time inference of the power modeling FFNN and show that the area overhead is negligible.

Keywords: Processor · Multicore · Power · Modeling · Estimation ·
Core-level · Artificial neural network · ANN · FFNN · Accuracy ·
Error · Overhead

1 Introduction

To take effective management decisions, both power and thermal (P&T) management of multicores depend on accurate run-time dynamic power consumption information at core-level. Due to the cost-prohibitive nature of actually
measuring core power, such run-time power information is usually derived from
predetermined power models [14] which use observable performance counters,

© Springer Nature Switzerland AG 2020
A. Orailoglu et al. (Eds.): SAMOS 2020, LNCS 12471, pp. 186–199, 2020.
https://doi.org/10.1007/978-3-030-60939-9_13

operating frequency and voltage as inputs. The performance counters are necessary to model the activity and thus indirectly the power consumption of each core. Apart from the spatial resolution (core-level), such dynamic power information also has to have a high time resolution (μs to ms) to be useful for P&T management of the processor [16,17]. Most dynamic power models with such spatial and time resolution commonly assume a linear relationship between performance counters and dynamic power and a nonlinear relationship between changes of the voltage/frequency state and dynamic power [2,4,6,9,18,21,22].

Previous works have shown that the relationship between performance counters and dynamic core power can also be nonlinear at core-level at least for low time-resolutions (1 s) [13]. Furthermore, for server level energy accounting with low time resolutions (0.5 Hz–1 Hz), multiple works have already proposed using ANNs for power/energy modeling to capture such nonlinear relationships [7,12,20,24]. However, increasing complexity of modern core architectures integrating hundreds of millions of transistors per core and the importance of effective P&T management increasingly necessitate fine-grained high accuracy power models capturing nonlinear performance counter/power relationships. We therefore investigate the use of FFNNs for high rate power estimations on core-level and the associated run-time inference overhead. A motivational example for using FFNNs is given in Fig. 1 showing core power on the y-axis and a time frame of 250 ms on the x-axis. PARSEC raytrace is executed and actual power is shown with the green line; estimated power based on a linear model is shown as the red line and estimated power based on an FFNN model is shown with the blue line. One can see that the FFNN model more accurately estimates the actual power consumption than the linear model thus minimizing estimation error which allows for more effective P&T management.

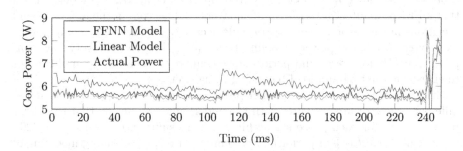

Fig. 1. Actual core power compared to power estimations using an ANN model and a linear model (Color figure online)

With this paper we make the following contributions toward fine-grained run-time power estimation of multicores:

– We explore FFNNs for power estimation on core-level with an estimation rate of 10 kHz.

- We optimize ANN hyperparameters, e.g. number of layers and neurons, with the goal of minimizing estimation error while avoiding overfitting.
- We show that relative estimation error decreases by 7.5% compared to a state-of-the-art linear modeling approach and by 5.5% compared to a multivariate polynomial regression model.
- We propose a micro-controller implementation for run-time inference for power estimation and discuss its negligible area overhead.

2   Related Work

A range of different methodologies for run-time dynamic power estimation on core-level or even on core-component-level for multicore processors have been proposed. Works which focus on a high estimation rates usually rely on linear models to describe the relation between performance counters and dynamic power and can be found for Intel or AMD multicore processors in [2,4,6], for IBM multicore processors in [9] and for embedded ARM multicore processors in [18,21,22].

McCullough et al. first identified non-linear power responses due to changing workloads in multicore power traces which have to be accounted for in power models [13]. They traced power consumption of an Intel Core i7, broke down power consumption on core-level and explored both linear and non-linear modeling techniques (polynomial regression and support vector regression). However, the sampling rate was comparatively low (1 Hz) and their non-linear models did not significantly improve upon linear models.

Further non-linear modeling techniques gained traction in the research area of power/energy modeling for datacenter systems and cloud servers. The first to propose ANNs for power modeling were Cupertino et al. [7]. They determined that a FFNN architecture with 2 hidden layers – 20 neurons in the first layer and 5 neurons in the second layer – to provide accuracy improvements compared to state-of-the-art linear power modeling techniques. However, the very low sampling rate 3 Hz for power and performance counter data limits the applicability to energy accounting and load balancing in datacenters.

In [10], ANNs were used to predict power consumption of applications across different processor architectures with the underlying assumption that the linear power models for each processor architecture are sufficiently accurate. In [20], the so called *additivity* of performance counters in regard to energy modeling of multicores is explored were additivity denotes the robustness of reusing a performance counter as model input for a wide range of applications. To determine the additivity of performance counters for their energy model generation, the use of linear, tree based and ANN models was investigated. However, parametrization and optimization of the neural network models is not discussed and the focus was on full system energy modeling with low estimation rates.

Another work exploring three different ANNs (FFNN, Elman and LSTM) for cloud server power modeling is given in [12] with BP and Elman having a single hidden layer with 25 neurons and the LSTM having 2 hidden layers with

10 neurons each. The resulting power model provides high accuracy at course-grained spatial (system-level) and time (1 Hz) resolution. In contrast to our work, core-level power models with high estimation rates (10 kHz) were not explored. Recurrent Elman neural networks have been proposed for course-grained power modeling of cloud servers where one hidden layer encodes power states and which exploits time series performance information [24]. Finally, for system design, the development of P&T management algorithms and power modeling algorithms, power simulators are often used, e.g. McPAT [11]. Although, the underlying principles of such power simulators are highly accurate, they cannot be used for runtime power estimation due to their large computational overhead.

In contrast to previous work, this paper focuses on generating FFNN-based power models accounting for non-linear effects with fine-grained spatial (core-level) and time (10 kHz) resolution with the resulting power estimations being applicable for run-time P&T management purposes. Extending the power estimations to the core-level and increasing the time resolution by four orders of magnitude, make a thorough investigation of the needed FFNN complexity – in regard to number of hidden layers and neurons – and the overhead for run-time inference necessary.

3   Feed-Forward Neural Networks for Power Modeling

Power modeling for runtime power estimation is inherently a regression problem with the desired power information as dependent variable and the performance counters as independent variables. We focus on dynamic core-level power information $P_{core,j}$ where j denotes the j-th core of the multicore processor. The core power is estimated during run-time through n performance counters PC_i with $0 \leq i \leq n$ all related to their respective cores. With actual $P_{core,j}$ not being observable for each individual core, we use the following approximation for the model generation step when only the j-th core is active at a time:

$$P_{core,j} = P_{pack} - P_{idle}. \tag{1}$$

Package-level power P_{pack} can be observed through instrumentation of the mainboard, i.e. actual power sensors, and P_{idle} is the idle power of the processor when no core is active. With only P_{pack} being actually observable, we generate different models (FFNN, polynomial, linear) for P_{pack} and subtract P_{idle} to derive core-level power consumption. Therefore, the PC_i and P_{pack} data used for model generation is reduced to timeframes where only a single core is active at a time to capture the power response of that particular core. As we only investigate a homogeneous multicore processor in this work, the power models for the j-th core can be generalized to any core of the system by using the performance counters of those cores as model input, respectively. The error (cost) function for generating the subsequent power models is then:

$$P_{pack,error} = |P_{pack,act} - P_{pack,est}| \tag{2}$$

where the subscripts $_{est}$ and $_{act}$ indicate estimated power and actual observed power, respectively.

3.1   ANN Architecture

There exist a multitude of ANN architectures, e.g. FFNN, Elman, LSTM, for modeling and prediction of non-linear functions and systems. With most fine-grained power models using linear regression models, we keep our analysis to comparatively simple ANN architectures. Our goal is to achieve higher estimation accuracies than with linear modeling techniques while adding as little additional modeling complexity and run-time overhead as possible. For this reason, we choose well-known feedforward networks which can theoretically model any nonlinear function according to the universal approximation theorem [8]. Similar to previous works, we do not use any input delay on the PC_i inputs, i.e. we do not generate any autoregressive models. While linear regression models are at risk of underfitting the underlying dynamic power relationship, FFNNs are at risk of both underfitting and overfitting the power relationship. With a finite amount of training data, FFNNs of sufficient size can fit each data point perfectly, i.e. memorize the data, while not actually learning the underlying relationship. In that case, the PC_i data is overfitted and the estimation errors on P_{core} for untrained PC_i data will be significant. Therefore, careful consideration has to be taken of the chosen hyperparameters of the FFNN which are distinguished between *algorithm* hyperparameters (learning related) and *model* hyperparameters (architecture related). For the algorithm hyperparameters, we train a number of networks for dynamic power estimation and compare both the resulting accuracy as well as training time and find that conjugate gradient backpropagation with Polak-Ribiére updates provide the best training speed/accuracy trade-off. As stop conditions for training the FFNN, we use the following:

- stop after 1000 training epochs OR,
- an MSE below 1% on the training data OR,
- a minimum performance gradient of $1 \cdot 10^{-5}$ OR,
- 5 subsequent failed validation tests where additional training leads to higher estimation errors on the validation data.

The question of how to determine the optimal FFNN model hyperparameters is still an ongoing topic of research, therefore, we follow best practices for the hyperparametrization. As a first step, the model hyperparameters have to be confined. For the activation function of the hidden neurons, we choose tanh after sweeping over a set of different activation functions and comparing estimation accuracy.

For the number of hidden layers and hidden neurons per layer, we align ourselves with the related work for coarse-grained power models for servers/datacenters and confine the hidden layer and hidden neuron hyperparameters as shown in Fig. 2. We explore one two-layered *shallow* network with 1–30 neurons per hidden layer. Note, that we explore all possible combinations of the number of hidden neurons per layer, i.e. 900 differently parameterized two-layered FFNNs. We further investigate one *mid-sized* network with 3 hidden layers where the number of neurons per layer can be any number of $1, 4, 7, 10, 13, 16, 19, 22, 25, 28$ and one *deep* network with 5 hidden layers where

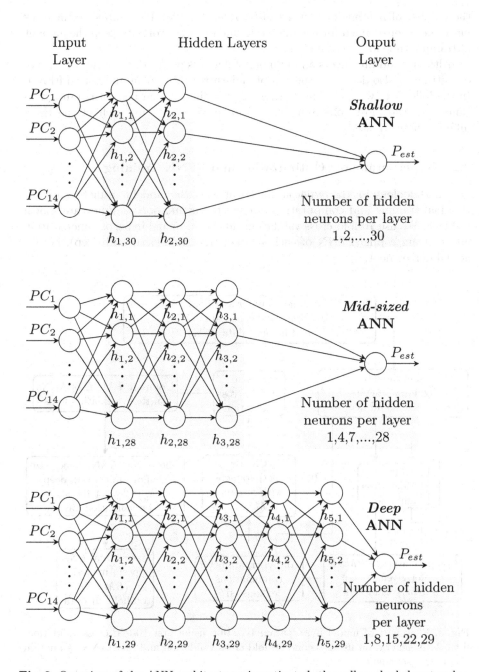

Fig. 2. Overview of the ANN architectures investigated; the yellow shaded rectangles indicate the ability to parameterize the number of hidden neurons per layer, i.e. from at least one hidden neuron per layer up to the given maximum number

the number of neurons per layer can be $1, 8, 15, 22, 29$. The number of neurons per layer is constrained for the mid-sized and deep networks to keep the amount of training time on a reasonable level.

Although, adding layers and number of neurons per layer increases the risk of overfitting, it also decreases the risk of underfitting due to an undersized FFNN. In the following, we show our methodology to find hidden neuron parametrizations with the most consistent estimation performance for each of the three different network sizes.

3.2   Hyperparameter Optimization and FFNN Training

Our methodology for the hyperparametrization of the model parameters and for the final training and computation of expected estimation accuracy are shown in Fig. 3. We use 10-fold cross validations for both, model hyperparametrization and to train a final FFNN of each size (shallow, mid-sized and deep), i.e. for actual deployment.

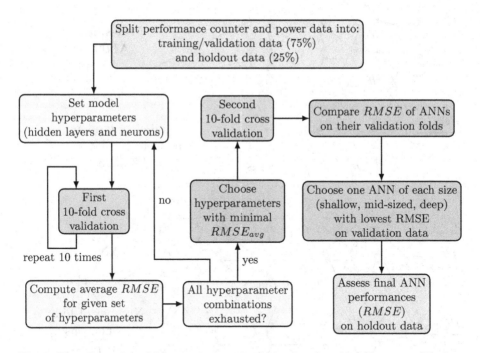

Fig. 3. Flowchart of model hyperparametrization using first 10-fold cross validation, final ANN generation using second 10-fold cross validation and final ANN estimation accuracy assessment

First, the traced PC_i and P_{pack} data is partitioned into a training/validation data set (75%) and a holdout data set (25%) such that the holdout data set is as diverse in regard to power behavior as possible. The holdout data set is neither used for hyperparametrization nor to train the three final FFNNs and can thus be used to determine the actual performance of these FFNNs on data they have not yet seen. For the hyperparametrization, we loop over all possible hidden neuron per layer combinations for each FFNN size (*shallow, mid-sized, deep*) and execute the first cross validation loop. In this loop, the training data set is further partitioned into 10 folds and each fold is used once for validation with the remaining folds being used for training the ANN. We repeat this step for each fold ten times to produce statistically significant results and to be able to remove outliers, i.e. diverging FFNNs. Thus, 100 FFNNs are generated for each possible model hyperparameter combination. After a full hyperparametrization run, the estimation error on the validation data is averaged for each hyperparameter over all folds. We then choose the hidden neuron parametrizations for each FFNN size with lowest average $RMSE$ under the assumption that these parametrizations provide the best general fit for the given performance/power data. The benefit of the repeated 10-fold cross validations lies in the robustness of the average $RMSE$ for the different hyperparameters and thus in choosing with high confidence good hyperparameters for generating the final FFNNs.

The hidden neuron parametrizations are then used in the second 10-fold cross validation step where we generate an FFNN for each training/validation fold combination, i.e. 10 FFNNs for each FFNN size (*shallow, mid-sized* and *deep*) and choose those FFNNs for testing which performed best on their corresponding validation data. We use the second cross validation to minimize the risk of selecting an overfitting FFNN from the first cross validation where 100 different FFNNs were generated for each hyperparameter. The risk of the FFNN with highest accuracy on their respective validation fold being overfitting is higher when 10 such FFNNs are available to chose from rather than just one. In the final step, we test the three chosen FFNNs on the holdout data to assess their potential dynamic power estimation performance in an actual deployment environment.

4   Experimental Setup

We use HotSniper [15], which is based on the Sniper multicore simulator [5] and expands the Sniper simulator with periodic power simulations using McPAT [11]. Sniper simulator uses interval simulation to speedup simulation times while providing good simulation accuracy. It is widely used for research of processor power/thermal management and power modeling, e.g. in [17,19]. Compared to a cycle-level simulator, an interval simulator focuses on accurately simulating performance changes due to stalls of the execution flow, while modeling performance on a higher abstraction layer when the execution flow is continuous. Our experimental framework simulates a 16-Core processor with Intel Gainestown core microarchitecture, with the details given in Table 1. We trace common performance counters similar to other state-of-the-art work, e.g. [2], with a sampling rate of 10 kHz. Some works use a larger number of performance counters – in

Table 1. Simulation framework

16-Cores (2 × 2 Tiles) with NoC Interconnect		
Intel Gainestown Core Architecture		
Memory Architecture		
L1 Caches	32 KB (private)	
L2 Caches	256 KB (private)	
L3 Caches	8 MB (shared per tile)	
Performance Information		
Processor Unit	Performance Counter	
Core	Instruction per Cycle	IPC
	# Branch Instructions	BPU
	# Floating Point Instructions	FP
	% C0 State Residency of a Core	C0
L2 & L3 Cache	# Load Instructions	LxLI
	# Store Instructions	LxSI
	# Load Misses	LxLM
	# Store Misses	LxSM
	% Cycles Lost due to misses	LxCLK
Workloads for Model Generation and Evaluation		
Suite	Benchmarks	
PARSEC [3]	blackscholes, bodytrack, canneal, dedup, streamcluster, swaptions, x264	
Splash-2 [23]	barnes, cholesky, fft, fmm, lu, ocean, radiosity, radix, raytrace	

the range of 50–100 – to estimate power due to the possibility of the estimation error decreasing with increasing number of performance counter inputs. However, processors commonly only support recording a small number of performance counters – in the range of 5–15 – at the same time [4]. We use the power and energy information provided by McPAT in our evaluation which generates power information on package, core and core component granularity with microsecond resolution. Finally, the benchmarks used for training the ANNs and generating reference power models are also given in Table 1.

5 Evaluation

5.1 Reference Power Models

We compare the estimation accuracy of the final FFNNs with the state-of-the-art linear approach published in [2] and a polynomial regression model as proposed by McCullough et al. [13]. For the linear model, we execute a set of microbenchmarks and the PARSEC/Splash-2 benchmarks on the system, trace P_{pack} and PC_i and generate a core-level linear regression model. Although [13] argues that a polynomial regression model was not able to accurately capture the non-linear power relationships – possibly due to overfitting – we still use it to test the hypotheses that our performance/power data could potentially be described well through polynomial regression and thus obviating the need for the complex ANN methodology. To generate the polynomial regression model, we use a similar methodology as described in Sect. 3 for FFNNs. First, we do repeated 10-fold cross validations to determine the best polynomial order and then generate the final polynomial regression model through another 10-fold cross validation choosing the polynomial model with the highest accuracy on its respective validation fold. We explored maximum polynomial orders of 1–6 for the independent PC_i inputs and found that a maximum polynomial order of 2 offered the best average estimation performance on the validation data.

5.2 Hidden Neuron Parametrization

We first look at the best model hyperparameters of the three hidden layer sizes and the average root mean squared error (RMSE) on the validation data from the 10-fold cross validation. For the three different FFNN sizes, the hidden neuron parametrization with lowest average RMSE is shown in Table 2. In addition the relative error to average core power is computed as $\frac{RMSE}{P_{avg}}$.

Table 2. Hyperparametrisation of shallow, mid and deep FFNNs with average RMSE on the randomized validation data

FFNN	Number of hidden layers	Neurons per hidden layer	Average RMSE	Relative error
Shallow	2	14-29	0.31 W	5%
Mid-sized	3	25-28-25	0.36 W	6%
Deep	5	22-08-22-15-15	0.33 W	6%

Shallow FFNNs with 2 hidden layers and 14 neurons in the first hidden layer and 29 neurons in the second hidden layer offer on average the best performance on the validation data. Both the mid and deep FFNN offer worse performance than the shallow FFNN on the validation folds. Additionally, we also show the relative estimation error of the actual core power.

5.3 Estimation Accuracy

We use the hyperparameters from Table 2 to generate three final FFNNs (shallow, mid, deep) using the second round of 10-fold cross validation. Note that for actual deployment in a multicore processor, we would only generate the *shallow* FFNN as it performed best on the validation data in the 10-fold cross validation. However, for providing an extensive performance overview and analysis we also show the performance of the *mid-sized* and *deep* FFNN. The estimation accuracy of the three resulting FFNNs is then determined on the holdout data, i.e. data which has neither been used for the hyperparametrization nor for training the FFNNs. Table 3 shows the RMSE and percentage errors of the three FFNNs, the model linear and the multivariate polynomial model as comparison.

Table 3. Estimation accuracy of FFNNs, linear model and polynomial model on the holdout data set

Model	RMSE	Relative error	MAPE
Shallow FFNN	0.26 W	4.5%	5.4%
Mid-sized FFNN	0.50 W	8.4%	8.0%
Deep FFNN	0.40 W	6.8%	7.0%
Linear Model [2]	0.75 W	12%	12%
Polynomial Model	0.60 W	10%	11%

From the FFNNs, the *shallow* one has the best estimation performance with the *mid-sized* and *deep* FFNN having worse error as was to be expected from the validation data. This shows – at least for FFNNs – that shallow structures with 2 layers are sufficiently complex to adequately capture the nonlinear performance/power relationships while FFNNs with more than 2 hidden layers start to suffer from overfitting. Compared to the state-of-the-art linear model, we observe a decrease in relative error of 7.5%. Such an estimation improvement can be significant for both short-term power (density) management and long-term thermal management. For example, an overestimation of the power consumption of 7.5% over a time range of ten milliseconds can lead to power-inefficient mapping and scheduling of tasks or an early end to frequency boosting by the power manager.

The best polynomial model had a an RMSE of 0.01 W on the validation data but an RMSE of 0.60 W on the holdout data which is not significantly better than the performance of the linear model. Compared to the polynomial model, the relative estimation error of the FFNN power estimator still decreases by 5.5%. The results of a *shallow* FFNN performing best as well as the best-suited polynomial order being 2, we interpret as the underlying non-linear performance counter/power relationship in itself being probably not overly complex. The comparatively bad polynomial model performance reconfirms the findings of McCullough et al. [13] that polynomial regression modeling very easily overfits the underlying performance/power data and is not well-suited to capture the non-linear relationships. In addition to the RMSE values and relative error values compared to average core power we also provide the mean absolute percentage error (MAPE) values in the final comparison shown in Table 3. Compared to the relative error, MAPE penalizes underestimations of the core power consumption stronger than overestimations of core power which could be advantageous for conservative power management algorithms. However, we do not observe significant qualitative differences between the relative error values and the MAPE values and have included MAPE for sake of completeness.

5.4   Run-Time Inference Overhead

To assess the computational and memory overhead of run-time inference of the FFNNs for producing a single power estimation, we first compute the necessary number of multiply accumulate (MAC) operations and the memory needed to store the neuron weights. The number of MAC operations is computed from the interconnections of each FFNN and the memory needed from the number of stored 32-bit weights values with both given in Table 4. Compared to the linear regression model, the *shallow* FFNN needs approximately between 60 times more MAC operations and 40 times more memory. Both, the computational and memory overhead are magnitudes higher for any FFNN implementation and we therefore discuss the feasibility and area overhead of a run-time inference implementation of the *shallow* FFNN in the following.

Table 4. Necessary computations and memory for a single power estimation/model inference

Model	Number of MAC operations	Memory in kBit
Shallow ANN	827	20
Mid-sized ANN	1971	56
Deep ANN	1426	39
Linear model [2]	14	0.5
Polynomial model	28	1.0

At least on IBM multicore processors, micro-controllers are integrated for both power estimation – so-called power proxies – and for power management purposes [9]. In the following, we approximate the transistor overhead for power estimations using the shallow ANN assuming integrated micro-controllers for power estimation. As a reference micro-controller, the 32-bit ARM Cortex M0 is well established, can be conservatively operated at 50 MHz with an implementation using less than 100k transistors [1]. In addition, the required SRAM to store the weights for the *shallow* ANN would add an additional 120k transistors. Each MAC operation and its associated load/store instructions takes 6 cycles on the M0 leading to approximately 5k cycles for a single inference of the shallow ANN, thus, power estimations could be executed with a periodicity of 100 μs.

Depending on the requirements of the P&T management, one micro-controller would be needed per core if 10 kHz power estimations are needed. Such a micro-controller implementation leads to an overhead of 250k transistors under conservative assumptions and has to be compared to the power estimations being used for a complex out-of-order core having hundreds of millions of transistors. The area overhead of – at maximum 0.25% – would decrease the average relative power estimation estimation error by 7.5%, translating to better P&T management and thus the possibility of higher compute performance and/or higher energy efficiency. Area overhead could be further decreased by custom logic for FFNN inference which would however remove programmability of the power estimator through firmware changes. Also, lower estimation rates in the range of 1 kHz would allow one power estimating micro-controller to serve multiple cores thus also decreasing area overhead.

6   Conclusion

In this paper, we investigate the use of FFNNs for fine-grained run-time power estimation on core-level with an estimation rate of 10 kHz. Suitable parametrizations of the number of hidden neurons per layer for three FFNN sizes (2, 3 and 5 hidden layers) were explored. To avoid underfitting non-linear relations between performance counters and dynamic power, and to avoid overfitting the training data, we used 10-fold cross validations for determining well-suited hidden neuron hyperparameters, and for the generation of the final three FFNNs for deployment. The *shallow* FFNN with 2 hidden layers proved to be most accurate on the validation data and decreased relative power estimation errors on the holdout data – data which was not used for training the FFNN – by 7.5% compared to a state-of-the-art linear model and by 5.5% compared to a multivariate polynomial regression model. Thus, shallow FFNNs are sufficient to capture non-linear relations between performance and power, thus providing significant improvements in accuracy for fine-grained, high-rate power estimations.

Furthermore, we propose a micro-controller-based implementation which allows the FFNN inference/power estimation to be executed at 10 kHz for each core with a maximum area overhead of 0.25% for large out-of-order cores. The higher run-time power estimation accuracy can be exploited by power and thermo management algorithms for more effective management decisions, e.g. power-density aware task mappings and frequency boosting.

Acknowledgments. This work was funded by the Deutsche Forschungsgemeinschaft (DFG, German Research Foundation) - Projektnummer 146371743 - TRR 89 "Invasive Computing".

References

1. ARM Limited: Cortex-M0 technical reference manual. Technical Report (2009)
2. Bertran, R., Gonzelez, M., Martorell, X., Navarro, N., Ayguade, E.: A systematic methodology to generate decomposable and responsive power models for CMPs. IEEE Trans. Comput. **62**(7), 1289–1302 (2013)
3. Bienia, C.: Benchmarking Modern Multiprocessors (2011)
4. Bircher, W.L., John, L.K.: Complete system power estimation using processor performance events. IEEE Trans. Comput. **61**(4), 563–577 (2012)
5. Carlson, T.E., Heirman, W., Eyerman, S., Hur, I., Eeckhout, L.: An evaluation of high-level mechanistic core models. ACM TACO **11**(3), 1–25 (2014)
6. Chadha, M., Ilsche, T., Bielert, M., Nagel, W.E.: A statistical approach to power estimation for x86 processors. In: Proceedings - 2017 IEEE 31st International Parallel and Distributed Processing Symposium Workshops, IPDPSW 2017 (2017)

7. Cupertino, L.F., Da Costa, G., Pierson, J.-M.: Towards a generic power estimator. Comput. Sci. Res. Dev. **30**(2), 145–153 (2014). https://doi.org/10.1007/s00450-014-0264-x

8. Huang, G.B., Chen, L., Siew, C.K.: Universal approximation using incremental constructive feedforward networks with random hidden nodes. IEEE Trans. Neural Networks **17**(4), 879–892 (2006)

9. Huang, W., et al.: Accurate fine-grained processor power proxies. In: IEEE/ACM MICRO (2012)

10. Kim, Y., Mercati, P., More, A., Shriver, E., Rosing, T.: P4: phase-based power/performance prediction of heterogeneous systems via neural networks. In: IEEE/ACM ICCAD (2017)

11. Li, S., Ahn, J.H., Strong, R.D., Brockman, J.B., Tullsen, D.M., Jouppi, N.P.: McPAT: an integrated power, area, and timing modeling framework for multicore and manycore architectures. In: IEEE MICRO (2009)

12. Lin, W., Wu, G., Wang, X., Li, K.: An artificial neural network approach to power consumption model construction for servers in cloud data centers. IEEE Trans. Sustain. Comput. **5**(3), 329–340 (2019)

13. McCullough, J.C., et al.: Evaluating the effectiveness of model-based power characterization. In: Usenix Atc (2011)

14. Möbius, C., Dargie, W., Schill, A.: Power consumption estimation models for processors, virtual machines, and servers. IEEE TPDS **25**(6), 1600–1614 (2014)

15. Pathania, A., Henkel, J.: HotSniper: sniper-based toolchain for many-core thermal simulations in open systems. IEEE Embed. Syst. Lett. **11**(2), 54–57 (2019)

16. Rapp, M., Pathania, A., Mitra, T., Henkel, J.: Prediction-Based Task Migration on S-NUCA Many-Cores. In: DATE (2019)

17. Rapp, M., Sagi, M., Pathania, A., Herkersdorf, A., Henkel, J.: Power-and cache-aware task mapping with dynamic power budgeting for many-cores. IEEE Trans. Comput. **69**(1), 1–13 (2019)

18. Rethinagiri, S.K., Palomar, O., Ben Atitallah, R., Niar, S., Unsal, O., Kestelman, A.C.: System-level power estimation tool for embedded processor based platforms. In: ACM RAPIDO (2014)

19. Samei, Y., Dömer, R.: Automated estimation of power consumption for rapid system level design. In: IEEE IPCCC (2014)

20. Shahid, A., Fahad, M., Manumachu, R.R., Lastovetsky, A.: Improving the accuracy of energy predictive models for multicore CPUs using additivity of performance monitoring counters. In: Malyshkin, V. (ed.) PaCT 2019. LNCS, vol. 11657, pp. 51–66. Springer, Cham (2019). https://doi.org/10.1007/978-3-030-25636-4_5

21. Su, B., Gu, J., Shen, L., Huang, W., Greathouse, J.L., Wang, Z.: PPEP: online performance, power, and energy prediction framework and DVFS space exploration. In: IEEE/ACM MICRO (2014)

22. Walker, M.J., et al.: Accurate and stable run-time power modeling for mobile and embedded CPUs. In: IEEE TCAD (2017)

23. Woof, S.C., Ohara, M., Torriet, E.: The SPLASH-2 programs: characterization and methodological considerations. In: ACM ISCA (1995)

24. Wu, W., Lin, W., He, L., Wu, G., Hsu, C.H.: A Power Consumption Model for Cloud Servers Based on Elman Neural Network. IEEE Transactions on Cloud Computing (2019)

From High-Level Synthesis
to Bundled-Data Circuits

Yoan Decoudu[1]([⊠]), Jean Simatic[2], Katell Morin-Allory[1], and Laurent Fesquet[1]

[1] Univ. Grenoble Alpes, CNRS, Grenoble INP, TIMA, 38000 Grenoble, France
{yoan.decoudu,katell.morin,laurent.fesquet}@univ-grenoble-alpes.fr
[2] HawAI.tech, 38000 Grenoble, France
jean.simatic@hawai.tech

Abstract. In order to spread asynchronous circuit design to a large community of designers, High-Level Synthesis (HLS) is promising option because it requires limited technical skills. Common HLS operations quickly provide a synchronous RTL description, which is usually split in two parts: a data-path and a control-path. In order to desynchronize such a circuit, the desynchronization process is only applied to the control-path, which is no more than a Finite State Machine (FSM). Our approach helps designers for quickly designing data-driven circuits while maintaining a reasonable cost, a similar area and a short time-to-market. To demonstrate our technique, the HLS tool, Catapult HLS from Mentor Graphics, has been used. Once the control-path has been extracted, the corresponding FSM is simply analyzed and desynchronized. On the other hand, the data-path is kept as it is. The resulting circuit is a bundled-data circuit requiring a particularly low design effort. Some samples illustrate the method and show its relevance in terms of area and performance.

Keywords: Event-driven circuits · Desynchronization · Low-power circuits · High-level synthesis

1 Introduction

Asynchronous circuits are today considered as relevant alternatives to synchronous design for many purposes. Indeed, unlike typical synchronous architectures, they have local synchronizations instead of a global synchronization signal. This brings several advantages depending on the implementation template: a reduced dynamic power consumption, robustness [2], low-voltage operations [9] or security. Despite all these favorable characteristics asynchronous circuits are not today widely spread in the industry, probably due to the lack of dedicated knowledge, know-how and EDA tools.

High-Level Synthesis (HLS) enables fast circuit design from a high-level description. This description, usually written in a C-like language, is compiled in order to synthesize a Register Transfer Level (RTL) description. The mostly

Grenoble INP–Institute of Engineering Univ. Grenoble Alpes

used commercial HLS tools cover from ASIC to FPGA implementations, but only generate classical synchronous circuits. For large circuits, this approach helps to explore several architectures and meet the required performances in terms of area, power and speed. Moreover, HLS demands few technical skills in hardware design. Therefore, this approach is ideal for spreading asynchronous circuits in the industry: it is an automated method, which implements asynchronous circuits without important changes in the standard design flow.

This paper proposes a new design method for synthesizing bundled-data circuits based on the use of most synchronous HLS tools. Our approach uses the HLS tool, Catapult HLS from Mentor Graphics, that partitions the resulting circuit into a data-path and a control-path. Then we only desynchronize the control-path, which is replaced by a specific asynchronous Finite State Machine (FSM). This leads to an asynchronous circuit synthesis requiring no specific knowledge on bundled-data circuits while taking advantage of the asynchronous logic features. Section 2 presents the bundled-data circuit principles and the related works on the HLS. Section 3 describes the proposed desynchronization method. Section 4 applies our method on a FIR Filter and a GCD calculator and then compares the synchronous circuits generated from Catapult and their asynchronous counterparts.

2   Related Works

2.1   Bundled-Data Circuits in a Nutshell

In this paper, we focus on a specific class of asynchronous circuits: the bundled-data circuits. In the sequel, we give a brief overview of this class of circuits [17,18].

Bundled-data circuits look very similar to synchronous circuits but the clock tree has been removed and replaced by a control circuit, whereas the data-path is kept as it is (see Fig. 1). The control circuit is locally composed of distributed controllers communicating with each others thanks to a 4-phase handshake protocol.

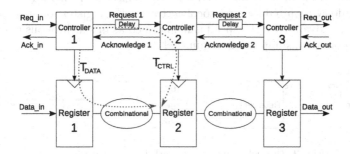

Fig. 1. Bundled-data circuit architecture.

The local timing assumptions in bundled-data circuits are between two connected controllers. Indeed, as shown in Fig. 1, the data must be sampled by the registers of the next pipeline stage register once the data computation is completed. Therefore the delay of the control path T_{CTRL} has to be longer than the computation in the data-path T_{DATA} in Fig. 1. Thus, it is necessary to add a delay element on the request signal for covering the logical gate delays. In the control path, the controllers are made with C-elements or Muller gates. Figure 2 shows its symbol and its truth table. This component allows the synchronization between 2 signals.

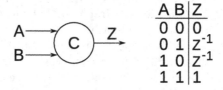

A	B	Z
0	0	0
0	1	Z^{-1}
1	0	Z^{-1}
1	1	1

Fig. 2. C-element truth table and symbol.

Late-Capture Protocol. There are many handshake protocols for bundled-data circuits offering different advantages. Most of them activate the registers when the request signal goes high. In order to meet the timing assumption requirements, it is mandatory to have a delay element greater than the critical logical path. In a 4-phase protocol, the cycle time is two times the delay because the request rising edge is propagating through the delay but also its falling edge during the return-to-zero phase. This leads to an important speed drop (2 times) compared to the synchronous version.

In order to be more efficient, a protocol activating the registers on the request falling edge is preferable such as the late-capture protocol [13]. Figure 3 shows the late-capture waveform. The request signal rising and falling edges are propagating through the delay before activating the registers. In this way, the delay is half of the delay required for a protocol activating the registers on its rising edge. This has two advantages: the speed is maintained as in synchronous circuits and the delay power consumption is minimized.

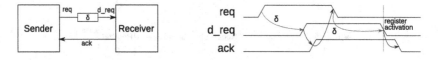

Fig. 3. Handshaking signals with late-capture protocol.

Figure 4 presents the Signal Transition Graph (STG) [3] of the late-capture protocol and its delay-insensitive implementation. This protocol decouples the handshake protocol at the input and at the output of the controller to enhance the speed of the communication. Hence, the late-capture protocol waits for the deactivation of the request R_{in} before activating the output request R_{out}.

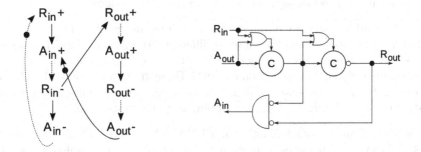

Fig. 4. (a) STG of a late-capture protocol. (b) Late-capture controller implementation.

2.2 High-Level Synthesis

HLS tools usually compile a high-level circuit description with no architectural nor timing information. This high-level description is synthesized into a RTL code. In addition, HLS is able to perform architectural exploration to optimize the design according to the design constraints. HLS is typically an attractive way to quickly design synchronous circuits implementing algorithms [4]. In case of asynchronous circuits, several tools already exist [16]. These tools use three different synthesis strategies.

Syntax Directed Translation. This strategy uses a dedicated high-level hardware description language (HDL) and map the code syntactic structures onto hardware components. For instance, the synthesis tools TiDE [10] and Balsa [1] translates the language syntax into handshake components. Circuit speed and area depend a lot on the designer's ability to write an optimized HDL code.

Pipelined Process Decomposition. HLS tools use intermediate representations of the algorithm to abstract and capture the function as independently as possible from the syntax. Data-driven decomposition [20] and CASH compiler [19] respectively use dynamic and static single assignment forms. These approaches are suitable for high-throughput applications as they generate highly pipelined components. But they are ill-adapted to typical IoT applications, which require low-power circuits and can afford low-speed.

Scheduling Based Flows. To enable optimization strategies, synchronous HLS is decomposed in distinct yet interdependent steps [4]. The main technical steps are allocation and scheduling, which can be done by different approaches depending on the design objectives. Most of the HLS tools use a control/data-path decomposition style. This approach fits well the HLS decomposition because the data-path results from the allocation, and the control-path from the scheduling. Following this model asynchronous HLS raises two issues:

- The scheduling time is continuous for asynchronous circuits. Thus, the optimal asynchronous scheduling may be different. An efficient algorithm is proposed in [8] that solves this question for two optimization criteria.
- For implementing the asynchronous FSM, there are many proposed architectures including locally-clocked [5,11] with optimized state coding, and one-hot state coding [15] allowing direct mapping from the state graph.

To the best of our knowledge, only the BUDASYN [5] flow, which only targets FPGA platforms, integrates a solution to both problems by implementing the algorithm of [8]. The FSM is a centralized locally-clocked implementation of an Extended Burst Mode (XBM) specification [21].

For asynchronous circuits, HLS tools help bridging the gap between circuit designer skills and the specific asynchronous techniques. Our approach is also based on a scheduling flow. However, the FSM is implemented thanks to interconnected distributed controllers. Compared to centralized implementations, such as locally-clocked FSMs, distributed AFSMs are likely less compact but offer a better scalability, ease the place and route operations, and are more appropriated for fine-grain pipelining.

This work is an improvement of the work presented in [12]. Moreover, our method is applied on a commercial tool, which allows more design possibilities. It relies on the synchronous tool Catapult from Mentor Graphics [7] for scheduling and allocation. It provides support for a standard programming language (a subset of ANSI C) and a wide set of possible transformations such as loop unrolling and pipelining. Catapult generates a synchronous synthesizable RTL code of the data-path and synchronous FSM. In order to generate an asynchronous control, the synchronous FSM is simply desynchronized.

3   Desynchronization Method

The HLS tool Catapult from Mentor Graphics generates a synchronous circuit divided in two parts: a control- and a data-path. This section presents the implemented method for desynchronizing the circuit just by replacing its control-path by its asynchronous counterpart. Therefore, the only modification of the data-path is the renaming of the flip-flop clock signal.

3.1   Desynchronization Principle

Figure 5 shows how the control-path and the data-path are interconnected within Catapult. The control-path activates multiplexers and enable signals on the flip-flops in the data-path. Each state is one-hot encoded. A dedicated signal controls the activated part of the data-path, represented by the signals C^M in Fig. 5.

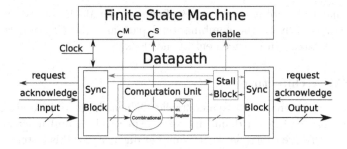

Fig. 5. Circuit architecture generated from catapult.

The next state is chosen at each cycle thanks to the signals C^S coming from the combinational part of the data-path.

In a circuit generated with Catapult, the synchronization between the system and the I/O is done thanks to a Synchronization Block (*Sync Block* in Fig. 5) and its handshake signals inserted at the input and output of the data-path. If the external environment does not activate the Synchronization Block, the *Stall Block* freezes the whole circuit including the FSM thanks to the signal *enable* in Fig. 5.

To desynchronize such a circuit, the FSM is replaced by an Asynchronous Finite State Machine (AFSM). In order to generate an AFSM, the RTL description is parsed to extract the FSM states. Thanks to this AFSM representation, a Petri Net modeling its behavior is generated. Then the Petri Net model is used for validating that the AFSM has no deadlocks and its liveliness is formally ensured. Once these verifications are done, an AFSM netlist is generated with late-capture controllers. The data-path is kept as it is. The unique modification removes the clock tree and substitutes the clock by the signals coming from the AFSM. By only substituting the FSM by an AFSM and connecting it to the data-path as presented in Fig. 6, the whole circuit behavior becomes asynchronous. Thus, the registers are only activated when needed (depending on the current AFSM state) while the computation results remain the same.

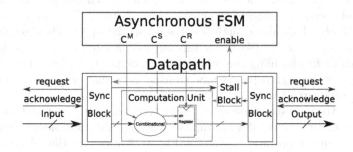

Fig. 6. Circuit architecture after the desynchronization.

Notice that there are now two types of control signals driven by the AFSM. The C^M signals activate the combinational part and the C^R signals directly activate the registers (in replacement of the clock).

3.2   AFSM Architecture

Each AFSM state corresponds to a controller. When there are several successors (respectively predecessor) a demultiplexer (respectively a multiplexer) component is used. Only one controller is activated at one because this latter represents a FSM state. Thus, the handshake protocol needs deactivating the previous controller before activating the next one. This is also a reason for choosing the late-capture protocol. The state activation begins with the request signal of the protocol. As the combinational part processes the data during the whole state duration, the signal C^M is activated on the request rising edge as shown in Fig. 7. According to our protocol, the data capture (represented by C^R) is initiated with the delayed request deactivation. Then the deactivation of C^M comes with the falling edge of the acknowledgement signal *ack*.

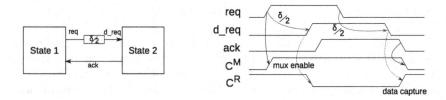

Fig. 7. State activation according to the handshake protocol.

Figure 8 shows an AFSM controller and its connection to the data-path. The signal C^R is connected after the delay on the request wire to ensure the local timing assumptions. As the registers sample on a rising edge, an inverter is added. Once the request is activated, the signal C^M immediately launches the computation. In this way, the local data-path has two times the delay duration for computing the data. The reset of C^M is done by an OR gate between the request and acknowledgement. As shown on Fig. 6, the AFSM can be frozen by the *Stall Block*, which also deactivates the whole data-path when no new data are available on the *Sync Block*. For this purpose, a latch has been added after each controller for disabling the request. Its clock pin is connected to the *Stall Block* output to be in transparent mode during the circuit operation and in latch mode when the circuit is idle.

In Fig. 8, the next states are chosen thanks to a demultiplexer and a selection signal C^S coming from the data-path. The design of a demultiplexer implementing the late-capture protocol is given on Fig. 9a. Notice that the selection signal is always valid when the request is deactivated. Therefore the selection coming from the data-path is not yet arrived on the request rising edge, which is propagated without control to the next branches. Thanks to a register, a delay and

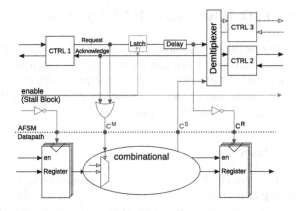

Fig. 8. Asynchronous FSM architecture.

a NAND gate, the request falling edge will only be transmitted to the selected branch. The delay ensures that the selection signal arrives first at the NAND input, so that the demultiplexer only activates one controller. A similar property should also be guarantied by the multiplexer. The latter just propagates the incoming request and acknowledges the adequate successor. Its implementation is given in Fig. 9b. Compared to the demultiplexer letting the request rising edge propagating to the next branches, the combinational logic transmitting the request to the next controller is not so obvious. Indeed, this functionality is obtained thanks to the equation shown in Fig. 9b.

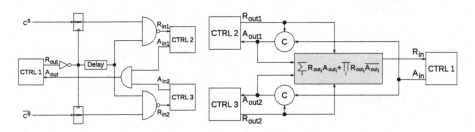

Fig. 9. (a) Demultiplexer architecture. (b) Multiplexer architecture.

The AFSM liveliness can be proven thanks to its Petri net model [14]. As only one token, representing the current state, evolves in the Petri net, the multiplexer and demultiplexer must generate only one token at their output. The deadlocks can also checked. In order to guarantee their absence, note that it is required to add a controller in each one-controller loop. This added controller will not be associated to C^M nor C^R. This case only happens when a state loops on itself.

4   Testcases: FIR Filter and GCD Calculator

In order to demonstrate our design flow, this section presents the desynchronization flow applied to a Greatest Common Divisor (GCD) calculator and a Finite
Impulse Response (FIR) Filter. They are first generated with Catapult and then
desynchronized. The area and speed performances have been evaluated in the
FD-SOI 28 nm technology from STMicroelectronics.

4.1   GCD Calculator

The GCD calculator uses the Euclid's algorithm (given in Fig. 10a) to compute
the GCD of two input numbers. The circuit FSM generated by HLS is shown
in Fig. 10b. State 1 recovers the input data, State 2 computes the data and State
3 sends the result. When desynchronizing, a Petri net of the FSM is constructed
to verify the liveliness and the absence of deadlocks. The self-loop on State 2
requires an additional controller to avoid deadlocks. Two GCD calculators have
been implemented: a 8-bit and a 64-bit. For both implementations, the control
path is exactly the same.

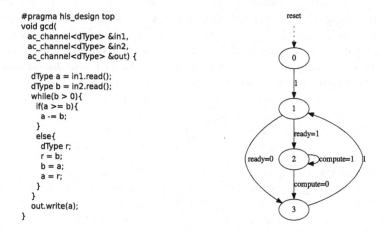

Fig. 10. (a) Source code of the GCD calculator. (b) GCD Calculator FSM.

4.2   FIR Filter

FIR Filters are very usual digital circuit. They process sampled data with filter
coefficients. Let x_i the ith sample of the input signal and h_i the ith coefficient of
the filter. The output sample y_k is given by Eq. (1):

$$y_k = \sum_i x_{k-i} h_i \qquad (1)$$

This equation has been implemented for a 8-bit filter written in C. We choose a sequential architecture with one multiplier and one accumulator. This leads to the architecture given in Fig. 11a. The samples (resp. coefficients) are stored in DL (resp. ROM) and then computed by MULT/ACC. The generated circuit by Catapult has a FSM with only two states (see Fig. 11b): a reset state 0 and a computation state 1. During the desynchronization, the Petri net is extracted as in the previous example and a controller is added to the self-loop on State 1.

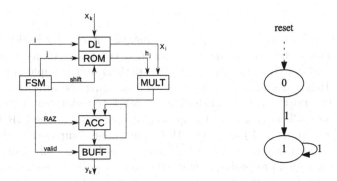

Fig. 11. (a) FIR Filter Architecture. (b) FIR Filter FSM.

4.3   Results

All the three circuits have been synthesized thanks to Design Compiler from Synopsys and validated with back-annotated logical simulations. The timing constraints are resolved thanks to the method described in [6] that takes advantage on the synchronous static timing analysis to check the specific timing constraints imposed by the asynchronous circuits. Thus, this allows us to use traditional EDA tools to synthesize and validate our circuits. Their synchronous counterpart have also been designed in order to compare them in terms of area and speed. For the FIR filter, the input signal is a pulse. For the GCD calculator, a random number generator generates the two input signals. The simulations use sufficiently long stimuli in order to average the results.

Area. Figure 12 reports the area of the circuits presented above. The area of the asynchronous circuits is a little bit larger than their synchronous counterparts. Indeed an asynchronous control circuit replaces the FSM. The extra-area of the AFSM results from a small increase of the FSM complexity. However, looking at the whole circuit, it is important to notice that the clock tree has not been implemented in the synchronous versions of the FIR and GCD circuits. The lack of the clock tree will impact unfavorably the comparison for the asynchronous circuits.

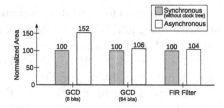

Fig. 12. Areas of the circuits normalized by the synchronous circuits.

Figure 12 reveals that the higher area increase is obtained with the 8-bit GCD calculator. The area is increased of 52% compared to its synchronous counterpart but, in this case, the tiny data-path is quite simple compared to the AFSM. Hence the area increase is huge. Changing the area ratio between the data-path and the control-path gives a completely different view. For the GCD, a 64-bit GCD only gives a 6% growth of the area. For the FIR filter, the FSM is rather simple and the data-path is quite huge compared to the control circuit. Therefore the area is only of 4% larger. As HLS is commonly used for designing large signal processing circuits, the control-path remains usually small compared to the data-path. Hence the area overhead will be negligible with most of applications designed with Catapult.

Speed. The synchronous circuit speed is imposed by the critical path, while, in asynchronous circuits, the speed results from an average of the stage speeds. Therefore the asynchronous circuits are faster than their synchronous counterparts, as shown in Fig. 13.

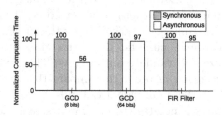

Fig. 13. Normalized computation time of the circuits.

The asynchronous FIR filter is a little bit faster with a speed increase of 5%. As the FSM remains in the same state during the computation (see Fig. 11b), only one controller activates the registers. Hence, the delay of the control circuit matches the circuit critical path. Therefore the speed of the two versions are almost the same.

For both GCD, the critical path corresponds to the computation stage, which is controlled by State 2 (State 2 is fed back on itself). Thus the performance strongly depends on the iteration number on State 2. For the 8-bit GCD, the computation requires a few iterations, so that the circuit often communicates with its environment activating the other states. Hence the performance enhancement is huge and reaches 44% compared to its synchronous counterpart. For the 64-bit GCD, the computation iteration number is larger and the system spends most of the time in State 2 where the critical path is. The speeds of the synchronous and asynchronous circuits are very similar and we only notice a slight speed increase of 3% for the asynchronous circuit.

5 Conclusion

For most of the designers, asynchronous design is challenging. Nevertheless, asynchronous circuits provide interesting features making them attractive for many applications. The proposed automated design flow takes advantage of the synchronous HLS from Mentor Graphics, Catapult HLS, to achieve asynchronous circuit design with very limited technical skills. This approach avoids learning HDL and keeps the design framework unchanged. This method is an opportunity for non-specialists to quickly design asynchronous circuits in a very standard framework.

The synthesized asynchronous circuits present a little area overhead, which has to be mitigated by the lack of the clock tree in the synchronous versions. The results also show a slight speed increase. As the results are strongly correlated to the FSM and data-path architectures, there is no doubt that a data-path mostly computing outside its critical path will enhance the speed of the asynchronous version. The worst case corresponds to the desynchronized circuits which only activate their critical path (our FIR filter).

Asynchronous circuits are well-suited for processing non-uniformly sampled signals and low-voltage applications thanks to their intrinsic robustness. Future work will target the design flow enhancement and the power analysis of the desynchronized circuits.

Acknowledgment. This work has been partially supported by the OCEAN12 European Project (Ecsel JU, Grant Agreement N°783127).

References

1. Bardsley, A.: Balsa: an asynchronous circuit synthesis system. Master's thesis, University of Manchester (1998)
2. Chang, K.L., Chang, J., Gwee, B.H., Chong, K.S.: Synchronous-logic and asynchronous-logic 8051 microcontroller cores for realizing the Internet of Things: a comparative study on dynamic voltage scaling and variation effects. IEEE J. Emerg. Sel. Top. Circuits Syst. **3**(1), 23–34 (2013)
3. Chu, T.A.: On the models for designing VLSI asynchronous digital systems. Integr. VLSI J. **4**(2), 99–113 (1986)
4. Coussy, P., Gajski, D., Meredith, M., Takach, A.: An introduction to high-level synthesis. IEEE Des. Test Comput. **26**(4), 8–17 (2009)

5. Garcia, K., Oliveira, D.L., d'Amore, R., Faria, L.A., Oliveira, J.L.V.: FPGA implementation of optimized XBM specifications by transformation for AFSMs. In: International Conference on ReConFigurable Computing and FPGAs (ReConFig), pp. 1–6 (2016)
6. Gimenez, G., Cherkaoui, A., Cogniard, G., Fesquet, L.: Static timing analysis of asynchronous bundled-data circuits. In: 24th IEEE International Symposium on Asynchronous Circuits and Systems (ASYNC), May 2018
7. Graphics, M.: Catapult HLS. Available: http://www.mentor.com
8. Hansen, J., Singh, M.: A fast branch-and-bound approach to high-level synthesis of asynchronous systems. In: 16th IEEE Symposium on Asynchronous Circuits and Systems (ASYNC), pp. 107–116 May 2010
9. Jorgenson, R.D., et al.: Ultralow-power operation in subthreshold regimes applying clockless logic. Proc. IEEE **98**, 299–314 (2010)
10. Nielsen, S., Sparsø J., Jensen, J., Nielsen, J.: A behavioral synthesis frontend to the Haste/TiDE design flow. In: 15th IEEE Symposium on Asynchronous Circuits and Systems (ASYNC), pp. 185–194 (2009)
11. Nowick, S.M., Dill, D.L.: Synthesis of asynchronous state machines using a local clock. In: IEEE International Conference on Computer Design: VLSI in Computers and Processors, pp. 192–197 (1991)
12. Simatic, J., Bastos, R.P., Fesquet, L.: High-level synthesis for event-based systems. In: 2nd International Conference on Event-based Control, Communication, and Signal Processing (EBCCSP), pp. 1–7 June 2016
13. Simatic, J., Cherkaoui, A., Bastos, R.P., Fesquet, L.: New asynchronous protocols for enhancing area and throughput in bundled-data pipelines. In: 29th Symposium on Integrated Circuits and Systems Design (SBCCI), pp. 1–6 Aug 2016
14. Simatic, J., Cherkaoui, A., Bertrand, F., Bastos, R.P., Fesquet, L.: A practical framework for specification, verification, and design of self-timed pipelines. In: 2017 23rd IEEE International Symposium on Asynchronous Circuits and Systems (ASYNC), pp. 65–72 May 2017
15. Sotiriou, C.R.: Direct-mapped asynchronous finite-state machines in CMOS technology. In: 14th Annual IEEE International ASIC/SOC Conference, pp. 105–109 (2001)
16. Sparsø J.: Current trends in high-level synthesis of asynchronous circuits. In: 16th IEEE International Conference on Electronics, Circuits, and Systems (ICECS), pp. 347–350 (2009)
17. Sparsø, J., Furber, S.: Principles of Asynchronous Circuit Design: a Systems Perspective, 1st edn. Springer Publishing Company, Boston (2010)
18. Sutherland, I.E.: Micropipelines. Commun. ACM **32**(6), 720–738 (1989)
19. Venkataramani, G., Budiu, M., Chelcea, T., Goldstein, S.C.: C to asynchronous dataflow circuits: an end-to-end toolflow. In: 13th IEEE International Workshop on Logic Synthesis (IWLS). Temecula, CA, June 2004
20. Wong, C., Martin, A.: High-level synthesis of asynchronous systems by data-driven decomposition. In: Design Automation Conference (DAC), pp. 508–513 June 2003
21. Yun, K., Dill, D.: Automatic synthesis of extended burst-mode circuits.i. (specification and hazard-free implementations). computer-aided design of integrated circuits and systems. IEEE Trans. **18**(2), 101–117 (1999)

Energy-Aware Partial-Duplication Task Mapping Under Real-Time and Reliability Constraints

Minyu Cui[1(✉)], Lei Mo[2], Angeliki Kritikakou[1], and Emmanuel Casseau[1]

[1] Univ Rennes, Inria, IRISA, CNRS, Rennes, France
minyu.cui@irisa.fr
[2] School of Automation, Southeast University, Nanjing, China

Abstract. An efficient task execution on multicore platforms can lead to low energy consumption. To achieve that, an Integer Non-Linear Programming (INLP) formulation is proposed that performs task mapping by jointly addressing task allocation, task frequency assignment, and task duplication. The goal is to minimize energy consumption under real-time and reliability constraints. To provide an optimal solution, the original INLP problem is safely transformed to an equivalent Mixed Integer Linear Programming (MILP) problem. The comparison of the proposed approach with existing energy-aware task mapping approaches shows that the proposed approach is able to find solutions when other approaches fail, achieving an overall lower energy consumption.

Keywords: Reliability · Task mapping · DVFS · Multicores · Real-time

1 Introduction

The execution of embedded applications on multicore platforms requires both in-time and reliable execution of tasks. In time-critical domains, tasks must finish before a given deadline. Meanwhile, their correct execution can be threatened by several sources, such as radiation [6] and electromagnetic interference [7], causing non-persistent *transient faults* (also called *soft errors*). Due to the technology size reduction and the increasing scaling of CMOS technology, the system has become more susceptible to soft errors [5]. To provide protection, the system reliability should be increased. To achieve that, tasks are executed with higher frequencies [8]. Another way is to apply fault-tolerance techniques at the system level, where tasks are replicated [2,4]. Nonetheless, these approaches increase the system energy consumption, which has become an important concern, especially for systems with limited energy budget, such as battery-powered or energy-harvesting devices [2–4], and green computing. To balance system performance and energy consumption, multicore platforms have been enhanced with Dynamic Voltage and Frequency Scaling (DVFS). However, by decreasing frequency and

© Springer Nature Switzerland AG 2020
A. Orailoglu et al. (Eds.): SAMOS 2020, LNCS 12471, pp. 213–227, 2020.
https://doi.org/10.1007/978-3-030-60939-9_15

voltage, systems become more susceptible to soft errors [9]. Therefore, adequate *mapping approaches* are required in order to obtain a reliable, in-time and energy efficient task execution on multicore platforms.

Table 1 depicts representative task mapping approaches, which decide the frequency assignment and the processor allocation to tasks, under Energy Budget (EB), Real-Time (RT) and Reliability (R) constraints. The goal is to maximize system reliability (max R), usually under an energy supply constraint [2–4], or to minimize energy consumption (min E), usually under a real-time [1,10,12] or reliability constraint [1,13,14]. Existing approaches execute only original tasks or, additionally, replicas of original tasks. A task is executed successfully, if at least one replica is executed without faults [1]. By executing several replicas on different processors, the probability of correct execution is increased, as it is unlikely that execution of all replicas fails [1,14,15]. Task replication can be either full (all tasks are replicated) or partial (selected tasks are replicated).

Table 1. Comparison with representative State-of-the-Art

Ref.	Objective		Task replicas		Platform		DVFS	Constraints		
	min E	max R	Full	Partial	Homo.	Hete.		EB	RT	R
[2]		✓			✓		✓	✓		✓
[4]		✓				✓		✓	✓	
[3]		✓	✓		✓		✓	✓	✓	
[15]		✓	✓			✓	✓	✓		✓
[10]	✓					✓	✓	✓		
[13]	✓					✓	✓	✓		✓
[1]	✓		✓		✓		✓		✓	✓
[14]	✓		✓			✓	✓			✓
[12]	✓			✓	✓		✓		✓	
Proposed	✓			✓	✓		✓		✓	✓

Task mapping approaches, that maximize reliability, consider i) only original tasks, through online heuristics [4] and static and dynamic algorithms [2], and ii) original and replicated tasks, when the number of replicas is known [3] and when the number of task replicas is also decided during the mapping process [15]. One category of the approaches, that minimize energy consumption, considers only original tasks, e.g., a decomposition algorithm is proposed under reliability constraints [13]. Mapping of original tasks on heterogeneous multicores is extended in order to provide a solution, where enough slack exist to re-execute a task in case of a single fault [10]. However, these approaches usually require high frequencies to satisfy the reliability constraints, increasing energy consumption. On top, even with the highest platform frequency, it may be impossible to satisfy the reliability constraints, leading to empty solution space. Another category considers both original and replicated tasks. Full replication approaches decide the number of replicas (at least one replica per task), e.g., for homogeneous [1] and heterogeneous [14] platforms. However, full replication leads to large energy consumption, combined with a negative impact on execution time; the end-times of tasks are delayed, due to the execution of task replicas. This impact may lead to empty solution space, when the real-time constraints are strict. Few approaches apply partial task replication. Usually heuristics are applied to select the tasks to be replicated, e.g., a heuristic that decides the tasks to be duplicated and their frequency [12], without considering reliability constraints. Our work belongs to this category and extends the State-of-the-Art (SoA) by optimally solving a combined task mapping problem, under both real-time and reliability constraints.

The goal of the proposed task mapping approach is to minimize system energy consumption by optimally and concurrently deciding the tasks to be duplicated, the frequency assignment per task and task allocation, on a homogeneous multi-core platform with DVFS, under both real-time and reliability constraints. The proposed approach considers the execution of a task to be safe, when it meets its reliability constraint. Otherwise the task is duplicated. As task duplication is applied only when the reliability constraint cannot be met, the number of duplicated tasks is reduced, reducing the negative impact on time and energy consumption. Our contribution is two-fold: i) the aforementioned task mapping problem is formulated as an Integer Non-Linear Programming (INLP), and ii) the INLP problem is safely transformed into a Mixed Integer Linear Programming (MILP) problem in order to be solved optimally. To support our contribution, we perform extensive experiments considering i) strict, medium and relaxed real-time constraints, and ii) strict and relaxed reliability constraints. From the obtained results, our approach is able to find more feasible solutions (on average, 31.77%) compared to approaches that always satisfy the reliability constraints without task replication, and consumes less energy (on average, 26.07%) compared to full duplication approaches. Especially for strict real-time constraints, our approach can achieve energy savings up to 51.56%.

The rest of the paper is organized as follows. Section 2 introduces the system model. Section 3 presents the proposed formulation of the duplication-based fault-tolerant mapping approach. Section 4 presents the evaluation results. Finally, Sect 5 concludes this study.

2   System Model

Task Model: We consider a set of N independent tasks, i.e., $\{\tau_1, \ldots, \tau_N\}$. For each task τ_i, C_i is the Worst Case Execution Cycles (WCEC). All tasks must be executed before a common deadline D, and no preemption occurs between different tasks executed on the same processor. Without loss of generality, in the rest of the paper, we assume that the release times of all tasks are at the start of the scheduling period.

Platform and Power Model: A multicore platform is considered with M homogeneous processors, i.e., $\{\theta_1, \ldots, \theta_M\}$. The multicore platform supports individual DVFS in task level and there are L different voltage/frequency (V/F) pairs $\{(v_1, f_1), \ldots, (v_L, f_L)\}$. When task τ_i is assigned with frequency f_l, its execution time is given by $t_i = \frac{C_i}{f_l}$. For each processor θ_m, the power consumption is modeled as the sum of static P_l^{sta} power and dynamic P_l^{dyn} power with frequency f_l [11], i.e., $P_l = P_l^{sta} + P_l^{dyn}$. The dynamic power consumption with voltage/frequency level (v_l, f_l) is given by $P_l^{dyn} = C_{eff} v_l^2 f_l$, where C_{eff} is the effective switching capacitance.

Fault Model and Reliability: We focus on soft errors that follow a Poisson Distribution with an average fault rate $\lambda(f)$ at frequency f, which can be modeled as $\lambda(f) = \lambda_0 \times 10^{d \frac{f_{max} - f}{f_{max} - f_{min}}}$, where λ_0 is the average fault rate corresponding to the maximum frequency f_{max}, d_0 is a positive constant, indicating the sensitivity of failure rate related to frequency scaling [8]. The reliability of a task τ_i, i.e., the probability of executing the task without any fault, follows the exponential model [8]. Hence, the task's reliability at frequency f_l is $r_i(f_l) = e^{-\varphi_i(f_l)}$, where $\varphi_i(f_l) = \lambda(f_l) \times t_i$, with t_i the execution time of task τ_i at frequency f_l [2,8,10]. If the reliability of task τ_i is larger than its reliability constraint, the execution is considered as reliable and the task reliability is not modified, $R_i = r_i(f_l)$. Otherwise, the task τ_i is duplicated and executed on different processors. The duplicated task is executed with same frequency as the original task, similar to [1,12,16], since using the same frequency in original and duplicated tasks yields similar energy consumption [16]. When the task is duplicated, its reliability is given by $R_i = 1 - (1 - r_i(f_l))^2$. As our approach is applied offline, with the goal of minimizing energy consumption, we consider only task duplication, i.e., a single replica per task, in order not to unnecessarily increase the platform workload, in case no faults occur. An mechanism can be applied, during execution, to further improve the energy consumption of our solution (by not executing the replica, when the first execution is correct), such as [17], and to deal with the low probability cases, where non-replicated tasks and both original and duplicated tasks are faulty, such as [18].

3   Duplication-Based Fault-Tolerant Mapping Approach (DFTMA)

Motivational Example: Before providing the mathematical formulation of the proposed Duplication-based Fault-Tolerant Mapping Approach (DFTMA), we provide a simple example to motivate our approach. Let us assume a single task with $C = 4 * 10^8$, a reliability threshold equal to 0.999 and the voltage/frequency levels of the platform from Table 4 in Sect. 4. Table 2 depicts the execution time (t), energy consumption $(E = P_l \times t)$ and reliability R, when only the original task is executed (columns $f_1 - f_6$) and when both original and its replica are executed (columns $2f_1 - 2f_6$). Table 2.a) enumerates all feasible solutions

Table 2. Motivational example

f_l	f_1	f_2	f_3	f_4	f_5	f_6	$2f_1$	$2f_2$	$2f_3$	$2f_4$	$2f_5$	$2f_6$
t	0.4994	0.4825	0.4677	0.4547	0.4431	0.4	0.9988	0.965	0.9444	0.9094	0.8862	0.8
E	2.1169	2.7905	3.6959	4.926	6.6141	8.9525	4.2338	5.581	7.3918	9.852	13.2282	17.905
R	0.9753	0.9909	0.9965	0.9985	0.9994	1	0.99939	0.99992	0.99999	0.99999	0.999999	1

a) Feasible solutions of three approaches under reliability constraint

DFTMA	$A_1=f_6$, $A_2=f_5$, $A_3=2f_4$, $A_4=2f_3$, $A_5=2f_2$, $A_6=2f_1$
FTM	$B_1=f_6$, $B_2=f_5$
FDM	$C_1=2f_6$, $C_2=2f_5$, $C_3=2f_4$, $C_4=2f_3$, $C_5=2f_2$, $C_6=2f_1$

b) Feasible and **optimal** solutions under reliability and deadline constraints

$\leq D$	0	0.4	0.4431	0.8	0.8862	0.9094	0.9444	0.965	0.9988
$D<$	0.4	0.4431	0.8	0.8862	0.9094	0.9444	0.965	0.9988	-
DFTMA	-	A_1	A_1,A_2	A_1,A_2	A_1,A_2	A_1,A_2,A_3	A_1,A_2,A_3,A_4	A_1-A_4,A_5	A_1-A_5,A_6
FTM	-	B_1	B_1,B_2	B_1,B_2	B_1,B_2	B_1,B_2	B_1,B_2	B_1,B_2	B_1,B_2
FDM	-	-	-	C_1	C_1,C_2	C_1,C_2,C_3	C_1-C_3,C_4	C_1-C_4,C_5	C_1-C_5,C_6

under only the reliability constraint for the approaches that i) apply full task duplication (FDM), such as [13], ii) must always satisfy the reliability constraint without duplication (FTM), such as [1,14], and iii) apply task duplication only when the reliability constraint cannot be satisfied (DFTMA), such as the proposed method. Table 2.b) explores how the deadline constraint (D) affects the feasible and optimal (highlighted in bold) solutions. Compared to DFTMA approach, existing approaches cannot find optimal solutions, due to strict reliability constraint (as FTM) or deadline constraint (as FDM), even for only a single task.

Mathematical Formulation: The goal is to minimize the total energy consumption of the system, subject to a set of reliability and real-time constraints. To achieve that we decide the: 1) frequency of original tasks (s); 2) duplication of original tasks (σ); 3) allocation of original tasks (q) and duplicated tasks (d). Table 3 summarizes the parameters and the variables of our formulation.

Table 3. Main notations

Parameters		Binary Variables	
M	number of processors	s_{il}	1 if task τ_i executes with frequency f_l 0 otherwise
N	number of tasks		
L	number of discrete V/F levels	q_{im}	1 if task τ_i executes on processor θ_m 0 otherwise
C_i	WCEC of task τ_i		
D	global deadline	σ_i	1 if task τ_i is duplicated 0 otherwise
(v_l, f_l)	the lth V/F level		
P_l	the lth power level of processor	d_{im}	1 if duplication of τ_i executes on θ_m 0 otherwise
R_i^{th}	task τ_i reliability constraint		

i) Frequency Assignment: Let $\mathbf{N} = \{1, \ldots, N\}$, $\mathbf{M} = \{1, \ldots, M\}$ and $\mathbf{L} = \{1, \ldots, L\}$. Since the platform provides individual DVFS, that can be applied per task, each task can only be assigned with one frequency level:

$$\sum_{l \in L} s_{il} = 1, \ \forall i \in \mathbf{N}. \tag{1}$$

ii) Task Duplication Decision: The reliability of task τ_i is expressed as $r_i = \sum_{l \in L} s_{il} e^{-\varphi_i(f_l)}$, where $\varphi_i(f_l) = \lambda(f_l) \times t_i$ and $t_i = \sum_{l \in L} s_{il} \frac{C_i}{f_l}$ (the execution time of task τ_i when executed with frequency f_l). Let R_i^{th} denote the reliability threshold of task τ_i. If $0 < r_i \leq R_i^{th}$, the task needs to be duplicated, $\sigma_i = 1$, else (i.e., $r_i > R_i^{th}$), only the original task is executed, thus, $\sigma_i = 0$. In order to describe this behaviour, the following Lemma is introduced.

Lemma 1. *Let x and y denote two discrete variables where $0 < x_{\min} \leq x \leq x_{\max} \leq 1$ and $0 < y_{\min} \leq y \leq y_{\max} \leq 1$. Let c denote a binary variable. Given the determination i) if $0 < x \leq y$, $c = 1$, and ii) if $x > y$, $c = 0$, then $\delta - (1 + \delta)c \leq x - y \leq 1 - c$, where δ is positive small value.*

Proof. Let $C_1 : \delta - (1 + \delta)c \leq x - y$ and $C_2 : x - y \leq 1 - c$. i) If $x < y$, then $x - y < 0$. For C_1, c must be 1. For C_2, c can be either 0 or 1. To satisfy C_1 and C_2 at the same time, then $c = 1$. If $x = y$, for C_1, c must be 1 due to $x - y = 0$ and $\delta > 0$. For C_2, c can be either 0 or 1. Similarly, we obtain $c = 1$. ii) If $x > y$, for C_1, c can be either 0 or 1. However, c must be 0 in C_2 due to $x - y > 0$. Hence, c must be 0 if $x > y$.

Since there are L pairs of voltage/frequency, for the values of r_i, then $r_i \in \{e^{-\varphi_i(f_1)}, \ldots, e^{-\varphi_i(f_L)}\}$. According to Lemma 1, the relationship between $R_i(f_l)$, R_i^{th} and σ_i is linearized as follows:

$$\delta - (1 + \delta)\sigma_i \leq \sum_{l \in L} s_{il} e^{-\varphi_i(f_l)} - R_i^{th} \leq 1 - \sigma_i, \ \forall i \in \mathbf{N}. \tag{2}$$

iii) Original task allocation: The original task τ_i is executed on one processor:

$$\sum_{m \in M} q_{im} = 1, \ \forall i \in \mathbf{N}. \tag{3}$$

iv) Duplicated task allocation: If a task τ_i is duplicated, the original and duplicated tasks should be allocated on different processors. The duplicated task is allocated only on one processor:

$$\sum_{m \in M} d_{im} = \sigma_i, \ \forall i \in \mathbf{N}, \tag{4a}$$

$$q_{im} + d_{im} \leq 1, \ \forall i \in \mathbf{N}, \ \forall m \in \mathbf{M}. \tag{4b}$$

v) Real-time Constraints: All (original and duplicated) tasks assigned on processor θ_m should be executed within a common deadline D:

$$\sum_{i \in N} q_{im} t_i + \sum_{i \in N} d_{im} t_i \leq D, \ \forall m \in \mathbf{M}, \tag{5}$$

where $t_i = \sum_{l \in L} s_{il} \frac{C_i}{f_l}$ is the execution time of task τ_i.

vi) Objective Function: As the duplicated task is executed with the frequency of the original task, their execution consumes the same energy. Therefore, the energy consumption of original task τ_i and its potential duplicated task is:

$$E_i = \sum_{l \in L} (1 + \sigma_i) s_{il} P_l \frac{C_i}{f_l}. \tag{6}$$

Based on Eq. (6), the total energy consumed by the system until the deadline is $E_s = \sum_{i \in N} E_i$. Based on the objective function and the aforementioned constraints, the Primal Problem (**PP**) is formulated as

$$\textbf{PP}: \quad \min_{s,q,\sigma,d} E_s \tag{7}$$

$$\text{s.t.} \begin{cases} (1), (2), (3), (4a), (4b), (5), \\ s_{il}, q_{im}, \sigma_i, d_{im} \in \{0, 1\}, \ \forall i \in N, \ \forall m \in M, \ \forall l \in L. \end{cases}$$

Since Eq. (5) and Eq. (6) include the nonlinear items $q_{im}t_i$, $d_{im}t_i$ and $\sigma_i s_{il}$, **PP** is an INLP problem, which is difficult to solve optimally. In order to find the optimal solution, and simplify the structure of problem, we equivalently transform **PP** to an MILP problem. By applying *variable replacement*, the nonlinear variable combinations are replaced and an equal to the original MILP formulation is obtained. To this end, we introduce the following Lemma:

Lemma 2. *Let b_1, b_2 and g denote binary variables. The nonlinear item $g = b_1 b_2$ can be replaced by i) $g \leq b_1$, ii) $g \leq b_2$ and iii) $g \geq b_1 + b_2 - 1$.*

Proof. The inequalities $g \leq b_1$ and $g \leq b_2$ ensure that g will be zero, if either b_1 or b_2 is zero. The equality $g \geq b_1 + b_2 - 1$ ensures that g becomes 1, if both variables b_1 and b_2 are equal to 1.

According to Lemma 2, we introduce the auxiliary binary variable h_{il} and let $h_{il} = \sigma_i s_{il}$. Then, Eq. (6) can be replaced by:

$$E_i = \sum_{l \in L} \left(s_{il} P_l \frac{C_i}{f_l} + h_{il} P_l \frac{C_i}{f_l} \right), \ \forall i \in N, \tag{8a}$$

$$- s_{il} + h_{il} \leq 0, -\sigma_i + h_{il} \leq 0, s_{il} + \sigma_i - h_{il} \leq 1, \ \forall i \in N, \ \forall l \in L. \tag{8b}$$

As a next step, $q_{im}t_i$ and $d_{im}t_i$ are linearized. Since $s_{il} \in \{0, 1\}$ and C_i is large enough, one cycle has a negligible impact on the solution. Thus, t_i are relaxed to continuous variables: $0 \leq t_i = \sum_{l \in L} s_{il} \frac{C_i}{f_l} \leq \overline{T_i}$, where $\overline{T_i} = \frac{C_i}{f_{min}}$. The following lemma is introduced:

Lemma 3. *Given two positive constants s_1 and s_2, there are two constraint spaces $P_1 = \{[t, b, x] | t = bx, -s_1 \leq x \leq s_2, b \in \{0, 1\}\}$ and $P_2 = \{[t, b, x] | -bs_1 \leq t \leq bs_2, t + bs_1 - x - s_1 \leq 0, t - bs_2 - x + s_2 \geq 0, b \in \{0, 1\}\}$, then $P_1 \rightleftharpoons P_2$.*

Proof. i) $P_1 \rightharpoonup P_2$: According to $t = bx$ and $-s_1 \leq x \leq s_2$, then $-bs_1 \leq t \leq bs_2$. Based on $-s_1 \leq x \leq s_2$ and $b \in \{0, 1\}$, then $(b - 1)(x - s_2) \geq 0$ and $(b - 1)(x + s_1) \leq 0$. Therefore, $t - bs_2 - x + s_2 \geq 0$ and $t + bs_1 - x - s_1 \leq 0$ hold. ii) $P_1 \leftharpoondown P_2$: When $b = 0$, $t = 0$ and $-s_1 \leq x \leq s_2$ according to P_2 space definition. When $b = 1$, then $-s_1 \leq t = x \leq s_2$ from P_2. Thus, $P_1 \rightleftharpoons P_2$.

Based on Lemma 3, the continuous variables $\chi_{im} = q_{im}t_i$ and $\xi_{im} = d_{im}t_i$ are introduced, replacing Eq. (5) by:

$$\sum_{i \in N} \chi_{im} + \sum_{i \in N} \xi_{im} \leq D, \ \forall m \in M, \tag{9a}$$

$$-\overline{T}_i q_{im} + \chi_{im} \leq 0, \ -t_i + \chi_{im} \leq 0, \ \overline{T}_i q_{im} + t_i - \chi_{im} \leq \overline{T}_i, \ \forall i \in N, \ \forall m \in M, \tag{9b}$$

$$-\overline{T}_i d_{im} + \xi_{im} \leq 0, \ -t_i + \xi_{im} \leq 0, \ \overline{T}_i d_{im} + t_i - \xi_{im} \leq \overline{T}_i, \ \forall i \in N, \ \forall m \in M. \tag{9c}$$

Therefore, the primal problem (7) is equally reformulated as follows:

$$\mathbf{PP1}: \min_{\substack{s,q,\sigma,d,h, \\ t,\chi,\xi}} \sum_{i \in N} \sum_{l \in L} P_l \frac{C_i}{f_l} (s_{il} + h_{il}) \tag{10}$$

$$\text{s.t.} \begin{cases} (1) \sim (3), (4a), (4b), (8b), (9a) \sim (9c), \\ -\sum_{l \in L} \frac{C_i}{f_l} s_{il} + t_i = 0, \ \forall i \in N, \\ s_{il}, q_{im}, \sigma_i, d_{im}, h_{il} \in \{0, 1\}. \\ 0 \leq t_i, \chi_{im}, \xi_{im} \leq \overline{T}_i, \ \forall i \in N, \ \forall m \in M, \ \forall l \in L. \end{cases}$$

Since all the variables (binary and continuous) are coupled linearly with each other, **PP1** is an MILP problem.

4   Experimental Results

Experimental Set-Up: The processor model is based on RISC-V Instruction Set Architecture (ISA). We have used a high-level C++ model with 32-bit RISC-V ISA and standard 5-stage pipeline, i.e., the open-source Comet processor [20]. To obtain realistic bounds for the WCEC, we analyse typical benchmarks, such as stringsearch, qsort, blowfish, and dikstra (MiBench suite [21]) and integer

Table 4. Platform and benchmark characteristics

v_l (V)	0.85	0.90	0.95	1.00	1.05	1.1
f_l (GHz)	0.801	0.8291	0.8553	0.8797	0.9027	1.0
C_{eff}		7.3249	8.6126	10.238	12.315	14.998	18.497
Main Memory Access Delay				200 cycles		

Benchmark	$WCEC_{iso}$ (Cyc.)	Num. Accesses	$WCEC_{inf}$ (Cyc.)
matmul int 32x32	3,313,958	371,957	226,488,158
matmul int64 32x32	4,055,289	507,133	308,335,089
qsort int 1000	875,616	184,089	111,329,016
qsort int64 1000	1,219,854	259,553	156,951,654
qsort softfloat 1000	1,745,122	185,437	113,007,322
dijkstra	766,369	117,151	71,056,969
blowfish	3,058,991	110,330	69,256,991
stringsearch	13,093,544	597,608	371,658,344

matrix multiplication (`matmul`). Through a measurement-based approach using Comet simulator, we count the number of execution cycles and memory access (Table 4). To obtaining safe and context-independent measurement, the sources of timing variability are eliminated [22], i.e., data-caches are considered disabled, the task is executed without interferences on a single core (WCEC_{iso}). Taking into account the number of cores, the number of memory accesses, and the delay of accessing the main memory, we compute WCEC_{inf} considering interferences. Regarding the DVFS, $L = 6$ voltage/frequency levels are used, based on the work of [19] considering 64 nm technology, as depicted Table 4.

To explore the ability to find optimal solutions and the solution quality, we performed a large and diverse set of experiments. More precisely, we tune the i) number of tasks, ii) WCEC, iii) reliability constraints and iv) deadline, considering 4 processors ($M = 4$). The failure rate constant has been set to $d_0 = 3$ and the initial failure rate $\lambda_0 = 5 \times 10^{-6}$ faults per second [8]. Three task sets are considered with N=10, 20 and 30 tasks. We generate the tasks WCEC randomly based on the measured WCEC values of Table 4, i.e., within the range $[1 \times 10^8, 4 \times 10^8]$, incorporating the cost of the DVFS switching mechanism. The deadline is given by $D = k \times \frac{N}{M} \times \frac{1}{2}\left(\frac{C_{max}}{f_{min}} + \frac{C_{max}}{f_{max}}\right)$, where k controls the range of the deadline, from tight deadlines up to more relaxed ones. The reliability constraint is randomly selected using Low Reliability Threshold (LRT) range $[0.9990, 0.9995]$ or a High Reliability Threshold (HRT) range $[0.9995, 1]$ based on the magnitude 10^{-3} of reliability target in [1]. Notice that, these numbers change only the values of the problem parameters, and not the problem structure. The evaluation is performed following the Once Tuning One Parameter (OTOP) approach, where only one parameter is modified at each experiment. Each experiment is repeated 20 times, modifying the WCEC and the reliability constraints. Each figure point presents the average result. In total, we have performed at least 12 (different deadline values) $\times$ 3 (number of tasks) $\times$ 20 (with different WCEC and reliability constraint) = 720 experiments, per approach.

The first set of experiments explores how the proposed approach behaves (energy consumption, percentage of duplicated tasks) with respect to i) real-time constraints and ii) reliability constraints. The second set of experiments compares the energy consumption, the feasibility (the percentage of the experiments where we obtained the optimal solution), the reliability improvement, and the estimation time, under reliability and real-time constraints for: i) the proposed Duplication-based Fault-Tolerant Mapping Approach (DFTMA), ii) a task mapping approach always satisfying the reliability constraint, without applying task duplication (formulated as **FTM**), similar to [13], and iii) a task mapping approach (formulated as **FDM**) always applying task duplication, similar to [1,14], when the number of replicas is set to two. We present results using LRT range, in order not to penalise the FTM approach. FTM under HRT constraint leads to many infeasible solutions. Since **FTM** and **FDM** are INLP problems, we apply the proposed transformation to convert them into an MILP problems, in order to be able to compare their optimal solutions. We have used Matlab 2018a to implement and solve (MILP solver) the problem formulation of DFTMA, FTM and FDM formulation. The simulations are performed on a quad-core 2.11 GHz Intel i7 processor and 16 GB RAM.

$$\text{FTM}: \quad \min_{s,q} \sum_{i \in N} \sum_{l \in L} s_{il} P_l \frac{C_i}{f_l}$$

$$\text{s.t.} \begin{cases} (1),(3), \\ \sum_{l \in L} s_{il} e^{-\varphi_i(f_l)} \geq R_i^{th}, \ \forall i \in N, \\ \sum_{i \in N} q_{im} t_i \leq D, \ \forall m \in M, \\ s_{il}, q_{im} \in \{0,1\}, \\ \forall i \in N, \ \forall m \in M, \ \forall l \in L. \end{cases}$$

$$\text{FDM}: \quad \min_{s,q,d} \sum_{i \in N} \sum_{l \in L} 2 s_{il} P_l \frac{C_i}{f_l}$$

$$\text{s.t.} \begin{cases} (1),(3),(4b),(5), \\ \sum_{m=1}^{M} d_{im} = 1, \ \forall i \in N, \\ s_{il}, q_{im}, d_{im} \in \{0,1\}, \\ \forall i \in N, \ \forall m \in M, \ \forall l \in L. \end{cases}$$

Real-Time Constraint: Figure 1a shows the energy consumption DFTMA, when the parameter k is tuned, from tight up to relaxed deadlines, with a reliability constraint within the LRT range. Figure 1a shows that more energy is consumed: i) when the task number N increases, and ii) when real-time constraints become tight (k decreases), since higher frequencies are required to meet the deadline. With k increasing, more slack exists, and a lower frequency (that still meets the reliability constraints) can be assigned, minimizing energy consumption. From a point and on ($k = 1.6$ for $N = 10$, $k = 1.4$ for $N = 20$, $k = 1.5$ for $N = 30$), the energy consumption is stable; the deadline is relaxed enough, and thus, it does not influence the global optimal solution.

Figure 1b shows the percentage of duplicated tasks by DFTMA. The number of duplicated tasks is low at tight deadlines; no slack exists, thus duplication cannot be applied and the deadline met at the same time. As k increases, slack is created, tasks are duplicated and lower frequencies are assigned, reducing energy consumption. With large enough deadline, almost all tasks are duplicated and executed with low frequencies.

Reliability Constraint: We further explore the behavior of DFTMA, when the reliability constraints belong to LRT and HRT regions. Figure 2 shows the obtained energy consumption, when $N = 10$ (Fig. 2a) and $N = 20$ (Fig. 2b). The energy consumption decreases with more relaxed deadlines. The HRT case

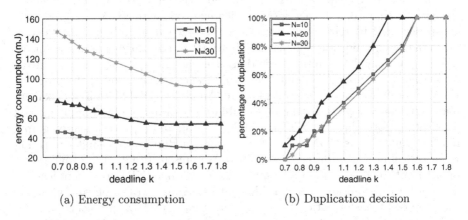

(a) Energy consumption   (b) Duplication decision

Fig. 1. Energy consumption and duplication decision for LRT.

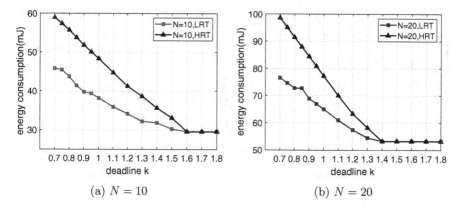

(a) $N = 10$ (b) $N = 20$

Fig. 2. Energy consumption considering LRT and HRT.

consumes more energy than LRT case under same conditions. As expect, when k is low, i.e., the deadline is strict, the strict reliability constraints require higher frequency to execute the tasks, which consumes more energy.

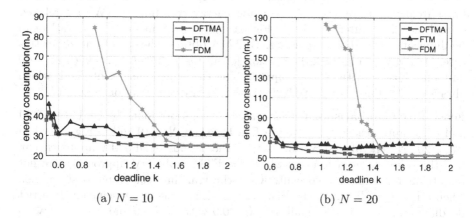

(a) $N = 10$ (b) $N = 20$

Fig. 3. Energy consumption comparison.

Energy Consumption Comparison: The energy consumption comparison of DFTMA, FTM and FDM approaches is depicted in Fig. 3a, with $N = 10$ and in Fig. 3b, with $N = 20$. A general observation is that the energy consumption obtained by DFTMA and FTM follows a similar trend. When the deadline is not strict, the energy consumption of DFTMA is less than the consumption of FTM. The FTM approach selects higher frequencies, since it requires to always satisfy the reliability constraints. On the contrary, DFTMA approach can exploit partial task duplication and use of lower frequencies in order to reduce energy consumption. The energy consumption of the FDM approach is much higher than

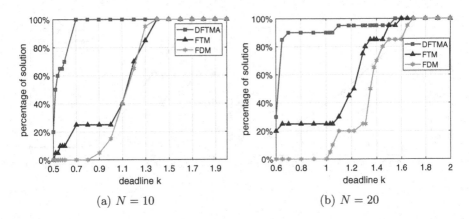

Fig. 4. Feasibility comparison

both DFTMA and FTM approaches, especially when the real-time constraints are strict (e.g., k within the range $[0.9, 1.4]$ in Fig. 3a). High frequencies are required when deadline is strict in order to execute both original and duplicated tasks before the deadline, leading to high energy consumption. As k increases, lower frequencies are assigned, reducing energy consumption. With a relaxed enough deadline (after $k = 1.6$ in Fig. 3a and $k = 1.5$ in Fig. 3b), all tasks can be duplicated with low frequencies. DFTMA obtains the same solution in this case. DFTMA decides task duplication for all tasks after $k = 1.6$ with $N = 10$ and after $k = 1.4$ with $N = 20$, approaching the same behavior of FDM, which always applies duplication, achieving lower energy consumption than FTM.

Feasibility Comparison: The percentage of solutions found by DFTMA, FTM and FDM approaches is depicted in Fig. 4a, when $N = 10$ and in Fig. 4b, when $N = 20$. A general observation is that the proposed DFTMA approach can find the solution, even in cases where the FTM and FDM approaches are not able to find a solution, especially when the real-time constraint is strict, i.e., when k has a small value. The FDM approach has the worst behavior. In strict deadline cases (when k is small, $k = 0.5$–0.9 with $N = 10$ and $k = 0.6$–1 with $N = 20$), FDM cannot find any solution. This is explained since the FDM approach applies duplication for each task, thus more time is needed to execute the original and the duplicated tasks, compared to both the FTM (no duplication) and the proposed DFTMA (partial duplication of tasks). Compared with FTM, the proposed approach performs generally better: in FTM approach, the reliability is a hard constraint that must be always satisfied, whereas in DFTMA, if the reliability constraint cannot be satisfied by original task execution, then a duplication task is applied to achieve a reliable execution. In this way, the proposed approach has a higher probability of finding the solution. Both in Fig. 4a and Fig. 4b, we can observe that when deadline becomes relaxed enough, after a given point (for example when $k = 1.4$ in Fig. 4a and $k = 1.7$ in Fig. 4b), all the three approaches can almost 100% provide a solution. This is possible since the deadline constraints, after these points, become loose enough and do not impact the feasibility of obtaining a solution.

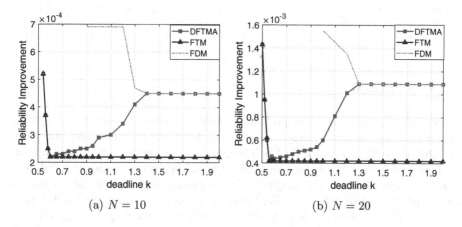

(a) $N = 10$ (b) $N = 20$

Fig. 5. Reliability improvement

Reliability Improvement (RI): Figure 5 shows the task reliability improvement above the reliability constraint, i.e., $RI = R_i - R_i^{th}$. The trend is the same for $N = 10$ and $N = 20$. For strict deadline, the RI is high for both DFTMA and FTM, due to the assignment of high frequencies, while FDM cannot find solutions. With deadline relaxing, FTM achieves a low RI, as it only requires to meet the reliability constraint. However, DFTMA exploits the time slack, duplicating tasks, increasing RI. Whenever FDM finds a solution, it has higher RI, due to full duplication. As k increases, DFTMA and FDM behave similarly.

Estimation Time: Table 5 depicts the time required to obtain the solutions. For all approaches, the stricter is the deadline, the higher is the estimation time. Even if the proposed approach requires a few more seconds it is able to find a significantly higher number of solutions. For instance, when $N = 10$ and $k = 0.5$, DFTMA requires 5.26 s more than FTM, but it finds solutions for 20% of the experiments, while the FTM finds very few ones. When $k = 0.7$, although the estimation time is similar, DFTMA is able to find optimal solutions for all experiments, while FTM found only 22% and FDM none. For the remaining cases, the estimation times are comparable. It should be stressed that as the approaches are applied offline, and thus, trading off a few more seconds in order to obtain optimal solutions is motivating.

Table 5. Estimation time (seconds) when at least one solution is found

	N = 10										N = 20							
k	0.5	0.6	0.7	0.8	0.9	1.0	1.1	1.2	1.3	1.4	1.0	1.1	1.2	1.3	1.4	1.5	1.6	1.7
DFTMA	8.36	0.14	0.13	0.05	0.16	0.19	0.06	0.06	0.09	0.06	114	1.23	0.16	0.13	0.13	0.2	0.05	0.06
FTM	3.1	0.06	0.11	0.03	0.13	0.06	0.02	0.03	0.03	0.02	10.75	0.56	0.11	0.08	0.06	0.14	0.02	0.02
FDM	–	–	–	–	179.03	23.81	0.05	0.03	0.02	0.03	–	94.7	20.66	0.09	0.03	0.02	0.09	0.11

5 Conclusion

In this paper, we studied the problem of task mapping by jointly solving task allocation, task frequency assignment, task duplication decision on multicore architectures enhanced with DVFS. The goal is to minimize energy consumption without violating the real-time constraint and taking into account the reliability. A safe transformation of the original INLP problem is applied to obtain an equivalent MILP problem, which is solved optimally. Through comparison of the proposed approach and two other energy-aware existing task mapping approaches, experimental results show that the proposed approach provides better trade-off between energy consumption and reliability, being able to find optimal solutions, even when existing approaches cannot. As future direction, the proposed strategy will be explored for heterogeneous architectures and for dependent task model.

Acknowledgement. This work has been founded by China Scholarship Council (CSC).

References

1. Haque, M.A., Aydin, H., Zhu, D.: On reliability management of energy-aware real-time systems through task replication. IEEE TPDS **28**(3), 813–825 (2017)
2. Zhao, B., Aydin, H., Zhu, D.: On maximizing reliability of real-time embedded applications under hard energy constraint. IEEE TII **6**(3), 316–328 (2010)
3. Zhou, J., et al.: Resource management for improving soft-error and lifetime reliability of real-time MPSoCs. IEEE TCAD **38**(12), 2215–2228 (2019)
4. Ma, Y., Chantem, T., Dick, R.P., Wang, S., Hu, X.S.: An on-line framework for improving reliability of real-time systems on 'Big-little' type MPSoC. In: IEEE/ACM DATE, pp. 1558–1101 (2017)
5. Ebrahimi, M., Evans, A., Tahoori, M.B., Seyyedi, R., Costenaro, E., Alexandrescu, D.: Comprehensive analysis of alpha and neutron particle-induced soft errors in an embedded processor at nanoscales. In: IEEE/ACM DATE, pp. 1–6 (2014)
6. Baumann, R.C.: Radiation-induced soft errors in advanced semiconductor technologies. IEEE TDMR **5**(3), 305–316 (2005)
7. Sudo, T., Sasaki, H., Masuda, N., Drewniak, J.L.: Electromagnetic interference (EMI) of system-on-package (SOP). IEEE TAP **27**(2), 304–314 (2004)
8. Zhu, D., Melhem, R., Mosse, D.: The effects of energy management on reliability in real-time embedded systems. In: IEEE/ACM ICCAD, pp. 35–40 (2004)

9. McPherson, J.W.: Reliability challenges for 45 nm and beyond. In: ACM DAC, pp. 176–18(2006)
10. Huang, K., et al.: Energy-efficient fault-tolerant mapping and scheduling on heterogeneous multiprocessors real-time systems. IEEE Access **6**, 57614–57630 (2018)
11. Chen, G., Huang, K., Knoll, A.: Energy optimization for real-time multiprocessor system-on-chip with optimal DVFS and DPM combination. ACM TECS **13**(3), 1–21 (2014)
12. Gou, C., Benoit, A., Chen, M., Marchal, L., Wei, T.: Reliability-aware energy optimization for throughput-constrained applications on MPSoC. In: ICPADS (2018)
13. Xie, G., Chen, Y., Liu, Y., Wei, Y., Li, R., Li, K.: Resource consumption cost minimization of reliable parallel applications on heterogeneous embedded systems. IEEE TII **3**(3), 1629–1640 (2017)
14. Xie, G., Chen, Y., Xiao, X., Xu, C., Li, R., Li, K.: Energy-efficient fault-tolerant scheduling of reliable parallel applications on heterogeneous distributed embedded systems. IEEE TSC **3**(3), 167–181 (2018)
15. Wang, S., Li, K., Mei, J., Xiao, G., Li, K.: A reliability-aware task scheduling algorithm based on heterogeneous computing systems. JGC **15**(1), 23–39 (2017)
16. Haque, M.A., Aydin, H., Zhu, D.: Energy-aware task replication to manage reliability for periodic real-time applications on multicore platforms. In: IEEE International Green Computing Conference, pp. 1–11 (2013)
17. Zheng, Q., Veeravalli, B., Tham, C.: On the design of fault-tolerant scheduling strategies using primary-backup approach for computational grids with low replication costs. IEEE TC **58**(3), 380–393 (2009)
18. Dubrova, E.: Fault Tolerant Design. Springer, New York (2013). https://doi.org/10.1007/978-1-4614-2113-9
19. Quan, G., Chaturvedi, V.: Feasibility analysis for temperature-constraint hard real-time periodic tasks. IEEE TII **6**(3), 329–339 (2010)
20. Rokicki, S., Pala, D., Paturel, J., Sentieys, O.: What you simulate is what you synthesize: designing a processor core from C++ specifications. In: IEEE/ACM ICCAD (2019)
21. Guthaus, M.R., Ringenberg, J.S., Ernst, D., Austin, T.M., Mudge, T., Brown, R.B.: A free, commercially representative embedded benchmark suite. In: International Workshop on Workload Characterization (2001)
22. Deverge, J., Puaut, I.: Safe measurement-based WCET estimation. In: WCET (2007)

A Quantitative Study of Locality in GPU Caches

Sohan Lal$^{(\boxtimes)}$ ⓘ and Ben Juurlink

Technische Universität Berlin, Berlin, Germany
{sohan.lal,b.juurlink}@tu-berlin.de

Abstract. Traditionally, GPUs only had programmer-managed caches. The advent of hardware-managed caches accelerated the use of GPUs for general-purpose computing. However, as GPU caches are shared by thousands of threads, they are usually a victim of contention and can suffer from thrashing and high miss rate, in particular, for memory-divergent workloads. As data locality is crucial for performance, there have been several efforts focusing on exploiting data locality in GPUs. However, there is a lack of quantitative analysis of data locality and data reuse in GPUs. In this paper, we quantitatively study the data locality and its limits in GPUs. We observe that data locality is much higher than exploited by current GPUs. We show that, on the one hand, the low spatial utilization of cache lines justifies the use of demand-fetched caches. On the other hand, the much higher actual spatial utilization of cache lines shows the lost spatial locality and presents opportunities for further optimizing the cache design.

Keywords: Data locality · GPU caches · Memory divergence

1 Introduction

GPUs have been very successful in accelerating general-purpose applications from different domains. The advent of hardware-managed caches further accelerated the use of GPUs for general-purpose computing by exploiting temporal and spatial locality. Caches reduce off-chip memory traffic and cut down pressure on memory bandwidth, however, using caches efficiently is a difficult task because a GPU employs a large number of threads, and GPU caches are small that lead to high contention and thrashing. In particular, there is a class of applications known as irregular applications that poorly utilize GPU caches. Irregular applications have memory divergence and/or control divergence, and they span a broad range of domains. GPUs issue concurrent memory accesses to consecutive addresses by coalescing memory accesses of threads in a warp. However, it may not always be possible to coalesce individual thread accesses due to scattered memory accesses that lead to memory divergence.

Memory divergence is known to cause many problems, including data over-fetch which can waste cache capacity, consume scarce resources such as MSHRs

© Springer Nature Switzerland AG 2020
A. Orailoglu et al. (Eds.): SAMOS 2020, LNCS 12471, pp. 228–242, 2020.
https://doi.org/10.1007/978-3-030-60939-9_16

and memory bandwidth, thus, further making it hard to utilize caches efficiently. As exploiting data locality is important for performance, there have been several studies to exploit the data locality in GPUs [7,15]. Moreover, the recent generations of GPUs have adapted the cache design to tackle issues such as data over-fetch caused by memory divergence. For example, Maxwell, Pascal, and Volta GPU architectures use sector caches to fetch only the sectors that are requested instead of always fetching all sectors of a cache line. We show that there is a higher locality in GPU caches than currently exploited by demand-fetched caches, offering opportunities for further optimizing the cache design for higher performance. Moreover, there is a lack of quantitative analysis of data locality and data reuse in GPUs. Therefore, in this paper, we quantitatively study the data locality and its limits in GPUs at different granularities. We observe that data locality is much higher than currently exploited by GPUs.

In summary, we make the following main contributions:

- We present a comprehensive, quantitative and limit study of locality in GPU data caches for memory-divergent workloads.
- We show that about 50% of cache capacity, and other scarce resources such as NoC bandwidth, memory bandwidth are wasted due to data over-fetch.
- We show that memory-divergent workloads have much higher locality than exploited by GPUs as locality gets destroyed due to cache thrashing.
- Our analysis shows that 57% of the cache lines are never re-referenced. However, the limit study shows that actually, only 30% of the cache lines are never re-referenced and 27% are evicted before re-reference.
- We show that the low spatial utilization of cache lines justifies the design decision to fetch sectors based on demand, however, the much higher actual spatial utilization of cache lines shows the lost spatial locality and presents opportunities for further optimizing cache designs.

The paper is organized as follows. In Sect. 2, we briefly discuss GPU data caches and classify locality. In Sect. 3, we explain the experimental setup. Section 4 presents the quantitative results. Section 5 describes related work. Finally, we conclude in Sect. 6.

2   Background on GPU L1 and L2 Data Caches

Traditionally, GPUs only had programmer-managed caches, however, with the advent of Fermi architecture, GPUs started using hardware-managed caches. In fact, the hardware-managed caches have accelerated the use of GPUs for general-purpose computing. There are several works which compared the performance of Tesla and Fermi GPUs and reported that hardware-managed caches play an important role in the higher performance of Fermi GPUs over Tesla GPUs [3,6,18]. GPU caches face different design challenges than CPU caches due to their different characteristics. For instance, write and allocation policies are quite different from CPU caches. The L1 data cache is only write-back for local accesses and write-evict for global accesses whereas in a CPU we either have write-back

Table 1. Summary of locality classification.

Locality category	Description
Intra-warp	Locality from threads of the same warp
Inter-warp	Locality from different warps
Intra-CTA	Locality from warps of the same CTA
Inter-CTA	Locality from different CTAs

or write-through caches. The allocation policy is usually no-write allocate for global accesses and write-allocate for only local accesses. The deviation in write and allocation policies is to cater to the different requirements of GPU workloads and smaller caches. GPU caches are shared by thousands of threads which make them a scarce resource and a victim of a lot of contention. Furthermore, due to the streaming nature of many GPU applications and smaller cache sizes, caches can suffer from thrashing and high miss rate. Therefore, exploiting locality in GPU caches is hard due to a large number of active threads and smaller caches. In fact, some works reported negative performance results with caches [7,14].

Thread-blocks or co-operative thread arrays (CTA) in NVIDIA terminology are independent units of scheduling on streaming multiprocessors (SMs) and a thread-block can be scheduled on any SM. This feature allows transparent scalability as simply more thread-blocks can be scheduled in parallel when more SMs are available and vice-versa. As thread-blocks can be scheduled on any SM, it is very hard to exploit inter-thread block locality at L1 caches because the L1 cache is private to an SM. For example, when two thread-blocks have inter-thread block locality but they are scheduled on different SMs, there is no way to exploit inter-thread block locality at L1. L2 cache is useful for exploiting inter-thread block locality in this case as L2 cache is shared among all SMs. Therefore, we have a relatively large L2 cache, which helps to filter requests to off-chip memory. L1 and L2 caches on GPUs are smaller than L1 and L2 caches in CPUs, but they have high bandwidth.

A typical cache line size is 128B in GPUs. The loads and stores were normally serviced at the granularity of a cache line until the Fermi architecture. However, starting from the Kepler architecture and subsequently, in other architectures such as Maxwell, Pascal, and Volta, the loads and stores can be serviced at 32B granularity. The 32B granularity is known as a sector. These architectures still have a data cache line size of 128B, but a cache line is divided into 4 sectors. There are byte masks, and on a miss, a cache will only fetch the 32B sectors that are requested. A full cache line is not automatically fetched, however, if all four sectors are requested, it is also possible to fetch a full cache line.

2.1 Locality Classification

As a thread block (also known as CTA), and a warp are the scheduling units in GPUs, we classify and study locality at thread block and warp level granulari-

Table 2. Summary of simulator configuration.

Parameter	Value	Parameter	Value
#SMs	16	Shared memory/SM	48 KB
SM freq (MHz)	822	L1 $ size/SM	16 KB
Max #Threads per SM	1536	L2 $ size	768 KB
Max #CTA per SM	8	# Memory controllers	6
Max CTA size	512	Memory type	GDDR5
#FUs per SM	32	Memory clock	2004 MHz
#Registers/SM	32K	Memory bandwidth	192.4 GB/s

ties. We classify the locality as *intra-warp locality* when a cache line is initially referenced by a warp and then re-referenced by the same warp. When a cache line is re-referenced by a different warp than the one initially requested the cache line, we classify such a locality as *inter-warp locality*. Similar to intra-warp and inter-warp locality, we classify the locality as *intra-CTA locality* and *inter-CTA locality*. Table 1 shows a summary of the locality classification.

3   Experimental Setup

In this section, we describe our experimental methodology.

3.1   Simulator

We use gpgpu-sim simulator for simulating different benchmarks [2]. We configure the simulator to have two level data caches with a cache line size of 128B. Table 2 summarizes the main configuration parameters of the simulator.

3.2   Benchmarks

Table 3 shows the benchmarks used for the experimental evaluation. We include benchmarks from the popular Rodinia benchmark suite [4] and CUDA SDK [13] that have memory divergence. From each benchmark, we select a single kernel launch with the highest memory divergence, and when a benchmark has multiple kernels, we only include kernels that have memory-divergence. A benchmark is memory divergent if all intra-warp memory accesses of a load or a store instruction cannot be coalesced into one (two) memory transaction(s) depending upon whether the coalescing is done at half (full) warp. We use coalescing efficiency to note the degree of memory divergence for each benchmark. The lower the coalescing efficiency, the higher the degree of memory divergence. The coalescing efficiency is given by the following equation:

$$\mathrm{CE} = \sum \mathrm{GMI} / \sum \mathrm{GMT}$$

Table 3. Memory-divergent benchmarks used for the experimentation. A benchmark with different subscripts designates distinct kernels of the same benchmark.

Name	Launch id	CE (%)	Description
histogram	36	3	Histograms for analysis [13]
kmeans1	1	6	k-means clustering [4]
scan1	11	5	Parallel prefix sum [13]
srad2_1	1	56	Speckle reducing anisotropic diffusion [4]
srad2_2	2	53	Speckle reducing anisotropic diffusion [4]
bfs	15	47	Breadth-first search [4]
ss1	9	11	Similarity score calculation [4]
b+tree1	1	75	Graph search [4]
b+tree2	2	75	Graph search [4]
srad1_1	5	70	Speckle reducing anisotropic diffusion [4]
srad1_2	11	79	Speckle reducing anisotropic diffusion [4]
mummergpu	1	7	Pairwise local sequence alignment [4]
storeGPU	1	41	Distributed storage systems [1]
mergesort1	2	5	Parallel merge-sort [13]
mergesort2	3	50	Parallel merge-sort [13]
mergesort3	41	67	Parallel merge-sort [13]
convSep1	1	50	Convolution [13]
convSep2	2	43	Convolution [13]
backprop1	2	64	Multi-layer perceptron training [4]
heartwall	2	54	Ultrasound image tracking [4]
hotspot	1	35	Processor temperature estimation [4]
leukocyte	3	51	Microscopy video tracking [4]

GMI is the total number of global memory instructions executed for a benchmark and GMT is the corresponding number of global memory transactions issued. When global memory instructions are equal to the global memory transactions, we have a case of perfect coalescing (100%), assuming 32-bit data is accessed by each thread. In the worst case, there can be one transaction issued per thread of a warp that corresponds to a coalescing efficiency of about 3% (1/32). Table 3 shows the coalescing efficiency of the benchmarks.

4   Results

In this section, we present the results of the quantitative study of L1 and L2 data caches. In Sect. 4.1, we present results for cache line reuse. Section 4.2 presents the analysis of the spatial utilization of cache lines. In Sect. 4.3 and Sect. 4.4, we study locality at warp and CTA levels, respectively.

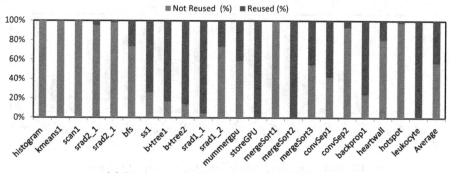

(a) L1 data cache lines reuse with 16KB size.

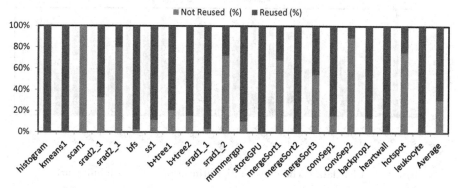

(b) Limit of L1 data cache lines reuse with with an infinite size.

Fig. 1. GPU L1 data cache lines reuse.

4.1 GPU Data Cache Lines Reuse Limit

Figure 1 shows the reuse of L1 data cache lines. Figure 1a shows the reuse of L1 data cache lines for 16 KB size. The figure shows that for several kernels such as *histogram*, *kmeans1*, *scan1*, the cache lines are evicted without any reuse. Only a few kernels such as *storeGPU*, *mergeSort2*, and *leukocyte* have all of the cache lines reused. The average cache line reuse is only 43%, which means that 57% of the cache lines are never re-referenced or gets evicted before re-reference.

In order to study the lost opportunities to reuse cache lines due to limited cache size, we also simulate a L1 data cache with infinite size. The infinite cache size here implies that once a cache line is brought to the cache, it never gets evicted. Figure 1b shows the L1 data cache lines reuse with an infinite size. The average cache lines reuse for the infinite L1 data cache is 70%, which shows that most of the kernels have high locality but current GPUs are unable to exploit the locality due to limited cache size. However, even with the infinite cache size, 30% of the L1 data cache lines have no data reuse.

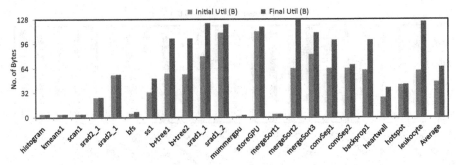

(a) L1 data cache lines spatial utilization with 16KB size.

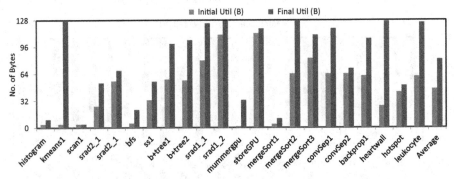

(b) Limit of L1 data cache lines spatial utilization with an infinite size.

Fig. 2. GPU L1 data cache lines spatial utilization showing data over-fetch.

4.2 GPU Data Cache Lines Spatial Utilization Limit and Over-Fetch

Figure 2 shows the spatial utilization of L1 data cache lines. Each kernel has two bars. The first bar shows the average initial utilization of a cache line, i.e., when a cache line is initially fetched. The second bar shows the average final utilization of a cache line, i.e., when a cache line is evicted. For calculating the spatial utilization, we use a bit vector of length equal to a cache line size. The bits corresponding to bytes that are requested at the time of fetching a cache line are initially set and the bit vector is updated whenever a cache line is reused until the cache line is finally evicted.

Figure 2a shows the spatial utilization of the L1 data cache lines for 16 KB cache size. The figure shows that for many kernels, the initial and the final utilization of cache lines is almost the same, which means there is a very low spatial utilization of L1 data cache lines. Only kernels such as *b+tree1*, *b+tree2*, *srad1*, *mergesort2*, *mergeSort3*, *convSep1*, *backprop1*, and *leukocyte* have significantly higher final utilization of cache lines. The average initial and final utilization of cache lines is 46B and 65B for all kernels. This implies that about 50% of the cache capacity, and other scarce resources such as network-on-chip bandwidth, L2 data cache bandwidth, etc., are wasted due to the data over-fetch.

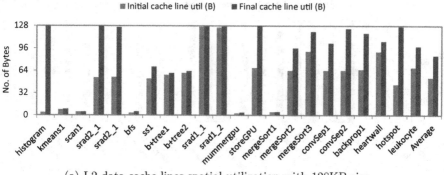

(a) L2 data cache lines spatial utilization with 128KB size.

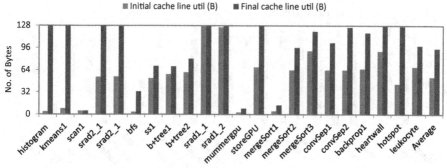

(b) Limit of L2 data cache lines spatial utilization with an infinite size.

Fig. 3. GPU L2 data cache lines spatial utilization showing data over-fetch.

The low utilization of cache lines could also be due to the limited cache capacity and high contention as a cache line may be evicted before it gets re-referenced again. To study the upper limit of the spatial utilization of cache lines, we simulate an infinite L1 data cache, which means a cache line once fetched to the cache never gets evicted. Figure 2b shows the final utilization of cache lines for an infinite L1 data cache. The figure shows that most of the kernels actually have higher spatial locality than exploited by the default cache size, however, GPUs are unable to exploit full spatial locality. The average final utilization of cache lines for the infinite L1 data cache is 81B, which is 24% higher than the default cache size. However, even with the infinite cache size, 36% of the cache capacity is still wasted. This implies that there is a potential for further improvements in the cache design.

There are two important conclusions that we can draw from the spatial utilization of cache lines. First, on the one hand, the low initial spatial utilization of cache lines justifies the sector cache design of Maxwell, Pascal, and Volta architectures. On the other hand, the much higher final spatial utilization of cache lines, as shown by our experiments, presents an opportunity for further optimizing cache designs. For example, if we only fetch the sectors on demand

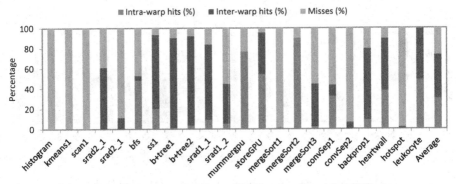

(a) Intra- and inter-warp locality of L1 data cache with 16KB size.

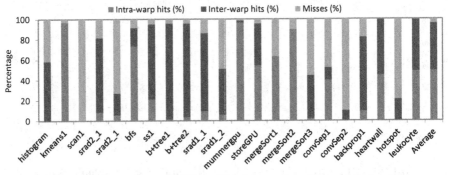

(b) Intra- and inter-warp locality of L1 data cache with an infinite size.

Fig. 4. Intra- and inter-warp locality of L1 data cache.

depending on the initial utilization of a cache line, we significantly lose the spatial locality present in the kernels. The initial sectors that need to be fetched for a memory load can be determined at the time of coalescing different memory requests of threads of a warp. If we only fetch the sectors as determined during coalescing, which is how it is done in recent GPUs, there will be significant lost opportunities for exploiting locality as our analysis shows that the final utilization of cache lines is much higher than the initial utilization of cache lines (see Fig. 2). One possible idea to exploit the lost locality is to investigate the use of spatial locality predictor for GPUs and then depending upon the prediction, fetch the predicted sectors.

We also did a similar kind of analysis for the L2 data cache. Figure 3 shows the spatial utilization of L2 data cache lines for 128 KB as well as infinite cache sizes. Figure 3a shows that the L2 data cache has better spatial utilization of cache lines compared to the L1 data cache. This is because the L2 data cache is shared by multiple processors. The average initial and the final utilization of cache lines is 54B and 85B, respectively. This means that 35% of the L2 data cache capacity is wasted, which is lower than the L1 data cache but still significant

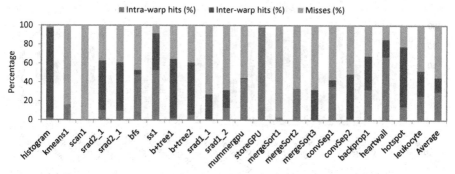

(a) Intra- and inter-warp locality of L2 data cache with 128KB size.

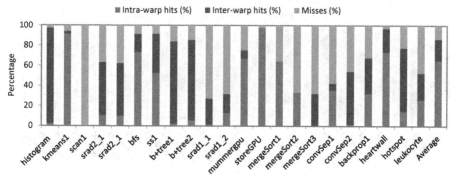

(b) Intra- and inter-warp locality of L2 data cache with an infinite size.

Fig. 5. Intra- and inter-warp locality of L2 data cache.

to look for further optimizations. The wastage of the L2 data cache is also a measure of wasted off-chip memory bandwidth. The average final utilization of cache lines is 95B for the infinite cache, which is almost 2.0× more compared to the average initial utilization of cache lines. The big difference between the initial and the final utilization of cache lines shows that pure demand-based sector fetching, implemented in GPU caches, needs to be revisited to improve their performance. The analysis also shows that we need more aggressive policies to properly utilize the L1 data cache than the L2 data cache.

4.3   Intra- and Inter-Warp Locality

As cache hits and misses are important metrics to evaluate a cache design, we also present hits and misses for both L1 and L2 data caches. We classify hits into two categories, *intra-warp* and *inter-warp hits*. As a warp is an important scheduling unit within an streaming multiprocessor, the hit ratio at a warp granularity provides crucial information that could be used for both scheduling warps and improving cache design.

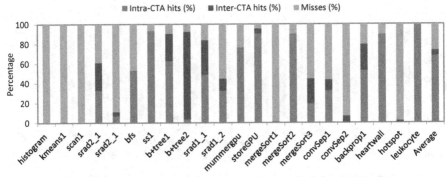

(a) Intra- and inter-CTA locality of L1 data cache with 16KB size.

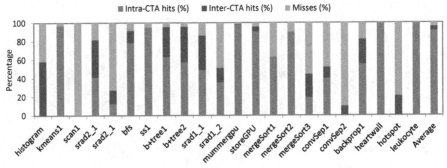

(b) Intra- and inter-CTA locality of L1 data cache with an infinite size.

Fig. 6. Intra- and inter-CTA locality of L1 data cache.

Figure 4 shows the intra- and inter-warp hits of L1 data cache. Figure 4a shows that the L1 data cache has 31% intra-warp and 43% inter-warp hits for 16 KB cache size. The miss rate is 26% which is quite high. In contrast to GPUs, CPUs have a hit rate typically between 95% to 97% for a L1 cache. As discussed earlier, it is extremely difficult to exploit data locality in GPU caches due to several factors such as small size, massive multithreading.

Figure 4b shows the intra- and inter-warp hits for the L1 data cache with the infinite size. The figure shows that the average hit rate is about 96%, which is close to a typical hit rate for a CPU L1 cache. Concretely, on an average, we have 50% intra-warp and 46% inter-warp hits. There are a couple of interesting observations. First, kernels actually have a significantly higher locality but the current GPUs are not able to fully exploit it. Second, in contrast to some existing work [15], which shows much higher intra-warp locality than inter-warp locality, we see that there is almost equal division between the intra-warp and inter-warp localities. This is possible for memory-divergent workloads as they have scattered memory accesses and threads from different warps (which contributes to inter-warp hits) can access the data from the same cache line. This can happen more frequently for memory-divergent workloads compared to regular workloads.

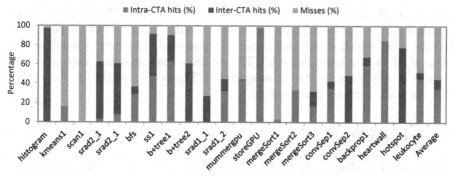

(a) Intra- and inter-CTA locality of L2 data cache with 128KB size.

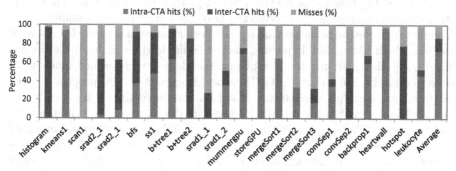

(b) Intra- and inter-CTA locality of L2 data cache with an infinite size.

Fig. 7. Intra- and inter-CTA locality of L2 data cache.

We also study the intra- and inter-warp locality for the L2 data cache. Figure 5 shows the intra- and inter-warp locality for the L2 data cache. The average intra-warp and inter-warp hits are 30% and 15%, respectively, for the 128 KB size, while for the infinite size, the average intra-warp and inter-warp hits are 65% and 21%, respectively.

An important point that is not evident after looking at the intra- and inter-warp locality is whether the warps belong to the same CTA or different CTAs (co-operative thread array aka thread block). This could also provide useful insight as CTAs are units of work distribution across different streaming multiprocessors. Moreover, the quantitative numbers further provide information on making scheduling decisions, for example, should we first schedule the warps from the same CTA or different CTAs.

4.4   Intra- and Inter-CTA Locality

Figure 6 shows the intra- and inter-CTA locality of the L1 data cache for 16 KB and infinite sizes. Figure 6a shows that on an average, there are 68% intra-CTA hits and 5% inter-CTA hits, which shows that a high percentage of inter-warp hits shown in Figure 4 are basically from warps within the same CTA. This is more evident when we look at the average numbers for the infinite L1 data cache.

On average, 91% hits are intra-CTA and only 5% are inter-CTA. Figure 7 shows a similar analysis for the L2 data cache. For the infinite L2 data cache, inter-CTA hits are 13%, which shows that there is a potential for better scheduling. For example, if we can schedule such CTAs on the same streaming multiprocessor, there is a possibility to exploit more inter-CTA locality at the L1 data cache that can lead to better performance.

5   Related Work

Related Work on Locality in GPU Caches: There are several works which report that hardware-managed caches play an important role in the higher performance of GPUs [3,6,18]. It is also well-known that exploiting locality is crucial in GPUs, otherwise, hardware-managed caches can also cause negative performance [7,14]. As sometimes, the use of caches can degrade performance, there have been several studies, which show that bypassing caches could lead to higher performance [5,9,11,19]. However, to the best of our knowledge, there is not much work done to quantify the locality in GPU caches. Rogers et al. [15] propose a cache aware warp scheduling mechanism, based on estimated intra-warp locality, to capture locality that is lost by other schedulers due to excessive contention for cache capacity. They reported that the majority of data reuse observed in highly cache sensitive benchmarks comes from intra-warp locality and therefore, give priority to intra-warp instructions to access L1 data cache. Li et al. [10] quantify the percentage of the inter-CTA reuse, which is based on the data reuse of all the memory requests generated from streaming multiprocessors before they enter L1 cache. In contrast, we present a comprehensive quantitative study of L1 and L2 data caches in GPUs, highlighting the gap between the locality exploited and the maximum locality actually present in workloads.

Related Work on Memory Divergence: Meng et al. [12] introduce dynamic warp subdivision (DWS), which allows a single warp to occupy more than one slot in the scheduler. Independent scheduling entities allow divergent branch paths to interleave their execution, and allow threads that hit to run ahead. The DWS does not improve memory divergence, but results in improved latency hiding and memory level parallelism. Tarjan et al. [17] propose adaptive slip, which allows a subset of threads from SIMD warps to continue execution while other threads in the same warp are waiting for memory. This provides benefits when runahead threads prefetch cache lines for lagging threads.

Zhang et al. [20] propose a software solution called G-Streamline to improve both irregular memory references and control flow. G-Streamline eliminates irregularity by enhancing the thread-data mappings on the fly. Sartori and Kumar [16] propose branch and data herding, which exploit error tolerance of applications to reduce memory divergence. Branch and data herding is based on the observation that many GPU applications produce acceptable outputs even if a small number of threads in a SIMD execution unit are forced to go down the wrong control path or are forced to load from an incorrect address. Lal et al. [8]

investigate performance bottlenecks in GPUs and show that several workloads have a high degree of memory divergence that can cause low performance.

6   Conclusions

GPUs are high throughput devices and can deliver peak performance in TFLOPs. However, due to several performance bottlenecks, the peak performance is often difficult to achieve. While caches play an important role in the higher performance of GPUs, they can suffer from thrashing, leading to high miss rate, in particular, caches can perform poorly for memory-divergent workloads. As exploiting data locality is crucial for performance, we conduct a quantitative study of data locality in GPU caches, showing the limits of locality for memory-divergent workloads. Our analysis shows that memory-divergent workloads have significantly higher locality, but the current GPUs are not able to fully exploit it. We show that 57% of the cache lines are never re-referenced, however, the limit study shows that only 30% of the cache lines are never re-referenced and 27% are evicted before re-reference. We further find that about 50% of the L1 data cache capacity is wasted due to data over-fetch. On the one hand, the low spatial utilization of cache lines, as exploited by GPUs, justifies the cache design to fetch sectors based on demand. On the other hand, the much higher actual spatial utilization of cache lines shows the lost spatial locality and presents opportunities for further optimizing cache design. We also study the locality at intra- and inter-warp levels and observe that, in contrast to previous studies, there is a significantly higher inter-warp locality at the L1 data cache for memory-divergent workloads, which can influence warp scheduling policies. Similarly, the locality analysis at the CTA level shows 13% inter-CTA hits at the L2 data cache, which shows the potential for better CTA scheduling across multiprocessors. In the future, we plan to use some of the key insights to improve GPU performance.

References

1. Al-Kiswany, S., Gharaibeh, A., Santos-Neto, E., Yuan, G., Ripeanu, M.: StoreGPU: exploiting graphics processing units to accelerate distributed storage systems. In: Proceedings of the 17th International Symposium on High Performance Distributed Computing, HPDC (2008)
2. Bakhoda, A., Yuan, G.L., Fung, W.W.L., Wong, H., Aamodt, T.M.: Analyzing CUDA workloads using a detailed GPU simulator. In: Proceedings of the IEEE International Symposium on Performance Analysis of Systems and Software, ISPASS (2009)
3. Cederman, D., Chatterjee, B., Tsigas, P.: Understanding the performance of concurrent data structures on graphics processors. In: Kaklamanis, C., Papatheodorou, T., Spirakis, P.G. (eds.) Euro-Par 2012. LNCS, vol. 7484, pp. 883–894. Springer, Heidelberg (2012). https://doi.org/10.1007/978-3-642-32820-6_87
4. Che, S., et al.: Rodinia: a benchmark suite for heterogeneous computing. In: Proceedings of the IEEE International Symposium on Workload Characterization, IISWC (2009)

5. Chen, X., Chang, L.W., Rodrigues, C.I., Lv, J., Wang, Z., Hwu, W.M.: Adaptive cache management for energy-efficient GPU computing. In: Proceedings of the 47th IEEE/ACM International Symposium on Microarchitecture, MICRO (2014)
6. Hong, S., Oguntebi, T., Olukotun, K.: Efficient parallel graph exploration on multi-core CPU and GPU. In: International Conference on Parallel Architectures and Compilation Techniques, PACT (2011)
7. Jia, W., Shaw, K.A., Martonosi, M.: Characterizing and improving the use of demand-fetched caches in GPUs. In: Proceedings of the 26th ACM International Conference on Supercomputing, ICS (2012)
8. Lal, S., Lucas, J., Andersch, M., Alvarez-Mesa, M., Elhossini, A., Juurlink, B.: GPGPU workload characteristics and performance analysis. In: Proceedings of the 14th International Conference on Embedded Computer Systems: Architectures, Modeling, and Simulation, SAMOS (2014)
9. Li, A., van den Braak, G.J., Kumar, A., Corporaal, H.: Adaptive and transparent cache bypassing for GPUs. In: Proceedings of the International Conference for High Performance Computing, Networking, Storage and Analysis, SC (2015)
10. Li, A., Song, S.L., Liu, W., Liu, X., Kumar, A., Corporaal, H.: Locality-aware CTA clustering for modern GPUs. In: Proceedings of the International Conference on Architectural Support for Programming Languages and Operating Systems, ASPLOS (2017)
11. Li, C., Song, S.L., Dai, H., Sidelnik, A., Hari, S.K.S., Zhou, H.: Locality-driven dynamic GPU cache bypassing. In: Proceedings of the 29th ACM on International Conference on Supercomputing, ICS (2015)
12. Meng, J., Tarjan, D., Skadron, K.: Dynamic warp subdivision for integrated branch and memory divergence tolerance. In: Proceedings of the 37th Annual International Symposium on Computer Architecture, ISCA (2010)
13. NVIDIA: CUDA: Compute Unified Device Architecture (2007). http://developer.nvidia.com/object/gpucomputing.html
14. Reguly, I.Z., Giles, M.: Efficient sparse matrix-vector multiplication on cache-based GPUs. In: Proceedings of the Innovative Parallel Computing, InPar (2012)
15. Rogers, T.G., O'Connor, M., Aamodt, T.M.: Cache-conscious wavefront scheduling. In: Proceedings of the 45th Annual IEEE/ACM International Symposium on Microarchitecture, MICRO (2012)
16. Sartori, J., Kumar, R.: Branch and data herding: reducing control and memory divergence for error-tolerant GPU applications. In: Proceedings of the 21st International Conference on Parallel Architectures and Compilation Techniques, PACT (2012)
17. Tarjan, D., Meng, J., Skadron, K.: Increasing memory miss tolerance for SIMD cores. In: Proceedings of the Conference on High Performance Computing Networking, Storage and Analysis, SC (2009)
18. Xiao, S., Lin, H., Feng, W.C.: Accelerating protein sequence search in a heterogeneous computing system. In: IEEE International Parallel and Distributed Processing Symposium, IPDPS (2011)
19. Xie, X., Liang, Y., Wang, Y., Sun, G., Wang, T.: Coordinated static and dynamic cache bypassing for GPUs. In: 2015 IEEE 21st International Symposium on High Performance Computer Architecture, HPCA (2015)
20. Zhang, E.Z., Jiang, Y., Guo, Z., Tian, K., Shen, X.: On-the-fly elimination of dynamic irregularities for GPU computing. In: Proceedings of the 16th International Conference on Architectural Support for Programming Languages and Operating Systems, ASPLOS (2011)

SPECIAL SESSION: Innovative Architectures for Security

CHASM: Security Evaluation of Cache Mapping Schemes

Fernando Mosquera[✉], Nagendra Gulur, Krishna Kavi, Gayatri Mehta,
and Hua Sun

University of North Texas, Denton, TX, USA
fernandomosquera@my.unt.edu

Abstract. Cache side-channel attacks have become a significant security threat across a variety of hardware architectures. By observing which
sets of a cache are accessed by the victim, the attacker gleans critical information about the address bits in the victim's access, thereby
revealing portions of secret keys used by encryption algorithms (or other
sensitive information). Fundamentally, this ability to deduce information
about addresses given the accessed sets depends on knowing (or discovering) how addresses are mapped to cache sets by hardware.

In this work, we evaluate the security of the various cache mapping
functions. Using an information-theoretic formulation, our framework
(denoted *CHASM*) estimates the number of address bits that are likely
leaked by different mapping schemes. Our analysis leads to several new
insights. One, all one-to-one schemes that map n set-index address bits
to 2^n set-indices leak all n bits. Two, based on memory footprint, programs often leak several additional (viz., tag) bits (e.g., AES leaks 39
bits out of 42 at L2). Three, tag bits leak even with the use of address
space layout randomization (16–33 bits). Four, the use of huge pages in
order to reduce pressure on TLBs increases leakage (5 additional bits
on average). Since many of these techniques have opposing impact on
performance and security, we use a new *security-delay* ratio metric to
jointly evaluate mapping schemes for both performance and security.

1 Introduction

Hardware security attacks have become a significant threat to the confidentiality
and integrity of data, including data residing on personal devices [4,26]. An
important sub-class of such security attacks is the cache side-channel attack[1].
Here, the attacker exploits the behavior of cache space across multiple executing
programs. By observing the differences in the timings of memory accesses to
cache memory locations (cache lines or sets), the attacker draws conclusions
about the addresses accessed by the victim. In most current multi-core systems,
it is trivially easy to identify the address bits used as a cache set. Knowing

---

[1] In this paper we do not directly address attacks based on speculative execution or
techniques to mitigate them.

© Springer Nature Switzerland AG 2020
A. Orailoglu et al. (Eds.): SAMOS 2020, LNCS 12471, pp. 245–261, 2020.
https://doi.org/10.1007/978-3-030-60939-9_17

the address bits accessed by the victim leads to knowledge about secret keys in cryptography applications [5]. This *address-as-data* side-channel has received significant attention from both attack and countermeasure standpoints [6,18,21, 27,31].

Mitigation techniques can broadly be classified as partitioning or randomization based. In partitioning-based techniques (for e.g., see [13,17,34]), the shared cache is partitioned such that each program uses its own cache partition (typically a subset of cache ways) and accesses to one partition do not result in any state changes to other partitions. While this method is effective at blocking some timing-based attacks[2], it brings a significant performance penalty: programs have varying demand for cache capacity and it is hard to impose efficient static partitioning regimes. Dynamic regimes, on the other hand, can reintroduce timing-based side-channels (e.g., see [34]) and generally require sophisticated governance mechanisms in hardware.

In randomization-based methods, the hardware obfuscates how memory addresses map to cache sets, making it harder for the attacker to translate a timing observation on a cache set to address bits used by the victim. Recent works (for e.g., [20,24]) have proposed to use encryption mechanisms at the last-level cache to map addresses to cache sets. Prior works (for e.g., see [9,15,16]) have also explored the use of non-trivial mapping functions for L1 and L2 caches, primarily from a performance improvement goal: to redistribute memory addresses across cache sets in order to reduce cache conflicts. Some of these schemes may also improve security.

In this work, we propose *CHASM* – an information-theoretic measure to evaluate the strength of various cache set mapping schemes. *CHASM* estimates the amount of information about memory addresses that a mapping scheme leaks: lower the estimated leakage, the stronger the security defense. Using this formulation, we evaluate several different cache set mapping schemes for private and shared caches. Using a combination of synthetic and real programs (SPEC, and cryptography), we establish the following:

– Schemes that are 1:1 mappings of the n set index address bits to 2^n sets, leak all n address bits.
– Information leakage is higher in programs with smaller memory footprints– higher order bits (tag bits, the bits not used for set index) do not vary significantly. For e.g., the *AES* benchmark leaks 39 bits (out of 42) at L2 cache when using traditional *Modulo* scheme[3] for mapping addresses to cache sets due to its small (<1 MB) footprint.
– Even for programs with larger foot prints, the non-uniformity of accesses to program addresses (see [22]) can leak information about the tag bits of programs.
– Address space layout randomization (see [23]) helps but is not sufficiently strong enough in reducing tag bit leakage. Despite using *ASLR*, programs still leak anywhere between 16 to 33 (out of 42) bits.

---

[2] Partitioning techniques do not prevent certain types of attacks [35].
[3] Mapping schemes are discussed in Sect. 3 and workloads in Sect. 5.

- Interestingly, the use of huge pages to reduce TLBs and page table sizes, actually results in higher leakage even for programs with large footprints. We observe additional 5 bits of leakage bits (average) with 2 MB pages.
- Using our proposed *security-delay* metric, we evaluate several mappings to identify schemes that are both more secure and better performing compared to the conventional baseline. Such metrics can be valuable in making quantitative decisions about performance-security trade-offs.

2   Background

Figure 1 provides an overview of a typical multi-core embedded processor architecture. Each core is provisioned with private L1 caches (L1 is split between data and instruction) followed by a large shared L2 cache. Depending on hardware scheduling and resource allocation, different programs share one or more caches. Programs that are co-located on the same core share private as well as shared caches. When hardware fine-grained scheduling techniques (such as Simultaneous Multi-Threading) are used, programs can concurrently execute on the same core sharing private data and instruction caches. Programs concurrently executing on different cores share the L2 cache. Thus, simultaneously executing programs affect (and are affected by) the performance of co-running programs: programs suffer additional cache misses due to interference.

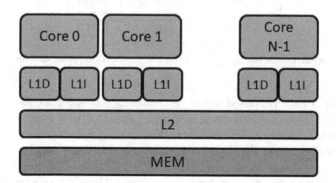

Fig. 1. Overview of multi-core embedded processor

This performance variation caused by sharing of private or shared caches is the basis of cache-based side-channel attacks. Depending on the level of access to the system, the attacker may share a private cache or the last-level cache with the victim. The attacker launches a covert attack on the victim by creating an information leakage channel from the victim to the attacker. Such a channel could be constructed in different ways based on system access, shared pages and observability. For illustration, in the PRIME+PROBE technique [35], the attack is deployed in three steps. In the first step, the attacker runs a spy process that fills the shared cache with its own data. In the second step, it lets the victim process execute. The victim brings its data to the shared cache, evicting some of the spy's cache blocks. In the third step, the attacker resumes the spy process accessing its data a second time. Cache misses of spy data (observed by timing the accesses) will indicate that the victim accessed the same set. This information is sufficient to reveal a portion of the address that the victim accessed.

In addition to PRIME+PROBE, several other attacks exist, such as FLUSH & RELOAD [31], EVICT & TIME [11] and so on. Various works have demonstrated the use of different levels of caches to create covert side channels [18]. At the heart of all of these attacks is the ability for the attacker to determine bits of the address accessed by the victim given the set that was accessed. The vast majority of existing hardware systems use the simple *modulo* mapping scheme to map addresses to cache sets: for a cache with $N = 2^n$ sets (organized as blocks of size $B = 2^b$ bytes), the cache controller uses the n bits $[b : b + n - 1]$ of the address to determine the set index. Figure 2 shows how the cache controller uses the a address bits to obtain the block offset, the set index and tag. Under this mapping scheme, if the attacker knows the set index, then (s)he knows the corresponding address bits. Despite this vulnerability, this scheme is the prevalent mapping scheme given its simplicity and low-cost of implementation.

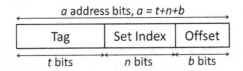

Fig. 2. Cache set mapping using the modulo mapping scheme

Researchers have proposed newer set mapping schemes that use some additional address bits, and applying a simple combinatorial function on these selected bits to compute a new set index. While most prior schemes were designed for higher performance, (by distributing the requests more evenly across cache sets to reduce cache misses), new schemes [20,24] have been proposed using a cipher to create pseudo-random hash maps from addresses to cache sets. In our evaluations we assume that the same address mapping is used for all processes. In a future study we will explore the use of different mappings for different processes and modifying mappings for a given process periodically.

Thus, given the central role that cache set mapping schemes play in mitigating cache side-channel attacks, our work proposes an information-theoretic framework for evaluating the security of cache set mapping schemes.

3 Evaluated Cache Set Mappings

In this section, we describe the various set mapping schemes that we explored. In addition to the *modulo* mapping scheme covered in the previous section (Fig. 2), we evaluate several representative schemes that are summarized in Table 1. We selected a representative set of mappings used in current systems or proposed by recent research. *For the purpose of describing these techniques we will assume 64-byte cache blocks.*

Table 1. Overview of cache set mapping schemes

Scheme name	Scheme description	Uses tag bits?	Usage
Rotate-3 [15]	Rotate-right the set-index address bits by 3 bit positions	No	L1, L2
XOR [15]	XOR the set-index address bits with least significant tag bits of address	Yes	L1, L2
Rotate-then-XOR	Rotate-right the set-index address bits by 1 bit position, and XOR the result with tag bits of address	Yes	L1, L2
Square-then-XOR	Square the tag bits of the address, and XOR the middle n bits of result with the n set-index address bits	Yes	L1, L2
Odd-Multiplier-7 [15]	Multiply the tag bits by 7, add to set-index address bits	Yes	L1, L2
Intel-Slice [32]	See description in [32]. Two-stage hash of cache slice	Yes	L2
CEASER	Encryption-based mapping scheme. See [24]	Yes	L2

The *Rotate-3* mapping uses the traditional n set index address bits $a_{(n+5)}$: a_6 and rotates these bits by three bit positions to produce the new set index ($[a_8, a_7, a_6, a_{n+5} : a_9]$).

The *XOR* scheme uses n bits of address from the cache tag portion to XOR them with the set index address bits. The XORed result is used as the set index. The use of the tag bits acts as a *pseudo-randomizer* resulting in obfuscating the mapping of addresses to cache sets. In practice, this technique introduces hardware implementation challenges at L1 as the use of virtual address tag bits for indexing has to be reconciled with coherence messages sent out using physical addresses. The tag bits are not guaranteed to be the same between virtual and physical addresses requiring some additional metadata to be maintained for correctly indexing into the L1 cache. However, this scheme is known to work effectively from a performance point of view as it distributes addresses more evenly across cache sets. The *Rotate-then-XOR* scheme first rotates the set index address bits and then XORs the rotated bits with the tag bits to compute the set index. The *Square-then-XOR* scheme first squares the tag address bits, then extracts the n bits in the middle of the result to XOR them with the set index address bits. While the squaring operation is hardware-expensive, if the number of bits is small (e.g., in the L1 cache) or the operation is invoked infrequently (for e.g., at lower-level caches), the overhead of this operation becomes tolerable[4]. The *Odd-Multiplier-7* scheme multiplies the tag bits by 7, and adds the result to the set index address bits. Modulo 2^n of the result is used as the set-index.

The *Intel-Slice* scheme is borrowed from Intel's implementation for the last-level cache in Sandy Bridge as outlined in [32]. In this scheme, the L2 is viewed as a collection of cache slices, and the computation of the slice ID is done using a two-stage function of the input address. CEASER [24] proposes the use of an encryption cipher implemented as a 4-stage Feistel network to translate the incoming physical address into an L2 cache set index[5].

We note that virtual addresses are used in mapping schemes used in the L1D cache since the majority of L1 caches are virtually-indexed while physical addresses are used in the L2 cache since L2 caches are almost always physically-indexed.

4   CHASM Formulation

We first describe how our formulation can be used followed by a description of the information leakage estimation technique.

4.1   Use Model

CHASM is not proposing a specific cache side-channel attack or a countermeasure. Instead, it provides a framework for assessing the strength of various cache mapping schemes in mitigating the disclosure of victim address bits. The typical use of *CHASM* is for the design and evaluation of new cache mapping schemes. Hardware architects can explore various mapping schemes (such as those described in Sect. 3) to identify the most secure schemes. Algorithm and OS developers can explore different software implementation techniques for how secure/vulnerable they are from a cache-based side-channel attack perspective.

CHASM formulation estimates the leakage of the victim's address bits given that the attacker knows which sets are being accessed by the victim. Tools such as the PIN tool for ARM [10] or Intel [19] can be used to collect a trace of a program's memory accesses. These traces are fed to a cache simulator that estimates information leakage using the *CHASM* formulation described next. The cache simulator implements the desired cache mapping schemes and provides statistical estimates of which address bits are leaked and the likelihood that a leaked bit is a 1 or a 0.

4.2   Information Leakage Estimation

The attacker's goal is to accurately predict the address bits used by the victim given that the attacker knows which set was accessed. We use an information-theoretic metric to estimate this leakage. An address bit a_i is estimated to be

---

[4] For small bit counts, a table lookup can be used.

[5] In the original work, this scheme was applied to the shared L3 cache.

leaked with probability 1, if every address that maps to a given set S in the victim program has the same value for bit a_i (either always zero or always one). Intuitively, this is stating the fact that an address bit value remains constant for all addresses that map to a given set, and an attacker can find the value of an address bit if he knows the set used. Additionally, correlations between address bits also reveal information. For instance, if address bit a_j is 1 whenever address bit a_i is 0, then knowing a_i, a_j can be predicted.

While the concept of *mutual information* (see [14, 29]) is widely used to define leakage in the presence of correlations, its computational complexity is high requiring multi-dimensional conditional probabilities to be estimated[6]. We define a simpler metric that uses only pair-wise correlations between address bits. Our metric computes both the individual per-bit leakage as well as correlated leakage in order to estimate the effective leakage.

Individual Leakage: If we denote the probability that a_i has a value of 1 when it maps to set S as $p_i = prob(a_i = 1|S)$, then the leakage of information regarding a_i is related to the entropy e_i of the bit, given by:

$$e_i = -p_i log(p_i) - (1 - p_i)log(1 - p_i) \qquad (1)$$

When p_i is either close to 0 or 1, then e_i is close to 0 (very small uncertainty). On the other hand, when p_i is close to 0.5, then e_i is close to 1. This individual bit leakage il_i is defined:

$$il_i = 1 - e_i \qquad (2)$$

A high value of il_i indicates that by simply knowing the set, bit a_i can be predicted.

Correlated Leakage: In almost all applications, lower-order address bits toggle more often than higher-order bits. Thus we compute correlations of bit a_j with all other previous bits a_{j-1} through a_6[7]. Let $SAME(i,j)$ denote the number of times that a_i and a_j have the same values among addresses mapping to set S. Let $DIFF(i,j)$ denote the number of times that a_i and a_j have different values. The correlation of a_j with a_i $(j > i)$ is defined:

$$c_{j,i} = 1 - \frac{min(SAME(i,j), DIFF(i,j))}{max(SAME(i,j), DIFF(i,j))} \qquad (3)$$

If the bits are strongly correlated or anti-correlated, then $c_{j,i}$ is close to 1. Thus we define the correlated leakage $cl_{j,i}$ of j due to i as:

$$cl_{j,i} = el_i \times c_{j,i} \qquad (4)$$

where el_i is the *effective leakage* of bit i defined in Eq. 5. The correlated leakage of a_j due to a_i is high if a_i has high effective leakage *and* a_j has high correlation

---

[6] In our case, leakage in bit i would depend on all other 40–50 bits requiring $2^{40} - 2^{50}$ probabilities to be estimated.

[7] We stop at a_6 as bits a_0 through a_5 are block offset bits that have no impact on cache mapping. In this paper we assume 64-byte cache blocks.

with a_i. We now define the effective leakage of a_j as:

$$el_j = max(il_j, cl_{j,j-1}, cl_{j,j-2}, .., cl_{j,6}) \tag{5}$$

Effective leakage of a_j is set to the maximum of its individual leakage, and its correlated leakages with preceding bits a_{j-1} through a_6. If a bit possesses strong (anti-) correlation with a preceding bit or suffers from high individual leakage, then its effective leakage is high.

We express the total leakage as a sum of the effective leakage contributions from all the relevant address bits: set-index bits and tag bits. This is given by:

$$L(S) = \sum_i el_i \tag{6}$$

where the summation is over all set index and tag address bits.

Ideally, the most secure mapping scheme leaks 0 bits of address information, while the weakest scheme leaks all tag and set index bits. For a given cache, the total information leaked is estimated as a weighted-average across all the sets, where $p(S)$ is the probability of an address mapping to set S.

$$L_{Cache}^{Avg} = \sum_s L(s)p(s) \tag{7}$$

The weighing by $p(S)$ ensures that sets that have received very few accesses do not skew the overall cache-level leakage metric. This also takes program characteristics into account: if a program exhibits a non-uniform use of cache sets, then that is useful information to the attacker and must be included in the metric.

We use this formulation to compare various cache set mapping schemes. If a set mapping scheme results in lower average information leakage (L_{cache}^{Avg}), then it is deemed to be more secure scheme.

4.3   Security-Delay Measure

Neither performance nor security alone is a useful measure. High performance under weak security is not desirable, and strong security with significant performance penalties is unacceptable. Therefore, we propose a new cache metric: *security-delay* ratio (denoted SD), defined as:

$$SD_{Cache} = \frac{(t+n)}{L_{Cache}^{avg}} \times \frac{1}{CPI} \tag{8}$$

This is a higher-is-better metric: lower CPI (Cycles Per Instruction) and lower leakage contribute to higher values of the metric. The $(t+n)$ term represents the maximum possible leakage and is used to normalize the security measure L_{Cache}^{Avg}. For example, if two schemes S_1 and S_2 have CPIs 2.0 and 1.5 with respective leakages of 20 and 30 bits (out of a maximum of 42^8), then their respective SD metrics are 1.05 and 0.933 suggesting that S_2 perhaps loses out on security a little too much (even though it is higher in terms of performance).

---

[8] As stated previously, we assume a 64-byte cache line size, and 48-bit addresses.

5   Experimental Methodology

We use a trace-based methodology for evaluating *CHASM*. Memory access traces of various workloads are collected using PIN [19] tool. These are virtual addresses that are suitable for L1 cache studies (L1 is VIPT - Virtually Indexed Physically Tagged). We also obtain corresponding physical addresses during the PIN tool execution by using a combination of Linux */proc/pagemap* and */proc/kpageflags* utilities [2]. Physical addresses are used for L2 cache studies (L2 is PIPT - Physically Indexed Physically Tagged). As is standard practice, we collect traces after skipping an initial warm-up period.

These traces are injected into Moola [25] - a multi-core, cache hierarchy simulator. The cache simulator is configured to match the Snapdragon Series 8 [7] cache configuration (L1D: 32 KB 4-way, L2: 2 MB, 8-way, all caches use 64B blocks). The cache simulator is modified to support all the cache mapping schemes listed in Table 1. The simulator is also enhanced to measure information leakage defined in Eqs. 7 and 8. Finally, the simulator reports the relevant statistics – cache performance, and information leakage.

Our workloads comprise synthetic programs, SPEC [12] benchmarks and off-the-shelf cryptography programs. Synthetic programs access consecutive elements of an array in a loop. By varying the size of the array, we observe the impact of memory footprint on security. We explore 6 different sizes and the corresponding workloads are denoted *synth_16KB*, *synth_128KB*, *synth_1MB*, *synth_8MB*, *synth_64MB* and *synth_512MB*. We use a subset of SPEC benchmarks that are memory-intensive: *bwaves, bzip2, cactusADM, GemsFDTD, leslie3d, libquantum, milc, mcf, soplex and zeusmp*. Our cryptography programs include *AES, RSA* and *SHA*. Traces collected from these programs are fed to the cache simulator and simulated for 10 billion memory accesses.

6   Results

We first evaluate L1D mapping schemes for their security using synthetic, SPEC and Cryptography benchmarks, followed by an evaluation of L2 mapping schemes.

6.1   Security of L1D Cache Mapping Schemes

Figure 3 plots the average information leakage (L_{Cache}^{Avg}, refer Eq. 7) from all address bits observed in synthetic programs across all the evaluated L1 mapping schemes.

These results clearly demonstrate that leakage reduces as memory footprint increases. Programs with smaller memory footprints leak many more bits (40 in *synth_16KB*) compared to programs with higher footprints (16 in *synth_512MB*). This is due to less variation in the address bit values in programs with smaller footprints. These results also reveal that every mapping scheme that uses only

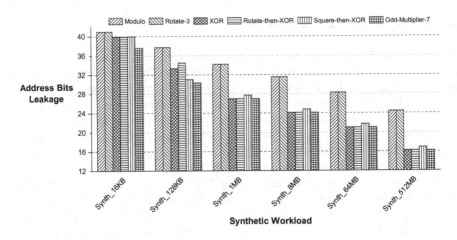

Fig. 3. Leakage of address bits in L1D on synthetic programs

the set-index portion of address bits to map the 2^n possible address bits to 2^n sets in a 1-1 function is *weak*: it reveals all n bits.

Next, we evaluate the leakage of information for selected SPEC and Cryptography workloads. Figure 4 plots this leakage across all mapping schemes. The first two schemes (that use only the set-index address bits for indexing) leak significantly more bits compared to schemes that leverage tag address bits for indexing. In particular, *AES* and *SHA* encryption programs show high leakage. This is attributable to their small memory footprints and lack of variation in tag bits, thereby enabling attackers to accurately estimate several address bits. Even if encryption routines are integrated into larger applications, as they are typically invoked in response to encryption requests, knowledgeable attackers can isolate these portions of code execution and attack them.

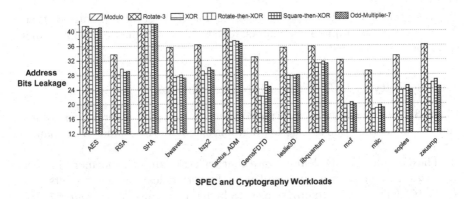

Fig. 4. Leakage of address bits in L1D on SPEC and crypto benchmarks

6.2   Leakage Under ASLR

Address Space Layout Randomization (ASLR, see [23]) is an OS feature that offers memory protection against attacks by randomizing the base addresses of various program sections such as the stack, heap and text. Across different runs of the same process, the OS places the process sections at different locations thereby making it harder for attackers to reliably determine addresses used by the victim via cache side-channel attacks.

In order to test the effectiveness of ASLR and to identify information leakage under ASLR, we ran our synthetic workloads 50 times each and obtained a merged trace for each workload[9]. By merging the address accesses from different runs of the same workload, we are able to capture the randomness introduced by ASLR and measure the resulting reduction in leakage.

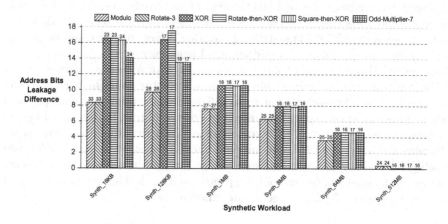

Fig. 5. Reduction in leakage with ASLR

Figure 5 reports our findings on the L1D cache by plotting the reduction in leakage by ASLR. Observe that this is a higher-is-better graph. The numbers above the bars are the absolute leakage values with ASLR. Overall, ASLR helps reduce the leakage of address bits. In particular, mapping schemes that use tag bits (last four bars for each workload) reduce leakage suggesting that a combination of such a mapping scheme operating under ASLR is effective. This is a positive result from a security standpoint – especially for programs with very small footprints. However, ASLR does not completely prevent leakage. As the numbers above the bars indicate, in small workloads (e.g., *synth_16KB*) despite ASLR, 15–30 bits leak.

This experiment reveals that a combination of including tag bits in computing set indices, coupled with the use of ASLR can provide a secure mapping scheme

---

[9] SPEC and Cryptography workloads exhibit similar trends and for brevity, we omit their details here.

preventing leakage of set-index bits. At the same time, ASLR is not strong enough to prevent leakage of several tag bits and a stronger scheme is needed to achieve this.

6.3   Security of L2 Cache Mapping Schemes

Figure 6 plots the leakage of the address bits in SPEC and Cryptography workloads[10]. These results are similar to synthetic workloads. Schemes incorporating the use of tag bits generally perform significantly better than schemes that do not. Cryptography workloads – due to their small footprints – leak more bits under all schemes (AES leaks a total of 39 bits – set-index+tag – under *Modulo*).

Impact of Page Size on Leakage. Large physical pages [1,3] (also called *superpages*, using page sizes of 2 MB through 1 GB) have been supported as a way to allocate and manage large contiguous chunks of physical memory efficiently. Large pages reduce TLB (Translation Lookaside Buffer) pressure and page-walk penalty by replacing many individual small page entries in a page table by a single entry. However, use of large pages comes with a security side-effect: all addresses that map to a large physical page have the same higher-order bits as compared to addresses that map to different non-contiguous small physical pages. Thus, using large pages can result in greater address bit leakage. In order to observe this, we compared two runs of a synthetic program – *huge_pages* allocates and uses huge (2 MB in our experiments) pages, while *small_pages* uses small (4 KB) pages. Figure 7 compares leakage of tag address bits in the L2 cache. Across all the schemes, the use of huge pages results in leaking several additional address bits (about 5 on average in our experiments).

6.4   Security-Delay Measure

We use the metric SD_{Cache} defined in Eq. 8 to study the joint effect of each scheme on performance and security. Figure 8 plots the percentage change in SD_{L1D} w.r.t the *modulo* baseline for SPEC and Crypto workloads for four mapping schemes on L1D. In workloads such as GemsFDTD, while *XOR* improves SD_{L1D} by as much as 49%, *Square-then-XOR* improves by only about 26%. On average (geometric mean), the *XOR* scheme performs the best. This evaluation shows that the SD_{Cache} metric is effective at capturing the joint performance & security impact of cache mapping schemes and can be used as a reliable indicator for future evaluations.

The above results and discussion indicate that hardware-wide static cache mapping schemes are leaky. Set-index bits are almost entirely revealed unless tag-based methods are used. Even then leakage still exists in smaller programs. Considerable leakage of tag bits occurs in all schemes even when ASLR is used.

---

[10] For lack of space, we omitted the *Rotate-3* scheme as its leakage is exactly the same as that of *Modulo*.

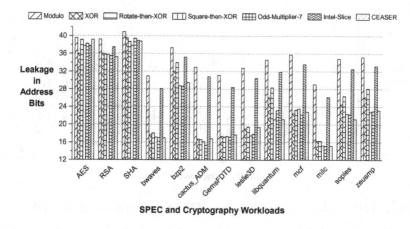

Fig. 6. Leakage of address bits in L2 on SPEC, cryptography workloads

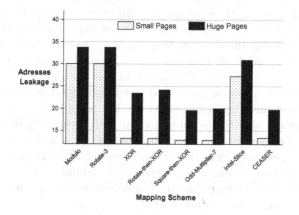

Fig. 7. Impact of huge pages

Large physical pages tend to leak even more. Large cache sizes also result in higher leakage. Our findings motivate the need for incorporating stronger mapping schemes that are either application-specific, or dynamic or both.

7   Related Works

Cache set mappings have received attention mainly from a performance perspective. These studies focus solely on performance and do not consider their security implication. The work in Kavi et al. [15] provides a comprehensive comparison of several mapping schemes used in low-associativity caches. The work in Givargis [9] explores mapping schemes that improve performance by considering correlations among address bits. Kharbutli et al. [16] explore the prime-modulo and prime-displacement mapping functions.

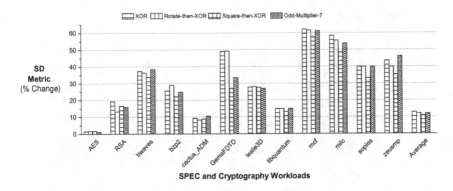

Fig. 8. L1D security-delay ratio metric of SPEC and cryptography workloads

The work in [24] explores the use of encryption-based mapping of physical addresses to LLC sets with emphasis on addressing security. In this work, the authors not only propose encryption but also re-encrypt and migrate cache blocks periodically to prevent the attacker from learning the encrypted mapping. Intel uses an undocumented hash function of the physical address bits to compute the last-level cache slice index. The details of this hash function were revealed in [20]. We evaluate these schemes in our work. ScatterCache [30] proposes a per-process keyed mapping scheme. Per-process mappings make inter-process attacks difficult but due to the mapping hardware overhead, they are feasible only at low-level caches. In contrast to these works, our work is not another cache mapping (or address randomization) scheme: rather, it provides a framework to evaluate the security of mapping schemes and highlights the role of program characteristics such as memory footprint in determining programs' vulnerability to microarchitectural side-channel attacks.

Address space layout randomization (ASLR) [23] was introduced by Linux as a guard against address-based attacks by randomizing the bases of text, stack, heap and mmap sections. It has however been shown that ASLR does not offer a strong defense [28].

Orthogonal to *CHASM*, Zankl et al. [33] provide a framework for detecting leakage of modular exponentiation software via instruction caches. The work in Doychev et al. [8] proposes *CacheAudit* - a framework for automatic static analysis of cache side channels. *CHASM* differs from this framework in that *CHASM* is driven by address traces factoring in aspects of the run-time system: physical addresses, use of large pages, ASLR and so on.

8 Conclusions

This work presented *CHASM* – a framework for evaluating strength of the security of cache mapping schemes. We evaluated several schemes at L1 and L2 caches under different system conditions (ASLR, large pages). Our evaluations reveal several insights about the vulnerabilities of cache mappings, including that smaller memory footprints leak more information, that non-uniformity of accesses leaks more information, that ASLR is only marginally effective and that "huge" pages leak more information. These findings indicate that more sophisticated techniques for hiding address mapping to cache sets are needed. Moreover, obfuscating techniques at the OS level as well as application/algorithm level are needed to increase the strength of countermeasures against side-channel attacks.

References

1. Huge Pages - The Linux Kernel Archives. https://www.kernel.org/doc/Documentation/vm/hugetlbpage.txt
2. Pagemap, From the Userspace Perspective. https://www.kernel.org/doc/Documentation/vm/pagemap.txt
3. Transparent Hugepage Support. https://www.kernel.org/doc/Documentation/vm/transhuge.txt
4. Ambrose, J.A., Ragel, R.G., Jayasinghe, D., Li, T., Parameswaran, S.: Side channel attacks in embedded systems: a tale of hostilities and deterrence. In: Sixteenth International Symposium on Quality Electronic Design, pp. 452–459, March 2015
5. Bernstein, D.J.: Cache-timing attacks on AES. Technical report (2005)
6. Bonneau, J., Mironov, I.: Cache-collision timing attacks against AES. In: Goubin, L., Matsui, M. (eds.) CHES 2006. LNCS, vol. 4249, pp. 201–215. Springer, Heidelberg (2006). https://doi.org/10.1007/11894063_16
7. Doweck, J., et al.: Inside 6th-generation intel core: new microarchitecture codenamed Skylake. IEEE Micro **37**(2), 52–62 (2017)
8. Doychev, G., Feld, D., Köpf, B., Mauborgne, L., Reineke, J.: CacheAudit: a tool for the static analysis of cache side channels. In: Proceedings of the 22nd USENIX Conference on Security, Series SEC 2013, pp. 431–446. USENIX Association, Berkeley (2013). http://dl.acm.org/citation.cfm?id=2534766.2534804
9. Givargis, T.: Improved indexing for cache miss reduction in embedded systems. In: Proceedings of the 40th Annual Design Automation Conference, Series, DAC 2003 (2003). https://doi.org/10.1145/775832.776052
10. Hazelwood, K.M., Klauser, A.: A dynamic binary instrumentation engine for the ARM architecture. In: Hong, S., Wolf, W.H., Flautner, K., Kim, T. (eds.) Proceedings of the 2006 International Conference on Compilers, Architecture, and Synthesis for Embedded Systems, CASES 2006, Seoul, Korea, 22–25 October 2006 (2006). https://doi.org/10.1145/1176760.1176793
11. He, Z., Lee, R.B.: How secure is your cache against side-channel attacks? In: Proceedings of the 50th Annual IEEE/ACM International Symposium on Microarchitecture, Series MICRO-50 2017, pp. 341–353. ACM, New York (2017). https://doi.org/10.1145/3123939.3124546
12. Henning, J.L.: SPEC CPU2006 benchmark descriptions. SIGARCH Comput. Archit. News **34**(4), 1–17 (2006). https://doi.org/10.1145/1186736.1186737
13. Intel: Introduction to Cache Allocation Technology in the Intel® Xeon® processor E5 v4 family (2016). https://software.intel.com/en-us/articles/introduction-to-cache-allocation-technology
14. Issa, I., Wagner, A.B., Kamath, S.: An operational approach to information leakage. CoRR, vol. abs/1807.07878 (2018). http://arxiv.org/abs/1807.07878
15. Kavi, K., Nwachukwu, I., Fawibe, A.: A comparative analysis of performance improvement schemes for cache memories. Comput. Electr. Eng. **38**(2), 243–257 (2012). https://doi.org/10.1016/j.compeleceng.2011.12.008

16. Kharbutli, M., Irwin, K., Solihin, Y., Lee, J.: Using prime numbers for cache index-ing to eliminate conflict misses. In: Proceedings of the 10th International Sym-posium on High Performance Computer Architecture, Series HPCA 2004, p. 288. IEEE Computer Society, Washington, DC (2004). https://doi.org/10.1109/HPCA. 2004.10015

17. Kiriansky, V., Lebedev, I., Amarasinghe, S., Devadas, S., Emer, J.: DAWG: a defense against cache timing attacks in speculative execution processors. In: Pro-ceedings of the 51st Annual IEEE/ACM International Symposium on Microarchi-tecture, Series MICRO-51, pp. 974–987. IEEE Press, Piscataway (2018). https:// doi.org/10.1109/MICRO.2018.00083

18. Liu, F., Yarom, Y., Ge, Q., Heiser, G., Lee, R.B.: Last-level cache side-channel attacks are practical. In: Proceedings of the 2015 IEEE Symposium on Security and Privacy, Series SP 2015, pp. 605–622. IEEE Computer Society, Washington, DC (2015). https://doi.org/10.1109/SP.2015.43

19. Luk, C.-K., et al.: Pin: building customized program analysis tools with dynamic instrumentation. In: Proceedings of the 2005 ACM SIGPLAN Conference on Pro-gramming Language Design and Implementation, Series PLDI 2005, pp. 190–200. ACM, New York (2005). https://doi.org/10.1145/1065010.1065034

20. Maurice, C., Le Scouarnec, N., Neumann, C., Heen, O., Francillon, A.: Reverse engineering Intel last-level cache complex addressing using performance counters. In: Bos, H., Monrose, F., Blanc, G. (eds.) RAID 2015. LNCS, vol. 9404, pp. 48–65. Springer, Cham (2015). https://doi.org/10.1007/978-3-319-26362-5_3

21. Mushtaq, M., Akram, A., Bhatti, M.K., Rais, R.N.B., Lapotre, V., Gogniat, G.: Run-time detection of prime + probe side-channel attack on AES encryption algo-rithm. In: 2018 Global Information Infrastructure and Networking Symposium (GIIS), pp. 1–5, October 2018

22. Nwachukwu, I., Kavi, K., Ademola, F., Yan, C.: Evaluation of techniques to improve cache access uniformities. In: 2011 International Conference on Parallel Processing, pp. 31–40, September 2011

23. Pax: Address space layout randomization ASLR (2003). http://pax.grsecuritynet/docs/aslr.txt

24. Qureshi, M.K.: CEASER: mitigating conflict-based cache attacks via encrypted-address and remapping. In: Proceedings of the 51st Annual IEEE/ACM Inter-national Symposium on Microarchitecture, Series MICRO-51, pp. 775–787. IEEE Press, Piscataway (2018). https://doi.org/10.1109/MICRO.2018.00068

25. Shelor, C., Kavi, K.: Moola: multicore cache simulator. In: 30th International Con-ference on Computers and Their Applications, CATA-2015 (2015)

26. Trilla, D., Hernandez, C., Abella, J., Cazorla, F.: Cache side-channel attacks and time-predictability in high-performance critical real-time systems, pp. 1–6, June 2018

27. Tromer, E., Osvik, D.A., Shamir, A.: Efficient cache attacks on AES, and coun-termeasures. J. Cryptol. **23**(1), 37–71 (2010). https://doi.org/10.1007/s00145-009-9049-y

28. Umbelino, P.: ASLR cache attack defeats address space layout randomiza-tion (2017). https://hackaday.com/2017/02/15/aslrcache-attack-defeats-address-space-layout-randomization/

29. Wagner, I., Eckhoff, D.: Technical privacy metrics: a systematic survey. CoRR, vol. abs/1512.00327 (2015). http://arxiv.org/abs/1512.00327

30. Werner, M., Unterluggauer, T., Giner, L., Schwarz, M., Gruss, D., Mangard, S.: ScatterCache: thwarting cache attacks via cache set randomization. In: Heninger, N., Traynor, P. (eds.) 28th USENIX Security Symposium, USENIX Security 2019, Santa Clara, CA, USA, 14–16 August 2019 (2019). https://www.usenix.org/conference/usenixsecurity19/presentation/werner

31. Yarom, Y., Falkner, K.: Flush+reload: a high resolution, low noise, L3 cache side-channel attack. In: Proceedings of the 23rd USENIX Conference on Security Symposium, Series SEC 2014 (2014). http://dl.acm.org/citation.cfm?id=2671225.2671271

32. Yarom, Y., Ge, Q., Liu, F., Lee, R.B., Heiser, G.: Mapping the intel last-level cache. Cryptology ePrint Archive, Report 2015/905 (2015). https://eprint.iacr.org/2015/905

33. Zankl, A., Heyszl, J., Sigl, G.: Automated detection of instruction cache leaks in modular exponentiation software. In: Lemke-Rust, K., Tunstall, M. (eds.) CARDIS 2016. LNCS, vol. 10146, pp. 228–244. Springer, Cham (2017). https://doi.org/10.1007/978-3-319-54669-8_14

34. Zhang, N., Sun, K., Shands, D., Lou, W., Hou, Y.T.: TruSpy: cache side-channel information leakage from the secure world on arm devices. Cryptology ePrint Archive, Report 2016/980 (2016). https://eprint.iacr.org/2016/980

35. Zhang, Y.: Cache side channels: state of the art and research opportunities. In: Proceedings of the 2017 ACM SIGSAC Conference on Computer and Communications Security, Series CCS 2017, pp. 2617–2619. ACM, New York (2017). https://doi.org/10.1145/3133956.3136064

DeePar-SCA: Breaking Parallel Architectures of Lattice Cryptography via Learning Based Side-Channel Attacks

Furkan Aydin[✉], Priyank Kashyap[✉], Seetal Potluri, Paul Franzon, and Aydin Aysu

North Carolina State University, Raleigh, NC 27606, USA
{faydn,pkashya2,spotlur2,paulf,aaysu}@ncsu.edu

Abstract. This paper proposes the first deep-learning based side-channel attacks on post-quantum key-exchange protocols. We target hardware implementations of two lattice-based key-exchange protocols—Frodo and NewHope—and analyze power side-channels of the security-critical arithmetic functions. The challenge in applying side-channel attacks stems from the single-trace nature of the protocols: each new execution will use a fresh and unique key, limiting the adversary to a single power measurement. Although such single-trace attacks are known, they have been so far constrained to sequentialized designs running on simple micro-controllers. By using deep-learning and data augmentation techniques, we extend those attacks to break parallelized hardware designs, and we quantify the attack's limitations. Specifically, we demonstrate single-trace deep-learning based attacks that outperform traditional attacks such as horizontal differential power analysis and template attacks by up to 900% and 25%, respectively. The developed attacks can therefore break implementations that are otherwise secure, motivating active countermeasures even on parallel architectures for key-exchange protocols.

Keywords: Deep-learning · Power side-channels · Lattice-based key-exchange protocols

1   Introduction

Key-exchange protocols enable computers to communicate over a public, insecure channel by establishing a secure session key. Lattice-based key-exchange protocols are versatile post-quantum alternatives, which have already found industry adoption even prior to the National Institute of Standards and Technology (NIST) post-quantum standardization. Google's Chrome Canary web browser, e.g., used NewHope, a post-quantum key-exchange (PQKE) protocol to provide a quantum-secure connection [9].

While lattice-based cryptography provides efficient implementations and quantum resilience, their implementations have shown vulnerability against

© Springer Nature Switzerland AG 2020
A. Orailoglu et al. (Eds.): SAMOS 2020, LNCS 12471, pp. 262–280, 2020.
https://doi.org/10.1007/978-3-030-60939-9_18

power side-channel attacks (SCAs) in the context of public-key encryption or digital signatures [3,16,32,37]. These attacks exploit the correlation between the power consumption of a cryptographic device and the secret-key dependent computations. Conventional attacks such as the differential power analysis (DPA) finds the secret-key by extracting this small correlation from noise through collecting a large number of traces. DPA on PQKE protocols is, however, impractical because these protocols generate a new secret-key for each key-exchange session. Therefore, the attacker is *limited to a single power measurement* for applying the SCA.

Recently, Aysu et al. [3] demonstrated that horizontal DPA against PQKE extracts the secret-key from a single power-trace. Others have likewise addressed this single-trace constraint through template attacks (TAs) [8,22,33,37]. However, all these works have focused on simple micro-controllers, such as ARM Cortex-M0 [8,22], Cortex-M4 [33], Cortex-M4F [37], or sequentialized hardware designs [3]. These attacks are expected to perform poorly on parallel hardware designs due to increased activity (i.e., algorithmic noise) [47] and their success rate is unknown.

In this paper, we extend power-based SCAs on lattice-based key-exchange protocols to parallelized hardware designs. We demonstrate the limitations of the existing attacks and address those limitations through power-based SCAs using deep-learning (DL) techniques. We use the NIST Round-2 version of Frodo [7] and NewHope [2] protocols as case studies. In addition to the industry attraction, both protocols are among the ongoing candidates of the NIST standards. We implement the security-critical operations of matrix and polynomial multiplication hardware that are the target of SCAs [3]. We implemented these hardware architectures at five distinct parallelization levels to evaluate success rate of side-channel attacks on different parallel architectures. Using signal processing and data augmentation techniques, we develop novel DL-based attacks on power measurements obtained from these hardware.

On a SAKURA-G Field Programmable Gate Array (FPGA) platform, our method is better than classical techniques such as horizontal DPA and TA by up to 150% and 11%, respectively, for Frodo and 900% and 25%, respectively, for NewHope. The results validate the superiority of DL-based attacks in breaking parallel hardware, which can otherwise be secure against earlier techniques. Therefore, there is a need to employ active countermeasures against sophisticated SCAs, even in the context of ephemeral keys and parallel hardware designs.

The major contributions of this paper are:

- We design parallel architectures of the arithmetic functions of Frodo and NewHope protocols using the latest, Round-2 specifications, and we show that the parallel architectures are still vulnerable to power-based SCAs.
- We develop DL-based single-trace SCAs and quantify that they are superior to classical techniques by up to 150% and 900%, respectively, for Frodo [7] and NewHope [2]. This shows that DL-based SCAs are able to generalize well to noisy implementations, namely parallel implementations.

– We evaluate the effect of the state-of-the-art SCA data augmentation techniques for DL [24] and reveal that they have marginal impact on accuracy while complicating the training process.

To the best of our knowledge, this is the first work to investigate DL-based SCAs on the next-generation encryption standards.

The rest of the paper is organized as follows. Section 2 provides the background and the prior work on power-based SCAs on lattice-based cryptography, DL-based SCAs, Neural Network (NN) classification, and Frodo and NewHope algorithms. Section 3 then introduces the novel DL-based SCAs we have developed in the context of lattice-based PQKE. Section 4 describes the parallelized hardware architectures under evaluation. Subsequently, Sect. 5 quantifies the proposed attack's improvement over the classical approaches and finally Sect. 6 concludes the paper.

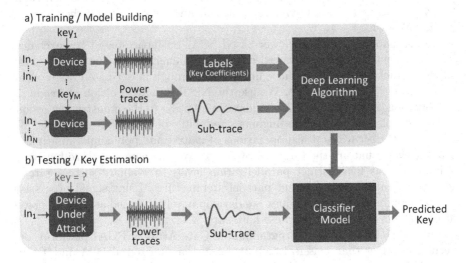

Fig. 1. Deep-Learning based SCAs illustrating a) training and b) testing phases.

2   Background and Prior Work

This section provides previous work and background information about power-based SCAs on lattice-based cryptography, DL-based SCAs, NN classification, and Frodo and NewHope protocols.

2.1   Power-Based SCAs on Lattice-Based Cryptography

The power consumption of an integrated circuit depends on the data being processed, and SCAs aim to extract this correlation. One of the most widely studied SCA on lattice-based cryptography is DPA [25]. To that end, it is a major threat that works in *unprofiled* settings: the attack analyzes changes occurring on traces (or sub-traces, which are pieces obtained from the same trace) under varying inputs and the fixed secret-key (or sub-keys, which are parts of the key). TAs, by contrast, are *profiled* attacks: the adversary builds multivariate probability density functions for targeted operations and uses them to estimate the secret-key [40]. TA thus requires having access to the target device and programming it with known keys prior to the attack.

Implementations of lattice-based cryptosystems have shown vulnerability to power-based SCAs [3,16,32,37,41]. Applying DPA on lattice-based PQKE protocols is, however, particularly challenging because the protocols generate a new secret-key for each key-exchange session; hence, the attacker is limited to a single power measurement. Aysu *et al.* addressed this challenge, for the first time, through horizontal DPA attacks, which exploited key-dependent, intermediate computations obtained within a single execution [3]. Others have shown TAs that work with a single-trace [8,22,33,37]. All these attacks, however, target serial software or hardware implementations and are expected to be less efficient on parallelized hardware designs because of the higher algorithmic noise.

2.2 DL-Based SCAs

The advantages of traditional machine learning approaches such as support vector machines (SVM) and random forests (RF) over DPA and TA have been highlighted in prior works [21,27]. However, there has been a surge in DL-based SCA-techniques to improve classification performance. Figure 1 outlines the method in such profiled attacks. During training, the adversary builds a profile of the device under different keys and inputs through a DL-based classifier, which then at test time estimates the secret-key. The primary underlying motivation of using DL is that it can apply filtering and alignment of traces in an automatic way, which was typically dealt with by ad-hoc methods known to side-channel experts. Several works have indeed used DL techniques to show how different methods can lend themselves to SCAs [18,24,29,34,38,45].

Unfortunately, all prior work on DL-based SCAs focuses on symmetric-key encryption functions such as AES and PRESENT or quantum-vulnerable cryptosystems such as RSA [12]. By contrast, we extend such attacks, for the first time, to PQKE.

2.3 NN Classification

The goal of any classifier is to take an input vector $\mathbf{x}$ and assign it to one of K discrete-classes $\mathcal{C}_k$, where $k = 1, 2, \ldots, K$. Figure 2 shows the DL-based classification to predict the secret-key. In our case, $\mathbf{x}$ refers to power-traces, and $\mathcal{C}_k$ corresponds to keys—the classifier is trained with this data.

NN consist of multiple layers of neurons with activation functions typically based on the rectified linear unit (ReLU) to model the non-linearity [31]. The network layers consist of an *input layer*, an *output layer*, and *hidden layers*. Neural networks that consist of multiple hidden layers are considered as deep

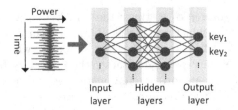

Fig. 2. DL-based classifier (Neural Network) taking samples of power-trace as an input and predicting a key as a label. Each sample in time domain of the power-trace is a neuron at the input layer and the ultimate prediction of the key guess is also a neuron at the output layer.

neural networks. The input layer represents the dimensions of the input data, e.g., the number of samples in a power-trace. The output layer tends to have as many neurons as the number of classes to predict. The number of hidden layers and the number of neurons in the hidden layers vary based on the task. For instance, to capture complex features of the input, we increase the number of layers or number of neurons in each layer, whereas, in the event of overfitting, we reduce the layers in the network or number of neurons per layer.

CNN. CNNs are a major class of DL techniques, which have shown better performance than classical approaches for image recognition [44]. A CNN is a special kind of neural network that is built for processing information that has a grid-like structure. Figure 3 shows a CNN, which consists of the following layers:

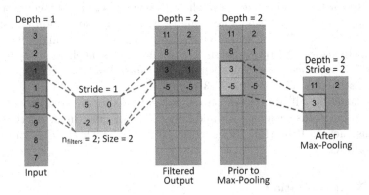

Fig. 3. Convolutional and pooling layers of a CNN. The input passes 2 filters of size 2, after which the output is sub-sampled using maximum pooling with a stride of 2.

- *Convolutional Layer.* The convolutional layer extracts features from the input while preserving the relationship between different pixels. In this layer, a filter of a certain size passes over the input and performs convolutions to produce a set of linear activations. The filter then moves by a fixed amount, referred to as the stride.

- *Pooling layer:* This layer follows the convolutional layer and sub-samples the produced feature map to make it invariant to small changes in the input [19]. Similar to the convolutional layer, a filter determines which values to sub-sample, and a stride length defines how much to move the filter. Pooling generally is either Maximum Pooling which takes the maximum of the values of the image in the filter area or average pooling which takes the average of all values in the filter.
- *Fully Connected Layer:* This layer predicts the probability distributions of the input over different classes. The function is a fully connected (dense) layer of neurons, with the outputs having a *Softmax* activation. This is because *Softmax* converts logits, which are raw scores of the output layer, to probabilities $S(y_i) = \frac{e^{y_i}}{\sum_j e^{y_j}}$, where y_i is the ith logits value [11].
- *Batch Normalization Layer:* During the training of neural networks, updating parameters of an earlier layer results in the parameters of a later layer to change. This phenomenon is known as the internal covariate shift [23], which results in slowing down the training by requiring the learning rates of the models to be small. Batch normalization addresses this problem by normalizing the parameters of the network layer-wise and readjusting the parameters and improving training time [23].
- *Dropout Layer:* Neural networks are difficult to train and often tend to over-fit to the training data. Dropout is a technique that addresses this problem by randomly dropping neurons (with their connection) during training which prevents the network from learning data from the training set only and improving the performance of the network [43].

2.4   Frodo and NewHope Algorithms

Frodo [7] and NewHope [2] are key-exchange protocols that allow two or more parties to establish a unique, symmetric key over an insecure medium. Parties communicate their share of the secret-key in such a way that the adversary eavesdropping on the exchanged information cannot recover the secret-key. Frodo and Newhope algorithms include arithmetic functions of matrix and polynomial multiplication, respectively, where the secret-key is multiplied with a known input. Hence, the SCA-security of the protocols can be evaluated by analyzing these operations [3].

Frodo and NewHope have different parameter options depending on the desired security level. We analyze Frodo and NewHope, which aim Security Level 5 in the NIST call for proposals. For Frodo, this corresponds to using matrices of sizes $n \cdot n$, $n \cdot \tilde{n}$, $\tilde{m} \cdot n$, and $\tilde{m} \cdot \tilde{n}$ where n, $\tilde{n}$, and $\tilde{m}$, are respectively, 1344, 8, and 8 with integer elements modulo 2^{16}. For NewHope, this corresponds to operating with polynomials of degree 1023 with integer coefficients modulo 12289.

Since breaking Frodo and Newhope is equivalent to successfully applying SCAs on matrix/polynomial multiplication [3], we focus on these operations with $\mathbf{A} \cdot \mathbf{S}$ and $\mathbf{a} \cdot \mathbf{s}$, where $\mathbf{A}$ (or $\mathbf{a}$) is the public value and $\mathbf{S}$ (or $\mathbf{s}$) is the secret sub-key. These multiplication functions use the same secret sub-keys more than one time in the computation; therefore, the attacker can extract the secret information from a single power-trace [3].

3   The Proposed DL-Based SCAs

This section presents the proposed DL-based SCAs and related challenges. First, we describe the adaptation of existing SCA-techniques based on time-series analysis. We then introduce our CNN based attack using power measurements. Finally, we elaborate on the hyper-parameter tuning of the trained models.

3.1   Neural Network Based Classification

Prior works have shown that time-series power measurements can be used to predict the Hamming weight (HW) or Hamming distance (HD) for an AES-128 8-bit implementation [28,38], which in turn discloses the secret-key. However, predicting these classes is difficult due to the imbalance of HW/HD in the dataset for a given implementation [35]. To address this issue of class imbalance, data balancing techniques have to be used to successfully attack AES [24]. However, in this work, instead of attacking intermediate computations or HW/HD, we attack a coefficient of the key, i.e., a sub-key. This allows the data-set to be balanced in terms of the key and thus ensures smooth training of the model.

Similar to the work by Kim et.al [24], we constructed a simple CNN architecture based on the performance observed on AES, namely a Visual Geometry Group (VGG) based architecture that has been proven to be highly effective for SCAs [24,38].

Our model consists of multiple convolutional layers with a fixed number of channels, followed by a maximum pooling layer. However, the model does not include a batch normalization layer after every pooling layer as we observe overfitting on the training set when we include it in the model. Prior to the last two layers, we flatten the output of the convolutional layer before feeding into a batch normalization layer. After the batch normalization layer, we feed the data into a dropout layer, with the probability of dropping certain connections with a probability of 0.5 during the training. After the dropout layer, we pass the flattened data into a fully connected layer before being passed to the final output layer. The final layer is also a fully connected and consists of 11 neurons for Frodo to predict the 11 possible sub-keys values (similarly, 33 neurons for NewHope). All the hidden layers have ReLU activations and the output layer has *Softmax* activations.

3.2   Hyper-parameter Tuning

Most DL algorithms come with a different set of parameters to control different aspects of the classification task. Hyper-parameter selection can determine the run-time and computational resources required by the algorithm to classify new data (which the algorithm has never seen). To find a set of hyper-parameters for the model, we evaluate the model on the validation set after every iteration and the network stops training when it achieves the highest validation accuracy. Once we find the highest validation accuracy, we re-train the model with the combined test and validation sets and evaluate it on the test set. To prevent overfitting of the CNN, the training stops when the accuracy does not increase after 5 training iterations. The network architecture, kernel size, stride length, filter size, learning rate, batch size and number of training iterations are all hyper-parameters for the CNN, which were tuned to find a suitable network architecture. Once we tune the hyper-parameters mentioned above for `Frodo-1`, we keep them fixed for the remaining implementations, including `NewHope`.

Figure 4 shows that the hyper-parameter tuning found a set of reasonable hyper-parameters as there is no evident overfitting/underfitting observed on the training and validation data.

Loss functions enable the network to determine how much to tune the parameters and are a measure of how well a specific algorithm models the data. The loss function in addition to an optimizer, which updates the weights during training to minimize the loss reduces the error in the model prediction. Accuracy is a metric for classification models use to determine how many classes it predicted correctly. It is the ratio of the total number of correct predictions to the total number of predictions made overall.

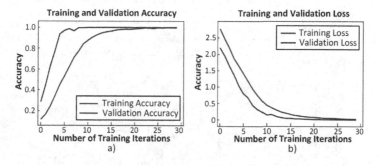

Fig. 4. a) The training and validation loss and b) The training and validation accuracy curves for `Frodo-1` which were used determine the hyper-parameters.

During the training process, `Frodo` takes a larger number of training iterations to converge on a high-accuracy solution as compared to `NewHope`. `Frodo` takes 30 iterations to converge on an optimal model whereas `NewHope` takes only 20 iterations.

4   The Proposed Hardware Architectures

To evaluate side-channel security, we implemented the security-critical arithmetic functions of matrix and polynomial multiplications – prior work have identified that the side-channel leakage of these functions results in session key recovery [3]. We proposed five architectures for these multiplications in Frodo and NewHope algorithms that support different parallelism. Since the proposed architectures process 1, 2, 4, 8, and 16 coefficients in parallel, we labeled these architectures as Frodo/NewHope-1, Frodo/NewHope-2, Frodo/NewHope-4, Frodo/NewHope-8, and Frodo/NewHope-16. The proposed architectures are based on the prior work [3], but has been modified for Round-2 parameters and extended for parallel computing. Figures 5 and 6 show the architecture details of the developed hardware designs for Frodo and NewHope, respectively. We colored the architectures with different colors in Figs. 5 and 6 in order to demonstrate the differences between each architecture clearly. Frodo/NewHope-1/-2/ -4/-8/-16, comprise different numbers of each hardware structure, respectively, 1, 2, 4, 8, 16. For example, Frodo-4 comprises 4 different target registers that are labeled as in bold red, respectively, target_0, target_1, target_2, and target_4.

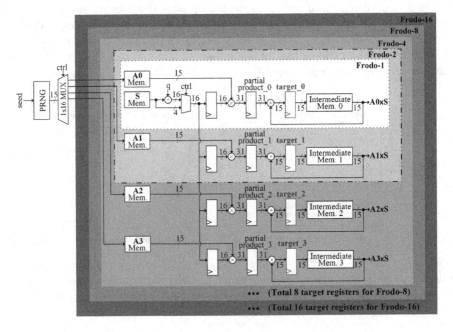

Fig. 5. Hardware architectures and operations under attack for Frodo. (Color figure online)

For Frodo, a pseudo-random generator produces public values (**A**) in the hardware. We used the Trivium algorithm [46] to create random numbers in order to minimize the hardware resource usage without sacrificing the security. After performing two's complement conversions of secret sub-keys (**S**), multiplier(s) that is the main processing unit of all architectures calculates partial products. Then, these partial products are accumulated to the previous value stored in intermediate memory. The `Frodo` designs use modular reduction with a power of two; thus, the modulo reduction is free. The accumulator sum is allowed to exceed q and will only be reduced modulo q since the modulus q is a power of two. In other words, it performs simply a truncation of the adder output to $\log_2 q$ bits.

The difference of `NewHope` compared to `Frodo` is that `NewHope` requires a full-scale reduction after the modular multiplication because the modular reduction is with the constant integer 12289. To that end, we used the *Barrett reduction* technique [30], which computes the modular reduction with two multiplications and a small, fixed number of subtractions. It also removes the errors within a fixed range by a sequence of subtractions and bound checking [3], which is between 0 and 12289×4. We implemented this operation before the intermediate memory updates in parallel to ensure a constant-time operation and reduce power side-channel leakage level of the design [3].

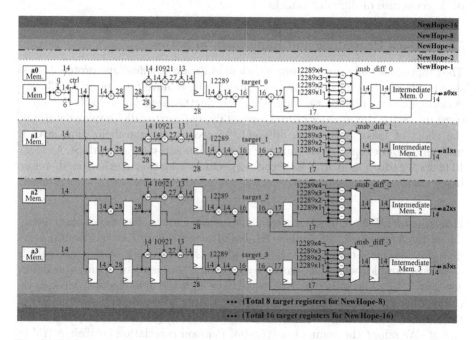

Fig. 6. Hardware architectures and operations under attack for `NewHope`. (Color figure online)

The main challenge of `Frodo` and `NewHope` is to implement these architectures in the memory-constrained devices. For example, the size of the matrix **A** requires 1024×1024×14 bits for the `NewHope` implementation. Since our target FPGA cannot store this amount of data into the memory, we resolve the resource limitation using the on-the-fly calculation approach [7] that enables the computation of **A·S**/**a·s** without accumulation in the hardware. Although

Number Theoretic Transform (NTT)-based polynomial multipliers are possible for NewHope, we use the regular (i.e. schoolbook) multiplication. Note that the regular multiplication has some advantages over NTT-based implementations in terms of critical path delay, or area- and power-efficiency [6,10,20,39]. But the regular multiplication is admittedly more susceptible to SCAs.

Frodo-1/-2/-4/-8/-16 and NewHope-1/-2/-4/-8/-16 are written in Verilog Hardware Description Language and mapped on to the Xilinx Spartan-6 XC6SLX75. We used Xilinx Integrated Synthesis Environment (ISE) version 14.7 with default settings for synthesizing, placing, and routing of the proposed designs.

5   Evaluation Results and Comparison

This section describes the measurement setup for our experiments and compares the success rate of different attacks.

5.1   Attack Procedure and Experimental Setup

The proposed attacks target multiplications of Frodo and NewHope protocols, and specifically the intermediate memory updates to remove false positives [3]. We perform a chosen-plaintext attack, where we vary the keys but keep the plaintext constant. Since the number of updates is different for parallel implementations, the effect of false positives is different. Moreover, the parallelization level is inversely proportional to the number of available sub-traces for all SCAs (e.g., 1344 for Frodo-1 and 672 for Frodo-2). Our evaluation method is therefore based on the comparison of the success rate vs. the number of sub-traces used.

Horizontal DPA. Our horizontal DPA attack follows the methodology introduced by Aysu et al. [3]. Unlike DL-based attacks and TAs, horizontal DPA does not require a training or profiling phase. It relies on a statistical analysis of several samples where the same keying material is used to operate on different data [42]. The sensitive data leaked through the side-channel depends on the number of bits switching in the registers. Our power models use the HD of the register to determine the expected (hypothetical) power consumption of the circuit. We adopt the common method of Pearson correlation coefficient [15] in our statistical analysis to compare the real power consumption values and the hypothetical power consumption values for each sub-key. Correlation trace $\rho_{i,j}$ for a sub-key guess i is defined as:

$$\rho_{i,j} = \frac{\sum_{d=1}^{D}(h_{d,i} - \bar{h}_i)(t_{d,j} - \bar{t}_j)}{\sqrt{\sum_{d=1}^{D}(h_{d,i} - \bar{h}_i)^2 \sum_{d=1}^{D}(t_{d,j} - \bar{t}_j)^2}} \tag{1}$$

where T data points of D number of traces. The hypothetical power consumption value to the appropriate sub-key is defined as h_d, i with $0 < d \leq D$ and real power-trace is defined as $t_{d,j}$ with $0 < j \leq T$. $\bar{h}_i$ and $\bar{t}_j$ represent the mean power estimate and the mean power-trace, respectively. The result of the Pearson correlation is between $[-1,1]$ and depicts the relationship between real power consumption values and the hypothetical power consumption values. Therefore, the maximum absolute correlation coefficient reveals the timing information of the DPA leakage.

TA. To perform a TA, we first create a "profile" of the device and apply this profile to find the secret sub-keys. In other words, we create a template of the device's operation and then apply this template to the attacked traces. The template is effectively a multivariate distribution that describes the key samples in the power-traces.

To reduce the number of samples and the size of the templates, we selected some special values in each trace that are called the point of interest (POI). In the literature, there are different kinds of approaches [4,5,17,42] to find the POIs that vary strongly between different key coefficients. We used the Sum of Squared Difference (SOSD) method that is one of the strongest approaches to improve the classification performance of the TA [17]. We have k different operations and i sample points in a number of traces named $t_1..t_k$. The mean power M and SOSD are calculated as follows:

$$M_{k,i} = \frac{1}{T_k} \sum_{j=1}^{T_k} t_{j,i} \tag{2}$$

$$SOSD_i = \sum_{k_1,k_2} \left(M_{k_1,i} - M_{k_2,i}\right)^2 \tag{3}$$

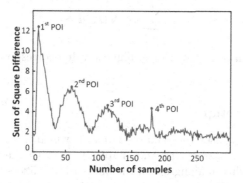

Fig. 7. An example of POI selection from SOSD results.

Figure 7 shows that there are four peak points for the SOSD. We picked these four peak points as POIs because the power variation of power consumption is maximum at these samples s_i. As an experiment, we used different number of POIs for our TA. However, using more than four POIs did not improve the success rate of TA for Frodo and NewHope because most of the time-samples in each sub-traces are not highly correlated with the sub-keys. Also, using all samples of traces makes an impractical template and decreases the classification performance due to high computational requirement [14,40]. We calculated average power μ_i in (4), variance of power v_i in (5), and covariance in (6) c_{i,i^*} at every pair of POIs (i and i^*) for creating covariance matrix in S_i (7).

$$\mu_i = \frac{1}{T_k} \sum_{j=1}^{T_k} t_{j,s_i} \tag{4}$$

$$v_i = \frac{1}{T_k} \sum_{j=1}^{T_k} (t_{j,s_i} - \mu_i)^2 \tag{5}$$

$$c_{i,i^*} = \frac{1}{T_k} \sum_{j=1}^{T_k} (t_{j,s_i} - \mu_i)(t_{j,s_i^*} - \mu_{i^*}) \tag{6}$$

$$S = \begin{pmatrix} v_1 & c_{1,2} & c_{1,3} & \cdots \\ c_{2,1} & v_2 & c_{2,3} & \cdots \\ c_{3,1} & c_{3,2} & v_3 & \cdots \\ \vdots & \vdots & \vdots & \ddots \end{pmatrix} \tag{7}$$

For the attack step, we calculated the multivariate normal probability density function (MVNPDF) using POIs of the attacked traces t_{j,s_i}, μ_i, and c_{i,i^*} results of the profiled devices. We summed the log of the normal distribution $\mathcal{N}$ to avoid precision issues that occur if the results of MVNPDF are too large or too small.

$$P_k = \sum_{j=0}^{k} \log \mathcal{N}(t_j, \mu, S) \tag{8}$$

The index of the matrix P_k with the highest value corresponds to the sub-key guess.

5.2   Evaluation Setup

Our evaluation setup uses the Sakura-G board, which has a Xilinx Spartan-6 XC6SLX75 FPGA for processing and enables measuring the voltage drop on a 1Ω shunt-resistor while making use of the onboard amplifiers to measure FPGA power consumption. We also use a low noise AC amplifier, which is a PA-203 amplifier from Langer EMV-Technik with 20 dB [26]. We collect power measurements using a PicoScope-3206D model oscilloscope at 500MS/s [36]. We then pre-process the raw power-traces to divide the entire power-trace into sub-traces, which capture the information about the device for one cycle of operation.

We train and evaluate DL-models on a computer with 64 GB of Random Access Memory (RAM), an NVIDIA 2080 Ti graphics card, and an Intel i7 9700K. We use the *TensorFlow* Graphics Processing Unit (GPU) [1] as the backend, with a *Keras* front end to train and evaluate all of the DL-models. We use a categorical cross-entropy as our loss function with *Adagrad* as the optimizer with a learning rate of 0.1 [13]. Using Adagrad allows the learning rate to be adjusted dynamically as the model is training, thus even with a large learning rate, the optimizer will update it to the appropriate value. The average time to train the models is around 10 minutes to achieve over 99% accuracy, similar to the prior work on AES [38].

5.3 Comparison Against Conventional Attacks

Figure 8 compares the proposed DL-based attack to horizontal DPA and TA. The DL-based attack achieves 100% accuracy whereas TA and horizontal DPA aren't able to attack the implementation successfully. The DL-based approach outperforms horizontal DPA and TA by up to 900% and 25% in terms of the attained success rate. This performance is attributed to the ability of the CNN to filter out the noise from the power-traces [24]. This quantifies that the proposed DL-based attack needs fewer samples to succeed and hence, can break even further parallelized designs where the conventional techniques would fail.

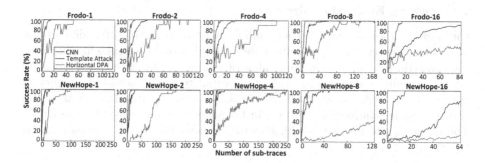

Fig. 8. Comparison of DL-based vs. classical SCAs on `Frodo` and `NewHope`.

Table 1. SNR (dB) for Frodo and NewHope traces at 1.5 MHz

Algorithm/Parallelization Level	1	2	4	8	16
Frodo	6.27 dB	5.64 dB	4.73 dB	3.15 dB	2.19 dB
NewHope	3.81 dB	3.31 dB	2.91 dB	2.61 dB	2.11 dB

Table 1 furthermore shows the SNR (dB) values of the captured traces for `Frodo` and `NewHope` implementations at a clock frequency of 1.5 MHz. As expected, the algorithmic noise increases with the increase in parallelization, which impacts the TA and the horizontal DPA. In other words, the TA and horizontal DPA results become worse with low SNR. As a result, there is a steady increase in the number of sub-traces required to attack the parallel implementations. The CNN attack, however, tolerates the algorithmic noise better than TA and horizontal DPA. Consequently, the number of required sub-traces for a successful attack varies between 10–17 sub-traces for the CNN.

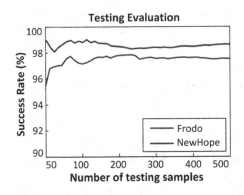

Fig. 9. The effect of testing size on ML SCAs on `Frodo-16` and `NewHope-16`.

5.4   Testing Evaluation Size

For most DL applications, there are millions of data points to both train and test the model. However, in Fig. 8 we limit the evaluation to 200 samples for each sub-key. Though, this is not a large number of samples we observe that evaluating more test samples does not degrade the overall test accuracy of the model as is seen in Fig. 9. As is evident from Fig. 9, the success rate plateaus after 100 and 200 testing samples per sub-key for `NewHope-16` and `Frodo-16` respectively. Thus a smaller testing set is sufficient to represent the overall accuracy of the model.

5.5   Data Augmented Vs Proposed Approach

We adapt our CNN to include a batch normalization layer at the input, followed by a layer of Gaussian noise. The addition of the batch normalization is necessary so that noise can be added to the normalized inputs. This acts as a regularization that is only active during the training of the model and has previously been used successfully to reduce any overfitting in SCA [24]. We train the two different models for `Frodo-16` and `NewHope-16` while varying the number of training samples used to create the model at 15 sub-traces. Due to the random noise at the inputs in the augmented case, training takes closer to 50 training iterations to produce a model with similar accuracy on the training set.

We observe in Fig. 10 that both models achieve similar results on the test set. As more data is made available, both models are able to learn the features of the power-trace more effectively. In fact, for both `Frodo-16` and `NewHope-16`, the augmented network has a slightly lower accuracy as compared to the regular CNN. Thus, we conclude that the data augmentation technique of adding random noise to the inputs does not improve the performance of the model in this setting as there are sufficient training samples that are able to capture the added noise. However, in an instance when the attacker has access to a limited number of traces, such a noise augmentation can provide a similar result.

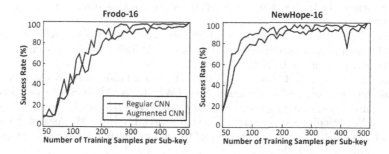

Fig. 10. Varying the training set size to train the regular CNN and a CNN with noise at the inputs to prevent overfitting for `Frodo-16` and `NewHope-16`.

6 Conclusions

As the industry and governments gear towards a post-quantum cryptography standardization, implementation security becomes an important issue in addition to the theoretical cryptanalysis of candidate algorithms. This paper analyzes the physical side-channel vulnerability of the hardware designs performing a fundamental arithmetic of lattice-based cryptography, which are among the prime candidates for post-quantum cryptosystems. We demonstrate the superiority of *deep learning* over classical methods and show that such attacks has a potential to break otherwise secure systems. Therefore, the paper illustrates the need to incorporate active security mechanisms against power side-channels even for the single measurement and parallel hardware use-cases.

Acknowledgements. This research is supported in part by the NSF under the Grants No. CNS 16-244770 (Center for Advanced Electronics through Machine Learning) and CNS 18-50373. NC State is an academic partner of Riscure Inc. and thanks them for providing hardware/software support for side-channel analysis. We acknowledge NVIDIA for their GPU donation and Xilinx for their FPGA donation.

References

1. Abadi, M., Agarwal, A., Barham, P., Brevdo, E., Chen, Z., et al.: TensorFlow: Large-Scale Machine Learning on Heterogeneous Systems (2015). https://www.tensorflow.org/, software available from tensorflow.org

2. Alkim, E., Ducas, L., Pöppelmann, T., Schwabe, P.: Post-quantum key exchange - a new hope. In: USENIX Security Symposium, pp. 327–343 (2016). https://www.usenix.org/conference/usenixsecurity16/technical-sessions/presentation/alkim

3. Aysu, A., Tobah, Y., Tiwari, M., Gerstlauer, A., Orshansky, M.: Horizontal side-channel vulnerabilities of post-quantum key exchange protocols. In: IEEE International Symposium on Hardware Oriented Security and Trust (HOST), pp. 81–88 (2018)

4. Gierlichs, B., Paar, C.: Templates vs. stochastic methods a performance analysis for side channel cryptanalysis. In: CHES (2006)

5. B. Gierlichs, L. Batina, P.T., Preneel, B.: Mutual information analysis. In: CHES (2008)

6. Bian, S., Hiromoto, M., Sato, T.: Filianore: better multiplier architectures For LWE-based post-quantum key exchange. In: ACM/IEEE Design Automation Conference (DAC), pp. 1–6 (2019)

7. Bos, J., Costello, C., Ducas, L., Mironov, I., et al.: Frodo: take off the ring! practical, quantum-secure key exchange from LWE. In: ACM SIGSAC Conference on Computer and Communications Security, pp. 1006–1018 (2016)

8. Bos, J.W., Friedberger, S., Martinoli, M., Oswald, E., Stam, M.: Assessing the feasibility of single trace power analysis of frodo. In: Selected Areas in Cryptography (SAC), pp. 216–234 (2018)

9. Braithwaite, M.: Google Security Blog: Experimenting with Post-Quantum Cryptography, July 2016. https://security.googleblog.com/2016/07/experimenting-with-post-quantum.html

10. Buchmann, J., Göpfert, F., Güneysu, T., Oder, T., Pöppelmann, T.: High-performance and lightweight lattice-based public-key encryption. In: ACM International Workshop on IoT Privacy, Trust, and Security, pp. 2–9 (2016)

11. Campbell, D., Dunne, R.A., Campbell, N.A.: On the pairing of the softmax activation and cross-entropy penalty functions and the derivation of the softmax activation function. In: Australian Conference on Neural Networks, pp. 181–185 (1997)

12. Carbone, M., et al.: Deep learning to evaluate secure RSA implementations. IACR Trans. Cryptographic Hardware Embedded Syst. **2019**(2), 132–161 (2019)

13. Chollet, F., et al.: Keras (2015). https://keras.io

14. Chong, T., Kaffes, K.: Hacking AES-128. SemanticScholar (2016)

15. Brier, E., Olivier, F.: Correlation power analysis with a leakage model. In: CHES (2004)

16. Espitau, T., Fouque, P.A., Gérard, B., Tibouchi, M.: Side-channel attacks on BLISS lattice-based signatures: exploiting branch tracing against strongswan and electromagnetic emanations in micro-controllers. In: ACM SIGSAC Conference on Computer and Communications Security, pp. 1857–1874 (2017)

17. Fan, G., Zhou, Y., Zhang, H., Feng, D.: How to choose interesting points for template attacks more effectively? Int. Conf. Trusted Syst. **9473**, 168–183 (2014)

18. Gilmore, R., Hanley, N., O'Neill, M.: Neural network based attack on a masked implementation of AES. In: IEEE International Symposium on Hardware Oriented Security and Trust (HOST), pp. 106–111 (2015)

19. Goodfellow, I., Bengio, Y., Courville, A.: Deep Learning. MIT Press (2016). http://www.deeplearningbook.org

20. Güneysu, T., Lyubashevsky, V., Pöppelmann, T.: Practical lattice-based cryptography: a signature scheme for embedded systems. In:CHES (2012)

21. Heuser, A., Zohner, M.: Intelligent machine homicide. In: Schindler, W., Huss, S.A. (eds.) COSADE 2012. LNCS, vol. 7275, pp. 249–264. Springer, Heidelberg (2012). https://doi.org/10.1007/978-3-642-29912-4_18

22. Huang, W.L., Chen, J.P., Yang, B.Y.: Power analysis on NTRU prime. IACR Trans. Cryptographic Hardware Embedded Syst. **2020**(1), 123–151 (Nov 2019). https://doi.org/10.13154/tches.v2020.i1.123-151, https://tches.iacr.org/index.php/TCHES/article/view/8395

23. Ioffe, S., Szegedy, C.: Batch normalization: accelerating deep network training by reducing internal covariate shift. In: International Conference on Machine Learning (ICML), pp. 448–456. PMLR (2015)

24. Kim, J., Picek, S., Heuser, A., Bhasin, S., Hanjalic, A.: Make some noise. unleashing the power of convolutional neural networks for profiled side-channel analysis. In: IACR Transactions on Cryptographic Hardware and Embedded Systems **2019**(3), 148–179 (2019). https://tches.iacr.org/index.php/TCHES/article/view/8292

25. Kocher, P., Jaffe, J., Jun, B.: Differential Power Analysis. In: Wiener, M. (ed.) CRYPTO 1999. LNCS, vol. 1666, pp. 388–397. Springer, Heidelberg (1999). https://doi.org/10.1007/3-540-48405-1_25

26. Langer EMV: PA 203 SMA Pre-amplifier. https://www.langer-emv.de/en/product/preamplifier/37/pa-203-sma-set-preamplifier-100-khz-up-to-3-ghz/518

27. Lerman, L., Bontempi, G., Markowitch, O.: Power analysis attack: an approach based on machine learning. Int. J. Appl. Cryptography **3**(2), 97–115 (2014)

28. Maghrebi, H.: Deep learning based side channel attacks in practice. IACR Cryptology ePrint Archive, Report 2019/578 (2019). https://eprint.iacr.org/2019/578

29. Maghrebi, H., Portigliatti, T., Prouff, E.: Breaking cryptographic implementations using deep learning techniques. In: Security, Privacy, and Applied Cryptography Engineering (SPACE), pp. 3–26 (2016)

30. Menezes, A.J., Van Oorschot, P.C., Vanstone, S.A.: Handbook of Applied Cryptography. CRC Press, July 2016

31. Nair, V., Hinton, G.E.: Rectified linear units improve restricted boltzmann machines. In: International Conference on International Conference on Machine Learning (ICML), pp. 807–814. PMLR (2010)

32. Oder, T., Schneider, T., Pöppelmann, T., Güneysu, T.: Practical CCA2-secure and masked Ring-LWE implementation. IACR Trans. Cryptographic Hardware Embedded Syst. **2018**(1), 142–174 (2018)

33. Pessl, P., Primas, R.: More practical single-trace attacks on the number theoretic transform. In: LATINCRYPT, pp. 130–149 (2019)

34. Picek, S., et al.: Side-channel analysis and machine learning: a practical perspective. In: International Joint Conference on Neural Networks (IJCNN), pp. 4095–4102 (2017)

35. Picek, S., Heuser, A., Jovic, A., Bhasin, S., Regazzoni, F.: The curse of class imbalance and conflicting metrics with machine learning for side-channel evaluations. IACR Trans. Cryptographic Hardware Embedded Syst. **2019**(1), 209–237 (2018), https://tches.iacr.org/index.php/TCHES/article/view/7339

36. Pico Technology: PicoScope 3206D Model Oscilloscope. https://www.picotech.com/oscilloscope/3000/picoscope-3000-oscilloscope-specifications

37. Primas, R., Pessl, P., Mangard, S.: Single-trace side-channel attacks on masked lattice-based encryption. In: CHES, pp. 513–533 (2017)

38. Prouff, E., Strullu, R., Benadjila, R., Cagli, E., Dumas, C.: Study of deep learning techniques for side-channel analysis and introduction to ASCAD database. IACR Cryptology ePrint Archive 2018, 53 (2018). http://eprint.iacr.org/2018/053

39. Pöppelmann, T., Güneysu, T.: Area optimization of lightweight lattice-based encryption on reconfigurable hardware. In: IEEE International Symposium on Circuits and Systems (ISCAS), pp. 2796–2799 (2014)

40. Rechberger, C., Oswald, E.: Practical template attacks. In: International Workshop on Information Security Applications, pp. 440–456 (2004)
41. Reparaz, O., Roy, S.S., Vercauteren, F., Verbauwhede, I.: A masked ring-LWE implementation. In: CHES, pp. 683–702 (2015)
42. Chari, S., Rohatgin, P.: Template attacks. In: CHES (2002)
43. Srivastava, N., Hinton, G., Krizhevsky, A., Sutskever, I., Salakhutdinov, R.: Dropout: a simple way to prevent neural networks from overfitting. J. Mach. Learn. Res. **15**, 1929–1958 (2014)
44. Sultana, F., Sufian, A., Dutta, P.: Advancements in image classification using convolutional neural network. In: International Conference on Research in Computational Intelligence and Communication Networks, pp. 122–129 (2018)
45. Timon, B.: Non-profiled deep learning-based side-channel attacks with sensitivity analysis. IACR Trans. Cryptographic Hardware Embedded Syst. **2019**(2), 107–131 (2019). https://tches.iacr.org/index.php/TCHES/article/view/7387
46. Tian, Y., Li, J.: On the Design of Trivium. Cryptology ePrint Archive, Report 2009/431, 2009, January 2009. http://eprint.iacr.org/
47. Zhang, L., Vega, L., Taylor, M.: Power side channels in security ICS: Hardware countermeasures. CoRR abs/1605.00681 (2016). https://arxiv.org/abs/1605.00681

Profiling Dilithium Digital Signature Traces for Correlation Differential Side Channel Attacks

Apostolos P. Fournaris[1]($\boxtimes$), Charis Dimopoulos[2], and Odysseas Koufopavlou[2]

[1] Industrial Systems Institute/Research Center ATHENA, Patras Science Park,
Patras, Greece
fournaris@isi.gr
[2] Electrical and Computer Engineering Department, University of Patras,
Rion Campus, Patras, Greece

Abstract. A significant concern for the candidate schemes of the NIST postquantum cryptography standardization project is the protection they support against side-channel attacks. One of these candidate schemes currently in the NIST standardization race is the Dilithium signature scheme. This postquantum signature solution has been analyzed for side channel attack resistance especially against timing attacks. Expanding our attention on other types of side-channel analysis, this work is focused on correlation based differential side channel attacks on the polynomial multiplication operation of Dilithium digital signature generation. In this paper, we describe how a Correlation Power Attack should be adapted for the Dilithium signature generation and describe the attack process to be followed. We determine the conditions to be followed in order for such an attack to be feasible, (isolation of polynomial coefficient multiplication inpower traces) and we create a power trace profiling paradigm for the Dilithium signature scheme executed in embedded systems to showcase that the conditions can be met in practice. Expanding the methodology of recent works that mainly use simulations for power trace collection, in this paper, power trace capturing and profiling analysis of the signature generation process was succesfully done on a, noisy, Commercial off-the-shelf ARM Cortex-M4 embedded system.

Keywords: Postquantum cryptography · Side channel attack · Secure embedded systems

1 Introduction

The research efforts in recent years are increasingly targeted towards the realization of a quantum computer. By exploiting properties that stem from quan-

This paper's work has received funding from the European Union's Horizon 2020 research and innovation programme CPSoSaware under grant agreement No 873718 and also the European Union's Horizon 2020 research and innovation programme CONCORDIA under grant agreement No 830927.

© Springer Nature Switzerland AG 2020
A. Orailoglu et al. (Eds.): SAMOS 2020, LNCS 12471, pp. 281–294, 2020.
https://doi.org/10.1007/978-3-030-60939-9_19

tum mechanics, these machines are able to bypass performance barriers traditional computers face. One key remark is that quantum computers are not able or designed to replace the existing computing paradigm, but to provide vast amounts of performance boost in specific applications powered by novel algorithms.

In the field of cryptography, Shor's algorithm [21] is able to solve the integer factorization problem in polynomial time when executed in a quantum computer thus breaking the majority of the public-key cryptography schemes currently deployed in many infrastructures. As quantum computer development is accelerating, new and quantum resilient schemes have emerged to replace the no-longer safe to use public-key algorithms like DSA, RSA and Elliptic Curve Cryptography. These new schemes are based on hard problems that retain their resistance even when paired against a quantum computer. The importance of discovering optimal postquantum cryptographic algorithms is demonstrated by, e.g., NIST's current call for post-quantum secure proposals [2] and the official recommendations regarding post-quantum security from the NSA [6]. Still, a fundamental security consideration in the postquantum cryptography schemes that may make them unsafe for real-world use is their vulnerabilities linked with the underlying implementation due to possible leakage from Side Channels (eg. power consumption or electromagnetic emission (EM) during processing, or timing delay). Side Channel leakage can be exploited by various relevant attacks including timing, power and EM attacks both simple or advanced ones []. Differential analysis attacks [11,13] constitute the most potent such attacks under an unknown implementation scenario while template [9,17] and Machine Learning attacks [15] are equally potent when a device under attack is in the full control of an attacker.

Lattice based cryptography (LBC) constitutes a very promising category of post-quantum cryptosystems that has a strong presence in the NIST postquantum cryptography contest [2] and can offer digital signatures, key exchange and encryption. Dilithium digital signature scheme [10] is one of the promising LBC proposal of the NIST content and can be implemented very efficiently since it has relatively small keys and parameters. It has been implemented with relative success in x86 based devices, in ARM based devices and also in hardware. There are several works that evaluate the Dilithium side channel attack resistance in emulated environments and provide generic leakage assessment results (eg. using the Welch t-test leakage assessment technique) but few works focus on specific attacks (like Differential Power Analysis or template based attacks [19]). Other works rely on protecting the scheme against side channel attacks (SCAs) but produce a considerable performance overhead [16]. It should be mentioned that very few works explore the potentials of DPA in the Dilithium Digital signature scheme in a practical level that include measurements. In general, works that collect side channel leakage from actual implementations, use dedicated side channel trace collection platforms like the Chipwhisperer boards [1] and not off-the-shelf devices that are found in real embedded systems [7,16]. Regarding Differential SCA on Dilithium, while the attack is considered possible due to the existence of linear operations in the Dilithium structure, there are no analytic and practical approaches on how to mount such an attack.

In this paper, the Dilithium signature generation operation is analyzed and interesting computation points are identified for mounting differential power analysis SCAs. The analysis is focused on the polynomial multiplication operation needed during the sample rejection loop of the algorithm (last loop iteration) regardless of the technique used to perform it (schoolbook polynomial multiplication, sparse matrix polynomial multiplication or Number Theoretic Transform (NTT) representation). Correlation Power Analysis (CPA) is a very promising type of attack to be mounted in the focused operation, so, in this paper, we describe how such an attack should be adapted for the Dilithium signature generation. It is concluded that a Dilithium based CPA attack is feasible, regardless of the polynomial multiplication technique that is used in the Dilithium implementation, as long as individual polynomial coefficient multiplication can be identified in the collected power traces. To evaluate the correctness of this assumption, in this paper, we showcase how to profile collected traces of Dilithium signature generation process even when those traces are captured from a Commercial, noisy, off-the-shelf (COTS) embedded system boards. The results verify that the identified, exploitable, interesting points are visible in the power trace signals and that they can be isolated so that CPA can be effectively mounted on Dilithium signature generation.

The rest of the paper is organized as follows. In Sect. 2 the Dilithium digital signature algorithm is described and how CPA can be mounted on the algorithm is presented in detail. In Sect. 3 the experimental process that was followed is presented and in Sect. 4 measurements for profiling Dilithium signature generation are described and analyzed. Finally, Sect. 5 concludes the paper.

2 Dilithium Postquantum Digital Signature Scheme

The Dilithium digital signature scheme [10] is one of the algorithms that participate in the second round in the NIST postquantum cryptography competition. Dilithium is a signature scheme based on the Fiat-Shamir with Abort framework [14] and is implemented with Modules. Thus, it can perform key generation, message signature generation and digital signature verification. The algorithm is using a variation of the Ring-LWE problem, i.e. the Module-LWE problem. It relies in rings R_q: $Z_q[X]/(X^n + 1)$ where q is an integer. Thus, all elements in R_q are polynomials of degree n that have coefficients belonging to Z_q. In Dilithium scheme $q = 2^{23} - 2^{13} + 1 = 8380417$ and $n = 256$. Typically, as in all lattice based cryptography schemes, in Dilithium, the public key is a $k \times \ell$ matrix A where all its elements belong to R_q (thus $A \in R_q^{k \times \ell}$). However, Dilithium private keys S_1, S_2 are vectors of $R_q^{\ell \times 1}$ and $R_q^{k \times 1}$ respectively. A potential side channel attacker is expected to be interested in the key generation and most importantly in the message digital signature generation operation since in it, the secret key of the Dilithium scheme is used (the digital signature is verified using the public key so no sensitive information is involved in digital signature verification). Thus, in this paper, our analysis is focused on the Dilithium digital signature generation process (Algorithm 2). For the sake of completeness, the Key generation process is also presented (Algorithm 1). The algorithm uses a series of specialized truncation procedures i.e. ExpandA/Decompose/HighBits/LowBits/Power2Round/MakeHint. The reader can refer to the original Dilithium paper for more information on those functions [10]. Also, Dilithium has several parameters apart from q and n that can be tuned in order to provide different levels of security (weak, medium, high etc.). The parameters are presented in Table 1. As suggested by its creators, all polynomial multiplications in Dilithium are performed using NTT. For this reason, the table A, Y, W, Z as well as S_1 and S_2 are transformed in their NTT equivalent. However, there are works indicating that working in the normal domain could also be efficient in some corner cases.

Algorithm 1: Dilithium Key Generation Algorithm

Output: $P_{key} : (T_1, \rho)$ $S_{key} : (\rho, \hat{\rho}, S_1, S_2, T)$

1 Choose a random ρ and $\hat{\rho}$ from $\{0,1\}^{256}$;
2 ExpandA to sample A using XOF with seed ρ ;
3 Randomly generate $S_1 \in R_\eta^{\ell \times 1}$ and $S_2 \in R_\eta^{k \times 1}$ using XOF with seed $\hat{\rho}$;
4 $T = A \cdot S_1 + S_2 \in R_q^{k \times 1}$;
5 $(T_1, T_0) = \text{Power2Round}_q(T, d) \in R_q^{k \times 1}$;
6 $P_{key} = (\rho, T_1)$;
7 $S_{key} = (\rho, \hat{\rho}, S_1, S_2, T_0)$;
8 **return** P_{key}, S_{key}

Algorithm 2: Dilithium Signature Generation Algorithm

Input: $S_{key} : (\rho, \hat{\rho}, S_1, S_2), T_0, m$
Output: $\sigma = (Z, H, C)$

1 ExpandA for A using a XOF with input ρ ;
2 $T_1 = \text{Power2Round}(T_0, d)$;
3 **Rejection sampling loop** ;
4 $\rho' = \{0,1\}^{256}$;
5 $Y = Sample(\rho')$ using XOF ;
6 $W = A \cdot Y$;
7 $W_1 = HighBits(W,)$;
8 $C = H\{\rho, T_1, W, m\}$;
9 $Z = Y + C \cdot S_1$;
10 $R_0 = Lowbits(W - C \cdot S_2, 2\gamma_2)$;
11 if $||Z||_{\inf} >= \gamma_1 - \beta$ go to 3 ;
12 if $||R_0||_{\inf} >= \gamma_2 - \beta$ go to 3 ;
13 if $||C \cdot T_0||_{\inf} >= \gamma_2$ go to 3;
14 $H = MakeHint(-C \cdot T_0, W - C \cdot S_2 + C \cdot T_0, 2\gamma_2)$;
15 **return** $\sigma = (Z, H, C)$

From an SCA adversary perspective, there are various computational points attacks can be mounted. In [16], the authors provide several such points of interest to be exploited in order to reveal the secret keys S_1 and S_2. More specifically, by attacking the rejection operation, an attacker can possibly extract partial information on the secret key during the key generation. Also in Algorithm 2, the matrix Y that is used for the signature generation or even on a rejected matrix Z can also leak information about the secret key [10]. Similarly, computations that are directly linked with S_1 and S_2 can also be targeted ie. the computation of $Z = Y + C \cdot S_1$ (targeting $C \cdot S_1$), $R_0 = Lowbits(W - C \cdot S_2, 2\gamma_2)$ (targeting $C \cdot S_2$) or $MakeHint(-C \cdot T_0, W - C \cdot S_2 + C \cdot T_0, 2\gamma_2)$.

Table 1. Dilithium parameters for various security levels [10]

	Weak	Medium	Recommended (high)	Very high
q	8380417	8380417	8380417	8380417
d	14	14	14	14
weight of c	60	60	60	60
$\gamma_1 = (q-1)/16$	523776	523776	523776	523776
$\gamma_1 = \gamma_1/2$	261888	261888	261888	261888
(k, ℓ)	(3,2)	(4,3)	(5,4)	(6,5)
η	7	6	5	3
β	375	325	275	175
ω	64	80	96	120
Public key size (bytes)	896	1184	1472	1760
Signature size (bytes)	1387	2044	2701	3366

2.1 On Side Channel Leakage of the Dilithium Secret Key

Inspecting the Dilithium specifications, reveals that the secret key S_1 and S_2 are polynomial vectors of ℓ and k elements respectively. Each polynomial, however, is not defined in the polynomial ring R_q but rather in $R_\eta : Z_\eta[X]/(X^n + 1)$ where $n = 256$ and η is a Dilithium parameter that, as seen in Table 1, is a small integer number (3 to 7). So, practically, each polynomial in the secret key vector has 256 coefficients that each of them is an integer with values $\{-\eta, \eta\}$. Furthermore, in the Dilithium scheme specifications C is a n degree polynomial, deriving from a hash function (SHAKE256) sampling, that has 60 non zero coefficients of $\{-1, 1\}$. Given the above facts, computation in line 9 and line 10 of Algorithm 2 can become somewhat predictable as long as the computation of $C \cdot S_1$ and $C \cdot S_2$ can be identified in the side channel leakage traces. More specifically, focusing on the last iteration of the rejection sampling loop (where the sampling is not rejected and C is obtained), an attacker, by knowing the C value, can make a hypothesis on the value of each coefficient of S_1 or S_2 polynomial and compute by using a power model (Hamming weight or Hamming distance) this hypothesis expected leakage when $C \cdot S_1$ or $C \cdot S_2$ results are stored in some ARM processor's register. Then, using a distinguisher function (eg. Pearson Correlation), the attacker can evaluate if this hypothesis is correct using the collected leakage trace from the actual computation of $C \cdot S_1$ or $C \cdot S_2$. The above methodology constitutes the core of various divide and conquer Differential Side channel attacks (e.g Differential Power Analysis, DPA or Correlation Power Analysis, CPA) [8,13].

Let's assume a function $F(X)$ that consists of T different intermediate operations $f_i(X_i)$ where $i : \{1,..T\}$ and each X or X_i is a set of $\mathbf{K}$ or k inputs respectively on $F()$ or $f_i()$ (eg. $X^{(i)} : \{I_1^{(i)}, I_2^{(i)}, I_3^{(i)}..I_k^{(i)}\}$). Consider also that some operation f_t uses as one of its input an unknown secret S to provide a result and that all other f_t inputs are known or can be computed from the provided $F(X)$ inputs X (ie. $f_t(X^{(t)})$ where $X^{(t)} : \{I_1^{(t)}, I_2^{(t)}..I_{k-1}^{(t)}, I_k^{(t)}\}$ and $I_k^{(t)} = S$). A Correlation based vertical side channel attack can be mounted as long as operation f_t can be identified in the $F(X)$ side channel signal.

A CPA can be mounted in three phases. Initially, we generate λ different, random, inputs X_j for $F(X)$, then perform $F(X_j)$ for each one of those inputs, collect the results and capture a side channel trace P_j for each one of those inputs ($j \in \{1, 2, 3, ..\lambda\}$). The samples on each one of the P_j traces that match the operation $f_t(x^{(t)})$ are isolated thus creating λ different $PK_j(f_t)$ useful traces with p samples each (one sample in each leakage trace is denoted in $PK_{j,v}$ where $v \in \{1, 2, ..d\}$). Apart from that, in the first phase, the intermediate inputs of f_t, denoted as $X_j^{(t)} : \{I_{1,j}^{(t)}, I_{2,j}^{(t)}..I_{k-1,j}^{(t)}\}$ ($I_{k,j}^{(t)} = S$ for all $j \in 1, 2, ..\lambda$), are computed for all X_j inputs or outputs of $F(X)$ (depending on how $F(X)$ is realized).

In the CPA second phase, the attacker creates a hypothesis h on the value of S, denoted S_h, for all possible X_j inputs of $F(X)$, then for each j input calculates the $f_t(X_{j,h}^{(t)})$ result where $X_{j,h}^{(t)} : \{I_{1,j}^{(t)}, I_{2,j}^{(t)}..I_{k-1,j}^{(t)}, S_{h,j}\}$ and generates its hypothetical side channel information using some model. In most cases, the dynamic power consumption leakage side channel information is used to mount an attack, so the Hamming Weight (HW) or Hamming distance (HD) model is adopted. Without loss of generality, in our analysis we adopt the Hamming Weight model, thus we compute the outcome of $f_t()$ for $X_{j,h}^{(t)}$ ($X_{j,h}^{(t)}$ is fully known if we include the hypothetical $S_{h,j}$ in the computation, and the hyphothetical leakage for $S_{h,j}$ would be $HWT_{j,h} = HW(f_t(X_{j,h}^{(t)}))$. The process is repeated with all possible h hypothesis of S thus m different $HWT_{j,h}$ hypothetical leakage values are obtained for each input $X_j^{(t)}$, where $h \in \{1, 2, ...m\}$. At the end of the second phase, $\lambda \times m$ different hypothetical leakage values are generated.

The third phase of the CPA attack, Pearson correlation is used as a distinguisher of false hypothesis based on the collected λ traces of d samples each. At the end of the computation, there should be one correlation value $r_{v,j}$ for each $v - th$ sample of each $j - th$ collected trace (where $v \in \{1, 2, ..p\}$ and $j \in \{1, 2, ..\lambda\}$. Pearson Correlation is performed using the following equation:

$$r_{v,j} = \frac{\sum_{w=0}^{\lambda}\left[(HWT_{w,v} - mean(HWT_{:,v})) \cdot (PK_{w,j} - mean(PK_{:,j}))\right]}{\sqrt{\sum_{w=0}^{\lambda}(HWT_{w,v} - mean(HWT_{:,v}))^2 \cdot \sum_{w=0}^{\lambda}(PK_{w,j} - mean(PK_{:,j}))^2}} \tag{1}$$

Thus, the outcome of the distinguisher operation would be a $p \times \lambda$ correlation matrix R. Each $j - th$ column of the R matrix corresponds to an S_j hypothesis. If some correlation value in the $j - th$ column is significantly higher that the other values on the same column then S_j hypothesis is correct (i.e the attacker winds the adversarial game by recovering S). In practice, a divide and conquer technique is applied in the above CPA approach, thus the attacker assumes that S can be partitioned into small components (eg. bytes) and focus his attack on an $f_t()$ operation that processes one S component at a time. Thus, CPA is repeated as many times as the S partitions.

Assuming that Dilithium signature generation acts as $F()$ operation, the various attack points identified in this paper and [16] can act as $f_t()$. Given the constrain that the $f_t()$ inputs be all known to the attacker apart from the secret S, the best match for CPA attack is the polynomial matrix multiplication of $C \cdot S_1$ or $C \cdot S_2$ (in line 9 and 10 of Algorithm 1 respectively) that happen at the last iteration of the rejection sampling loop (i.e where C, R_0 and Z are not rejected or the $C \cdot S_2$ in the $MakeHint$ operation (at line 14 of Algorithm 1). In all the above cases, C has a known value (is part of the digital signature σ) with $HW(C) = 60$ while the unknown secret S_1 or S_2 is a polynomial vector of ℓ or k elements that have small coefficients $(-\eta,)$. Thus, the CPA secret can be partitioned in individual polynomials and furthermore in individual coefficients so that using the divide and conquer technique the attacker can repeatedly retrieve individual coefficient values of S_1 or S_2 by partitioning, collecting traces and analyzing individual operations within $C \cdot S_1$ or $C \cdot S_2$ computation. Note, however, that this process is highly related to the technique used for performing the $C \cdot S_1$ or $C \cdot S_2$ computation. The first technique to be used, officially proposed in the Dilithium scheme specifications [10], is the number theoretic transform (NTT) technique, where all polynomial are transformed in the NTT domain, then their coefficients are multiplied and the result is transformed from the NTT to the normal domain. The second technique is the schoolbook and the sparse polynomial multiplication, on the normal polynomial domain, which, given the small values of the polynomial coefficients, might yield better performance in certain corner cases over area-constrained devices, due to its simplified control logic [12,18,20]. Additionally, since the signature component has to be generated in the normal domain, use of the schoolbook or the sparse polynomial multiplier technique does not need the NTT and inverse NTT computations.

Regarding the second technique, using the schoolbook method on polynomials $C(y)$ and $S_1(y)$ (or $S_2(y)$ respectively) can be performed if the following formula is used:

$$c(y) \cdot s_1(y) = \left[\sum_{i=0}^{n-1}\sum_{j=0}^{n-1} c_i \cdot s_{1,j} x^{i+j}\right] \bmod \langle x^n + 1 \rangle = \sum_{i=0}^{n-1}\sum_{j=0}^{n-1}(-1)^{\lfloor\frac{i+j}{n}\rfloor} c_i \cdot s_{1,j} x^{i+j \bmod n} \tag{2}$$

Observing the above equation from the attacker's perspective reveals that as long as identifying and focusing on the side channel trace samples related to each computation of $c_i \cdot s_{1,j}$ is feasible, a CPA attack can be performed efficiently. Given that each c_i coefficient is a value between $(-1, 1)$ and that each $s_{1,j}$ is a value $(-\eta, \eta)$ the λ number of hypothetical values is small (based on Table 1 $\lambda \leq 15$) and the computations to find a hypothetical f_t result are simple. Thus, it can be concluded that this technique should be avoided in an unprotected Dilithium signature generation software or hardware implementation.

When the NTT technique is adopted in a Dilithium scheme implementation, both C and S_1 (or S_2) are represented in the NTT domain during the $C \cdot S_1$ or $C \cdot S_2$ computations. Assuming that $\hat{C}$ and $\hat{S}_1$ are the NTT versions of C and S_1 then performing $C \cdot S_1$ is as simple as performing $\hat{c}_i \cdot \hat{s}_{1,j}$ between the NTT coefficients of the polynomials and then applying a q modulo reduction on the result. These two operations are done sequentially thus each one of them may have a distinct presence in the power trace signal that can be assigned as $PK_{j,v}$. In fact, based on the conceptualization of CPA, an attacker is interested only on the operation $\hat{c}_i \cdot \hat{s}_{1,j}$ to act as $PK(f_t)$. However, in the NTT representation of all polynomial coefficients belong to Z_q (and not Z_η or Z_2) thus there will be $\lambda = q$ different hypothesis for $\hat{s}_{1,j}$ which may make the computational overhead of CPA considerable (i.e the correlation matrix). There are, however, research works suggest that this is feasible [22].

3   Experimental Process

Dilithium is highly optimized, in terms of performance, compared to other postquantum lattice based cryptography digital signature schemes and can be efficiently executed, apart from x86 machines, in ARM based processors of the cortex M family. In the previous section's analysis, it was shown that CPA is possible on the polynomial multiplications that involve the polynomials of S_1 and S_2, however, it was highlighted that the attack is feasible as long as the leakage samples of such operation can be identified and collected from the overall Dilithium signature generation function. This feat might be easily accomplished in a controlled environment (for embedded systems) like an emulator or a dedicated side channel assessment platform (eg. Chipwhisperer) but can be considerably more difficult in Commercial off-the-shelf (COTS) boards. In this section, a road map on how to collect and profile the appropriate traces for CPAs on COTS embedded system devices is proposed and described in detail. The trace analysis is made for NTT based implementations of Dilithium since they seem harder to attack (based on the previous section's analysis).

Setup: For our profiling experiments, the Post-quantum cryptographic library PQClean [4] was utlized, offering clean standalone implementations of most post-quantum schemes that are included in the NIST post-quantum project [2]. Aiming mostly towards the embedded system domain, the STM32 ST-Nucleo-F401RE [5] board was used as a testbench for the deployment of the Dilithium signature scheme. It features an ARM Cortex-M4 microprocessor that is currently being used by a plethora of embedded devices globally, making it an ideal reference system benchmark.

While the Dilithium signature scheme is being executed through the PQClean library, a probe is connected to the IDD current measurement jumper provided by the Nucleo, capturing the power consumption of the device. This power measurement signal is transferred through a pre-amplifier to a PicoScope 5000D Series Oscilloscope [3], which collects the generated traces with a sampling rate of 1 GS/s. Moreover, two additional probes are active throughout this process and connected to the GPIO pins of the Nucleo board. These probes act as trigger signals (one main, one secondary), assisting the oscilloscope to capture in a timely manner the correct portion of the received data. The secondary trigger is utilized as a marker to quickly identify the different operations of the signature scheme that are being computed at any given moment.

4   Profiling Process and Results

4.1   Methodology

Before commencing the profiling process, the PicoScope 5000D oscillator is configured properly in order to generate an additional math channel plot. This generated trace includes a measurement of the average value collected through multiple single-time signature samples. After sufficient number of these samples has been gathered (usually 100 single execution traces), this averaging process creates a clearer final trace with significantly less amount of noise, where the operations of the underlying computed signature generation scheme can be identified in a much easier manner compared to a single trace.

The signature generation algorithm as described by Algorithm 2 is being executed once every second, using the same randomly generated public-private key pair and the same message to be signed. This small delay allows the oscillator to conveniently capture the signal and add it to the averaging trace. As mentioned earlier, using the PQClean library's default implementation, the executed code can be viewed in Fig. 1, where the primary trigger signal is active throughout the duration of the whole signature generation process.

```
/* Generate Dilithium2 signature */
   main_trigger = 1;

   sign_ret = PQCLEAN_DILITHIUM2_CLEAN_crypto_sign_signature(signature,
       (size_t*)sizeof(signed_message), message, sizeof(message),
       secret_key, secondary_trigger);

   main_trigger = 0;
```

Fig. 1. PQClean Dilithium2 signature generation code snippet.

4.2   Signal Trace Acquisition

The complete Dilithium signature generation trace is presented in Fig. 2, where the blue upper plot represents a single signature generation capture, while the green plot is the averaging trace as described above. The red plot is the primary trigger, marking the beginning and end of the signature generation process. It can be observed by both plots how the algorithm is comprised of sequential rejection sampling loops (Step 3 to 13 of Algorithm 2), as well as the points in time when the $C \cdot S_1$ critical operation using the S_1 vector of the secret key is being computed inside the specific rejection loops.

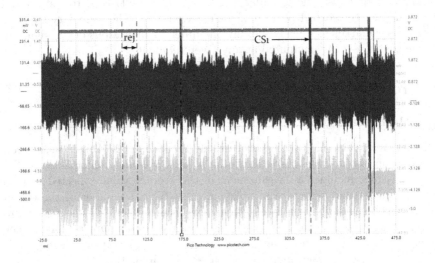

Fig. 2. Dilithium signature trace. (Color figure online)

By using the secondary trigger probe, the beginning and end of each individual process can be monitored. The first major one to be examined is the complete rejection loop as seen in Fig. 3. The various steps of the rejection loop are clearly visible in the averaging trace, starting with the Y *Vector Sampling* (Step 5), continuing with the matrix vector multiplication $W = A \cdot Y$ (Step 6) and the decomposing of the W matrix (Step 8). In the remainder of the rejection loop, one can observe the critical operations $C \cdot S_2$ and $C \cdot S_1$ involving the hidden coefficients S_2 and S_1 of the secret key respectively.

The $C \cdot S_2$ operation as is viewed in Fig. 3 is comprised of 4 distinct areas. This remark denotes the selection as default by the PQClean library of the value $k = 4$ of the Module-LWE which represents the number of rows of any given sample, as it is represented as a matrix of small polynomials A instead of a unique polynomial A. Focusing the secondary trigger towards one of those areas, the resulting trace portion $c_i \cdot s_{2,j}$ is presented in detail in Fig. 4.

Regarding the S_1 part of the secret key, the same logic is applied as in the $C \cdot S_2$ operation, with the main difference made apparent by looking at the trace

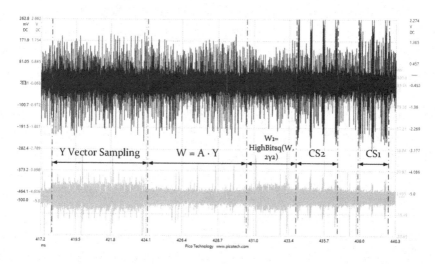

Fig. 3. Rejection loop trace.

associated with the selection of the value $l = 3$ as a parameter that represents the columns of the Module. The operation is, thus, repeated 3 times, each using a different part of the matrices. A sample code snipped mapped from the PQClean operation is presented in Fig. 5, denoting the activation of the secondary trigger during each of the 3 loops. The $c_i \cdot s_{1,j}$ operation leakage is clearly seen in Fig. 6 while being differentiated from the adjacent computational leakages happening prior or after $C \cdot S_1(i)$. It should be noted at this point that the chosen rejection loop used in this analysis, is based on is the last rejection loop executed on the full signature generation algorithm, where all the conditions described in the Steps 11–13 of Algorithm 2 have been successfully met to generate the final signature value. Note also that our triggering involves only the polynomial multiplication in the NTT domain and the corresponding Montgomery reduction for one element of the S_1 vector. Matching the polynomial multiplication happening in the NTT domain coefficient per coefficient with the trace in Fig. 6 reveals that each trace peak corresponds to one coefficient multiplication $\hat{c}_i \cdot \hat{s_{1,j}}$ and can be directly used in the CPA approach described in the previous section

Given the generated traces for all the Steps that the Dilithium signature generation algorithm is consisted of and based on the security aspects of those operations as described in Sect. 2.1, it can be concluded that for medium security parameters shown in Table 1, a possible attacker can identify and extract the critical operations $c_i \cdot s_{1,j}$ and $c_i \cdot s_{2,j}$. This fact constitutes a valid requirement for an impacting realization of a possible CPA attack on the polynomial multiplication of the polynomials S_1 and S_2. It can be noted by observing at Figs. 6 and 4 the distinct waveform pattern produced by $c_i \cdot s_{1,j}$ and $c_i \cdot s_{2,j}$ polynomial operations.

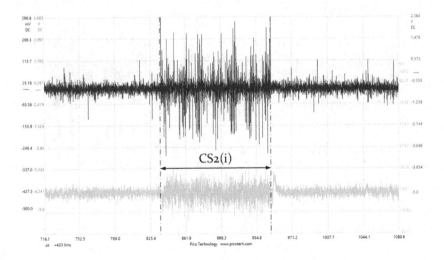

Fig. 4. $c_i \cdot s_{2,j}$ operation trace.

```
/* Compute z, reject if it reveals secret */
    for (size_t i = 0; i < L; ++i) {
        secondary_trigger = 1;
        PQCLEAN_DILITHIUM2_CLEAN_poly_pointwise_invmontgomery(&z.vec[i],
            &chat, &s1.vec[i]);
        secondary_trigger = 0;
        PQCLEAN_DILITHIUM2_CLEAN_poly_invntt_montgomery(&z.vec[i]);
    }
```

Fig. 5. PQClean $C \cdot S_1$ computation code snippet.

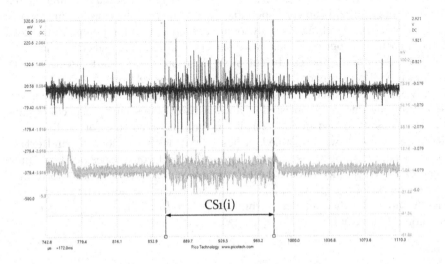

Fig. 6. $c_i \cdot s_{1,j}$ operation trace.

5   Conclusion

In this paper, an analysis on the Dilithium signature generation operation was done in order to identify interesting points for side channel analysis. We focused on the polynomial multiplication operation needed during the sample rejection loop of the algorithm (last loop iteration). In the paper, we also described how to perform CPA side channel attacks on this Dilithium operation regardless of how such operation is implemented. Our goal was to show that CPA is feasible as long as individual polynomial coefficient multiplication is traceable in collected power side channel information. By collecting traces from a COTS embedded system device that executes Dilithium Digital Signature generation on ARM Cortex M4 processor, we were able to demonstrate that indeed the polynomial operation is visible in the traces. Thus, it can be verified that the described attack is possible as long as the attacker has an analyzer/computer that can process the hypothesis values in correlation with the collected samples (as CPA dictates) for high bit length hypothesis data. As future work, we plan to perform the attack on extensive number of power trace datasets collected from the COTS device and evaluate the efficiency of the attack in relation to the number of such traces.

References

1. ChipWhisperer, NewAE Technology Inc. https://www.newae.com/chipwhisperer
2. NIST post-quantum cryptography project. https://csrc.nist.gov/projects/post-quantum-cryptography
3. PicoScope 5000D series oscillator. https://www.picotech.com/oscilloscope/5000/flexible-resolution-oscilloscope
4. PQClean library. https://github.com/PQClean/PQClean
5. STM32 ST-Nucleo-F401RE. https://os.mbed.com/platforms/ST-Nucleo-F401RE/
6. NSA/IAD. CNSA Suite and Quantum Computing FAQ. https://www.iad.gov/iad/library/ia-guidance/ia-solutions-for-classified/algorithm-guidance/cnsa-suite-and-quantum-computing-faq.cfm (2016)
7. Barthe, G., Belaïd, S., Espitau, T., Fouque, P.A., Rossi, M., Tibouchi, M.: GALACTICS: Gaussian sampling for lattice-based constant- time implementation of cryptographic signatures, revisited. In: Proceedings of the 2019 ACM SIGSAC Conference on Computer and Communications Security, CCS 2019, pp. 2147–2164. Association for Computing Machinery, New York, NY, USA (2019). https://doi.org/10.1145/3319535.3363223, https://doi.org/10.1145/3319535.3363223
8. Brier, E., Clavier, C., Olivier, F.: Correlation power analysis with a leakage model. In: Joye, M., Quisquater, J.-J. (eds.) CHES 2004. LNCS, vol. 3156, pp. 16–29. Springer, Heidelberg (2004). https://doi.org/10.1007/978-3-540-28632-5_2
9. Chari, S., Rao, J.R., Rohatgi, P.: Template attacks. In: Kaliski, B.S., Koç, K., Paar, C. (eds.) CHES 2002. LNCS, vol. 2523, pp. 13–28. Springer, Heidelberg (2003). https://doi.org/10.1007/3-540-36400-5_3
10. Ducas, L., et al.: Crystals-Dilithium: a lattice-based digital signature scheme. IACR Trans. Cryptographic Hardware and Embed. Syst. 238–268 (2018)

11. Fournaris, A.P., Koufopavlou, O.: Protecting CRT RSA against fault and power side channel attacks. In: 2012 IEEE Computer Society Annual Symposium on VLSI, pp. 159–164 (2012)

12. Güneysu, T., Lyubashevsky, V., Pöppelmann, T.: Practical lattice-based cryptography: a signature scheme for embedded systems. In: Prouff, E., Schaumont, P. (eds.) CHES 2012. LNCS, vol. 7428, pp. 530–547. Springer, Heidelberg (2012). https://doi.org/10.1007/978-3-642-33027-8_31

13. Kocher, P., Jaffe, J., Jun, B.: Differential power analysis. In: Wiener, M. (ed.) CRYPTO 1999. LNCS, vol. 1666, pp. 388–397. Springer, Heidelberg (1999). https://doi.org/10.1007/3-540-48405-1_25

14. Lyubashevsky, V.: Fiat-shamir with aborts: applications to lattice and factoring-based signatures. In: Matsui, M. (ed.) ASIACRYPT 2009. LNCS, vol. 5912, pp. 598–616. Springer, Heidelberg (2009). https://doi.org/10.1007/978-3-642-10366-7_35

15. Maghrebi, H., Portigliatti, T., Prouff, E.: Breaking cryptographic implementations using deep learning techniques. IACR Cryptology ePrint Archive 2016, 921 (2016). http://eprint.iacr.org/2016/921

16. Migliore, V., Gérard, B., Tibouchi, M., Fouque, P.-A.: Masking Dilithium. In: Deng, R.H., Gauthier-Umaña, V., Ochoa, M., Yung, M. (eds.) ACNS 2019. LNCS, vol. 11464, pp. 344–362. Springer, Cham (2019). https://doi.org/10.1007/978-3-030-21568-2_17

17. Papachristodoulou, L., Fournaris, A.P., Papagiannopoulos, K., Batina, L.: Practical evaluation of protected residue number system scalar multiplication. IACR Trans. Cryptographic Hardware Embed. Syst. 2019(1), 259–282 (2018). https://doi.org/10.13154/tches.v2019.i1.259-282. https://tches.iacr.org/index.php/TCHES/article/view/7341

18. Pöppelmann, T., Güneysu, T.: Towards efficient arithmetic for lattice-based cryptography on reconfigurable hardware. In: Hevia, A., Neven, G. (eds.) LATIN-CRYPT 2012. LNCS, vol. 7533, pp. 139–158. Springer, Heidelberg (2012). https://doi.org/10.1007/978-3-642-33481-8_8

19. Primas, R., Pessl, P., Mangard, S.: Single-trace side-channel attacks on masked lattice-based encryption. In: Fischer, W., Homma, N. (eds.) CHES 2017. LNCS, vol. 10529, pp. 513–533. Springer, Cham (2017). https://doi.org/10.1007/978-3-319-66787-4_25

20. Pöppelmann, T., Güneysu, T.: Area optimization of lightweight lattice-based encryption on reconfigurable hardware. In: 2014 IEEE International Symposium on Circuits and Systems (ISCAS), pp. 2796–2799 (2014)

21. Shor, P.W.: Polynomial-time algorithms for prime factorization and discrete logarithms on a quantum computer. SIAM J. Comput. 26(5), 1484–1509 (1997). https://doi.org/10.1137/S0097539795293172

22. Tunstall, M., Hanley, N., McEvoy, R.P., Whelan, C., Murphy, C.C., Marnane, W.P.: Correlation power analysis of large word sizes. In: IET Irish Signals and Systems Conference (ISSC), pp. 145–150 (2007)

S-NET: A Confusion Based Countermeasure Against Power Attacks for SBOX

Abdullah Aljuffri[1,2(✉)], Pradeep Venkatachalam[1], Cezar Reinbrecht[1], Said Hamdioui[1], and Mottaqiallah Taouil[1]

[1] Delft University of Technology, Delft, The Netherlands
{A.A.M.Aljuffri,P.Venkatachalam,C.R.WedigReinbrecht,
S.Hamdioui,M.Taouil}@tudelft.nl
[2] King Abdulaziz City for Science and Technology, Riyadh, Saudi Arabia
aaljuffri@kacst.edu.sa

Abstract. Side channel attacks are recognized as one of the most powerful attacks due to their ability to extract secret key information by analyzing the unintended leakage generated during operation. This makes them highly attractive for attackers. The current countermeasures focus on either randomizing the leakage by obfuscating the power consumption of all operations or blinding the leakage by maintaining a similar power consumption for all operations. Although these techniques help hiding the power-leakage correlation, they do not remove the correlation completely. This paper proposes a new countermeasure type, referred to as *confusion*, that aims to break the linear correlation between the leakage model and the power consumption and hence confuses attackers. It realizes this by replacing the traditional SBOX implementation with a neural network referred to as S-NET. As a case study, the security of Advanced Encryption Standard (AES) software implementations with both conventional SBOX and S-NET are evaluated. Based on our experimental results, S-NET leaks no information and is resilient against popular attacks such as differential and correlation power analysis.

Keywords: S-NET · Side channel analysis · Neural network · SBOX · Advanced Encryption Standard

1 Introduction

Since it was selected by National Institute of Standards and Technology (NIST) in 2001 as the official standard for block cipher cryptography [1], Advanced Encryption Standard (AES) gain a massive adoption in network communication protocols [2]. Nowadays AES is the most widely used symmetric encryption algorithm [2]. Hence, it is attractive for attackers to comprise keys which may lead to massive data breaches. A recent study made by IBM and Ponemon Institute showed that the average cost of a single data breach is estimated to be

© Springer Nature Switzerland AG 2020
A. Orailoglu et al. (Eds.): SAMOS 2020, LNCS 12471, pp. 295–307, 2020.
https://doi.org/10.1007/978-3-030-60939-9_20

$3.86 million [3], not to mention the additional reputation damage. Theoretically, AES is considered to be resistant against all attacks with the exception of brute force attacks. However, attackers found means to compromise the security of such algorithms based on their implementation [4]. One of the most popular techniques to retrieve the key is by analyzing the physical characteristics such as power consumption known as side channel attack (SCA). SCA poses a serious threat to the security of current encryption algorithms. As a consequence, the implementations of these algorithms have to be reevaluated and secure implementations have to be developed.

The current developed countermeasures can be classified into two groups referred to as *randomization* and *blinding*. Randomization aims at obfuscating the power consumption irrespective of the executed operation, while blinding aims at leveling the power consumption (i.e., keep as constant as possible) during the encryption/decryption. *Randomization* was first proposed in 1999 by Chari et al. [5] shortly after the first power attack was introduced in 1998 [6]. The authors split the operation using a random factor known as masking. However, this masking technique does not protect against second-order power attacks [7]. Higher order masking [8] was thereafter introduced to defend against the attacks; unfortunately, it decreased the performance significantly without guaranteeing protection. Other randomization countermeasure techniques such as dummy delay insertion [9] and shuffling [10] were also proposed. These techniques made attacks harder but could not necessarily prevent them [11,12]. In the second group of countermeasures, i.e. *blinding*, also several countermeasures have been proposed. In [13] the authors proposed dual-rail logic, a technique where all input and output signals of a gate also have complementary values. Hence, the technique balances the number of transitions. Another example of *blinding* consists of duplicating the design where one part operates on the original message while the other on the complementary message [14]. However, both these techniques still leak information due two reasons. First, a difference in load capacitance between the two complementary logic gates may cause an unbalanced power leakage for different input values. Second, different arrival times of signals leaks information as well [15]. Hence, both *randomizing* and *blinding* countermeasures are susceptible to power attacks as both techniques are focusing on covering the problem instead of solving it. To solve the leakage issue, the linear correlation between the power consumption and leakage model must be broken.

This paper proposes a radical new countermeasure type that aims to break the linear correlation between the power consumption and the leakage model. We realize this by substituting the SBOX operation of AES with a neural network which we call S-NET (short for substitution neural network). Due to the chaotic nature of S-NET and removal of the linear power-leakage relation, we classify this countermeasure as *confusion*. The main contributions of this paper can be summarized as follow:

- Proposal of S-NET: a new countermeasure based on *confusion*. It nullifies power attacks by invalidating the existing power-leakage models.

– Implementation of S-NET. This includes designing, training, and testing of an appropriate neural network.
– Validating S-NET security using conformance testing by applying signal-to-noise ratio analysis as a leakage assessment and evaluation style testing by applying key ranking analysis based on the most popular power attacks.

The rest of the paper is organized as follows. Section 2 provides a background on SBOX, side channel attacks, and neural networks. Section 3 explains the confusion countermeasure and the methodology applied to design S-NET. Section 4 validates its security. Section 5 discusses the benefits and limitations of S-NET. Finally, Sect. 6 concludes this paper.

2   Background

This section provides a background on SBOX, the most targeted component in SCA and the different SCA types. Thereafter, it introduces neural networks.

2.1   Substitution Box (SBOX)

An SBOX (or so called SubByte in AES) is an essential nonlinear substitution operation that is used in every block cipher. The purpose of an SBOX is to create confusion, i.e., to obscure the relationship between the private key and the ciphertext [16]. Among all the operations in block ciphers, the SBOX leaks the most information; hence it is typically the target of side channel attackers. The SBOX in AES has an 8-bit input and works as follows [1]:

1. The multiplicative inverse of the 8-bit input is calculated based on the finite Galois Field $GF(2^8)$ and the irreducible polynomial $p(x) = x^8 + x^4 + x^3 + x + 1$.
2. The intermediate result of the previous step is transformed using a predefined affine transformation.

To speed the calculations up, typically a 256-input Look-Up Table (LUT) is used containing pre-calculated values. Note that AES also contains other operations such as AddRoundKey MixColumns, and ShitfRows [1]. However, these are less relevant for side channel attacks and hence not addressed.

2.2   Side Channel Analysis

Side channels are observable characteristics such as time, power consumption, electromagnetic radiation, light, noise, heat, etc. that may leak secret information unintentionally. By analyzing these characteristics, i.e., perform a side channel attack, cryptographic keys can be retrieved [17]. Most of these type of attacks are non-invasive, as the observable characteristics can be observed from outside the chip and hence SCA attacks are relatively cheap. From the SCA attacks, power attacks are the most popular ones and hence the topic of this paper. Power attacks are statistical analysis of the power consumption measurements at an intermediate target (e.g., SBOX operation) that are correlated to a leakage model. Leakage models make assumptions on how the secret information is leaked based on the operations and switching activity. Examples are [18]:

- hamming weight: HW = ones(Intermediate AES function)
- hamming distance: HD = ones(plain-/ciphertext $\oplus$ HW)

The function ones() represent the number of ones in a byte, while Intermediate AES function is the targeted function of the AES ecnryption/decryption process. Examples are:

- AddRoundKey = $plaintext \oplus key$
- SubByte = $SBOX[plaintext \oplus key]$
- LastRound = $SBOX^{-1}[ciphertext \oplus key]$

Power attacks can be classified in non-profiled and profiled attacks. Each class is briefly explained next.

- **Non-profiled power attacks:** in these attacks, an attacker gets access to a target electronic device that runs a cryptographic algorithm. Thereafter, he or she tries to perform a key recovery by correlating a leakage model with obtained power traces during the execution of the cryptographic algorithm. Famous examples of this type of attacks are Differential Power Attack (DPA) [6] and Correlation Power Attack (CPA) [18].
- **Profiled power attacks:** unlike the non-profiled attacks, in these attacks, an attacker holds a device under his control similar to the target device in order to build a leakage template. Thereafter, he or she takes advantage of this template to exploit the leakage of the target device and performs a key recovery. Famous examples of these types of attacks are template based power attacks (TBA) [19] and Deep Learning based Side Channel Attacks (DL-SCA) [20].In this paper we will focus only on non-profiled attacks.

2.3   Neural Network

A neural network (NN) is a simplified mathematical representation of a biological network of neurons, where each biological neuron is represented by an artificial neuron [21]. In its simplest form, an NN consists of a single node; it is also know as a Logistic Regression (LR) model that consists of two steps. First, it calculates $\sum_{i=1}^{n} x_i w_i + bias$; here x_i presents the ith input value and w_i its associated weight. Subsequently, a nonlinear activation function is applied. The output of this model is a probabilistic decision. More complex NNs can be constructed by forming a network of multiple layers of neurons to form the so-called Multilayer Perceptron (MLP). MLP mainly consists of three types of layers. The first layer is called the input layer and serves as the data entry point to the neural network. The second type of layer is called the hidden layer. The hidden layers of the NN are responsible for the extraction of features of the input data. The size of

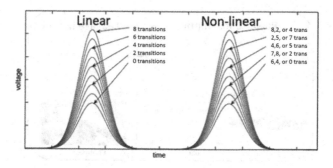

Fig. 1. Linear power-leakage correlation (modified from [23]).

the hidden layers is specified by the width and depth; the width represents the number of neurons in each layer while the depth refers to the number of layers. The final layer is called the output layer and is responsible for making decisions.

NNs can be used to map any finite or continues mathematical function independent of its complexity. According to the Universality Approximation Theorem (UAT) [22], a feed-forward neural network with a single hidden layer with a finite number of neurons and an arbitrary activation function can be used to approximate any continuous function. As the SBOX described in Sect. 2.1 is based on mathematical functions, it can theoretically be implemented using a neural network. In the next section we describe how we achieve this.

3   S-NET: A Countermeasure Based on Confusion

This section explains the *confusion* countermeasure, the idea behind S-NET and finally, the methodology to design it.

3.1   Confusion: Invalidating the Leakage Model

In side channel analysis (SCA), an attacker correlates the power consumption with a leakage model assuming a linear relation between them. In other words, a higher power consumption results in a larger hamming weight/distance as illustrated in the left part of Fig. 1. Hence, the different hamming weights/distances are traceable in the power traces. Note that the countermeasures based on randomization and blinding try to make this harder, but are typically not able to completely hide this linear relation when statistical analysis are performed. The reason for this is that these countermeasures only try to modify the power consumption, as shown in the left part of Fig. 2. On the other hand, it would be much more difficult for attackers to analyze power traces when the relation between the hamming weight/distance is nonlinear with the actual power consumption as the right part of Fig. 1 shows. In such a scenario, based on the message-key combination, different hamming weights/distances might have the same power consumption and message-key combinations with the same hamming weights/distances

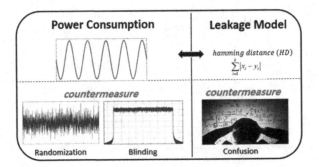

Fig. 2. Visual explanation of the confusion concept.

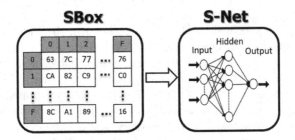

Fig. 3. SBOX representation in S-NET

might have a different power consumption; hence, attacks based on hamming weight/distance are confusing and not effective. The reason for this is that such a countermeasure confuses the leakage in relation to the power consumption. Therefore, this countermeasure targets the leakage model as illustrated in the right part of Fig. 2.

Note that the implementation of S-NET inherits the non-linearity from the stochastic properties of neural networks. Generally any mathematical function that tries to break the linear power-leakage behaviour can be categorized as a countermeasure based on confusion.

3.2   Motivation Behind S-NET

Besides their stochastic properties, neural networks also have other benefits. Neural networks can be considered to a certain degree as black boxes as it is unclear how their internals precisely work. This property makes neural network based implementations difficult to be characterized. Hence, finding a good leakage model against it is extremely hard.

3.3   Design Methodology

Figure 3 shows the concept of S-NET. S-NET implements the SBOX operation using a neural network without affecting the remaining AES operations. The size and weights of the neural network can be achieved by iterating over three steps, namely design, training, and optimization until a satisfying solution is reached. Thereafter, in the final and fourth step, the neural network is integrated with the other parts of AES. Each step is described in detail next.

1. Designing S-NET: This step describes the methodology used to define the sizes of the input, output and hidden layers of S-NET.

The SBOX is typically represented by the look-up-table (LUT) shown in left side of Fig. 3. The LUT contains 256 elements arranged in a table with 16 rows and 16 columns. The row index is specified by the first 4 input bits and the column index by the latter 4 input bits. Since a neural network is not a table, S-NET is designed differently. The input layer of S-NET is fixed to 8 neurons, each representing a single bit of the input, respectively. To improve the resilience against attacks, only a single neuron in the output layer has been used that generates the output byte of the SBOX. The size of the hidden layer, i.e., its width and depth, depends on how easy it is for the neural network to learn the content of the LUT. We have tried different widths and depths to find the optimal solution in term of computation and memory efficiency. We observed that the cheapest solution from a computational and memory point of view consists of using a single hidden layer for two reasons: 1) as the inputs are binary, no multiplications are required in the hidden layer, and 2) by reducing the depth to a single layer, data can be represented using less number of bits. Note that the range of intermediate values increases for a larger depth.

2. Training S-NET: This step describes the training process and how the weights and biases of S-NET are determined. Usually the data set consists of three subsets during the training of a neural network. One subset is used for the training of the network, one for the validation of the network, and one for evaluating the performance after the training is completed. However, in case of S-NET, only a single data set is used for training. The validation and evaluation are not needed as S-NET must be 100% functional, i.e., it must generate correct outputs for all 256 SBOX inputs.

3. Optimizing S-NET: This step describes the optimization techniques used to increase the performance and reduce the overhead of S-NET.

The computational complexity and memory overhead of neural networks make them undesirable solutions for both hardware and software applications. Therefore, to reduce the cost of the proposed solution, multiple optimization techniques are applied before, during, and after the training process. These techniques are highlighted next.

Integer Weights: It is well understood that integer operations have a significant performance benefit in comparison with floating point operations. Therefore, the weights of the neural network are rounded to the nearest integers after the training phase. After this step, all the inputs of the SBOX are reevaluated to guarantee correct operation.

Constrain Weights: The neural network typically produces a wide range of values for the weight set and hence floating point numbers are used by default during training. An implementation of a neural network in hardware and software would be more optimal if the weight set is restricted to a limited number of bits. In S-NET, we fixed the sizes of the weights to 16 bit integers, thereby speeding up the operations and lowering the memory overhead, especially when customized hardware operations are used.

Reduce Multiplications: Multiplications are one of the most expensive operations in the neural network. For this reason, S-NET is designed to have a single hidden layer where no multiplications are needed as the input neurons are represented by a single bit. In the output layer, the number of multiplication is reduced by setting a threshold for the weight. Any weight value below this threshold is skipped. Hence, it results in a lower computational overhead.

Use Simple Activation Functions: Each neuron contains an activation function. The input to this activation is equal to the sum of the product of the inputs and weights of the neuron plus the bias. Many functions have been used as activation function such as tanh, sigmoid, Rectified Linear Unit (ReLU), etc. The computational complexity of these functions varies. In our design we intentionally chose Relu for the hidden layer and no activation function in the final layer to achieve simplicity in both software and hardware implementations.

4. Integrating S-NET in this final step, the designed S-NET component is integrated into the AES implementation by replacing the conventional SBOX.

4   Validation

This section describes the platform and validates the security of S-NET by analyzing the power traces using evaluation and conformance style testing.

4.1   Experiment Setup

To validate the proposed concept of the countermeasure, we compare the security of an unprotected and protected software implementation of AES128, where the protected implementation uses S-NET. The software implementations run on the Chipwhisperer board from NewAE Technology Inc [24]. It is a development board that comes with the Atmel XMEGA microcontroller as target device. We used the unprotected open source AES128 implementation that comes with the board as our reference for the unprotected AES128 implementation. The power consumption is measured with an ADC that is integrated in the development board. Finally, the development board is connected to a computer to control the execution and storage of the power traces.

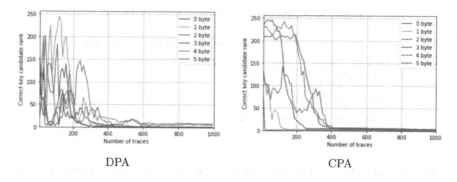

Fig. 4. Ranking analysis results of unprotected SBOX implementation

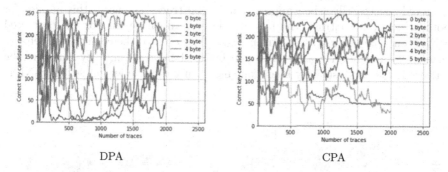

Fig. 5. Ranking analysis results of S-NET implementation

4.2   Results Analysis

To analyze the security of both the unprotected and protected AES implementations, two analysis methods are applied. They are referred to in literature as evaluation-style and conformance-style testing.

First, in evaluation-style testing traces are examined based on real attacks scenarios, preferably by advanced state-of-the-art attacks. They reveal whether the implementations are resilient against these attacks or not. Here, we limit ourselves to the most famous power attacks; they are: differential power analysis (DPA), and correlation power analysis (CPA). Second, in conformance-style testing the traces are checked to meet certain leakage requirements, without considering attacks. Examples of such analysis are TVLA [25] and signal-to-noise ratio (SNR) analysis [26]. Due to space limitations, we only limit ourselves to SNR analysis. The results of both analysis methods are provided next.

Evaluation-style Testing: Two popular attacks (i.e. DPA and CPA) are performed on the recorded traces of the unprotected and protected implementations.The traces are generated based on fixed keys. For each attack, we evaluate the rank of the correct sub-key values (i.e., 8 bits of the 128-bit key). A rank of zero means that the attacker is able to retrieve the correct sub-key, while a rank

Table 1. Number of correctly predicted sub-keys

	Unprotected		Protected (S-NET)	
Leakage Model & Attack	DPA	CPA	DPA	CPA
HW(AddRoundKey)	0	0	0	0
HW/HD(SubByte)	16	16	0	0
HW/HD(LastRound)	16	16	0	0

of 255 represents the lowest confidence of guessing the right sub-key. Figure 4 shows the rank analysis of the first 6 bytes for both attacks for the unprotected implementation. The figure clearly shows, as expected, that the sub-key can be retrieved successfully when approximately 400 traces are used; this applies for both attacks. In contrast, the two attacks were unsuccessful for the protected S-NET implementation as shown in Fig. 5. The rank of the correct key behaves chaotically and never reaches zero and hence the correct sub-key could not be retrieved. The analysis have been done using only a single weight set for S-NET.

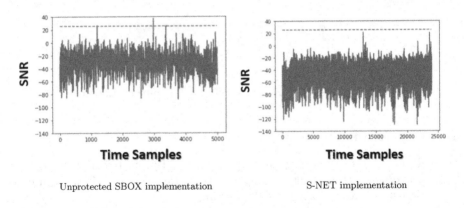

Unprotected SBOX implementation   S-NET implementation

Fig. 6. SNR analysis results

Conformance-style Testing: Figures 6a and 6b show the SNR analysis of the unprotected and protected implementation, respectively. The traces for the analysis are generated based on random keys. The maximum SNR value of both figures differs. For the unprotected case, a high SNR value of 37.6 is observed around sample 3000 which is higher than the considered threshold value (which equals 25 [27]); hence, information leaks. However, for the protected case, the highest observed SNR value is 21.5 around sample 14000, which is below the minimum threshold value. Hence, it is hard to extract the secret key.

The results based on both evaluation-style and conformance-style testing clearly show that S-NET is secure against CPA and DPA power attacks. This can also be seen in Table 1. In the protected case, we were not able to recover any of the sub-key values. However, for the unprotected case, all the 16 sub-keys were successfully retrieved for attacks based on SubByte and LastRound (see Sect. 2.2), for both DPA and CPA using both hamming distance (HD) and hamming weight (HW).

5   Discussion

This work proposes a new countermeasure type against SCA. Based on our experiments, we conclude the following:

Security: S-NET provides a unique solution to the leakage problem which is different from the randomization and blinding techniques, as it tries to break the linear correlation between power consumption and leakage model. It has additional benefits as it makes characterization difficult due to the inherent nature of neural networks.

Performance: The software implementation of S-NET has a large timing overhead. The protected AES runs 75 times slower than the unprotected AES implementation. However, this delay overhead is comparable to other countermeasures such as masking where the timing overhead is larger than 100x [28].

Hardware Implementation: One way to speed-up S-NET is to implement the neural network in hardware. In hardware, S-NET can be implemented in a single or a couple of cycles which increases the performance. However, it might impact the area overhead negatively.

Optimization: To tackle the area and performance issues two possible solutions can be investigated. The first method is based on the usage of emerging memory technologies. Several articles already showed that neural networks implemented with resistive memories have a huge area reduction compared to CMOS implementations [29]. Another way of trying to improve the performance is by looking at other (mathematical) functions that create a nonlinear power-leakage correlation. In case such a function exists, its implementation is most likely cheaper than using a neural network.

Applicability: Due to its widely usage, the SBOX of AES has been used to implement S-NET. However, the S-NET countermeasure technique can be easily applied to other block ciphers such as Data Encryption Standard (DES), Blowfish, Towfish, etc. In addition to that, it can be used to secure lightweight encryption systems such as PRESENT, which lately are gaining increasing attention due to increase in Internet-of-Things (IoT) applications.

Analysis: In this paper we proved that S-NET was able to secure AES against power attacks. However, other side channel attacks such as timing and electromagnetic field have not been investigated. Nevertheless, we believe that they are less powerful than power attacks.

6   Conclusion

This paper introduced a new countermeasure type against side channel power attacks referred to as *confusion*. In contrast to blinding and masking, that try to hide the leakage, confusion countermeasure solves the leakage problem by removing the linear correlation between the power consumption and leakage model. We realized this by deploying a neural network, referred to as S-NET. The experimental results showed that S-NET is immune against DPA and CPA. However, the performance results showed a 75 times higher execution time than the conventional implementation. Overall, S-NET has the potential to replace existing countermeasures due to its high security.

Acknowledgments. This work was labelled by the EUREKA cluster PENTA and funded by Dutch authorities under grant agreement PENTA-2018e-17004-SunRISE.

References

1. NIST: Announcing the advanced encryption standard (AES). Fed. Inf. Process. Stan. Publ. **197** 3 (2001)
2. Leech, D.P., et al.: The economic impacts of the advanced encryption standard, 1996–2017. NIST (2018)
3. IBM: 2019 Cost of a Data Breach Report: IBM Security (2019).https:// databreachcalculator.mybluemix.net/. Accessed 23 Sept 2019
4. Ors, S.B., et al.: Power analysis attack on an ASIC AES implementation. In: ITCC (2004)
5. Chari, S., et al.: Towards sound approaches to counteract power-analysis attacks. In: Wiener, M. (ed.) CRYPTO 1999. LNCS, vol. 1666, pp. 398–412. Springer, Heidelberg (1999). https://doi.org/10.1007/3-540-48405-1_26
6. Kocher, P., et al.: Differential power analysis. In: Wiener, M. (ed.) CRYPTO 1999. LNCS, vol. 1666, pp. 388–397. Springer, Heidelberg (1999). https://doi.org/10. 1007/3-540-48405-1_25
7. Messerges, T.S.: Securing the AES finalists against power analysis attacks. In: Goos, G., Hartmanis, J., van Leeuwen, J., Schneier, B. (eds.) FSE 2000. LNCS, vol. 1978, pp. 150–164. Springer, Heidelberg (2001). https://doi.org/10.1007/3-540-44706-7_11
8. Coron, J.S., et al.: Higher-order side channel security and mask refreshing. In: Moriai, S. (ed.) FSE 2013. LNCS, vol. 8424, pp. 410–424. Springer, Heidelberg (2014). https://doi.org/10.1007/978-3-662-43933-3_21
9. Durvaux, F., et al.: Efficient removal of random delays from embedded software implementations using hidden Markov models. In: Mangard, S. (ed.) CARDIS 2012. LNCS, vol. 7771, pp. 123–140. Springer, Heidelberg (2013). https://doi.org/ 10.1007/978-3-642-37288-9_9
10. Luo, P., et al.: Towards secure cryptographic software implementation against side-channel power analysis attacks. In: ASAP (2015)
11. Durvaux, F., et al.: Cryptanalysis of the CHES 2009/2010 random delay counter-measure. IACR Cryptol. ePrint Arch. **2012**, 38 (2012)
12. Veyrat-Charvillon, N., et al.: Shuffling against Side-channel attacks: a comprehensive study with cautionary note. In: Wang, X., Sako, K. (eds.) ASIACRYPT 2012. LNCS, vol. 7658, pp. 740–757. Springer, Heidelberg (2012). https://doi.org/10. 1007/978-3-642-34961-4_44

13. Tiri, K., et al.: A dynamic and differential CMOS logic with signal independent power consumption to withstand differential power analysis on smart cards. In: 28th European Solid-State Circuits Conference (2002)

14. Ambrose, J.A., et al.: MUTE-AES: a multiprocessor architecture to prevent power analysis based side channel attack of the AES algorithm. In: ICCD (2008)

15. Fang, X., et al.: Leakage evaluation on power balance countermeasure against side-channel attack on FPGAs. In: IEEE HPEC (2015)

16. Shannon, C.E.: Communication theory of secrecy systems. The Bell Syst. Tech. J. **25**(4), 656–715 (1949)

17. Zhou, Y., Feng, D.: Side-channel attacks: ten years after its publication and the impacts on cryptographic module security testing. http://eprint.iacr.org/2005/388. Accessed 23 Sept 2019

18. Brier, E., et al.: Correlation power analysis with a leakage model. In: Joye, M., Quisquater, J.-J. (eds.) CHES 2004. LNCS, vol. 3156, pp. 16–29. Springer, Heidelberg (2004). https://doi.org/10.1007/978-3-540-28632-5_2

19. Chari, S., et al.: Template attacks. In: Kaliski, B.S., Koç, K., Paar, C. (eds.) CHES 2002. LNCS, vol. 2523, pp. 13–28. Springer, Heidelberg (2003). https://doi.org/10.1007/3-540-36400-5_3

20. Maghrebi, H., et al.: Breaking cryptographic implementations using deep learning techniques. In: IACR Cryptology ePrint Archive (2016)

21. Hassoun, M.H.: Fundamentals of Artificial Neural Networks. MIT Press, Cambridge (1995)

22. Csáji, B.C.: Approximation with artificial neural networks. Master's thesis, Eötvös Loránd University, Hungary (2001)

23. Standaert, F.-X.: Introduction to Side-Channel Attacks. Springer, Boston (2010). https://doi.org/10.1007/978-0-387-71829-3_2

24. N. T. Inc: Chipwhisperer-Lite two part board. http://store.newae.com/chipwhisperer-lite-cw1173-two-part-version/. Accessed 31 Jan 2020

25. Becker, G., et al.: Test vector leakage assessment (TVLA) methodology in practice (2011). https://pdfs.semanticscholar.org/. Accessed 23 Sept 2019

26. Mangard, S.: Hardware countermeasures against DPA – a statistical analysis of their effectiveness. In: Okamoto, T. (ed.) CT-RSA 2004. LNCS, vol. 2964, pp. 222–235. Springer, Heidelberg (2004). https://doi.org/10.1007/978-3-540-24660-2_18

27. N. technology inc: Measuring SNR of Target. https://chipwhisperer.readthedocs.io/en/latest/tutorials/pa_intro_3-openadc-cwlitearm.html/. Accessed 13 May 2020

28. Rivain, M., Prouff, E.: Provably secure higher-order masking of AES. In: Mangard, S., Standaert, F.-X. (eds.) CHES 2010. LNCS, vol. 6225, pp. 413–427. Springer, Heidelberg (2010). https://doi.org/10.1007/978-3-642-15031-9_28

29. Sun, J.: CMOS and memristor technologies for neuromorphic computing applications. Technical report, University of California at Berkeley (2015)

Risk and Architecture Factors in Digital Exposure Notification

Archanaa S. Krishnan[1(✉)], Yaling Yang[1], and Patrick Schaumont[2]

[1] Virginia Tech, Blacksburg, VA 24060, USA
{archanaa,yyang8}@vt.edu
[2] Worcester Polytechnic Institute, Worcester, MA 01609, USA
pschaumont@wpi.edu

Abstract. To effectively trace the infection spread in a pandemic, a large number of manual contact tracers are required to reach out to all possible contacts of infected users. Exposure notification, a.k.a. digital contact tracing, can supplement manual contact tracing to ease the burden on manual tracers and to digitally obtain accurate contact information. We study how risk emerges in security, privacy, architecture, and technology aspects of exposure notification systems. We provide potential overhead in using Bluetooth-based systems and discuss the architectural support required for other types of systems, and we wrap up with a discussion on architecture aspects to support these solutions.

Keywords: Exposure notification · Contact tracing · Privacy preserving · Privacy friendly architectures

1 Introduction

In recent months, the SARS-CoV-2 virus has infected four million people claiming over 250,000 lives. At the onset of the SARS-CoV-2 virus infection, the governments around the world placed entire states under lockdown to prevent the spread of the infection. Although this strategy was effective in curtailing the spread of the infection, it has adversely affected other aspects of life, increased the unemployment rate, stressed the medical infrastructure, affected the global supply chain, created both food shortage, and brought about food waste. To ease the lockdown and to support long-term infection management, governments are next considering and implementing a test-trace-isolate strategy. The aim of this strategy is, first, to reduce the infection rate and, second, to limit the confinement to exposed individuals and communities instead of countrywide lockdown. The effectiveness of this strategy depends on widespread testing and contact tracing.

The main goal of contact tracing is to interrupt ongoing transmission, reduce the spread of infection, and study the epidemiology of the infection in a particular population. Contact tracing has been effectively used against tuberculosis, sexually transmitted diseases, vaccine preventable diseases, bacterial and

© Springer Nature Switzerland AG 2020
A. Orailoglu et al. (Eds.): SAMOS 2020, LNCS 12471, pp. 308–319, 2020.
https://doi.org/10.1007/978-3-030-60939-9_21

viral infections. The World Health Organization has used contact tracing to prevent transmission of infection. It is performed by public health workers in three steps [33]. First, the public health workers, a.k.a contact tracers, work with infected individuals to identify contacts by revisiting their movements before the onset of illness. Second, all potential contacts of the infected individual are informed of their contact and advised about early care. Third, contact tracers periodically follow-up with the contacts for signs of symptoms and test for the illness.

In this paper, we focus on digital contact tracing and its security and privacy. We refer to digital contact tracing as *exposure notification* [36]. We present the components required to build a secure and privacy friendly exposure notification system through the following contributions:

- We study the state-of-the-art proposals in privacy preserving solutions and differentiate their architectural and privacy design.
- We analyze the risks involved in exposure notification. In particular, we analyze the security and privacy risks involved in collecting location data.
- We consolidate open research challenges in security and privacy friendly architectures for the exposure notification system. We present a roadmap to achieve secure and private architectures that may serve useful beyond the COVID-19 pandemic.

Organization: The rest of the paper is organized as follows. Section 2 presents the state-of-the-art exposure notification proposals and their security and privacy design. Section 3 provides a classification of risks involved in exposure notification based on several factors. Section 4 studies the role of architecture in designing, selecting, and implementing these proposals. Section 5 summarizes a few open research questions and presents an agenda to achieve secure and privacy friendly architectures.

2   Summary of Proposals

2.1   Preliminaries

We generalize exposure notification systems as follows. The main parties involved in exposure notification systems are the app users, health authorities, and back-end servers. The system is implemented as a mobile app and it operates in three phases [13] - collecting user location data, reporting infected user location data to the server, and computing exposure risk. Exposure risk is used to identify if any user was in contact with one or more infected users. We refer to app users who have tested positive for infection as infected users and the remaining as uninfected users. We refer to all types of contact information with its timestamp of collection as location data in the rest of the paper unless explicitly differentiated.

Architectural Differences in Exposure Notification: The proposed exposure notification systems can be broadly differentiated based on the architecture used to collect contact information. The architecture includes Bluetooth, geolocation, QR code, WiFi access point, or a combination of these techniques. The difference in architecture can be mostly observed in phase one of the system operation. For example, Bluetooth-based systems collect the Bluetooth pseudo IDs scanned from encountered phones whereas QR code-based systems collect the codes scanned from the visited public facilities. In all types of notification systems, the timestamp is used to mark the start of the required retention period for contact data. In notification systems other than Bluetooth-based ones, the timestamp is also a required parameter to properly define the location coordinates of users in space and time. Bluetooth ping-based systems are directly between users, and hence do not require space/time location coordinates.

Security Models Used in Exposure Notification: A majority of the existing proposals use a semi-trusted, also called honest-but-curious, server. Such a server is assumed to not add or remove information shared by infected users, but the server will not protect the privacy of all users [9]. The privacy of users in such models is independent of the trust placed in the server as the server only stores anonymized user data. In exposure notification systems, a central authority, such as the health authority, maintains the server. Based on the trust in the central authority, the proposals are broadly classified as centralized and decentralized models, with a notable difference in phase three of the system operation. In a *decentralized model*, the exposure risk is computed locally, by the user's mobile app, without revealing uninfected user's location data to the server. In a *centralized model*, the exposure risk is computed by the server and it notifies each user who queries.

2.2 Existing Deployments

There are several apps deployed by governments and academia/private sector. All the government apps are based on the centralized model, where the server is trusted to an extent to maintain user privacy and to compute the exposure risk [16,25,28,29,34,35]. Only a few of the governments have published their reference implementation [25,28,34], where Singapore's effort is notable for its transparency in reference implementation, underlying protocol [18], and privacy design. Even though the exposure notification initiatives were conceived to protect the citizens, it creates an avenue for exploiting their privacy when there is a lack of transparency in design, implementation, and evaluation. Recently, Arogya Setu, the app from the Indian government, was hacked to reveal the infection rate at any location with a precision of a meter [32]. The apps deployed by academia and private sector [6–9,12,15] are based on the decentralized model and are well documented with reference implementation, white papers, and open discussion on improving their privacy. A majority of them are based on the protocols discussed below.

2.3   Exposure Notification Protocols

Decentralized Privacy-Preserving Proximity Tracing (DP-3T) [9], Privacy-Sensitive Protocols And Mechanisms for Mobile Contact Tracing (PACT) [23], Private Automated Contact Tracing - the PACT protocol [11], the TCN(temporary contact number) protocol, and the Apple—Google collaboration framework [24] are proposals for secure and decentralized Bluetooth based tracing that minimize security and privacy risks in digital exposure notification. ROBust and privacy-presERving proximity Tracing protocol (ROBERT) [13] is a centralized protocol with similar design and federated servers. These designs guarantee user privacy by generating ephemeral random pseudo IDs using AES and SHA-2 based algorithms. Bluetooth based protocols only relying on anonymous pseudo IDs, are susceptible to various risks discussed in Sect. 3.

Epione [44] and TraceSecure [20] propose techniques beyond using ephemeral pseudo IDs to protect user privacy in Bluetooth-based systems. The former uses private information retrieval (PIR) with homomorphic or symmetric encryption, whereas the latter uses a set-based protocol with public key encryption and additive homomorphic encryption.

The privacy of GPS based proposals, such as PrivateKit [10], Safe-Trace [14]and [21,43], differ from Bluetooth-based proposals because geolocation data itself is not anonymized. Instead, they rely on private set intersection (PSI), PIR, homomorphic encryption, and multi-party computation(MPC) protocols to achieve user privacy, similar to the approach of TraceSecure [20] and Epione [44].

3   Risks in Exposure Notification

Figure 1 illustrates the potential attacks that exploit the risks presented in this section. Replay, trolling, linkage, coercion, eavesdropping, collusion, deanonymization, battery drain, and tracing attacks are discussed by Gvili [27] and Vaudenay [45]. Denial of Service(DoS), BleedingBit [41], and BlueBorne [40] attacks are particular to Bluetooth technology.

3.1   Security Risks

Integrity Based Risks: An uninfected user may add bogus location data to their location data to check if a particular location or user is infected. A malicious infected user may add bogus location data to their location data before they share it with the exposure database. A malicious server may modify the exposure database. The server may add bogus location to induce false positives or the server may delete certain locations to induce false negatives. The former could be used to create panic in a certain location and the latter may be exploited by certain services such as cafes and restaurants to delete their location data from the database to maintain a steady influx of customers. Integrity based risks may be exploited for trolling attacks, replay attacks, and to stigmatize infected users.

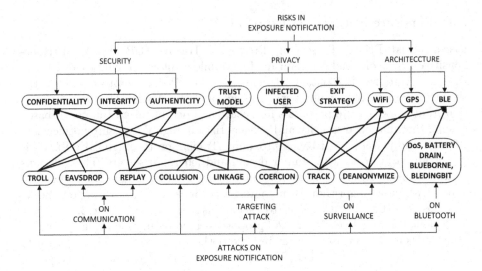

Fig. 1. A flow chart of risks in and attacks [27,40,41,45] on exposure notification systems

Authenticity Based Risks: The authenticity of the exposure database and exposure risk notification is at risk. Unverified uploading of location data to the exposure database can be exploited to upload bogus location data to the server. An attacker may impersonate the server and provide false positive and false negative exposure notification to users. The same attacker may also send malicious exposure database entries to the user and influence the user to compute a false positive/negative exposure notification. These risks may be exploited for trolling attacks.

Confidentiality Based Risks: An attacker can passively observe the communication between the app and the server. The attacker can obtain the location data when it is shared with the server. The attacker may also have access to the victim's terminal device, from which the stored location data may be extracted. All unencrypted data is vulnerable to the attacker. This data can be used for replay attacks, linkage attacks, and coercion threats.

3.2 Privacy Risks

Server Trust Model Risks: All the exposure notification proposals use a server in a centralized or decentralized trust model to store anonymous location data. In both centralized and decentralized models, a malicious server may introduce bogus location data to aid in trolling attacks, as described in authenticity based risks [37]. It may also store the metadata, such as source IP address, related to users, and break user anonymity. This can be further exploited by the server to build social graphs of the users without their consent. A social graph represents the relationship between app users which leaks user privacy. A server in the centralized model compares infected user location data and uninfected user location data to compute exposure risk. An untrusted centralized server has access to all user location data, which can be exploited by the central authority to sell location data for profit. The server trust model is inherently derived from the assumed attacker model. The attacker (app user or a third party) may collude with the server to perform collusion attacks to deanonymize location data using metadata, to obtain the social graph of all users, and obtain location data of all users. Collusion attacks may also be used to exploit the inherent risks of MPC protocols based exposure notification systems [43].

Infected User Privacy Risks: In decentralized exposure notification proposals, the infected user's location data is broadcasted to the public. The attacker can associate location data of each user with an identifier when there is a match in location data between the attacker's app and public database, the attacker is able to identify the infected user using their identifier. This may be exploited to target a particular victim, where the attacker only interacts with the victim and has location data only from the victim. When this location data is compared with the public database the attacker is able to identify if the victim is infected or not [27,45]. This risk could be exploited to deanonymize the infected user using linkage attacks and perform one-entry attacks [13]. A potential solution is not to publish the location data of infected users, but to have a federated server perform the exposure risk calculation using both user and infected user location data. This type of solution has its own risks mentioned above.

Sunset Provision Risks: The purpose of exposure notification systems is to limit the spread of an infection. Without preset deadlines to stop contact tracing, these systems may be exploited to track users beyond the scope of infection control.

3.3 Architecture and Technology Risks

Bluetooth Based Risks: A majority of proximity tracing proposals [9,11,13, 23,25] are based on Bluetooth technology. Bluetooth can be exploited to attack the exposure notification system by extending Bluetooth discoverability using a directional antenna. The attacker can create false positive contact data and to potentially perform trolling attacks. Using Bluetooth, an attacker can attack the general operation of a user's mobile phone as the Bluetooth is always on for the operation of exposure notification systems. Bluetooth is vulnerable to Denial of Service (DoS) attacks where the attacker can flood a victim's Bluetooth with a large volume of messages. The device consumes power in analyzing these messages, storing valid messages in memory which overloads the memory, and discarding invalid messages. This may drain the battery on the mobile phone, keep the phone occupied and lead to slow or no response to its regular operation. Bluetooth-based exposure notification system may be used to exploit Bluetooth vulnerabilities such as BleedingBit [41] and BlueBorne [41] which affects regular mobile phone operation. It is also vulnerable to passive tracking and identity exposure [19].

WiFi Access Point Based Risks: WiFi Access Point based proximity tracing systems [17] keep track of the network identifiers of WiFi Access Points. If the attacker has access to these network identifiers and their collection timestamp, they can identify the exact location of the user which leaks user privacy [42].

Geolocation Based Risks: When exposure notification proposals use geolocation based location data, they have access to the absolute user location data. The geolocation data is a commodity to be sold which can be used to construct social grahphs. This maybe exploited as a monitoring tool by nation state and corporations.

4   Role of Architecture

Tracing geolocation data, such as GPS, is considered to be intrusive and in wrong hands, it may be used to track the user. The attacker can use geolocation data to discern a victim's home address, workspace, their daily activities, and social interactions. Short-wavelength technology based proximity tracing was thought to be an alternative to GPS based contact tracing. The ubiquitousness of mobile phones with Bluetooth technology was an off-the-shelf solution adopted by a majority of exposure notification systems. In this section, we analyze the role architecture and technology plays in the design and choice of exposure notification proposals. We provide back-of-the-envelope calculations for the cost of using Bluetooth in exposure notification. We present the architectural requirements for using geolocation based location data for privacy friendly designs.

4.1   Bluetooth, Privacy, and Overhead

The privacy of the user is guaranteed in Bluetooth-based proposals by using ephemeral and random pseudo IDs, typically generated using SHA-2 [9], AES [24] or a pseudo random function [11]. Although modern mobile phone technology is equipped with hardware acceleration for AES and SHA-1, it is optimized for computation on large data. Since the IDs are typically 16B they can be generated with minimal overhead in software. Bluetooth Low Energy (BLE) is the recommended Bluetooth technology to be used in implementing these proposals. BLE is known for consuming low energy when compared to Bluetooth Classic by essentially operating in sleep mode. Table 1 lists the potential overhead of deploying the Google—Apple framework [24] in iPhone 5S. We differentiate the overhead based on two Bluetooth operation - broadcasting and scanning. We compute the broadcasting overhead with a 0.25 s broadcast interval, the recommended broadcast interval is between 0.2–0.27 s [24]. The scanning overhead is computed at an assumed scan interval of 1 s. For simplicity, we only consider the storage overhead of the BLE IDs without the timestamp and other metadata.

The overhead is listed in terms of the size of memory required based on a 14-day retention period and the percentage of battery drain per hour for each Bluetooth operation. The broadcasted ID storage includes the Temporary Exposure Keys (TEK) used to compute the Rolling Proximity Identifiers(RPID) in the past 14-days. Since TEKs are computed daily, the net broadcast ID storage overhead is computed as a product of TEK size in bytes (16B) and the number of days in retention period (14 days) which comes to 224B. The scanned ID storage is computed as a product of the scanned ID size (16B), number of contacts per day (assumed to be 1000), and number of days in retention period (14 days), which equals 224,000B.

The percentage battery drain is computed using technical reports from Aislelabs [1]. iPhone 5 S is equipped with a 1560 mAh battery [2]. When BLE broadcasts its RPIDs at 0.25s broadcasts interval, it uses 0.013% battery per hour [5]. The same iPhone uses 3.75% battery per hour to scan for incoming RPIDs in 1s scan interval [4]. During each scan operation, the phone may detect multiple beacons and process them which could be attributed to a higher battery drain during scanning. The percentage battery drain for Bluetooth operations can be reduced by increasing the broadcast and scan intervals [3], but this may adversely affect the protocol operation.

We highlight that Bluetooth communication is not free even in BLE. Apart from the proximity communication and storage overhead, there are overheads in communicating with the server, computing new IDs, and computing exposure risk.

Table 1. An example of overhead incurred by the Google—Apple framework in iPhone 5S. ID storage size includes the keys used to derive the broadcasted IDs and the scanned IDs in 14-days. The percentage battery drain was computed using Aislelabs technical reports [4,5]. *We assume 1000 contacts/day and a 1 s scan interval

14-day retention	Broadcast Overhead @ 0.25s interval	Scan Overhead @ *1s interval	Units
ID storage size	224	*224,000	B
Battery drain	0.013	3.75	%/hr

4.2   Hardware Acceleration for Privacy Protection

Apart from relying on AES and SHA-256 for security, some proposals use MPC protocols, PSI, and PIR to protect user privacy [37,43]. They use garbled circuits [44] and homomorphic encryption [20] as their underlying cryptographic primitives in their protocol design. There are several advantages to these protocol designs. First, it protects infected users from deanonymization. Since these proposals do not reveal any information about infected users, an attacker cannot infer infected users from their contacts. Second, homomorphic encryption based solutions are effective in using geolocation data without compromising user privacy. Third, homomorphic encryption solutions may be post-quantum secure, which is an added benefit in designing futuristic applications.

A major drawback in implementing such proposals is the computational overhead involved both at the app and the server side. For example, homomorphic computations generate large ciphertext with a message expansion factor of more than two [39]. The encryption, decryption, and evaluation using homomorphic encryption algorithms are also time consuming. Modern mobile phones are only equipped with cryptographic hardware acceleration for AES and SHA-1 or they are equipped for software acceleration for the same using custom instructions. Hardware acceleration for garbled circuit [30] and homomorphic encryption [38] exists only in academic literature. HEAX [38] is a novel architecture for homomorphic computation on encrypted data. It contains hardware modules for high throughput Number Theoretic Transform(NTT), homomorphic multiplication, and key switching. Prior work on hardware implementation for homomorphic encryption mostly designed accelerators for large number [47], polynomial [31] or integer [22] multiplication.

While the ubiquitousness of Bluetooth technology in mobile phones has lead to its widespread adaptations in privacy preserving proposals, the dearth of garbled circuit and homomorphic hardware may be attributed to the reason behind their limited use in the same field.

4.3 Secure Location Data Storage

A few security risks from Sect. 3 can be exploited by the attacker when they have access to read and to write local location data storage. The attacker may add bogus locations to the exposure database to perform trolling attacks. They can add targeted location data to check the infection data of a particular location or user. They can coerce a victim to reveal their location data [45]. These risks and attacks can be avoided if the location data is stored securely, without access to the attacker or even the app user. If the local data storage is encrypted and authenticated, the security risks can be avoided. Vaudenay [45] suggests using Trusted Platform Module(TPM) to prevent coercion threats and trolling attacks, which is also suggested in the DP-3T proposal [9]. Trusted Computing Group (TCG) has platform-specification for implementing TPM in mobile platforms for secure storage and execution [26]. If mobile phones are equipped with secure storage, a trusted exposure notification app may use this secure storage to store local location data.

5   Towards Secure and Privacy Friendly Architectures

The state-of-the-art proposals summarized in Sect. 2 are by no means a comprehensive list. And not all the 'privacy-protecting' proposals actually protect all user privacy [46]. We list a few challenges that persists in many proposals.

First, the security of location data is completely ignored or mentioned in passing as the proposals mainly focus on user privacy. Second, the user privacy is not protected irrespective of infection status and is mostly not protected from malicious central authority. Third, multi-hop transmission of the SARS-CoV-2 virus is failed to be traced by Bluetooth-based systems as these systems only account for human-to-human transmission. And finally, there is lack of details on implementing and maintaining honest-but-curious servers in both centralized and decentralized models.

The existence of these challenges may be attributed to the lack of architectural support to achieve security and privacy in mobile phones. The presence of secure storage and its access to trustworthy apps can help solve the first challenge. The second and challenges are addressed in a few proposals [20,37,43,44], but their practicality may be hindered by the overhead incurred by their privacy protection solution. These solutions use garbled circuits and homomorphic encryption in MPC, PSI and PIR based protocols to both protect infected user privacy and protect geolocation data. They may be viable in the presence of hardware acceleration for their cryptographic primitives. The availability of homomorphic hardware acceleration will not only be useful for exposure notification, as homomorphic encryption and computation is considered post-quantum secure. In the age of mobile phones with multiple lens and advanced software for night vision photography, why are they not equipped with acceleration to support secure and privacy friendly applications?

Acknowledgements. This work was supported in part by NSF grant 1704176 and NSF grant 2028190.

References

1. Aislelabs. https://www.aislelabs.com/
2. Apple iPhone 5S: technical specification. https://www.gsmarena.com/
3. iBeacon and Battery Drain on Phones: a technical report (2014). https://www.aislelabs.com/reports/ibeacon-battery-phones/
4. iBeacon Battery Drain on Apple vs Android: a technical report (2014). https://www.aislelabs.com/reports/ibeacon-battery-drain-iphones/
5. The Hitchhikers Guide to iBeacon Hardware: a comprehensive report by Aislelabs (2015). https://www.aislelabs.com/reports/beacon-guide/
6. CoEpi: Community epidemiology in action (2020). https://github.com/Co-Epi/
7. Covid Watch: slowing the spread of infectious diseases using crowdsourced data (2020). https://github.com/covid19risk
8. CovidSafe (2020). https://github.com/CovidSafe
9. Decentralized privacy-preserving proximity tracing (2020). https://github.com/DP-3T/documents
10. MIT PrivateKit (2020). https://privatekit.mit.edu/
11. PACT: private automated contact tracing (2020). https://pact.mit.edu/
12. PrivateKit: SafePaths (2020). https://privatekit.mit.edu/
13. ROBust and privacy-presERving proximity tracing protocol (2020). https://github.com/ROBERT-proximity-tracing/documents

14. Safetrace API: Privacy-first contact tracing (2020). https://safetraceapi.org/
15. WeTrace, a privacy focused mobile COVID-19 tracing App (2020). https://github.com/WeTrace-ch/WeTrace
16. Alderson, E.: Aarogya Setu: The story of a failure (2020). https://medium.com/@fs0c131y/aarogya-setu-the-story-of-a-failure-3a190a18e34
17. Altuwaiyan, T., Hadian, M., Liang, X.: EPIC: efficient privacy-preserving contact tracing for infection detection. In: 2018 IEEE International Conference on Communications, pp. 1–6. IEEE (2018). https://doi.org/10.1109/ICC.2018.8422886
18. Bay, J., et al.: BlueTrace: a privacy-preserving protocol for community-driven contact tracing across borders (2020). https://bluetrace.io/
19. Becker, J.K., Li, D., Starobinski, D.: Tracking anonymized bluetooth devices. PoPETs **2019**(3), 50–65 (2019). https://doi.org/10.2478/popets-2019-0036
20. Bell, J., Butler, D., Hicks, C., Crowcroft, J.: TraceSecure: towards privacy preserving contact tracing. CoRR abs/2004.04059 (2020). https://arxiv.org/abs/2004.04059
21. Berke, A., Bakker, M., Vepakomma, P., Larson, K., Pentland, A.S.: Assessing disease exposure risk with location data: a proposal for cryptographic preservation of privacy (2020)
22. Cao, X., Moore, C., O'Neill, M., Hanley, N., O'Sullivan, E.: High-speed fully homomorphic encryption over the integers. In: Böhme, R., Brenner, M., Moore, T., Smith, M. (eds.) FC 2014. LNCS, vol. 8438, pp. 169–180. Springer, Heidelberg (2014). https://doi.org/10.1007/978-3-662-44774-1_14
23. Chan, J., et al.: PACT: privacy sensitive protocols and mechanisms for mobile contact tracing. CoRR abs/2004.03544 (2020). https://arxiv.org/abs/2004.03544
24. Google, Apple: privacy-preserving contact tracing (2020). https://www.apple.com/covid19/contacttracing/
25. Government, S.: TraceTogether (2020). https://www.tracetogether.gov.sg/
26. Group, T.C.: TPM2.0 mobile reference architecture, December 2014. https://trustedcomputinggroup.org/resource/tpm-2-0-mobile-reference-architecture-specification/
27. Gvili, Y.: Security analysis of the COVID-19 contact tracing specifications by Apple Inc. and Google Inc., Cryptology ePrint Archive, Report 2020/428 (2020). https://eprint.iacr.org/2020/428
28. Israel Ministry of Health, I.M.: Hamagen: COVID-19 exposure prevention app (2020). https://github.com/MohGovIL/hamagen-react-native
29. North Macedonia Ministry of Health, N.M.M.: StopKorona! (2020)
30. Järvinen, K., Kolesnikov, V., Sadeghi, A.-R., Schneider, T.: Garbled circuits for leakage-resilience: hardware implementation and evaluation of one-time programs. In: Mangard, S., Standaert, F.-X. (eds.) CHES 2010. LNCS, vol. 6225, pp. 383–397. Springer, Heidelberg (2010). https://doi.org/10.1007/978-3-642-15031-9_26
31. Jayet-Griffon, C., Cornelie, M., Maistri, P., Elbaz-Vincent, P., Leveugle, R.: Polynomial multipliers for fully homomorphic encryption on FPGA. In: International Conference on ReConFigurable Computing and FPGAs, ReConFig, pp. 1–6. IEEE (2015). https://doi.org/10.1109/ReConFig.2015.7393335
32. National Informatics Centre, I.: Arogya Setu (2020). https://www.mygov.in/aarogya-setu-app/
33. Organization, W.H.: What is contact tracing and why is it important? (May 2017)
34. Ministry of Digital Affairs of Polland, M.: ProteGo Safe (2020)
35. Norwegian Institute of Public Health, N.I.: Smittestopp app (2020)

36. Reed, H.: Digital contact tracing and alerting vs exposure alerting (22 Apr 2020). https://harper.blog/2020/04/22/digital-contact-tracing-and-alerting-vs-exposure-alerting/

37. Reichert, L., Brack, S., Scheuermann, B.: Privacy-preserving contact tracing of COVID-19 patients. Cryptology ePrint Archive, Report 2020/375 (2020). https://eprint.iacr.org/2020/375

38. Riazi, M.S., Laine, K., Pelton, B., Dai, W.: HEAX: an architecture for computing on encrypted data. In: ASPLOS 2020: Architectural Support for Programming Languages and Operating Systems, pp. 1295–1309. ACM (2020). https://doi.org/10.1145/3373376.3378523

39. Saputro, N., Akkaya, K.: Performance evaluation of smart grid data aggregation via homomorphic encryption. In: 2012 IEEE Wireless Communications and Networking Conference, pp. 2945–2950. https://doi.org/10.1109/WCNC.2012.6214307

40. Seri, B., Vishnepolsky, G.: BlueBorne (2017)

41. Seri, B., Vishnepolsky, G., Zusman, D.: BleedingBit: the hidden attack surface against BLE chips (2019). https://info.armis.com/rs/645-PDC-047/images/Armis-BLEEDINGBIT-Technical-White-Paper-WP.pdf

42. Tang, Q.: Privacy-preserving contact tracing: current solutions and open questions. Cryptology ePrint Archive, Report 2020/426 (2020). https://eprint.iacr.org/2020/426

43. Tjell, K., Gundersen, J.S., Wisniewski, R.: Privacy preservation in epidemic data collection. CoRR abs/2004.14759 (2020). https://arxiv.org/abs/2004.14759

44. Trieu, N., Shehata, K., Saxena, P., Shokri, R., Song, D.: Epione: lightweight contact tracing with strong privacy. CoRR abs/2004.13293 (2020). https://arxiv.org/abs/2004.13293

45. Vaudenay, S.: Analysis of DP3T. Cryptology ePrint Archive, Report 2020/399 (2020). https://eprint.iacr.org/2020/399

46. Vaudenay, S.: Centralized or decentralized? the contact tracing dilemma. Cryptology ePrint Archive, Report 2020/531 (2020). https://eprint.iacr.org/2020/531

47. Wang, W., Huang, X.: FPGA implementation of a large-number multiplier for fully homomorphic encryption. In: 2013 IEEE International Symposium on Circuits and Systems, pp. 2589–2592. https://doi.org/10.1109/ISCAS.2013.6572408

SPECIAL SESSION: European Projects on Embedded and High Performance Computing for Health Applications

European Projects on Embedded and High Performance Computing for Health Applications

The rise of IoT systems, coupled with the availability of large scale computational resources accessible to a wider range of industrial and research actors is leading to the emergence of new application scenarios such as biomedical machine learning and in silico drug design, with great interest focusing on applications of AI, Machine Learning, and DeepLearning to health.

As a result, several collaborative research projects across Europe have brought together computer science and electronics teams to cooperate with bioengineers and health specialists. These projects span across the entire computing continuum, targeting both embedded medical devices and high-performance computing systems.

In this special session, the selected project reflect this spectrum, and cover a wide range of technologies, including: an application leveraging environmental and wearable sensors to provide advice to improve the quality of the working environment for the ageing population from the WorkingAge project; software methodologies to manage technical debt – a key issue for reducing development costs and malfunctioning risks – in implanted medical devices from the SDK4ED project; a benchmark suite for Computer Vision and AI applications from the RECIPE project; and a framework for developing AI applications for a wide range of medical and biomedical high performance applications from the DeepHealth projects.

These technologies have the potential to become the building blocks for a future generation of effective, reliable, and low-cost biomedical systems powered by AI techniques to support an increasingly ageing population in remaining healthy and active.

July 2020   Giovanni Agosta

VGM-Bench: FPU Benchmark Suite for Computer Vision, Computer Graphics and Machine Learning Applications

Luca Cremona[✉], William Fornaciari, Andrea Galimberti, Andrea Romanoni, and Davide Zoni

Politecnico di Milano, P.zza Leonardo da Vinci, 32, 20133 Milan, Italy
{luca.cremona,william.fornaciari,
andrea.galimberti,andrea.romanoni,davide.zoni}@polimi.it

Abstract. With the Internet-of-things revolution, embedded devices are in charge of an ever increasing number of tasks ranging from sensing, up to Artificial Intelligence (AI) functions. In particular, AI is gaining importance since it can dramatically improve the QoS perceived by the final user and it allows to cope with problems whose algorithmic solution is hard to find. However, the associated computational requirements, mostly made of floating-point processing, impose a careful design and tuning of the computing platforms. In this scenario, there is a need for a set of benchmarks representative of the emerging AI applications and useful to compare the efficiency of different architectural solutions and computing platforms. In this paper we present a suite of benchmarks encompassing Computer Graphics, Computer Vision and Machine Learning applications, which are greatly used in many AI scenarios. Such benchmarks, differently from other suites, are kernels tailored to be effectively executed in bare-metal and specifically stress the floating-point support offered by the computing platform.

Keywords: Benchmarks · Machine learning · Artificial intelligence · Floating-point · FPU.

1 Introduction

In the Internet-of-Things era, the embedded computing platforms are in charge of an ever increasing number of tasks. Novel and complex applications ranging from the Artificial Intelligence (AI) to the computer graphics domain emerged, and they are constantly evolving to improve the QoS perceived by the final user. The computational power required by such tasks pushed to the limit the efficiency requirement for the embedded platforms that are in charge of their execution, since frequently such devices are battery-powered. In particular, most of the AI applications are dominated by floating-point arithmetic computations, which represent a major contribution to the energy consumption. Traditionally,

A. Orailoglu et al. (Eds.): SAMOS 2020, LNCS 12471, pp. 323–335, 2020.
https://doi.org/10.1007/978-3-030-60939-9_23

the benchmark suites are employed to deliver a set of representative applications to compare the efficiency of different computing platforms in a way that is reproducible and consistent. Furthermore, they are the key factor enabling the design of energy saving methodologies for any class of computing devices, single-core [33], multi-cores [32] and HPC [23] architectures, or specific arithmetic accelerators [34].

The state-of-the-art reports different benchmark suites tailored to stress specific aspects of the computing platform. SPLASH-2 [29] and PARSEC [8] are employed to stress the multi-threading and multi-tasking capabilities of the computing platform, while SPEC applications [3] target single-threaded performance. Moreover, AI [27] and machine learning [17] benchmark suites are available for High-Performance Computing (HPC) platforms only. However, the critical drawback of any benchmark suite targeting AI applications is the abstraction layer, since each application in the suite assumes the presence of an Operating System as well as power-consuming resources, e.g., GPUs. The typical IoT scenario is different, there are RISC CPUs where few hardware accelerators are employed to offload the most intensive computational tasks from the main CPU. Moreover, the efficiency requirements impose to avoid the use of a fully-fledged OS, which is frequently replaced by a run-time library and a set of low-level peripheral drivers [2,4]. A valuable benchmark suite for this scenario, should provide bare metal applications to stress the computing capabilities of the target embedded systems, with specific emphasis on the floating-point support, given its increasing relevance in nowadays AI applications.

Contributions - This paper illustrates a set of benchmarks targeting three of the most critical application domains in the IoT era: machine learning, computer graphics and computer vision. Instead of delivering complete applications for each class, every benchmark in the proposed suite targets a different computationally intensive brick of a possible bigger application that falls in one of the three considered classes. In a nutshell, our benchmark suite is *representative* of a wide set of popular application domains, can be employed on *bare metal* without the impact and disturbance of an operating system and, finally, the focus on kernels (micro-benchmarks) allows to dramatically reduce the *execution time* of the test, enabling the possibility of an effective *design space exploration*. Such lightweight configuration is also suitable to analyze low-end computing architectures, such those typically employed for IoT applications. The complete benchsuite, together with a detailed description of each application is available as open source at [1]. To show in practice the value of this benchmark suite, results are collected on a RISC-V System-on-Chip platform meant for IoT. In particular, we demonstrated the impact on the efficiency due to the amount of floating-point resources available on the target device. The rest of the paper is organized as follows. Section 2 examines the state-of-the-art benchmark suites for image processing and machine learning applications. Section 3 presents the proposed benchmark suite and describes the algorithms behind each application. Section 4 is an example of usage of the benchmark suite which analyzes the error rate of the application when varying the precision threshold and the number of truncated bits in the mantissa of their floating-point representation. Section 5 drawn some concluding remarks.

2   Related Works

The state-of-the-art contains several benchmark suites targeting computing platforms ranging from the embedded to the HPC domains. In particular, each benchmark suite allows to assess different aspects of the target computing platform.

Considering high-end embedded platforms and HPC systems, PARSEC [8] and SPLASH-2 [29] applications are meant to stress the multi-threading and multi-tasking capabilities of the computing platform. Differently, SPEC-CPU2006 benchmarks [3] are used to assess single-threaded performance. We note that applications in those benchmark suites spread over different domains, since they are conceived for general-purpose computing platforms. However, their complexity and the requirement of running on top of an Operating System (OS) make such suites not viable for the assessment of both low-end embedded platforms and in-development devices. The former, i.e., low-end embedded devices, in general do not necessarily exploit an operating system while the latter, i.e., in-development devices, are usually executed by RTL simulators or on prototype boards for which the software ecosystem, e.g., OS and drivers, is not mature enough to support OS-based applications.

To this extent, several general-purpose benchmark suites emerged to assess different embedded system figures of merit. Such applications are usually written in ANSI-C and are meant to to be executed in bare-metal. [14] proposes the Worst-Case Execution Time (WCET) benchmark suite to assess the real-time performance of the considered computing platform. [15] presents a set of open source general-purpose applications, covering security, telecommunication, consumer and networking domains, for which the required computational power and the input size are optimized for the execution on embedded devices.

The AI momentum fueled the proposal of different benchmark suites and frameworks specifically focused on the machine learning, computer graphics and computer vision domains. CortexSuite [27] is a brain-inspired benchmark suite containing a set of applications and algorithms pertaining machine learning, natural language processing and computer vision, also including real-world datasets. The MLBench [17] benchmark suite specifically focuses on machine learning algorithms, such as the Bayes classifiers. However, the applications in both CortexSuite and MLBench are not suitable to be executed in bare-metal mode, thus preventing their use during the microarchitectural design stage in the hardware design flow.

To overcome such limitations, we present the *VGM-Bench* suite. It contains 12 kernel applications targeting three different application domains: computer vision, computer graphics and machine learning. Each application is written in ANSI-C and can be executed in bare-metal. Moreover, the default datasets are sized according to the need of executing the applications where the computing platform is either prototyped, i.e., FPGA-implemented, or still under design, hence simulated using an RTL simulator.

3   Benchmarks Details

This section provides an overview of our bench-suite, organized according to the realm of application: Computer Vision, Computer Graphics and Machine Learning. We briefly describe the rationale behind each benchmark, its impact on the state of the art systems and its implementation. Moreover, we discuss whether a benchmark: (i) makes intensive use of floating-point computation and, (ii) traces back to a classification procedure, meaning that we expect it to be more resilient to floating-point errors. Apart from the description of its functionality, each benchmark is described in terms of two properties: floating-point intensiveness and type of application. The floating-point intensiveness measures the percentage of FP-instructions in the benchmark, while the type labels each benchmark as a classification application, or not. We note that the performance of FP-intensive applications strongly depends on the floating-point support, either hardware or software, offered by the computing platform. Moreover, classification applications are less sensitive to low-precision floating-point formats than non-classification ones.

3.1   Computer Vision

Computer Vision addresses the problem of processing one or more images to infer a wide variety of information from the captured scene. For this category, we present four applications which are especially useful while recovering 3D models from images, for instance for augmented reality, environment mapping or camera localization.

Zero-means Normalized Cross Correlation (ZNCC) - It is a widely adopted kernel to compute the correlation between the patches of two images patches. Such kernel is employed in Stereo Matching [11] and 3D reconstruction [22]. The proposed benchmark compares two patches considering of the fountain P-11 dataset [26] as default input set. Images are grayscale converted and, then, encoded as a bi-dimensional integer array where each element corresponds to a pixel whose value is in the interval $[0, 255]$. The expected output of ZNCC is a floating-point between -1 and $+1$. We note that the kernel procedure performs several FP sums and multiplications, therefore it is floating-point intensive.

Ray-Triangle Intersection - It is a fundamental kernel to estimate the color of each pixel in rendering applications and 3D volumetric reconstruction problems. Given a ray R originating from O and the triangle T, the idea is to apply a transformation such that the transformed ray R' is aligned with the x-axis and the transformed triangle T' lays on the yz-plane. Then, the ray-triangle intersection is simply given by the y z coordinates of the transformed point O'.

If its corresponding barycentric coordinates are inside T' then the intersection test has success. The proposed benchmark considers 5 rays and 4 triangles and tests the ray-triangle intersection for each pair, totaling 20 tests. Each test has a binary output, thus making the kernel a classification application.

Kalman Filtering - It is a widely used estimation tool that aims at predicting a series of the state of a process taking as input a series of noisy measurements and the initial state. In Computer vision and Robotics, it plays an important role, especially when dealing with Simultaneous Localization and Mapping (SLAM) [12] and Parallel Tracking and Mapping (PTAM) [16] problems. To this extent, the benchmark mimics the localization case of study in which the state consists of the 3D position and the 3D velocity of a robot. We generated the ground truth trajectory with a constant velocity model, where the velocities are (10 unit/s, 5 unit/s, 2 unit/s) and the measurements are derived from those trajectory perturbed by a Gaussian noise $\nu \sim \mathcal{N}(0, 1)$. The kernel does not falls into the category of classifier kernels. Moreover, the majority of the instructions are due to matrix indexing operations, thus making the kernel an FP-mild one.

K Nearest Neighbor - Finding the K nearest neighbor of a query data $\mathbf{y} \in \mathrm{R}^n$ among a set of elements distributed in the R^n space is a key ingredient of many Computer Vision algorithms, e.g., when computations involve 3D point clouds. Given a set $\mathcal{F}$ of elements, i.e., features, $\mathbf{f} \in \mathcal{F} \subset \mathrm{R}^n$, and a distance function $dist(\cdot, \cdot)$, the k nearest neighbors of a query $\mathbf{y} \in \mathrm{R}^n$ is the set of features $(\hat{\mathcal{F}}_k = \mathbf{f}_1, ..., \mathbf{f}_k) \in \mathcal{F}$ such that $\nexists \mathbf{f} \in \mathcal{F} \setminus \hat{\mathcal{F}}_k$ and $\mathbf{f}_k \in \hat{\mathcal{F}}_k, dist(y, f) < dist(y, \mathbf{f}_k)$. A simple and effective way to implement this algorithm is to store the features in an array and order the array up to the k-th position as in the selection sort method. The proposed kernel is fed with a set of 100 features and tests 20 query points. The output is a binary value for each query, i.e., found or not, thus making the algorithm a classifier. We also note that the kernel involves a balanced mix of floating point instructions together with indexing operations, i.e., integer instructions.

3.2   Computer Graphics

Computer graphics is the branch of computer science that creates, manipulates and stores geometric objects (modeling) and their images (Rendering). In the proposed bench-suite, we identify four key procedures belonging to this category.

Laplacian Smoothing - It is adopted as a fairing step of many computer graphics algorithm, extended by several methods and applied in variational mesh refinement algorithms to implement a smoothing energy term [22]. The proposed benchmark is fed with a deformed sphere made up of 77 vertices and 150 faces. The output is a set of new vertex positions obtained by the smooting process. In addition to this, even if the core of the application is essentially an average of float vertices positions, the application highly rely on indexing operations to retrieve the coordinates of the vertices to be processed at each step.

Facet Normals - Given a 3D mesh, its facets normals are exactly the normal vectors of the plane where each facet lays. They can be computed through the cross product applied for each facet of a mesh. This computation is conceptually easy however, normals constitute a fundamental building block of the computation of lighting in computer graphics rendering pipelines, [9]; they can also be the basis for vertex normal computation [18] which is, in turn, a relevant issue for many rendering operations. Moreover facets normals computation is fundamental during the mesh refinement operation proposed in most of of the works cited in the previous section This benchmark uses as input a sphere with 77 vertices and 150 faces. The expected output is an array of 3D vectors (no classification), 150 in our case, each vector is the normal of the facet with the corresponding index. Even in this case the number of indexing operation to access to vertices positions is significant compared to the floating point ones.

Facet Subdivision - Facet subdivision aims at refining the resolution of the mesh. Given a triangular mesh several approaches have been adopted to improve the resolution of the mesh while smoothing its shape [25]. However, in some situations, there is a need for disentangled resolution increase and smoothing. In such cases, a very common approach turns the facets of the mesh in a 1-to-4 pattern [28]; in this benchmark, we implemented the 1-to-4 pattern as follows. First, we copy the input vertices into the output vector of vertices V_{out}. For each vertex, we store a vector which is populated whenever a new vertex is added to split one of the adjacent facets. For each facet, and each of its three edges, we check from the vector associated to the ending vertex v_{min} whose index is smaller if the mid-point exists; otherwise, we create it and we add it to the last empty element of the vector associated with v_{min}. The four new triangles are then created by adding the indices of the original and the new vertices to I_{out} coherently, where I_{out} is the array of indices building up the facets of the output mesh.

The input of this benchmark is a portion of a sphere with 39 vertices and 58 facets, and the expect output a mesh with 135 vertices and 232 facets, therefore a mix of index (integer output) and vertices positions (float output). Facet subdivision involves many indexing operation both to access to vertices positions and to define the new vertices and their connectivity inside the new mesh; floating point operations is limited to the vertex averaging.

Self Intersections - Mesh self-intersections are those facets belonging to the same mesh and intersecting with each other. So, given mesh Γ containing a set of facets $\mathcal{F}$, we define two facets $f_1, f_2 \in \mathcal{F}$ as self-intersecting if they intersect each other; the set mesh self-intersections $\hat{\mathcal{F}}$ contains all facets f_i such that $\exists f_j \neq f_i \in \hat{\mathcal{F}}$ with which it has an intersection. Self-intersections are usually considered an issue especially since they are an unrealistic representation of a real-world surface. For this reason, several Computer Graphics algorithms, especially those modifying the mesh shape, requires the detection of self-intersection to get rid of them or preemptively avoid a certain mesh deformation that would produce them [30]. Similarly in Zaharescu et al., [31] evolves a mesh to refine its appearance, and at the same time checks which are the self-intersections and they fix them.

To implement self-intersection detection we check if, each facet intersects one of the others using the triangle-triangle intersection algorithm proposed by Möller [19]. The benchmark takes as input a mesh made up of 47 vertices and 72 facets. The mesh has been intentionally designed with 16 self-intersecting facets.

Therefore, the procedure performs binary classification for each facet. However the number of floating-point operation is significant, due to the triangle-triangle intersection test.

3.3 Machine Learning

Machine learning is an application of artificial intelligence (AI) that provides systems the ability to automatically learn and improve from experience without being explicitly programmed. Machine learning focuses on the development of computer programs that can access data and use it to learn for themselves. VGM-Bench suite proposes four benchmarks to address this field.

Linear Regression - It is one of the most basic and relevant Machine Learning tools whose aim is to fit a linear model into a set of labeled data. Given a set $\mathbf{x}$ of input data and the corresponding $\mathbf{y}$ labels, the goal is to find a linear model $\mathbf{y} = \theta_1 \mathbf{x} + \theta_2$ that is the better represents the input-label relationship, i.e., it minimizes the mean-squared error. Linear regression is one of the simplest machine learning methods which is the basis of some more complex approaches [20]. The benchmark is made up of 67 sets of 100 points where a linear 2D model has to be fit. The output of linear regression, as suggested by the name is float (no classification) and is composed by a good balance of indexing and floating points operations.

k-Means - It is a classical clustering algorithm widely adopted for data analysis or compression. Given a number K of clusters, and a set of input data $\mathbf{x}$, K-means aims at finding the position of the centroids of the clusters and to which each input data has to be associated. In the following, we describe the algorithm considering the input data as points in the space. the same procedure can be applied to whatever input data belonging to $\mathbf{R}^n$. K-means is an Expectation-Maximization method that minimizes the function:

$$ J = \sum_{i=1}^{m} \sum_{k=1}^{K} w_{ik} \left\| x^i - \mu_k \right\|^2 \tag{1} $$

where $w_{ik} = 1$ if point i is associated to cluster k, otherwise $w_{ik} = 0$, x_i the i-th input point and μ_k the k-th the cluster centroid. Therefore it alternates between an Expectation and a Maximization step. After initializing the position of each centroid μ_k, usually spread uniformly in the domain of the input data, in the Expectation step it minimizes J w.r.t. w_{ik} keeping μ_k fixed. In the maximization step, K-means minimizes J w.r.t. μ_k keeping w_{ik} fixed, i.e., In other words, it recomputes the centroids according to the new assignments in w_{ik}. In the benchmark, two clustering problems are reported with 5 centroids and 9 input points. Since the aim is to choose which point belongs to which centroid, k-means traces back to classification. Even in this case the procedure is made up of a balanced mix of floating point and indexing operations.

Q-learning - Q-Learning is one of the most popular algorithms of Reinforcement learning, i.e., the branch of Machine learning in which an agent interacts with the environment and it has to learn how to reach a specific goal, knowing that a reward is associated with certain actions. A reinforcement learning problem is often described as a Markov Decision Process. We define a set of states (S) a set of actions (A) that the agent can take, a transition probability $P(s, s')$ of going from s to s' and a reward function $R_a(s', s)$ of going from s' to s with an action a. Q-learning is a reinforcement learning algorithm that seeks to find the best action to take given a state; more in general, Q-learning looks for the policy $\pi(a, s)$, i.e., the probability that an action a has to be applied given a state s. To do so, a table state-action, named q-table, is kept updated as the agent explores the environment. In general, giving an agent starting in a state s_1, it takes an action a_1 and receives a reward r_1 and ends in a state s_2. To choose a_1 either the agent chooses randomly, or it considers the action that according to the q-table will give the highest expected reward. The choice between these two alternatives is the well-known trade-off between exploration and exploitation. This process is usually iterated multiple times for all the states until convergence. Let notice that the random number adopted to choose the random action, have been extracted in advanced and saved in an array, to obtain deterministic results. In the proposed benchmark we consider a Markov decision Process with 6 states, where the sixth is the goal. The input is just the Markov Decision Process (MDP) description and the expected output is the updated q-table. The computation involves many matrix multiplication therefore a significant amount of indexing operations, i.e., integer instructions, compared to the FP ones.

Long-Short Term Memory - Long-Short Term Memory (LSTM) Neural Network is a special kind of Recurrent Neural Networks (RNN) that in addition to the short term dependencies learned by RNN, it also aims at learning long-term ones [13]. Such networks usually process input sequences as strings of text, and output some kind of prediction, depending on the task and depending on the training data. The idea in LSTM is to have the so-called cell, where each element of the input is processed; then, it uses input, output and forget gates to learn dependencies among data. At the end of this process, to map the hidden state of dimension $h \times 1$ to the desired dimension d_o, e.g. a single predicted value, a linear layer is added after the output of the hidden layer. In the benchmark we implemented all matrix and vector operations, the *sigmoid*, the *tanh* and so the exponential function. In the proposed application we can find a neural network aimed for time-series predictions, where the input is a series of 20×1 vector $(d = 20)$ elements, and we use a single hidden layer of dimension $h = 32$. To generate the data we followed the procedure described in [5] and we trained our model with PyTorch [21].

The output of LSTM is a prediction of the temporal series (no classification). LSTM involves numerous floating point operations but also significant amount of indexing operations, especially due to array and matrix multiplications.

4   Experimental Evaluation

As already mentioned, most of the nowadays IoT devices are battery-powered and cost-sensitive. Thus, during the design of the computing platforms, it is important to consider both the size and the computing power of all the components of the system.

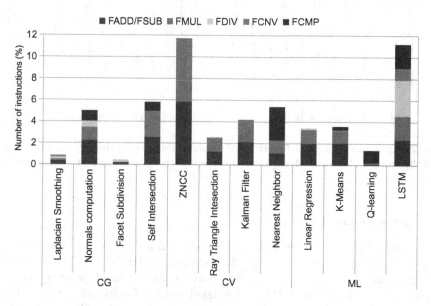

Fig. 1. Floating point instructions mix for the proposed benchmarks. Results are collected from a RISC-V compliant platform employing a custom CPU embedding the hardware FPU from the ORPSoC-v3 project.

In particular, one of the most critical components of the CPU is the FPU (Floating Point Unit). Especially in small embedded processors, its power consumption can represent up to 40% of the overall count. As a consequence, it is crucial the sizing of the FPU operands, to prevent the cost of a full-size FPU implementation. To this purpose, we will show the benefit of using our suite to tackle this type of problem, by considering a representative use case. The analysis is split over two sections. The experimental setup is described in Sect. 4.1, while the experimental results are discussed in Sect. 4.2.

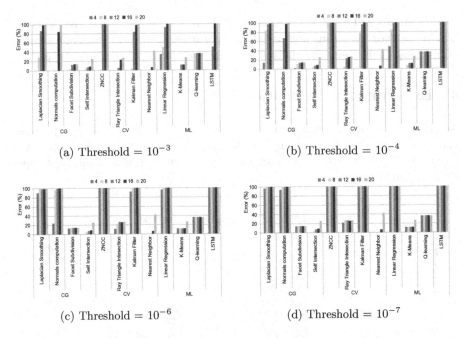

Fig. 2. Error rate of the benchmark applications when varying the precision threshold and the number of truncated bits in the mantissa of their floating-point representation.

4.1 Experimental Setup

We employed the System-on-Chip (SoC) presented in [24] as our reference computing platform. The SoC embeds a fully-compliant RISC-V CPU that features a single-issue, in-order, 5-stage pipeline, and implements the Integer (I), Integer Multiplication and Division (M) and Single-Precision Floating-Point (F) RISC-V 32-bit ISA extensions. The floating-point unit adopted in this processor has been taken from the ORPSoC-v3 project and has been adapted to comply with the RISC-V extension specification. The applications have been simulated on the considered processor using the *xsim* RTL simulator, within the *Xilinx Vivado 2018.2* design suite, and by setting a 50 MHz clock frequency. The floating-point instruction mix has been extracted through continuous monitoring of the performance counters implemented in the processor (more details can be found in [1]).

4.2 Experimental Results

Figure 1 shows the floating-point instruction mix for the bench-suite: for each application on the X axis, we plot the stacked percentages of the different types of floating-point instructions on the Y axis. Figure 2, instead, reports the number of errors generated by the applications when truncating the mantissa of the floating-point operands. This truncation is mimicking a possible reduction of the operand size to investigate if a smaller FPU can be adopted to reduce the size and power consumption of the device. Given a certain accuracy threshold varying from 10^{-3} to 10^{-7} ((a), (b), (c), (d)), each plot displays the normalized percentage of results not satisfy the desired accuracy. We consider 5 cases, truncating from 4 to 20 bits of the 23-bit mantissa.

From these two figures, we can notice that there is no correlation between the percentage of floating-point instructions in the application with the number of errors generated. For example, ZNCC has 11.8% of floating-point instruction against the 0.8% of Laplacian Subdivision, but the number of error generated is around 100% when truncating more than 8 bits of mantissa. The number of errors depends more on the application algorithm rather than on the number of truncated bits. For example let us consider a classifier, this applications returns a boolean or an integer (number of the class) value, e.g., in the case of Ray Triangle Intersection, it returns true if the ray intersects the triangle, false otherwise. It doesn't consider the position of the intersection or the incidence angle, so even if there are errors due to the truncations, the final result, in most cases, can be correct anyway. This consideration becomes fundamental when there is a need to use an FPU dedicated for a specific type of algorithm: in this case the number of bits for the mantissa can be tailored to meet its specific requirements. Lets considering again, as an example, Facet Subdivision, Self Intersection, Ray Triangle Intersection, Nearest Neighbour and K-Means. We can notice that the number of errors does not increase significantly when decreasing the required precision. In fact, the average error percentage for these applications goes from close to 18% up to around 22%. The other applications, since their final outputs are floating-point values, are more sensitive to the reduction of the number of bits used to represent the mantissa of the operands, pulling the number of errors rapidly up to the maximum value. Thanks to the use of our benchmark suite exploiting selected micro-kernels, this design space exploration has been carried out in less than two hours on a Xeon E5-2650 V3 running @2.3 GHz.

5   Conclusions

In this paper we propose *VGM-bench*, a benchmark suite containing bare-metal applications coming from computer vision, computer graphics and machine learning areas. These applications aim to stress the whole hardware architecture of the target computing platform, with a special focus on the floating point unit, and can be particularly useful during the prototyping phases of a design. To show the effectiveness of VGM-bench, the full suite has been simulated on a 32-bit RISC-V CPU [24] leveraging Xilinx Vivado 2018.2 design suite, to perform an extensive design space exploration. In addition to the analysis of the mix of floating-point instructions generated by the proposed benchmarks, we explored the impact of different mantissa truncations on the results accuracy, since this aspect is related to the cost and power consumption of embedded processors. Such design optimization has taken less than 2 h of simulation on a mid-range desktop, thus making such optimization step fully affordable. The source code of the bench-suite is available for free download at [1], together with a complete description of each application.

Acknowledgments. Work supported by the H2020 FET-HPC project "RECIPE", G. A. no. 801137. More information can be found in [6,7] and [10].

References

1. Lamp: Lightweight application-specific modular processor. http://www.lamp-platform.org
2. Freertos (2003). https://www.freertos.org
3. Spec cpu2006 (2006). https://www.spec.org/cpu2006/
4. Mbed (2009). https://www.mbed.com/
5. LSTMS for time series in pytorch (2019). https://www.jessicayung.com/lstms-for-time-series-in-pytorch/. Accessed 05 Aug 2019
6. Agosta, G., et al.: The RECIPE approach to challenges in deeply heterogeneous high performance systems. Microprocess. Microsyst. **77**, 103185 (2020). https://doi.org/10.1016/j.micpro.2020.103185. ISSN 0141-9331
7. Agosta, G., et al.: Challenges in deeply heterogeneous high performance systems. In: 2019 22nd Euromicro Conference on Digital System Design (DSD), August 2019. https://doi.org/10.1109/DSD.2019.00068
8. Bienia, C.: Benchmarking Modern Multiprocessors. Ph.D. thesis, Princeton University, January 2011
9. Fan, W., Wang, K., Cayre, F., Xiong, Z.: 3D lighting-based image forgery detection using shape-from-shading. In: 2012 Proceedings of the 20th European Signal Processing Conference (EUSIPCO), pp. 1777–1781. IEEE (2012)
10. Fornaciari, al.: Reliable power and time-constraints-aware predictive management of heterogeneous exascale systems. In: Mudge, T.N., Pnevmatikatos, D.N. (eds.) Proceedings of the 18th International Conference on Embedded Computer Systems: Architectures, Modeling, and Simulation, Pythagorion, Greece, 15–19 July 2018, pp. 187–194. ACM (2018). https://doi.org/10.1145/3229631.3239368
11. Geiger, Andreas., Roser, Martin, Urtasun, Raquel: Efficient large-scale stereo matching. In: Kimmel, Ron, Klette, Reinhard, Sugimoto, Akihiro (eds.) ACCV 2010. LNCS, vol. 6492, pp. 25–38. Springer, Heidelberg (2011). https://doi.org/10.1007/978-3-642-19315-6_3
12. Geneva, P., Maley, J., Huang, G.: An efficient SCHMIDT-EKF for 3d visual-inertial slam. In: Proceedings of the IEEE Conference on Computer Vision and Pattern Recognition, pp. 12105–12115 (2019)
13. Greff, K., Srivastava, R.K., Koutník, J., Steunebrink, B.R., Schmidhuber, J.: LSTM: a search space odyssey. IEEE Trans. Neural Networks Learn. Syst. **28**(10), 2222–2232 (2016)
14. Gustafsson, J., Betts, A., Ermedahl, A., Lisper, B.: The mälardalen wcet benchmarks - past, present and future. In: Proceedings of the 10th International Workshop on Worst-Case Execution Time Analysis, July 2010
15. Guthaus, M.R., Ringenberg, J.S., Ernst, D., Austin, T.M., Mudge, T., Brown, R.B.: Mibench: a free, commercially representative embedded benchmark suite. In: 2001 IEEE International Workshop Proceedings of the Workload Characterization, 2001. WWC-4, pp. 3–14. WWC 2001 (2001)

16. Klein, G., Murray, D.: Parallel tracking and mapping for small ar workspaces. In: Proceedings of the 2007 6th IEEE and ACM International Symposium on Mixed and Augmented Reality, pp. 1–10. IEEE Computer Society (2007)

17. Leisch, F., Dimitriadou, E.: mlbench: Machine Learning Benchmark Problems, r package version 2.1-1 (2010)

18. Max, N.: Weights for computing vertex normals from facet normals. J. Graph. Tools **4**(2), 1–6 (1999)

19. Möller, T.: A fast triangle-triangle intersection test. J. Graph. Tools **2**(2), 25–30 (1997)

20. Montgomery, D.C., Peck, E.A., Vining, G.G.: Introduction to Linear Regression Analysis, vol. 821. Wiley, Hoboken (2012)

21. Paszke, A., et al.: Automatic Differentiation in Pytorch (2017)

22. Romanoni, A., Matteucci, M.: Mesh-based camera pairs selection and occlusion-aware masking for mesh refinement. Pattern Recogn. Lett. **125**, 364–372 (2019)

23. Sansottera, A., Zoni, D., Cremonesi, P., Fornaciari, W.: Consolidation of multi-tier workloads with performance and reliability constraints. In: 2012 International Conference on High Performance Computing Simulation (HPCS), pp. 74–83 (2012). https://doi.org/10.1109/HPCSim.2012.6266893

24. Scotti, G., Zoni, D.: A fresh view on the microarchitectural design of FPGA-based risc cpus in the IoT era. J. Low Power Electron. Appl. **9**, 19 (2019). https://doi. org/10.3390/jlpea9010009

25. Shiue, L.J., Jones, I., Peters, J.: A realtime GPU subdivision kernel. In: ACM Transactions on Graphics (TOG). vol. 24, pp. 1010–1015. ACM (2005)

26. Strecha, C., von Hansen, W., Van Gool, L., Fua, P., Thoennessen, U.: On benchmarking camera calibration and multi-view stereo for high resolution imagery. In: Computer Vision and Pattern Recognition, pp. 1–8. IEEE (2008)

27. Thomas, S., et al.: CortexSuite: a synthetic brain benchmark suite. In: International Symposium on Workload Characterization (IISWC), October 2014

28. Vu, H.H., Keriven, R., Labatut, P., Pons, J.P.: Towards high-resolution large-scale multi-view stereo. In: Computer Vision and Pattern Recognition, pp. 1430–1437. IEEE (2009)

29. Woo, S.C., Ohara, M., Torrie, E., Singh, J.P., Gupta, A.: The splash-2 programs: characterization and methodological considerations. In: Proceedings of the 22nd Annual International Symposium on Computer Architecture, pp. 24–36. ISCA 1995

30. Xu, J., Sun, Y., Zhang, L.: A mapping-based approach to eliminating self-intersection of offset paths on mesh surfaces for CNC machining. Computer-Aided Design **62**, 131–142 (2015)

31. Zaharescu, Andrei., Boyer, Edmond, Horaud, Radu: TransforMesh : a topology-adaptive mesh-based approach to surface evolution. In: Yagi, Yasushi, Kang, Sing Bing, Kweon, In So, Zha, Hongbin (eds.) ACCV 2007. LNCS, vol. 4844, pp. 166–175. Springer, Heidelberg (2007). https://doi.org/10.1007/978-3-540-76390-1_17

32. Zoni, D., Cremona, L., Fornaciari, W.: All-digital control-theoretic scheme to optimize energy budget and allocation in multi-cores. IEEE Trans. Comput. **69**(5), 706–721 (2020). https://doi.org/10.1109/TC.2019.2963859

33. Zoni, D., Cremona, L., Fornaciari, W.: All-digital energy-constrained controller for general-purpose accelerators and cpus. IEEE Embedded Syst. Lett. **12**(1), 17–20 (2020). https://doi.org/10.1109/LES.2019.2914136

34. Zoni, D., Galimberti, A., Fornaciari, W.: Flexible and scalable FPGA-oriented design of multipliers for large binary polynomials. IEEE Access **8**, 75809–75821 (2020). https://doi.org/10.1109/ACCESS.2020.2989423

Decision Support Systems to Promote Health and Well-Being of People During Their Working Age: The Case of the WorkingAge EU Project

Rosa Maria Resende de Almeida[6], Adriana Grau Aberturas[6],
Yolanda Bueno Aguado[6], Maurizio Atzori[1], Alessandro Barenghi[3],
Gianluca Borghini[2], Carlos Alberto Catalina Ortega[5], Sara Comai[3],
Raquel Losada Durán[6], Mariagrazia Fugini[3], Hatice Gunes[4],
Basam Musleh Lancis[5], Gerardo Pelosi[3]([✉]), Vincenzo Ronca[2],
Licia Sbattella[3], Roberto Tedesco[3], and Tian Xu[4]

[1] Università di Cagliari - DMI, Cagliari, Italy
atzori@unica.it
[2] BrainSigns s.r.l., Rome, Italy
{gianluca.borghini,vincenzo.ronca}@brainsigns.com
[3] Politecnico di MIlano - DEIB, Milan, Italy
{alessandro.barenghi,sara.comai,mariagrazia.fugini,gerardo.pelosi,
licia.sbattella,roberto.tedesco}@polimi.it
[4] University of Cambridge - DCST, Cambridge, UK
{hatice.gunes,tian.xu}@cl.cam.ac.uk
[5] Instituto Tecnológico de Castilla y León, Burgos, Spain
{carlos.catalina,basam.musleh}@itcl.es
[6] Fundación INTRAS, Valladolid, Spain
{rra,aga,yba,rld}@intras.es

Abstract. The WorkingAge project aims at improving the psycho-physical condition of workers, with a special focus on ageing subjects. In this context, a Decision Support System, based on a hybrid data-driven/model-driven approach, fed with data coming from environmental and wearable sensors, aims to provide personalised advises to the worker. In this paper we briefly present the WorkingAge project and architecture, and then focus on the decision-making pipeline that, starting from raw data, generates the advises.

Keywords: Occupational Safety · Decision support systems for health at work · Suggestion of health strategies · Occupational ontology

1 Introduction

The increasing longevity of population in industrialized countries is shifting the age distribution of the workforce. However, the aging process can lead to physio-

This project has received funding from the European Union's Horizon 2020 research and innovation programme, under grant agreement N. 826232.

A. Orailoglu et al. (Eds.): SAMOS 2020, LNCS 12471, pp. 336–347, 2020.
https://doi.org/10.1007/978-3-030-60939-9_24

logical and cognitive changes that can affect the well-being and quality of life of workers. Workplace design and organizational strategy can play a pivotal role in maximizing the comfort and performance of occupants, as well as in promotion healthy habits in working/living environments.

The ongoing EU project WorkingAge (Smart Working environments for all Ages - https://www.workingage.eu/) – WA for short – focuses on these issues and promotes healthy habits in working environments targeting people aged over 45. The aim of the project is to achieve a better understanding of well-being at work and of factors that may inhibit or deteriorate prolonged employment [9]. The Working Age Of Wellbeing (WAOW) tool is under development to provide workers with assistance in their everyday routine in the form of recommendations, risks avoidance and reminders. The WAOW tool monitors the worker's behavior, health data and preferences through continuous data collection using Internet of Things (IoT) devices – sensors, interaction tools, wearable devices – to provide recommendations on working habits, physical activities and social relations. The core of the WAOW tool environment is a Decision Support System (DSS), a reasoning system about the worker conditions and for early detection of possible issues. The DSS supports workers in taking effective and personalized decisions and interventions based on a set of measured indicators.

The paper is organized as follows. Section 2 reports related work; Sect. 3 provides an overview of the WAOW tool; Sect. 4 introduces the intervention strategies to improve workers' well being; Sect. 5 introduces the WAOW Ontology-based data model; Sect. 6 shows how the DSS provide recommendations to the workers; finally, Sect. 7 outlines conclusions and future work.

2   Related Work

Safety and well-being at work is recognized to be highly related to social, economic, and environmental conditions [19]. These should be enhanced to improve health and well aging [12], in the line of what recommended by the Occupational Health and Safety (OHS) management system standard[1] described in [6]. An interesting overview of problems related to aging and well-being at work and in societal environments is given in [13].

Working, even at a relatively advanced age, is considered good to maintain physical and mental health [10]. However, not all workers benefit of favorable conditions, due to dangerous or stressing work environments. Moreover, ageing and shrinking of work forces [2] worsen the work conditions of many classes of workers, due to staff shortage and lack of expertise in young generations [1]. New working and living conditions are encouraged in many studies and experiences, centered around concepts of autonomy and quality of life [4,8] The WAOW tool can be classified as a Self-Management Occupational Safety and Health Supervision System (SMOSHS System) [3]. The tool is being designed considering DSS issues, in order to adapt its interface and functions to the user, in the line of

---

[1] https://www.bsigroup.com/en-GB/Occupational-Health-and-Safety-ISO-45001/.

what proposed in [15] and considering that the partners involved in experiments apply procedures compliant with GDPR.

Coming to the DSS, in the last years, DSSes have become quite popular in health services, to enhance interaction between patients and their physicians [16], in social care [5], and in many other areas, using technologies which commonly draw on an existing knowledge base of evidence and guidelines to provide logical reasoning-based expert advice. In [21], a DSS is described for workers with disabilities who are more sensitive for stress at work and for the injuries connected with non-adequate workplaces. Based on ontologies, many DSSes have been developed for business decision making, or for cyber-physical systems [17,18], which are very similar to our application area. In fact, these systems tightly integrate software, human, and physical components with the need to satisfy constraints on performance and safety of the monitored activities, exhibiting a high degree of automation for the management of their functionalities and decision making processes. In general, there is a strong need for semantic models of the involved application domains. In such a context, the clinical domain [14] witnesses an increasing demand to develop knowledge-based DSSs employing medical knowledge and expertise coming from different ontologies.

3   The WAOW Tool

The main goal of the WA project is designing and developing the WAOW tool. Such tool provides feedback to the employers by means of warnings and advises. Furthermore, the WAOW tool collects information useful to perform changes in the workplace that may lead to an increased level of comfort for the workers and new solutions to promote flexible and sustainable job longevity measures. The WAOW tool is focused on the usage of innovative Human Computer Interaction (HCI) methods, including augmented reality, virtual reality, gesture/voice recognition and gaze tracking. It will measure the user's psychological/emotional/health state, collect data about the environmental conditions of her/his workplace, and will provide advises taking into consideration also gender, ethics and security aspects. The WAOW tool architecture can be divided into three parts (see Fig. 1). Firstly, there are numerous sensors that are deployed in the workplace or worn by the worker in order to acquire all the information (Raw data) required by the system; notice that, another input source is provided by questionnaires administered to the worker by means of the WA App, running on the worker's phone. These pieces of information are then sent via Wi-Fi or Bluetooth to the Edge Cloud (the second part of the architecture) to be processed by means of different algorithms to the end of computing a relatively small set of High-Level information regarding the well-being status of the workers. Finally, High-Level information is sent to the WA App, where it is stored into the Ontology and processed by the DSS, which generates advises to the worker (see Sect. 6 for details).

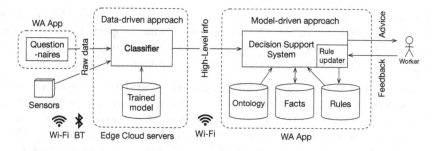

Fig. 1. The WAOW tool decision making pipeline.

4   The Intervention Strategy

The WA project intends to develop an *e-coach* system of interaction to implement an intervention program with workers over 45 years to prolong their work ability and autonomy, reduce strain in different working conditions and promote well-being throughout different areas of their lives, promoting an inclusive approach to the health at work. It seeks to increase awareness of workers on aspects such as ergonomic conditions, occupational hazards, stress and its effects on health, providing the worker with the knowledge and skills to reduce negative effects or adopt healthier and safer behaviors.

The WA Intervention Framework is pillared on well-known models, such as the CDC Workplace Health Model, the Plan-Do-Check-Act (PDCA) cycle adopted by the Occupational Safety and Health Administration for the certification process of the OHSAS 18001 management standard, and the Integrated Risk Management (IRM) model, a set of practices and processes supported by a risk-aware culture. It considers the multi-factorial nature of subjective well-being and work ability to ensuring a holistic and comprehensive approach to the individual. The WA Intervention Strategy designed so far considers wellness on physical, emotional, intellectual, occupational, social and environmental dimensions. The integrated approach fosters awareness on psycho-social and ergonomic risk prevention measures, seeking to promote attitudinal and behavioral changes towards healthy lifestyles. From this perspective, WA addresses four major areas of intervention: *Ergonomics & Physical environment* (which promotes adequate work postures and encourages healthy work habits), *Worker's health and personal characteristics* (which encourages the user to follow and/or acquire health promotion and disease prevention strategies), *Psycho-social factors* (which aims at increasing the self-awareness about cognitive and emotional states of activation or discomfort) and *Lifestyle & Health habits* (which promotes the acquisition and maintenance of healthy lifestyle habits). The goal of the WA Interventions is not limited to leveraging the power of technology for recommend practices for safety and health but also for general well being. Taking advantage of the technological concept of WA the proposed intervention approach aims to change the way the workers see and take care of their health, helping to better understand their own health, improving self-awareness of well-being, and changing how workers access to assessment data and advice. For employers, WA provides many opportunities for smarter health and well-being support. In the development of the WA Intervention Framework and Strategies, a multidisciplinary team of expert professionals designed the intervention around the following pillars.

Framework for Stress and Strain Assessment and Intervention. Strain is an essential aspect for assessing the effects of work on a given person describing her/his reactions to the set of working conditions. Stress describes the external characteristics of a work situation that influences the working person. These include, for example, physical and organizational working conditions. Within the WAOW tool, there will be different sensors used to measure *physical* (muscular, skeletal, cardiovascular and somatic) and *psychological* (mental and emotional) strain, as defined in [20]. The analysis of these measures lets the WAOW tool to generate a personalized advice, which aims at improving the worker's condition, based on the strain typology.

WA focuses the design of the intervention in a goal-oriented approach, where coaching is "essentially about helping individuals regulate and direct their interpersonal and interpersonal resources to better attain their goals" [11]. Specific, Measurable, Achievable, Relevant Time bound (SMART) goals will be progressively tuned around the user profile, promoting behavioral changes, improving the healthy habits of the worker, taking into account behavioral, environmental and personal factors. Moreover, a specific set of interventions will be developed to meet the different SMART goals along the WA tool usage.

The Recommendation System. The DSS, incorporating the framework depicted above, will generate the appropriate recommendation. Relevant information for the DSS will come from measurements, from SMART goals and from questionnaires (see Sect. 6). The DSS will propose an advice at any moment, and/or in response to a specific measure, indicative of a possible risk to the user's health. The recommendations are focused on ergonomics, psycho-educational and emotional activation control techniques, and behavioural modification.

5   The Ontology

The WA Ontology represents the data model for the High-level information samples generated by Edge Cloud servers. Starting from such pieces of information, the DSS will generate personalized advices to the workers.

The Ontology is represented by means of the OWL2 DL language. In the OWL language, a concept is represented as a *class*, if it can be seen as a set; the relationships between classes are named *object properties*; the attributes belonging to a class are named *datatype properties*; finally, *individuals* define the instances of a class, i.e., elements of a set. For providing the best privacy, the resulting OWL file is stored on the worker's phone, into the WA App.

In our Ontology each datatype property corresponds to a specific High-level information, and whenever a new High-level information is added to the Ontology, a new individual is created. In the following, we describe the five parts that compose our Ontology, using a simple graphical language, where squares represent classes, arcs show object properties and "pins" depict datatype properties. A dotted square denotes a "link" to a class that is described into other drawings.

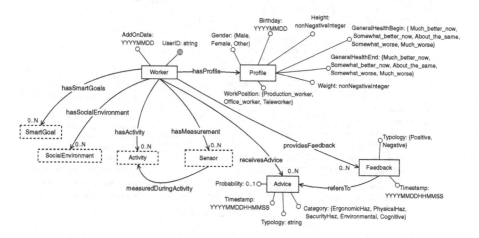

Fig. 2. Description of the worker, and related classes.

Worker. This part is the "core" of the Ontology and describes the profile of the worker, as well as the connections to all the relevant information provided by other parts of the Ontology (see Fig. 2). The Worker class, together with the Profile class, describe the basic characteristics of the worker. Notice that UserID is described as a *key* for the class Worker, meaning that such a datatype property will be used by the WAOW tool to identify a specific worker. A worker is associated with zero or more advices, and can provide a corresponding feedback. advices are associated with a probability; this is due to the fact that any High-level information is, in general, generated by data-driven classifiers. We leverage that characteristic by providing not only the classifier output (which corresponds to a High-level information to be stored into the corresponding datatype property of a specific class) but also the related probability. Thus, the ProbLog engine can provide a *probabilistic* advice; such probability can be seen as a *reliability score* associated with the advice. Finally, the worker is associated with several sensor measurements, social environments, activities, and SMART goals. Note that a sensor measurement happens in the context of a given activity; in fact, a worker can be measured at the workplace or during free time.

Sensor. This is the most complex part of the Ontology and describes the High-level information samples calculated from the Edge Cloud servers, about a worker. The taxonomy in Fig. 3 shows the sensor typologies that the WAOW tool leverages for collecting information about the worker and her/his environment. Each measurement is provided with a timestamp and a probability value; over the time, we collect an ordered sequence of High-level information samples, of

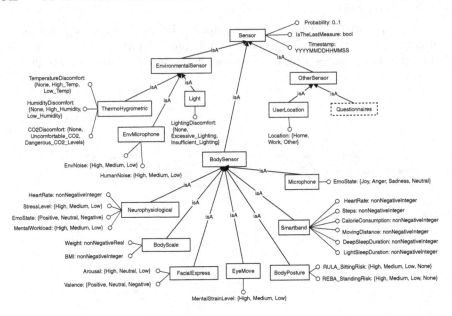

Fig. 3. Information derived from several body and environmental sensors (`Questionnaires` class omitted).

various typologies, associated with various reliability values (adopting the same interpretation described for advices). The DSS will reason on this sequence. Sensors are subdivided into environmental sensors, body sensors, and other typologies (which include questionnaires and user location). Questionnaires, which will be administered to the worker by means of the WA App, are considered as a special case of sensors, and provide daily, weekly or monthly "measurements".

Activity and Social Environment. The class named "Activity" describes the relevant characteristics of the activity associated with a worker. Worker's activities are split into two main parts, as Fig. 4 shows: `Task` and `FreeTime`. In fact, the WAOW tool will measure workers at the working place, and during their activities at home or in other places. By "social environment" we mean the relevant social characteristics of the working environment as captured by classes in Fig. 5.

SMART Goals. This part describes the so-called SMART goals about healthy habits that the worker is encouraged to adopt (see Fig. 6). According to the worker's context, a `SmartGoal` will be set for each individual worker. The Ontology stores the current state of the individual worker as well as the goals that are identified to be met by the worker. These personalized goals can help the workers improve their working and living conditions. The Class `GoalState` shows the worker's progress towards the set SMART goal, which is updated weekly. These goals are mostly related to nutrition, sleep, and social relations, and aim

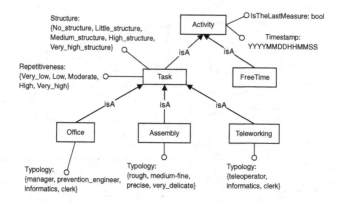

Fig. 4. Information about activities of the worker.

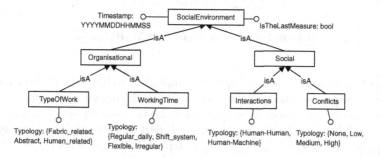

Fig. 5. Information about social characteristics of the working environment.

at challenging the workers in terms of behavioural change, and of motivating them to adopt a healthier lifestyle.

6   The Decision Support System

One of the central components of the WAOW tool is the DSS; such a system supports the worker while dealing with working activities. The DSS we developed is based on a model-driven approach – in particular, it's a rule-based engine – but it is able to work with the results of the Edge Cloud algorithms, which generate a probabilistic output. Thus, the whole "decision-making pipeline", as Fig. 1 shows, is actually based on a hybrid data-driven/model-driven approach. We opted for this design as for the models working on Raw data we found feasible corpora that permitted to leverage data-driven models. For generating advices, however, no feasible corpora existed, and creating our own dataset was not an option. Thus, we decided for a model-based approach. Model-driven approaches refer to methods that are able to reason over existing and infer new knowledge based on a given model of the domain at hand. These solutions are often referred to as *expert systems*. A typical model is often expressed as a set of *rules*, which

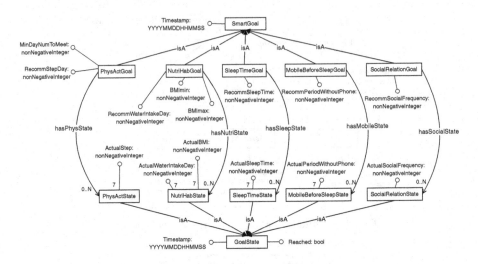

Fig. 6. Information about the SMART goals.

describe how to derive new *facts*, as it happens in well-known declarative programming languages like Prolog. Declarative model-driven approaches are also used for case-based reasoning, to provide insights based on previously occurred instances. Given a model, the computation is performed by the reasoning engine, that applies the model to user-provided data to infer new knowledge regarding the domain.

Research in model-based reasoning focus in various areas, including the core engine optimizations, debugging, expressivity of rules and knowledge representation in general. Recent research included uncertainty in their proposed models, leading to engines able to handle probabilistic rules [7]. In the design of the WAOW tool, we determined that uncertainty was needed in order to represent aspects of the model which cannot be predicted in a deterministic way. For instance the confidence that an expert may give to a specific suggestion, or the measure of a sensor, may not be always equal to 100%. This is why we chose ProbLog as the inference engine for the DSS.

ProbLog. ProbLog [7] is a probabilistic logic programming proposed by the DLAI group at the KU Leuven University (Belgium), heavily inspired by Prolog. It reuses the Prolog syntax but allows probabilistic labeling of rules and facts, allowing not only inference of certainly-true facts (according to the usual declarative models), but also derive the level of confidence for that specific inferred fact. An interesting property of ProbLog is that it does not require to specify an exact Bayesian Network, relying instead on a sort of best-effort approximation whenever some nodes and edges of the full causal graph are missing. It can also compute marginal probabilities of any number of ground atoms in the presence of evidence, therefore recomputing probabilities whenever new data is provided. This is important since in many real applications, including those in the context of the WA project, many aspects of the causal dependencies cannot be modeled exactly, and so a level of approximation must be handled by the tool. As the original Prolog, ProbLog uses procedural interpretation of Horn clauses, in this case labeled with probabilities. As we show next, we use these probabilistic rules to model scenarios in the context of working environments.

The DSS. As Fig. 1 shows, the DSS is fed by High-Level information generated by the data-driven models running into the Edge Cloud. The Ontology acts as a data model with the aim of describing all the possible worker's physical, cognitive and emotional states.

The DSS leverages the OWL definition of the Ontology to check for correctness and consistency the coming High-level information. Individuals, however, are not described in terms of OWL syntax elements: for best efficiency, they are directly created as probabilities facts, following the ProbLog syntax. The outputs of the DSS will be highly supported by the Interventions platform, described in Sect. 4. The suggestions and interventions implemented in the WAOW tool are provided by experts. Such suggestions and interventions proposed to the user will be implemented as probabilistic rules by the DSS: the selection is carried out taking into account the probability associated to each worker's state. Such a probability is modulated by the High-Level information provided by each sensor integrated into the WAOW tool and by the feedback provided by each worker toward the interaction with the DSS.

The rules leveraged by the DSS will consider different factors that may affect the well-being of the worker, such as the environment (e.g., loudly, incorrect lighting), wrong behaviour at work (e.g., use of wrong tools or used in a wrong way, posture), worker's habits and state (including out-of-work elements such as food, sleep). The DSS will interact with different entities integrated in the WAOW tool. In particular, the DSS will receive in input the descriptions of the worker's physical and mental states, with the support of the Ontology, and will produce recommendations based on the worker's current *state* and on her/his *history* (both stored by the DSS as probabilistic facts). Notice that the worker can provide feedback to the DSS which, in turn, can update the rules to customise them to the worker's preferences. For instance, if a given suggestion in the past (e.g. the use of earmuffs) did not produce an expected benefit (e.g. "decrease in user stress recorded through sensors"), the DSS may then explore other suggestions with the given user (e.g., "take a pause of X minutes").

Action Rules: A Simple Example for User Suggestions. Let's assert, in Prolog, that Jack is a worker and every worker is also a person:

```
worker(jack).
person(X) :- worker(X).
```

The left hand side of the rule is called *head*, the right hand side is the *body*. Uppercase X is a variable. Whenever the body holds, the head holds too. With this simple representation, the DSS can automatically infer that Jack is a person, that is, `person(jack)` holds. In our experiments, we modelled many possible aspects of different working environments, from worker profile – for example, education or activity typology – to time constraints, and even complex behavioural knowledge; as an example, the following rule:

```
0.3::suggestion(take_pause,W) :-
        worker(W), isShown(stressed,W),
        env(env_discrete_volume_serious_hazard),
        isUsing(W,use_noise_reduction_safety_ear_muffs).
```

generates the `take_pause` suggestion whenever a worker in an excessively loud environment is stressed despite using safety ear muffs, giving to the rule a weight of 0.3. The final probability associated to the suggestion takes into account the probability associated to each proposition in the rule body. More than one suggestion could be generated by the DSS. Thus, the associated probability helps in ranking them and select the best one. Moreover, if the selected suggestion is associated with a probability lower than a given threshold, the DSS could simply give up, avoiding to flood the worker with useless advices. Finally, the generated suggestion – for example, `take_pause` – is translated into human language: "The working area is too noisy and you look tired, it's time to take a pause."

7   Conclusion

The paper has described the WA project and tools, aimed at providing smart assistance to elder workers. The paper has focused on the Ontology and the DSS portions of WA, which will generate recommendations about risk avoidance and well-being at work. Experiments about DSS are being conducted via in-company use cases, testing the proposed solutions by collecting sensor data and by improving the learning and smart capabilities of the DSS.

References

1. Birkel, H.S., et al.: Development of a risk framework for industry 4.0 in the context of sustainability for established manufacturers. Sustainability **11**(2), 384 (2019)
2. Calzavara, M., Battini, D., Bogataj, D., Sgarbossa, F., Zennaro, I.: Ageing workforce management in manufacturing systems: state of the art and future research agenda. Int. J. Prod. Res. **58**(3), 729–747 (2020)
3. Chen, H., Hou, C., Zhang, L., Li, S.: Comparative study on the strands of research on the governance model of international occupational safety and health issues. Saf. Sci. **122**, 104513 (2020)
4. Cheng, Z., Nielsen, I., Cutler, H.: Perceived job quality, work-life interference and intention to stay. Int. J. Manpow. **40**, 17–35 (2019)
5. Cresswell, K., et al.: Investigating the use of data-driven artificial intelligence in computerised decision support systems for health and social care: a systematic review. Health Inform. J. **26**, 2138–2147 (2020)
6. Darabont, D.C., Bejinariu, C., Baciu, C., Bernevig-Sava, M.A.: Modern approaches in integrated management systems of quality, environmental and occupational health and safety. Calitatea **20**(S1), 105 (2019)

7. Fierens, D., et al.: Inference and learning in probabilistic logic programs using weighted Boolean formulas. Theor. Pract. Log. Program. **15**(3), 358–401 (2015)

8. Fitzpatrick, M.D., Moore, T.J.: The mortality effects of retirement: evidence from social security eligibility at age 62. J. Public Econ. **157**, 121–137 (2018)

9. Fugini, M., et al.: WorkingAge: providing occupational safety through pervasive sensing and data driven behavior modeling. In: Proceedings of the 30th European Safety and Reliability Conference and the 15th Probabilistic Safety Assessment and Management Conference. Research Publishing (2020)

10. Golightley, M., Goemans, R.: Social Work and Mental Health. SAGE Publishing, Thousand Oaks (2020)

11. Grant, A., Stober, D.: Evidence Based Coaching Handbook: Putting Best Practices to Work for Your Clients. Wiley, Hoboken (2006)

12. Grosch, J.W., Scholl, J.C.: Designing age-friendly workplaces: an occupational health perspective. In: Czaja, S.J., Sharit, J., James, J.B. (eds.) Current and Emerging Trends in Aging and Work, pp. 429–451. Springer, Cham (2020). https://doi.org/10.1007/978-3-030-24135-3_22

13. Kalteh, H.O., Mortazavi, S.B., Mohammadi, E., Salesi, M.: The relationship between safety culture and safety climate and safety performance: a systematic review. Int. J. Occup. Saf. Ergon. **24**, 1–11 (2019)

14. Lodh, N., Sil, J., Bhattacharya, I.: Graph based clinical decision support system using ontological framework. In: Mandal, J.K., Dutta, P., Mukhopadhyay, S. (eds.) CICBA 2017. CCIS, vol. 776, pp. 137–152. Springer, Singapore (2017). https://doi.org/10.1007/978-981-10-6430-2_12

15. Mabkhot, M.M., Amri, S.K., Darmoul, S., Al-Samhan, A.M., Elkosantini, S.: An ontology-based multi-criteria decision support system to reconfigure manufacturing systems. IISE Trans. **52**(1), 18–42 (2020)

16. Moreira, M., Rodrigues, J., Korotaev, V., Al-Muhtadi, J., Kumar, N.: A comprehensive review on smart decision support systems for health care. IEEE Syst. J. **13**(3), 3536–3545 (2019)

17. Pease, S.G., et al.: An interoperable semantic service toolset with domain ontology for automated decision support in the end-of-life domain. Future Gener. Comput. Syst. **112**, 848–858 (2020)

18. Petnga, L., Austin, M.: An ontological framework for knowledge modeling and decision support in cyber-physical systems. Adv. Eng. Inform. **30**(1), 77–94 (2016)

19. Roughton, J., Crutchfield, N., Waite, M.: Safety Culture: An Innovative Leadership Approach. Butterworth-Heinemann, Oxford (2019)

20. Arbeitswissenschaft. Springer, Heidelberg (2018). https://doi.org/10.1007/978-3-662-56037-2_9

21. Vujica Herzog, N., Harih, G.: Decision support system for designing and assigning ergonomic workplaces to workers with disabilities. Ergonomics **63**(2), 225–236 (2020)

Technical Debt Management and Energy Consumption Evaluation in Implantable Medical Devices: The SDK4ED Approach

Charalampos Marantos[1], Angeliki-Agathi Tsintzira[2],
Lazaros Papadopoulos[1(✉)], Apostolos Ampatzoglou[2],
Alexander Chatzigeorgiou[2], and Dimitrios Soudris[1]

[1] School of Electrical and Computer Engineering,
National Technical University of Athens, Athens, Greece
{hmarantos,lpapadop,dsoudris}@microlab.ntua.gr
[2] Department of Applied Informatics, University of Macedonia,
Thessaloniki, Greece
angeliki.agathi.tsintzira@gmail.com,
{ampatzoglou,achat}@uom.edu.gr

Abstract. The design constraints of Implantable Medical Devices (IMD), such as the low energy consumption, impose significant challenges to application developers. Software tools that improve the quality of the source code by means of technical debt management and provide energy consumption estimations are useful to IMD application developers for addressing such challenges. In this work, we demonstrate the effectiveness of tools that manage the technical debt and provide energy consumption estimations applied to an IMD application for seizure detection.

Keywords: Technical debt · Energy consumption · Implantable Medical Devices · Embedded systems

1 Introduction

The Implantable Medical Devices (IMDs) are objects surgically inserted into the human body for medical purposes [7]. They are used to treat conditions such as cardiac disorder, epilepsy, numerous autoimmune diseases and psychological disorders (among others), thus contributing to the normal quality of patient's lives. Nowadays, IMDs are a common part of modern medical care, support physicians to diagnose and treat diseases and enable the quality of life of patients.

The design requirements of IMDs include the small volume in terms of size and weight, long lifespan, low energy consumption, high biocompatibility and reliability [8]. As the clinical demand for IMDs increases, addressing design and efficiency challenges is even more urgent. From application development perspective, increasing the quality of source code (improving maintainability and

A. Orailoglu et al. (Eds.): SAMOS 2020, LNCS 12471, pp. 348–358, 2020.
https://doi.org/10.1007/978-3-030-60939-9_25

reusability) and evaluating the energy efficiency contribute to meeting the afore-mentioned challenges.

The SDK4ED platform integrates a number of toolboxes for application developers of embedded systems that enable the optimization of various source code qualities, such as the source code maintainability (e.g. the management of technical debt), the security and the energy consumption optimization[1]. Additionally, it identifies trade-offs between the optimization of the maintainability, security and energy qualities at application source code-level and enables decision support. More specifically, the toolboxes are the following: i) Technical Debt Management ii) Security iii) Energy consumption iv) Forecasting and v) Decision support. The toolboxes recommend source-to-source optimizations, while the decision support toolbox provides guidance to developers about the optimizations that should be applied based on user-selected priorities.

In this paper, we leverage specific tools from the SDK4ED platform to efficiently manage the technical debt of a seizure detection IMD application and estimate the energy consumption. Therefore, this work contributes to the evaluation of the SDK4ED tools on a real-word use case from the IMD domain and we reach interesting conclusions.

The rest of the paper is organized as follows: Sect. 2 provides more details about the SDK4ED tools used in the present work, as well as related work about the technical debt management and energy consumption approaches in the IMD domain. Section 3 describes the implementation of the tools in the IMD application and in Sect. 4 we draw conclusions.

2   Related Work

Technical debt (TD) in software engineering refers to the additional maintenance costs caused by quality compromises which are often taken for short-term benefits during the software development process. The TD metaphor which was first coined in 1992 by Ward Cunningham [6] has proved highly effective as a means of conveying to nontechnical product stakeholders the need for what we call "refactoring" [9]. The concept of Technical Debt Management (MTD) encompasses all processes that should be undertaken by software development teams to identify, measure, prioritize and repay TD.

Embedded systems form a software-intensive domain where platform-specific run-time constraints such as performance, energy consumption and memory usage, have to be strictly satisfied. However, embedded systems exhibit long lifetime expectancy, often beyond a decade, resulting in intense maintenance activities. To limit the effort spent on maintenance, companies could invest in boosting design-time quality through the management of TD. A case study involving seven embedded software industries revealed that quality attributes such as functionality, reliability, and performance are indeed given higher priority compared to managing TD [3]. However, developers of embedded software

---

[1] The SDK4ED platform: https://sdk4ed.eu/.

clearly acknowledge the need for low TD on components that are expected to have a longer lifetime [3].

Energy efficiency challenge for IMDs is usually addressed through approaches such as energy harvesting [10] and the design of ultra-low power hardware devices [1]. For instance, the integration of dedicated hardware blocks that perform the computational expensive operations, as well as frequency and voltage scaling are typical techniques applied at OS/hardware-level to improve energy efficiency [7]. However, source-to-source energy optimization techniques, such as cache utilization improvement, which are widely applicable in embedded systems are also applicable in the IMD domain. The tools used in the context of this work enable such optimizations by providing relevant information about the energy efficiency of the application. More specifically, the SDK4ED tools for energy consumption optimization extend advanced machine-learning techniques described in the literature for estimating energy consumption [5,11] and identifying acceleration opportunities [2].

3   Technical Debt and Energy Consumption Evaluation

3.1   Overview of the Application and Source Code

The use-case application targets modern Implantable Medical Devices (IMDs), which are battery-powered embedded devices with high safety and reliability standards. These devices are designed to operate for long time (up to 10 years) implanted in the human body. To support the treatment capabilities of these devices, they are equipped with wireless transceivers, able to communicate with external reader/programmer or a base station for local and/or remote monitoring of patient health, performing a device test, reading sensors, updating device settings.

The application provides primary implant functionality, e.g. Neurostimulation, seizure detection, cardiac pacing etc. More specifically, the application performs the following tasks:

- The sensor (ECoG/EEG) values are received via ADC periodically (using interrupts)
- An FIR filter operation is performed on the input samples. This filter accurately approximates a continuous complex Morlet wavelet
- Based on the filter output a decision whether the seizure is detected or not is made
- Optogenetic or electrical stimulus are applied via GPIO in order to suppress the seizure.

3.2   Technical Debt Management

Methodology. In this subsection we present the methodology that has been followed to measure the levels of Technical Debt for the software that belongs to the Implantable Medical Devices application domain.

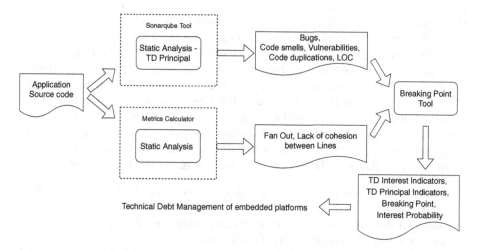

Fig. 1. Tool flow for technical debt management

In the context of the SDK4ED platform, Technical Debt management consists of monitoring all key aspects of TD, namely Principal, Interest and Interest Probability. Figure 1 graphically depicts the tool flow of TD management (TDM). TDM toolkit relies on three tools: i) SonarQube ii) Metrics Calculator and iii) Breaking point tool.

SonarQube is considered by many the world's leading software quality dashboard. It is based on the SQUALE method and: (a) contrasts the source code of an application with a set of predefined rules, so as to identify violations called code smells, and (b) for each identified violation it calculates a remediation time that is required to resolve it. The sum of the remediation time for all identified violations is recorded as the SQUALE index, representing TD principal. In addition, SonarQube calculates the number of bugs, vulnerabilities and the percentage of duplicated code.

The Metrics Calculator has been developed in the context of SDK4ED with the purpose of calculating maintainability metrics for object oriented and non-object oriented software. For non-object oriented languages (like C) it calculates coupling (Fan out) and cohesion (Lack of cohesion between Lines) per file. Fan out refers to the number of modules called from a file and Lack of cohesion between Lines represents the coherence between all possible pairs of lines of code of a method (aggregated at file level as an average). For object oriented languages (like Java) it calculates 10 metrics: Message-passing couple (MPC), Depth of inheritance tree (DIT), Number of children (NOCC), Response for class (RFC), Lack of cohesion in methods (LCOM), Weighted methods per class (WMPC), Data abstraction coupling (DAC), Number of methods (NOM), Lines of Code (LOC), Number of Properties (NOP).

The results of SonarQube and Metrics Calculator are being used as input to the Breaking Point tool to calculate TD Interest and the time point at which the accumulated interest will exceed TD principal (breaking point) and Interest Probability. TD Interest is calculated based on the FITTED Framework [4]. The FITTED framework has been introduced to measure software sustainability, which is the ability of a system to meet *"the needs of the present without compromising the ability of future generations to meet their own needs"*. FITTED measures this as the period in which the cumulative interest is lower than the saved principal. When cumulative interest is equal to the saved principal the system is on its breaking point which means that any savings resulting from the decision to not repay TD will vanish due to increased maintenance effort during evolution. To calculate TD Interest, FITTED suggests the following steps:

1. identify the five artifacts that are most structurally similar to the artifact under consideration
2. based on the values of the selected object-oriented metrics for all structurally similar artifacts, compile an artificial optimal one
3. calculate the average distance of the artifact under analysis from the artificial optimal one–this distance is referred as the ratio of additional maintenance effort
4. calculate the average maintenance product (i.e., lines of code maintained) in each version
5. multiply the ratio of additional maintenance effort with the average maintenance product (extract from past changes on the artifact under analysis)
6. divide the previous outcome with the average lines of code maintained in one hour, so as to retrieve the interest in minutes; and
7. calculate interest in currency using the same hourly rate as in principal calculation.

Finally, Interest probability is a measure of how frequently a file changes in the sense that a file that changes frequently adds more debt (interest).

Results. In this subsection we present the results on TD quantification, focusing on TD Principal, TD Interest and Interest Probability for the target system. The results are summarized in Table 1.

The TD Principal varies across system files; in relative terms on can identify file 'reader.cpp' as the one holding the largest principal. This particular file requires 302$ to fix the 29 identified code smells. Even more important is the fact that it also exhibits the highest interest (9.68$) and a very high interest probability (0.8). In other words, this file violates several of the rules checked by SonarQube, its metrics indicates that the maintainability is quite low and has a high probability of being changed in the subsequent version. All these signals provide an imminent risk which should be mitigated by the development team. Similar observations can be made for file 'cisc.cpp'.

In terms of the particular code smells that appear in the code, SonarQube indicates for example that more unit tests should be added so as to increase coverage. For file 'reader.cpp' one of the most demanding issues reads *'92 more lines of code need to be covered by tests to reach the minimum threshold of 65.0% lines*

Table 1. Technical Debt Management output

Source file	TD principal	TD interest	Interest probability	Code smells	LOC	Complexity
api.cpp	92	0	0	7	93	15
api.h	50	0	0	15	11	0
body.cpp	14	0	0	4	11	2
body.h	10	0	0	1	1	0
resources/imdcode_v1.3/imdcode.c	191	0	0	17	111	26
resources/imdcode.c	183	0	0	18	111	26
main.cpp	53	0	0	7	53	6
misty1.c	148	0	0	7	145	15
misty1.h	65	0	0	16	58	0
reader.cpp	302	9.68	0.8	29	206	25
reader.h	9	0	0	3	1	0
sec_primitives.cpp	23	2.8	0.25	3	24	4
sec_primitives.h	19	0.7	0.25	5	3	0
sims.cpp	14	0	0	4	11	2
sims.h	10	0	0	4	1	0
sisc.cpp	280	30	0.87	26	199	24
sisc.h	9	0	0	3	1	0

coverage'. Such an issue requires substantial effort to be resolved (estimated by SonarQube to 3 h 4 min). Another striking issue, which also contributes heavily to the total principal, is code duplication. For file 'reader.cpp' *2 duplicated blocks of code must be removed* requiring an estimated time of 30 min.

On the other hand, one can observe files with relative high TD Principal (such as imdcode.c) but without any TD Interest or Interest Probability. This is due to the fact that this file has been introduced in the last version and thus it has never been the subject of change. Thus, to be certain whether the development team will face maintainability issues, one should probably wait for data from further revisions. However, we need to note that files with high Principal, but low Interest (that have been maintained for some versions) are usually assigned a low priority for TD management.

These findings imply that a software development team wishing to manage TD in its products, shouldn't focus only on selected figures, but seek a combined interpretation of the findings. In other words, maintenance problems are probable for files with a high TD principal, substantial interest and non-negligible interest probability.

It is well known that all contemporary software systems evolve frequently over time. Thus, beyond the analysis of the current snapshot of each system, it makes sense to observe the evolutionary trends of TD-related concepts. In Figs. 2a and 2b we plot the evolution of Principal/Interest and Breaking Point across system versions, respectively.

From Fig. 2b, we can observe that the system is slightly deteriorating over time, in terms of TD principal, presenting some high spikes (introduction of considerable TD principal at once) in version 4 and 8. Its interest remains rela-

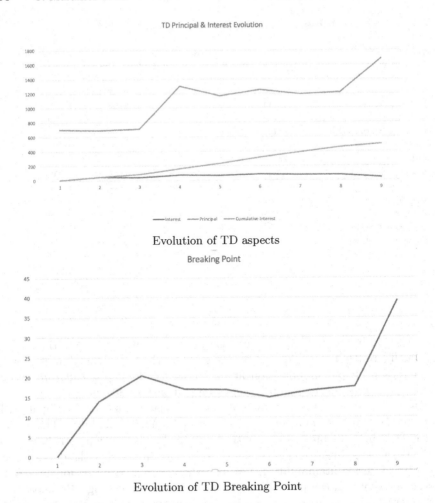

Evolution of TD aspects

Evolution of TD Breaking Point

Fig. 2. Evolution of TD aspects and evolution of TD breaking point

tively stable; nevertheless, the cumulative interest is naturally increasing almost linearly, as the interest of each version is added to the already existing interest.

However, the evolution of the Breaking Point in Fig. 2b reveals a rather healthy project status: The Breaking Point, i.e. the time at which the accumulated interest will exceed the TD Principal lies for most of the versions 20 versions ahead. The Breaking Point is doubled in the final version. This is primarily due to the addition of new code in the last version, which increases Principal - see Fig. 2a (resulting in additional rule violations being detected by SonarQube). However, it seems that the new code has not introduced additional interest, which possibly implies that it is well designed in terms of coupling and cohesion. Considering the rather short history of the project (9 versions), a

Breaking Point of 40 version indicates that the development team is not expected to face significant additional maintenance costs in the near future.

3.3   Energy Consumption Evaluation

Figure 3 shows the tool flow of for energy consumption estimation and optimization. It consists of three tools: i) Hotspots identification ii) Acceleration opportunities identification and iii) Energy consumption estimation.

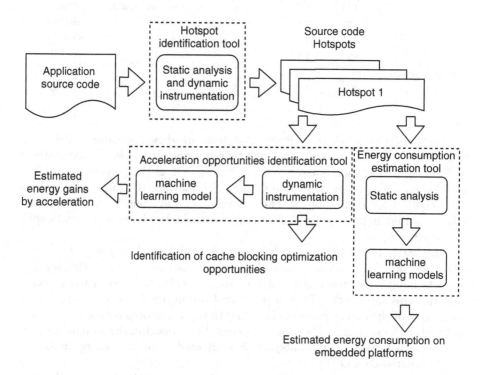

Fig. 3. Tool flow for energy consumption estimation and optimization.

The *hotspot identification* tool parses the application source code and uses dynamic instrumentation to identify the parts of the application that are computationally expensive in terms of CPU cycles. The main purpose of the tool is to provide the parts of the application source code in which optimizations are expected to have major impact in energy and/or performance. From technical perspective, the hotspot identification tool is based on CLANG and on the Cachegrind tool from the Valgrind benchmark suite. CLANG is used to identify loops and functions through source code static analysis. Valgrind performs dynamic instrumentation and estimates the number of CPU cycles across the application in line-by-line granularity. By combining the outputs of the static analysis and Cachegrind the CPU cycles spent in each loop and function are estimated. The most computationally expensive loops and functions of the application source code are the "hotspots".

Table 2. Hotspot identification output

Hotspot	Line start	Line end	CPU cycles	Cache miss	Function name	Source file
Function-level granularity						
1	218	705	5 %	16 %	main	imdcode.c
2	106	153	4 %	0 %	misty1_encrypt_block	misty1.c
3	32	44	3 %	9 %	fi	misty1.c
4	191	211	3 %	0 %	cmac	imdcode.c
5	47	62	4 %	0 %	fo	misty1.c
Loop-level granularity						
1	202	206	3 %	0 %	-	imdcode.c

The results of the IMD application analysis are shown in Table 2. 5 computationally expensive functions are identified and one critical loop. The starting and ending line of each hotspot is reported, as well as the percentage of CPU cycles spent in each one. Based on Cachegrind analysis, the cache miss ratio is also reported for each hotspot. Thus, developers may consider applying optimizations that improve cache utilization (e.g. cache blocking) in hotspots with high cache miss ratio.

The hotspots are further analyzed by the *acceleration opportunities identification* tool. This tool is based on dynamic instrumentation techniques. It extracts information from each hotspot, such as ILP level and memory access pattern. This information feeds a machine learning model, which provides an estimation of the energy gains of offloading the specific hotspot on a GPU accelerator. For the specific application no acceleration opportunities were identified. In other words, none of the hotsposts is estimated to provide energy gains by being executed on a GPU.

The *energy consumption estimation* tool, processes the hotspots through source code static analysis and extracts information from the assembly instructions, such as the type of instructions and their sequence. This information is the input of a machine learning model that estimates the execution time and the energy consumption. The tool can provide estimations for any embedded platform provided that the dataset will be prepared and the model will be trained for each one.

Table 3 shows the energy consumption and execution time estimation for a number of ARM-based embedded platforms. Energy consumption model was trained for A-57 and M0+ only. However, the execution time model was trained for all embedded platforms of Table 3. The selected CPUs belong to the Cortex A family (A-57 and A-72) and to the Cortex M family, which mainly targets microcontrollers. Developers may exploit these results by selecting the most suitable platform, based on the design constraints. For example, by deploying the

Table 3. Time and Energy estimation of various platforms integrating different ARM CPU architectures

Platform (CPU)	Time (us)	Energy consumption (mJ)
Nvidia Tegra TX1 (ARM Cortex A-57)	16	0.09
Raspberry Pi 4 (ARM Cortex A-72)	17.5	-
Arduino Nano 33 IOT (ARM Cortex M0+)	1400	0.0008

IMD application on Arduino Nano, execution time is traded for very low energy consumption.

4 Conclusions

Both TD analysis and energy consumption tools aim at assisting application developers in the process of maintaining and optimizing the application source code. More specifically, the analysis of TD does not aim at characterizing a software system as well- or poor-performing. Rather, it can serve the purpose of raising warnings about repeating code or design inefficiencies, such as lack of unit tests or duplicate chunks of code. The development team, considering also the change frequency of the affected files, can value the merit of such warnings, and proceed to code quality improvements. The application of the SDK4ED platform on the IMD application revealed that a unified view of TD principal, interest and interest probability can help to quickly identify and prioritize code quality improvements on selected artifacts so as to increase their maintainability.

The energy consumption analysis set of tools identify critical parts of the application and provide energy consumption and execution time estimations for various embedded platforms. Thus, developers may obtain estimations in a fast and convenient way and identify performance vs. energy trade-offs by application deployment in various architectures. As presented in the previous section, the IMD application is not suitable for acceleration, however, interesting execution time vs. energy trade-offs have been identified through static analysis at instruction-level for three different ARM-based architectures.

Acknowledgement. This work has received funding from the EU's Horizon 2020 research and innovation programme, under grant agreement No. 780572 (SDK4ED, www.sdk4ed.eu). The authors would like to thank the group of Ass. Prof. Christos Strydis at Erasmus MC, Netherlands for providing the implantable medical devices application.

References

1. Ahmed, S., Kakkar, V.: An electret-based angular electrostatic energy harvester for battery-less cardiac and neural implants. IEEE Access **5**, 19631–19643 (2017)

2. Alavani, G., Varma, K., Sarkar, S.: Predicting execution time of CUDA kernel using static analysis. In: 2018 IEEE International Conference on Parallel & Distributed Processing with Applications, Ubiquitous Computing & Communications, Big Data & Cloud Computing, Social Computing & Networking, Sustainable Computing & Communications (ISPA/IUCC/BDCloud/SocialCom/SustainCom), pp. 948–955. IEEE (2018)

3. Ampatzoglou, A., et al.: The perception of technical debt in the embedded systems domain: an industrial case study. In: 2016 IEEE 8th International Workshop on Managing Technical Debt (MTD), pp. 9–16 (2016)

4. Ampatzoglou, A., Michailidis, A., Sarikyriakidis, C., Ampatzoglou, A., Chatzigeorgiou, A., Avgeriou, P.: A framework for managing interest in technical debt: an industrial validation. In: Proceedings of the 2018 International Conference on Technical Debt, TechDebt 2018, pp. 115–124. Association for Computing Machinery, New York (2018). https://doi.org/10.1145/3194164.3194175

5. Bazzaz, M., Salehi, M., Ejlali, A.: An accurate instruction-level energy estimation model and tool for embedded systems. IEEE Trans. Instrum. Meas. **62**(7), 1927–1934 (2013)

6. Cunningham, W.: The WyCash portfolio management system. SIGPLAN OOPS Messenger **4**(2), 29–30 (1992). https://doi.org/10.1145/157710.157715

7. Kakkar, V.: An ultra low power system architecture for implantable medical devices. IEEE Access **7**, 111160–111167 (2018)

8. Khan, W., Muntimadugu, E., Jaffe, M., Domb, A.J.: Implantable medical devices. In: Domb, A.J., Khan, W. (eds.) Focal Controlled Drug Delivery. ADST, pp. 33–59. Springer, Boston, MA (2014). https://doi.org/10.1007/978-1-4614-9434-8_2

9. Kruchten, P., Nord, R.L., Ozkaya, I.: Technical debt: from metaphor to theory and practice. IEEE Softw. **29**(6), 18–21 (2012)

10. Kumar, V., Kakkar, V.: Miniaturized resonant power conversion for implanted medical devices. IEEE Access **5**, 15859–15864 (2017)

11. Mendis, C., Renda, A., Amarasinghe, S., Carbin, M.: Ithemal: accurate, portable and fast basic block throughput estimation using deep neural networks. In: International Conference on Machine Learning, pp. 4505–4515 (2019)

Distributed Training on a Highly Heterogeneous HPC System

Jose Flich[1(⊠)], Carles Hernandez[1], Eduardo Quiñones[2], and Roberto Paredes[1]

[1] Universitat Politècnica de València, València, Spain
jflich@disca.upv.es, carherlu@upv.es, rparedes@dsic.upv.es
[2] Barcelona Supercomputing Center, Barcelona, Spain
equinones@bsc.es

Abstract. During the recent years HPC systems are being targeted as suitable systems to run DeepLearning workloads. In that respect, a number of machine learning libraries exist targeting different HPC computing platforms. In the context of the European DeepHealth project, the European Distributed Deep Learning library (EDDL) and the European Computing Vision library (ECVL) have been developed. These libraries target heterogeneous HPC systems including multi/many-core processors (CPUs), GPUs and FPGAs. In this paper we describe the approach followed within the project to exploit HPC resources in an efficient and transparent manner with special focus on FPGAs. The complete process is hidden from the end user perspective, allowing a simplification on the complexity to run DeepLearning workloads on heterogeneous systems.

1 Introduction

Traditionally, computing systems have always relied on the use of multi/many-core processors (CPUs) for the effective computation of challenging applications. High-end commercial or proprietary CPUs combined with high-performance interconnects (either standard such as InfiniBand or proprietary) has been the default approach followed by specialized large companies and academia. This has been a valid solution while power consumption and energy dissipation were not a concern. However, as the complexity and integration capacity of CPUs (and in a minor extent the interconnect) grew, the impact of power consumption and energy dissipation became apparent and CPUs were no longer regarded as the only one competitive general-purpose solution. This effect is exacerbated by the increasing size (in terms of nodes and cores) being used on new HPC systems.

This led to the adoption of new technologies and to the emergence of heterogeneous computing. In such a system, different types of computing devices, each with different power consumption and performance trade-offs are used in combination. Heterogeneous computing systems rely on different architectures and have the capability to suit specific problem definitions and particular programming approaches. Indeed, although some devices may achieve lower performance when compared with others, they can be more power and energy efficient, leading to a more efficient computation process (GFLOPS per Watt).

© Springer Nature Switzerland AG 2020
A. Orailoglu et al. (Eds.): SAMOS 2020, LNCS 12471, pp. 359–370, 2020.
https://doi.org/10.1007/978-3-030-60939-9_26

One of the first common adoptions we see in large HPC systems is the combination of CPUs with high-end GPUs. They are common nowadays. Although GPUs were initially designed for image processing related computations, their massive data-parallelism is very well suited for HPC workloads with intensive utilization of algebraic computations. Although power consumption of GPUs can be on par with the one exhibited by CPUs, certain applications can achieve one or two orders of magnitude (if not more) of performance improvement when compared with CPUs, and so exhibiting higher performance per Watt unit.

One application field in which GPUs are specially suited for, is Artificial Intelligence (AI) computing. Nowadays, AI applications are on the raise and this has been enabled by the utilization of GPUs for the training and inference process of complex neural network models. In particular, we have seen a boost of new neural network models and types of network layers, together with the use of larger and more complex datasets for which high-end GPUs (or alternative acceleration approaches) showing TFLOPS performance numbers are required. Moreover, the use of large HPC systems composed of dozens or hundreds of parallel nodes combining CPUs and GPUs, and interconnected with high-performance networks, allows to efficiently distribute and speed-up training operations, facilitating the adoption of AI in new applications and domains.

While systems with nodes combining CPUs and GPUs are common place, we can also see other types of heterogeneous components being approached and embedded into large system configurations. This is the case of manycore accelerators (one clear example is the Intel Xeon Phi which later was discontinued) and the adoption of FPGAs. In this later case, FPGAs, which are electronic devices allowing their architecture to be completely configured, can be adapted and optimized to solve specific problems. FPGAs are massively used in embedded systems domains and low-latency applications such as robotics, networking, and cryptography.

In the context of HPC and cloud systems, FPGAs have been successfully deployed in large systems such as the Microsoft's Catapult project where FPGAs have been used and adapted to the Bing search engine, showing significant performance/Watt boost and lower latency when compared to traditional HPC systems. The effective integration of FPGA devices to build new HPC architectures has also been the target of several research projects such as MANGO [5] and RECIPE [2].

Although FPGAs are very appealing due to their adaptation and reconfigurability properties, they need to be mastered appropriately to get performance improvements in the majority of application domains. Indeed, FPGAs are not raw systems allowing massive parallelism such as GPUs and do not offer generalization such as CPUs. FPGAs, are very efficient in specific application domains where floating point is not of vital need and simpler arithmetic and logic operations of reduced precision are used. Nevertheless, last FPGA devices have been also adapted for HPC utilization including new internal macro blocks such as hardened FPU units (e.g. Altera FPGAs) and AI accelerator engines (e.g. Xilinx

Versal boards). This, indeed, looks like a natural path to allow FPGAs better adapt to HPC applications while keeping power consumption still low.

Despite the clear benefits of heterogeneous computing, it also challenges the programmability of HPC systems. As exposed above, the different accelerator devices are programmed with different programming models with the objective of exploiting the performance capabilities of each. Therefore, it is of paramount importance to select the most appropriate programming model for each device, while maintaining the productivity in the software development of the whole HPC systems. In other words, the performance benefits of heterogeneous computing cannot preclude the programmability of the system.

1.1 DeepHealth Project

In this paper we bet for an efficient use of FPGAs combined with GPUs and CPUs for running distributed training and inference AI workloads. We describe in this paper the approach followed within the DeepHealth project [6] to achieve such goal.

The DeepHealth project is funded by the EU [6] and aims to develop a set of open source deep learning (European Distributed DeepLearning Library; EDDL) and computer vision (European Computer Vision Library; ECVL) for their use in applications related with medical images and diagnosis of diseases. Up to seven industrial and academic AI platforms and fourteen use cases are included in the project (e.g. alzheimer's disease, skin cancer, dementia, ...).

The project also deals with the interaction and synergies that occur when applying AI related workloads on an HPC infrastructure. Indeed, one of the main goals of the project is the effective and efficient deployment of training processes for neural networks targeting the use cases and using their datasets running on an HPC system.

Although there are existing platforms and tools to deploy distributed training on top of large systems made of CPUs and GPUs, the main goal of the project is to obtain new solution that is specifically optimized for medical applications and can be easily deployed in current and future HPC systems.

1.2 Programming Complexity

One of the most significant adoption barriers for new devices, such as GPUs and FPGAs, specially for FPGAs, is their programming complexity and the interaction with the CPUs. Nowadays, heterogeneous computing follows the *host-device* paradigm, in which the CPU (the host) is the resource responsible of orchestrating the computation offload to the different devices, e.g., initiating the memory transfers between the main memory and the memory device, launching the acceleration kernels, synchronizing them with the main program. Although GPUs are not complex devices from the programming perspective (as they rely mostly on massive data parallel threads), they usually require dedicated programming models (e.g., CUDA, OpenCL) designed to exploit the performance capabilities of the GPU. More exacerbated is the case of FPGAs for which there exist a wide variety of programming alternatives and abstraction levels of different complexity, despite OpenCL is being increasingly used to program the host-FPGA interactions.

As an example, the way GPU programming complexity is hidden in the EDDL is similar to the one used in TensorFlow [1] and when combined with Keras [4]. The expert user defines its neural network model and its training process and only needs to set the target device where it wants to run it. Therefore, in our design, we embed all the complexities of dealing with GPUs, CPUs, and FPGAs within the EDDL and ECVL libraries, selecting the most appropriate programming model to fully exploit the performance capabilities of each device, as well as optimising the host-device interaction for an efficient execution in terms of memory transfer and synchronization mechanisms.

These programming complexities are completely hidden for expert users working AI applications of a particular domain (e.g. health) since they are usually not experts in heterogeneous computing and only familiar with high abstraction level programming languages (e.g. python). By doing so, the expert user can leverage from HPC systems features without the need to worry about how his/her code will run and where.

To sum up, in this paper, we present the methodology implemented within DeepHealth to support the distribution of the training and inference process on an heterogeneous HPC system.

2   Abstracting Hardware Resources in the EDDL

The ambitious goal of EDDL is to cover most of the commonly used deep learning functionalities running with different hardware accelerators offering tailored implementations that can be efficiently executed on CPUs, GPUs, and FPGAs. These hardware accelerators can be selected by the user by means of what we call *Computing Service* (CS).

The EDDL API is centered around the concept of a *Tensor* and the *Neural Network* model. The *Tensor* class concentrates all what concerns tensors – e.g., matrix element-wise and linear algebra operations. Moreover, this class plays the role of Hardware Abstraction Layer (HAL): models and tensors will be created and initialized on the device(s) specified by the CS selected by the user. In this sense the network definition and training procedure is defined by the user independently of the CS selected where all the computation will be performed.

Furthermore, EDDL allows the parallel execution of training operations. In this case, the neural network workload can be distributed among multiple nodes, each featuring different acceleration devices. The DeepHealth project relies on the COMPSs distributed framework [3] (see Sect. 3.2 for further details) in a way transparent to the programmer. Additionally, EDDL includes *ad hoc* methods for serializing weights and gradients in order to facilitate the network update in the distribution version of the training operation.

3   Workload Distribution in Heterogeneous HPC Systems

In this section we describe the approach followed for the efficient distribution of the training process on an HPC system with heterogeneous components such as CPUs, GPUs, and FPGAs.

3.1   General Overview

The DeepHealth aims at reducing the execution time of the training process by exploiting the inherent data parallelism of input data. To do so, the input dataset is distributed over the different targeted nodes and each node is in charge of training the model with the assigned dataset part. Later, the different models trained in isolation must be combined which requires exchanging either the model (parameters) or the parameter's gradients between the nodes.

The approach relies on a hierarchical structure. At the top level, the end user launches the training process. For this, the application uses the EDDL and ECVL libraries. Then, the training process is distributed on the set of nodes in the system. Each node can be compounded of different types of components such as GPUs and FPGAs. Even, each node can have a different number of such components. Figure 1 shows the initial situation describing the problem addressed. On the upper part of the figure we can see the training/inference process represented as a set of batches.

Each batch includes the dataflow defined by the neural network which combines tensors and kernels. The kernels are the specific computing functions that need to be computed following the dataflow defined by the neural network. The tensors are the memory data used for different types of information. In particular, input data is stored in tensors and they are filled from the dataset. Output data represents the produced output of each training/inference process. Network tensors are temporal tensors defined for each network layer and shared data refers to tensors which need to be shared by the different nodes running a distributed training process. These typically will store the weights and bias of the neural network.

On the lower part of the figure we can see the hardware where the training process has to be mapped to. The figure illustrates an example where CPUs, GPUs and FPGAs are randomly placed on different nodes. However, we can see all combinations are represented on at least one node. One particular aspect to notice is the fact that each node always has at least one CPU. Therefore, GPUs and FPGAs are used as accelerator devices from the CPU standpoint.

Figure 2 shows a mapping solution potentially performed by our approach. The different training batches are assigned to a different node, each one with a different configuration based on the configuration of each node. In addition, on each node, different sets of devices are assigned. Typically, devices of the same type are used on each node but we can also see nodes where the three types of devices are assigned to train a batch cooperatively. Indeed, the process can also be split between the different components, meaning that not only one component is in charge of the training of a batch but all heterogeneous components can

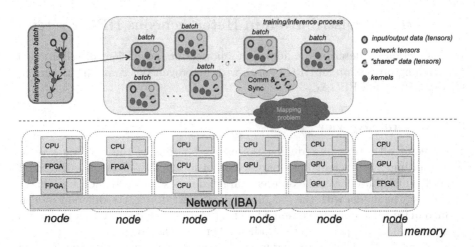

Fig. 1. Overall approach in DeepHealth for efficient distributed training on a set of heterogeneous devices.

collaborate on the training or inference process altogether. This is specially true when dealing with FPGAs, as will be described later.

3.2 Distributed Computing via COMPSs

The COMPSs distributed framework [3], developed and owned by BSC, offers a portable programming environment based on a task model, whose main objective is to facilitate the parallelization of sequential source code written in Java or Python programming languages, in a distributed and heterogeneous computing environment. In COMPSs, the programmer is responsible of identifying the units of parallelism (named *COMPSs tasks*) and the synchronization data dependencies existing among them by annotating the sequential source code (using *annotations* in case of Java or standard *decorators* in case of Python). COMPSs enables the software development at a very low cost because of two main reasons: (1) the model is based on sequential programming on top of popular programming languages (i.e., Java, Python and C/C++), meaning that users do not have to deal with the typical duties of parallelization and distribution (e.g., thread creation, data distribution, fault tolerance, etc.); and (2) the model abstracts the application from the underlying distributed infrastructure, hence COMPSs programs do not include any detail that could tie them to a particular platform (e.g., deployment or resource manager) boosting portability among diverse computing infrastructures.

Figure 3 shows a source code snipped (simplified for readability purposes) of the parallelization of the EDDL library training operation with COMPSs. COMPSs tasks are identified with a standard Python decorator @task (lines 1 and 5). The IN, OUT and INOUT arguments define the data directionality of function parameters. By default, parameters are IN, and so there is no need

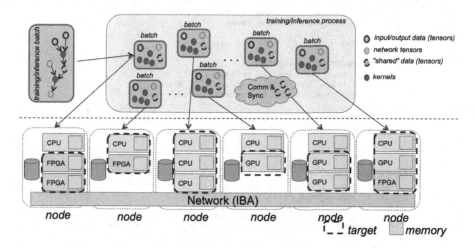

Fig. 2. Mapping example of training process to hardware resources.

to explicitly specify IN parameters. Moreover, when a task is marked with is_replicated=True (line 1), the COMPS task is executed in all the available computing nodes for initialization purposes; otherwise, it executes on the available computing resources. The train iterates over num_epochs epochs (line 14). At every epoch, num_batches batches are executed (line 15), each instantiating a new COMPSs task (line 16) with an EDDL library train batch operation. All COMPSs tasks are synchronized at line 18 with compss_wait_on, and the partial weights are collected. The gradients of the model are then updated with the partial weights at line 20.

The task-based programming model of COMPSs is then supported by its runtime system, which manages several aspects of the application execution and keeps the underlying infrastructure transparent to the programmer. The COMPSs runtime is organised as a master-worker structure:

- The *master*, executed in the computing resource where the application is launched, is responsible for steering the distribution of the application and data management.
- The *worker(s)*, co-located with the Master or in remote computing resources, are in charge of responding to task execution requests coming from the Master.

One key aspect is that the master maintains the internal representation of a COMPSs application as a Direct Acyclic Graph (DAG) to express the parallelism. Each node corresponds to a COMPSs task and edges represent data dependencies (and so potential data transfers). As an example, Fig. 4 presents the DAG representation of the EDDLL training operation presented in Fig. 3.

Based on this DAG, the runtime can automatically detect data dependencies between COMPSs tasks: as soon as a task becomes ready (i.e., when all its data

```
1.  @task (is_replicated = True)
2.  def build (model):
3.    # The model is created at each worker
4.    [...]
5.  @task(INOUT = weights)
6.  def train_batch(model, dataset):
7.    # A train operation is executed at each worker
8.    # on the model and the dataset passed
9.    [...]
10. def main():
11.   # A new model is created
12.   net = eddl.model([...])
13.   build(net)
14.   for i in range(num_epochs):
15.     for j in range(num_batches):
16.       weight[j] = train_batch(net,dataset)
17.     # Synchronize all weights from workers
18.     compss_wait_on(weight)
19.     # Update weights on the model
20.     update_gradients(net,weight)
```

Fig. 3. A (simplified) snipped of pyEDDLL training operation parallelised with COMPSs.

dependencies are honoured), the master is in charge of distributing it among the available workers, transferring the input parameters before starting the execution. When the COMPSs task is completed, the result is either transferred to the worker in which the destination COMPSs task executes (as indicated in the DAG), or transferred to the master if a compss_wait_on call is invoked.

3.3   Heterogeneous Computing via FPGAs

In the DeepHealth project the use of FPGAs is also supported. Each specific kernel function implemented in the EDDL/ECVL libraries is complemented with an specific FPGA kernel. Currently, the two libraries support around 200 kernel functions. Although not all the functions are worth being implemented on an FPGA device, the libraries have been provisioned with full support. The reason to provide the full coverage is to enable a dynamic execution of the training/inference process where some kernel functions run on the CPU (and potentially on the GPU) whereas others run on the FPGA.

For each kernel function we define two basic running modes, which can be selected for each specific kernel individually. In the *cpuemu* running mode the kernel runs on the CPU while the data is in the FPGA memory. In the *fpga* running mode the kernel runs on the FPGA device. The *cpuemu* is used to avoid using the FPGA for a kernel not worth being run on the FPGA. This is the case, for instance, of floating-point intensive operations (which can better run on GPUs) or initialization kernel functions which are seldomly used in a training process. The process of offloading and moving data to/from the different devices is supported by OpenCL-based runtime deployed in the system. We use the Xilinx runtime (XRT) for those devices currently supported by Vitis and a modified version of the same libraries to support the FPGA devices included in the MANGO prototype.

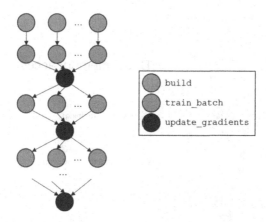

Fig. 4. DAG representation of the application presented in Fig. 3.

The two libraries enable the selection of the running mode for each kernel function. The selection is performed at compilation time. Indeed, the two libraries can be recompiled for specific configurations where the same functions run either on CPU/GPU or on FPGA.

We use Xilinx development tools to implement the FPGA kernel functions. In particular, kernels are described in C with specific Xilinx pragmas and implemented using high-level synthesis (HLS) tools. The two libraries are provided with each kernel function together with a running test for the specific kernel. The compilation process of FPGA kernels usually takes several hours. To speed up the compilation of the libraries we potentially create a repository of compiled FPGA kernels with different FPGA targets and optimizations.

The *fpga* running mode is complemented with the three typical running modes in FPGAs. In particular, we use the *swemu* mode to test the functional validity of the FPGA kernel. This mode can be used together with the end user application to test whether the FPGA kernel impacts on training accuracy. Then, once the kernel is functionally validated, we run the *hwemu* mode to test performance of the kernel in an isolated environment. Additionally, we use Vitis Analyzer to test its timing and resource utilization. We enter the design process by iterating on these two modes for a particular kernel until it is no longer optimized. Then, we use the *hw* mode and test the kernel using the FPGA and with the kernel embedded into the EDDL/ECVL libraries and the end user application using the libraries.

One key aspect when using FPGAs is the decision about which kernels should be running on the FPGA and which ones should be running on the CPU or GPU. This decision is affected by the neural network topology being exercised and by the input dataset size. In order to address this issue, the two libraries have been enhanced with the support for profiling statistics. Each function kernel referenced by the training process from the EDDL/ECVL libraries is tracked and accounted. The training process, at the end, shows the list of kernel functions

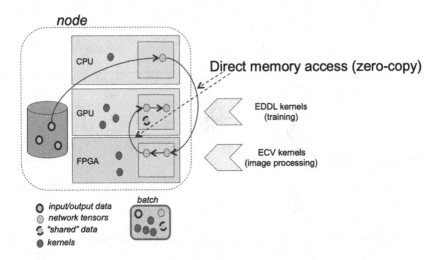

Fig. 5. Combined example with ECV library running on FPGA and EDDL library running on GPU.

run with associated information of number of instances and accumulated time used. Notice that this can be obtained when using either the CPU or the FPGA (and the FPGA with either *cpuemu* or *fpga* running mode). This enables to identify the kernel functions used by each target application and to assess which kernels perform better either on CPU or on FPGA.

Figure 5 shows a potential example where we can exploit the efficiency of FPGAs and the efficiency of GPUs in the DeepHealth project. In particular, the two libraries are instantiated to run on different devices. The ECVL library, providing support for image processing, uses the FPGA to perform data augmentation and other image kernels on the input dataset of the training process. As these algorithms are pixel-based, FPGAs offer superior performance than GPUs for some of the kernels. Then, the produced new images are used by the GPU which runs EDDL kernels performing floating-point intensive operations. Notice that at the node level all memory accesses should be performed with zero-copy operations (i.e. not involving intermediate transfer to the CPU host) by using GPUdirect and a similar technology for the FPGAs. We will adapt FPGA runtime and hardware support to enable direct FPGA transfers.

3.4 Memory Management

One key aspect of this hybrid computation between heterogeneous devices relies on the data location and data sharing. Indeed, deciding where the data lies and moving data between memories of the different devices may compromise final performance of the solution. In order to address this issue, both the EDDL and ECVL libraries keep buffers for each tensor on each possible device used in the training process. For instance, for each tensor used in the training process a buffer is created and managed on the FPGA device and a temporal buffer is also allocated on the CPU memory.

Let us consider an example in which the FPGA is used to perform computation c_1 and the CPU performs c_2 on the same set of tensors. When the kernel c_1 is invoked, the EDDL/ECVL library triggers the FPGA kernel and provides the pointers to the input and output tensor. The operation is finished and the result is stored on the FPGA DDR memory. Instead, when c_2 is invoked, the EDDL/ECVL library performs a copy of the tensor from FPGA DDR memory to CPU memory and then triggers the CPU kernel, which uses the pointers to the just copied buffer in CPU memory. Then, once the kernel finishes the results are potentially copied back to the FPGA DDR memory. Notice this buffer copy procedure can be obtained also with frameworks such as OpenCL. In our case, the EDDL/ECVL library keeps track of the location of the produced data, and, potentially reduces memory transfers if two kernels are run in sequence with the same set of tensors.

This memory management strategy will be optimized in the future with the support of direct memory access of the CPU to FPGA DDR memory. This is similar to the GPUdirect technology. This will enable the CPU to assist the FPGA in specific kernel functions. Indeed, the memory copy between FPGAs and CPUs will be avoided by using direct memory access.

4   Target HPC Infrastructures

In the DeepHealth project different systems will be targeted for demonstration of the distributed training process implemented on the EDDL/ECVL libraries. Besides the well-known Marenostrum supercomputer we will also target the FPGA-based MANGO prototype.

4.1   Marenostrum 4

The fourth generation of the Marenostrum supercomputer, managed and hosted at the Barcelona Supercomputer Center (BSC) features 48 racks with 3456 nodes, each featuring two 24-core Intel Xeon Platinum processors running at 2.1 GHz. The whole cluster sums up a total of 165,888 processors and 390 Terabytes of main memory, and is capable of reaching a peak performance of 11.15 PetaFLOP/s. The nodes are interconnected by a low-latency Omnipath network with a fully connected fat-tree topology.

4.2   MANGO Prototype

The MANGO prototype is the result of a previous European project [5] which targeted FPGAs as emulation infrastructure for HPC architectures. Once concluded, the MANGO prototype is being adapted for computation purposes and will be used in DeepHealth. The MANGO prototype is set of eight clusters of FPGAs connected to four end nodes. Each FPGA cluster is compounded of 12 high-end FPGAs and 8 DDR memories strategically located within the cluster. The 12 FPGAs and 8 DDR memories are interconnected physically and all can be reached through a PCIe connection to the associated node. In total, 96 FPGAs are used in the prototype.

5   Conclusions and Future Work

This paper describes the approach followed in the DeepHealth project to enable a flexible and efficient utilization of HPC resources in the context of AI applications. We have presented how the EDDL abstracts hardware devices and enables the combination of several computing platforms using a single API. In that respect, we have put special emphasis on how to deal with FPGA resources in a transparent manner. Finally, we have also shown how the training process can be distributed in highly heterogeneous HPC systems using COMPSs. Is part of our future work the development of communication mechanisms that allow the direct communication between different computing devices.

Acknowledgment. This project has received funding from the European Union's Horizon 2020 research and innovation programme under grant agreement No. 825111.

References

1. Abadi, M., et al.: TensorFlow: large-scale machine learning on heterogeneous systems (2015). http://tensorflow.org/. Software available from tensorflow.org
2. Agosta, G., et al.: Challenges in deeply heterogeneous high performance systems. In: 22nd Euromicro Conference on Digital System Design, DSD 2019, Kallithea, Greece, 28–30 August 2019, pp. 428–435. IEEE (2019). https://doi.org/10.1109/DSD.2019.00068
3. Badia, R.M., et al.: Comp superscalar, an interoperable programming framework. SoftwareX **3–4**, 32–36 (2015)
4. Chollet, F., et al.: Keras (2015). https://github.com/fchollet/keras
5. Flich, J., et al.: MANGO: exploring manycore architectures for next-generation HPC systems. In: Kubátová, H., Novotný, M., Skavhaug, A. (eds.) Euromicro Conference on Digital System Design, DSD 2017, Vienna, Austria, 30 August–1 September 2017, pp. 478–485. IEEE Computer Society (2017). https://doi.org/10.1109/DSD.2017.51
6. DeepHealth Project: Deep-Learning and HPC to Boost Biomedical Applications for Health (2019). https://deephealth-project.eu/. Accessed 27 July 2020

Author Index

Printed in the United States
By Bookmasters